"GOD IS DEAD."

With these words of Friedrich Nietzsche, modern existentialism can be said to have begun. Born out of social chaos and the havoc of war, it proclaims a world where man is essentially alone and "condemned to be free." Rejecting all traditional values and social customs, it sees life as something which each man must in some way make for himself out of the depths of his own being. Totally accepting the horrors and the basic meaninglessness of life, it nonetheless propounds a philosophy of hope based on man's struggle to achieve an authentically human existence.

This book represents one of the most far-reaching anthologies of existentialist writings ever published. Covering the whole range of existentialist thought from Kierkegaard to Merleau-Ponty, it constitutes a searching exploration of the nature of man's existence.

H. J. BLACKHAM

is a graduate of Birmingham University. He has been Secretary of the Ethical Union, and, since 1963, Director of the British Humanist Society. His publications include **Six Existentialist Thinkers, The Human Tradition** and **Political Discipline in a Free Society.**

BANTAM MATRIX EDITIONS

reality, man and existence:

essential works of existentialism

•

edited and with an introduction
by H. J. BLACKHAM

•

BANTAM BOOKS
NEW YORK/TORONTO/LONDON

REALITY, MAN AND EXISTENCE:
ESSENTIAL WORKS OF EXISTENTIALISM
A Bantam Matrix Edition / published February 1965
2nd printing
3rd printing

ACKNOWLEDGMENTS

Sören Kierkegaard. Reprinted from Concluding Unscientific Postscript *by Sören Kierkegaard, translated by David Swenson and Walter Lowrie, by permission of Princeton University Press. Copyright, 1941, Princeton University Press.*

Karl Jaspers. "Philosophy and Science" first appeared in PARTISAN REVIEW, *Volume 16, number 9, Summer 1949, pp. 871–884. Reprinted by permission of* PARTISAN REVIEW.

Karl Jaspers. "The Origin of the Contemporary Philosophical Situation," reprinted from Reason and Existenz *by Karl Jaspers by permission of Farrar, Straus & Company, Inc. Copyright, 1955, by The Noonday Press. Also reprinted by permission of Routledge & Kegan Paul Ltd.*

Gabriel Marcel. "An Essay in Autobiography," from The Philosophy of Existence *by Gabriel Marcel, translated by Manya Harari. Reprinted by permission of Harvill Press, Ltd., London.*

Gabriel Marcel. "Sketch of a Phenomenology and a Metaphysic of Hope," from Homo Viator *by Gabriel Marcel. Reprinted by permission of Editions Aubier Montaigne, Paris, and Victor Gollancz, Ltd. English translation Copyright Emma Crauford 1951.*

Gabriel Marcel. "Lineaments de l'Expose," from Être et Avoir *by Gabriel Marcel. Reprinted by permission of Editions Aubier Montaigne, Paris. From* Being and Having *by Gabriel Marcel, translated from* Être et Avoir *by Katharine Farrer, Dacre Press: A. & C. Black Ltd., London.*

Martin Buber. Quotations from the authorized English translation of Buber's I and Thou *(1937 edition) are given with the permission of the publishers, T. & T. Clark, Edinburgh.*

Martin Buber. "Dialogue" and "What is Man," reprinted with permission of The Macmillan Company from Between Man and Man *by Martin Buber. © and also by permission Routledge & Kegan Paul Ltd.*

Werner Brock. "An Account of Being and Time*," taken from a treatise by Dr. Werner Brock (who was a pupil of Heidegger at the University of Freiburg) from* Existence and Being *by Martin Heidegger, Copyright, 1949, Vision Press Ltd., London. Also reprinted by permission of Henry Regnery Co., Chicago.*

Jean-Paul Sartre. "L'imaginaire," from Psychology of Imagination *by Jean-Paul Sartre, Copyright, 1940, by Philosophical Library, Inc.*

Jean-Paul Sartre. From Being and Nothingness (L'être et le néant) *© Editions Gallimard, 1943. Also reprinted by permission of Methuen & Co., Ltd.*

Maurice Merleau-Ponty. From Phenomenology of Perception, *translated by Colin Smith. © and by permission of Routledge & Kegan Paul Ltd. Also reprinted by permission of Humanities Press, New York, 1962.*

Maurice Merleau-Ponty. From In Praise of Philosophy, *translated by John Wild and James M. Edie ("Northwestern University Studies in Phenomenology and Existential Philosophy," pp. 34–41). Copyright © 1962, by Northwestern University Press.*

Bantam Books are published by Bantam Books, Inc., a subsidiary of Grosset & Dunlap, Inc. Its trade-mark, consisting of the words "Bantam Books" and the portrayal of a bantam, is registered in the United States Patent Office and in other countries. Marca Registrada. Bantam Books, Inc., 271 Madison Avenue, New York 16, New York.

PRINTED IN THE UNITED STATES OF AMERICA

CONTENTS

AN INTRODUCTION TO EXISTENTIALIST THINKING

Provenance

Did it all begin with Kierkegaard and Nietzsche, those two nineteenth-century originals and "exceptions" to whom existentialist philosophers constantly refer? Existentialism is not a philosophical "school" founded by these masters. In any case, they are independent sources; they did not communicate. Constant reference to them does not mean constant deference to them. Other names have been highly important, pre-eminently Kant, but also Schlegel and Husserl in Germany; and in France, Maine de Biran and Bergson were influences which helped to form Marcel's thinking before he had heard of Kierkegaard. Indeed, most of the great names in philosophy appear frequently in the pages of existentialist writings, including some of the pre-Socratics, notably Heraclitus, in whom these latest thinkers have encouraged a revival of interest. Above all, existentialism is not a school because it is not a system of philosophy which can be worked at and taught. Its exponents philosophise and incite others to do likewise.

Nevertheless, Kierkegaard and Nietzsche are the revolutionary heroes of existentialist thinking. Perhaps it seems outrageous to import the language of violent political action into a peaceful field of academic study, but there was an outrage to describe if these two amateurs were a disturbing influence that changed the course of philosophy, as Jaspers has said. Merleau-Ponty, in his inaugural lecture, *Éloge de la Philosophie,* quotes Bergson, writing in 1935: "I call *amateur* in philosophy him who accepts just as they are the terms of a customary problem . . . to philosophise to serious purpose would consist here in *creating* the formulation of the problem and in *creating* the solution. . ." For Nietzsche, as also for Kierkegaard, the philosopher is a representative man of his time who says what the problems really are as he comes to grips with them in his own life. He may not be a professor; but the professor may be operatively only an artisan, a bright student bred in the skills of an intellectual craft. A man who believes that his eternal happiness is staked upon his thinking is not in an academic frame of mind, dealing with intellectual puzzles. If he is playing a game, it is for the highest stakes. Pascal was superlatively capable of enjoying the excitements of the intellectual life, and no less capable of taking a big question seriously as a matter of eternal moment, even when he posed the issue too literally as a gambling throw. Kierkegaard in the mid-nineteenth century is still in this position of believing that his eternal happiness is the issue at stake in his thinking. But, equally, Nietzsche, who does not believe that his eternal happiness is in question, and who does believe that human mortality gives the thinker the freedom to experiment with his life, feels himself desperately involved in his thinking since [illegible] decide the terms of his tenure of life and to make u[illegible] mind on what to do about them; and nobody can help him.

The philosopher is an exception insofar as he is engaged in what has been called an unusually persistent attempt to think clearly. He will also be an exception if he lives with his problem in such a way as to become his problem, unlike a Hume who disturbs complacency and then retires to the realities of backgammon and the society of modest women—although he too may change the course of philosophy. Kierkegaard and Nietzsche were exceptions in both senses: they lived their problems in the Greek manner and devoted their minds to reflection upon them. They were exceptional but also representative because their problems were problems of their time. Existentialist thinking was conditioned by three nineteenth-century situations: (1) the situation in philosophy, following Kant and Hegel and the advance of the sciences; (2) the situation for Christianity after the Enlightenment; and (3) the situation of the person lost in the masses of a progressive society, one among many, isolated and organized.

(1) Kant had shown the limited reach of reason, competent to organize intersubjective experience but not able to know the object in itself. Hegel had exalted the competence of reason by restoring the old theme, putting reason back into nature and history. In these analyses consciousness-in-general became aware of an object-of-knowledge, or the Absolute became an object to itself, but in neither case did the real personal self in its body and situation encounter the independent objects of its experience. On the other hand, positivists, wholly preoccupied with the objects of empirical

knowledge, ignored metaphysical issues and their own assumptions, and thought of the thinking mind, when they thought of it at all, as a thing among things. A return was required from abstractions and reductions to existential realities.

(2) The human situation itself was put in question by the challenge of the Christian faith and the challenge to the Christian faith. The challenge to the faith was an alarming threat from several quarters: critical philosophy, biblical criticism, and the advancing sciences. There might still be the complacent assumption on the one hand that Christianity was the revealed and established truth, guaranteed by the saints and the church, and by common consent; with the complacent assumption on the other hand that Christianity was now shown to be a fable, outgrown by mankind in the positivist age. However, the challenge to the faith forced the issue, so that both this and the challenge of the faith had to be taken seriously by thinking minds. A decision was called for, and the nature of that decision was brought into the center of attention.

(3) The drive toward equality, taken together with the objectivity of the sciences, the division of labor, and the ubiquitous encroachment of the machine, threatened a deflation of personality, a reduction to equivalence—human sand, in Nietzsche's rhetorical image. This situation might be given a sociological analysis, as by Marxists, or a religious or philosophical analysis, as by existentialists—and the various personalists in Britain and elsewhere influenced by Lotze and reacting against both Hegel and materialism.

The perils to and the requirements of the person involved in these situations, insofar as he reflects upon them, raise the question of human reality: man becomes a question to himself; and this is a main preoccupation of existentialist thinking.

Characteristics

In regard to these three situations of the time, in philosophy, in religion, and in society, existentialism is characterized by a refusal of the alternatives posed, idealism or positivism or materialism, a dogmatic faith or a dogmatic rationalism, individualism or collectivism. These established oppositions are not rejected because they are extreme, in the sense of being one-sided, but because they cover up the extreme nature of the problems. They are not merely wrong solutions; they propose the wrong kind of solution. They dispose of the problems, in one way or another, whereas these are problems which cannot be disposed of because they make the human condition. Existentialism is a literature of extreme situations. Man is an extreme piece of nature, an animal that makes promises, that answers for the future. Historical extreme situations, such as the situation of the disciples after the crucifixion of their master or the situation of the member of the Resistance in the Nazi torture chamber, are not exceptional, for they represent and reveal the real situation in which we all are all the time. The solutions achieved in practice—religious faith, loyalty to civilized values—are not achieved once for all nor by one for all: they remain forever decisions to be made and remade by one and all. Philosophical questions cannot be disposed of by established answers, as problems are removed in science, generally speaking, for all and once for all. To answer these questions in this way is an abuse of thinking.

Any metaphysical system must be radically mistaken insofar as it claims to represent Being, reducing it to the categories of thought. For it is then like the blueprint for a machine, and we are not related to the world as a whole as we are to a machine which we design and make. We exist in the world, and our thinking is existentially involved in our situation. Being includes object and subject and is not included in the point of view of a subject. Conceptual thinking can serve only to show that Being is unthinkable. The ontological problem, then, (*what is what is?*) is not of a kind that can ever be solved by any attempt to say what Being is. This conclusion does not necessarily exclude the problem from any further consideration; rather, it alters our understanding of the nature of the problem. We may ask, not what Being is, but how we may possibly approach or encounter or experience or "hear" or decipher Being, or bring Being to light. The answer to such a question is not in propositional terms, but in terms of attitudes, expectations, preparations, removal of inhibitions, even techniques.

Similarly, the question of religious faith cannot be settled on evidence. God is not an hypothesis, and faith cannot be falsified by any conceivable experience. The question of faith has to be settled at risk ("out upon the deep, over seventy thousand fathoms"), solely on one's own responsibility: it is answered by decision, response, trust, and fidelity, rather than by opinions for which there is good evidence. God is addressed, not expressed. Or God is dead, and the full consequences have to be digested. The question is not simply whether or not God exists, but what believing or disbelieving in God means. A total personal response is called for, of one kind or another, not merely a learned response, the answer in the catechism—or the textbook—however authorized or supported.

Who am I, the thinker capable of such decisions? I come into existence as thinker after I have become aware of the "other," of my body, of the world. The object of knowledge is thus given to me before I am given to myself. The *cogito* of Descartes is not the primordial situation in which I establish my existence and from which I set out to find the world. On the contrary, having found the world, I come to myself and find that I am in the world but not of it, in the sense that I am able to separate myself from it in thought and intention. Human reality is "awareness of" and "intention to" and thus constitutes itself and constitutes the world for itself in its thoughts and projects—whether deliberate or not. I am totally responsible for my world because I give it meaning by my thoughts and projects, totally responsible in the sense of being solely responsible and in the sense of being responsible for all of it.

Yet also I find myself inserted into a ready-made world, a going concern, with routes, signposts, indicators, and a public voice directing me to assigned positions. Everything is to hand, formed for purposes not my own, and I assume a destiny provided for me in this elaborately established order. Existentialist literature is rich in descriptions of this public world in which human reality is liable to be lost and apt to hide from itself.

Human reality, then, is constituted by an ability to separate itself from what is there and to project itself beyond what is there; unlike things, which are and remain solely what they are in the world.

I am not my life, my fate. Or, rather, I am not wholly that. I can turn from my actualities to my potentialities, and it is then that I encounter myself. But what is this nonempirical self? The accounts vary and are often obscure. For Sartre, it is nothing: I am "not that," I am "no thing," I am not even what I am aware of as myself, for that has become my past, a thing. For Marcel, this nonempirical real self to which I withdraw is not an abstract self to be identified with reason, a thinking self, the self of the philosophers; it is, rather, aspiration, invocation, response, a creative engagement of the self in relation to something other. This real self is pure possibility unless and until it realizes and establishes itself in decisions; it comes into existence only in coming to decisions. What kind of decisions? All kinds; but above all, the acknowledgment that decisions are required of me, the awakening to my unlimited responsibility, the shift from the animal and the aesthetic to the ethical—the responsible and the responsive. The recognition that I am alone and totally responsible, "condemned to be free" in Sartre's phrase, is accompanied by dread, anguish, "angst." The sheer incomprehensibility of our existence, its *essential* unknowability, shatters all rational security and may induce "nausea." Face to face with the human condition from which nothing and nobody can save anybody, the person in dread begins his "authenticity."

I am never relieved of responsibility; I cannot rest on my laurels; if I was a hero yesterday, that is in question again today; there is no decision once for all; I cannot take refuge in what "is done," nor in what is required, nor in thought-out principles: insecurity, care is our lot. Thinking which brings this home to me is valid; thought taught as "results" gives out a security which can never be ours. This insecurity, however, is the condition of spontaneity, vitality, passion, creativity, the condition of human life and living; whereas all our securities are states of death.

Although I am alone in my singleness and in the responsibility which attaches to that, I am given to myself in thought in separation from the "other," and thought separates here what are related. In Buber's thinking, "I and Thou" in meeting become and transcend themselves. They are no longer subject and object, "I-It." They recover the primary *a priori* relatedness in which they are given together, before the object is given to the subject and the subject to himself, as "I-It." The meeting is exchange, not identification, mutual unmediated presence.

Buber's account of the meeting of "I and Thou" is his own, but it can be paralleled in the others. What is common is that the "other" cannot be reduced to an object; or, rather, although the other is an object to me, as I am to another, this is an external illusory aspect of a reality which cannot be seized in itself as an object, which, as subject, is inaccessible by constitution, and cannot be assimilated nor appropriated—nor eliminated. I can try to communicate with the Other; I can "meet" the Other as a "presence"; I cannot know the Other as an object.

Transactions of this kind, encounters and communications with myself as human reality, with the Other as Thou, and, possibly, with God or Being, bring into existence personality and community. It follows that the person is not merely the individual, and the community is not merely the collective. Person and community have always to be realized and are never fully nor finally achieved. Individualism and collectivism are not opposed ideals or claims; they belong together: the collective is a herd of individuals; the individual is in the herd because he is isolated and lost. On the other hand, the person finds the responsible independence in which he is "given" to himself, and meets the Other on the same ground in community. This "community" does not necessarily mean "harmony." Communication may involve conflict when it is authentic, but the conflict is then necessary and "loving."

Certain discontinuities in experience, or levels of Being, are discriminated in this thinking. There is the world of objects which are *there,* for study or observation or use, the objects of science or manufacture or administration, including of course man in these contexts. There is the world of persons, the world of decisions and "meetings"—including of course human beings trying to escape from themselves or the Other, from the human condition. There is for most of these thinkers, in some form, the transcendental world of Being-in-itself, encompassing subject and object and therefore inaccessible to thought but capable of being encountered in certain ways. The failure to make and sustain these necessary distinctions, the assimilation of Being to one level, is the typical error of idealism as of positivism or materialism. Reduction is the capital philosophical error.

Method

Every philosopher seeks to establish his statements by some method, and in turn his statements are examined in the light of the method he has used to establish them. Indeed, philosophy proper is largely a question of choosing or devising and justifying a method, and philosophies are largely distinguished by their methods. Thus there has been dialectical thinking, deductive and inductive thinking, critical analysis, linguistic analysis, symbolic logic, and phenomenology, to name only some of the methods of philosophic thinking. Methods may be expository or may be used to validate statements or may constitute the structure of the philosophical system or may claim to represent the structure of thought as such or the structure of Being. Any or many of these possibilities may be found in any one method as used by a philosopher; and of course any philosopher may use more than one method. Logic and metaphysics in the history of philosophies have been characteristically interdependent, for the logic has usually depended upon some assumption about or insight into the structure of Being and has then been used to elaborate a system of Being or a systematic description of Being. This is as true of Epicurus as of Plato or Aristotle, of Occam as of Leibnitz or Descartes; it is notoriously true of Hegel, but it is also true of such thinkers as Kant and Husserl, who do not claim to speak about Being, the world as it is in itself; for this position, too, involves a judgment about Being, even if it is only a suspension of judgment, since the decision to suspend judgment is a certain understanding of the situation which determines the method.

What method is involved in existentialist thinking? Kierkegaard employs a dialectical method in the development of his entire authorship. This is mainly expository, for he employs it, and his "Socratic" irony, to refuse "results," to force the reader back on himself, to force the issue and afterward to keep the question open; but this in turn is required by a certain understanding of the situation in which the thinker is placed, the "existential" situation. Nietzsche engages in "perspective" thinking, looking at things experimentally from different points of view. Jaspers concentrates on developing a logic of philosophizing, distinct from the logic of the sciences, and this develops into a concentration on the history of philosophy: "In order to preserve our philosophical consciousness—the content of thousands of years of philosophizing, the right to carry through the kind of philosophical thinking which sustains our life—I have tried to understand what methods of thinking have actually been used in philosophy since time immemorial." Marcel distinguishes "secondary reflection" as the special tool of philosophical research. Primary reflection is analytic, giving us the specialized sciences; secondary reflection is recuperative, restoring the unity of experience by an inner reshaping of thought by which it escapes from the images and ideas with which it tends to become identified and facilitates participation in and responsiveness to existence.

Phenomenology is the method most commonly associated with existentialism; and it is distinctively the method of Heidegger, Sartre, and Merleau-Ponty, students of Husserl. In a general sense, phenomenology is merely description of phenomena as observed, and existentialist literature is rich in classical descriptions of human phenomena. With Edmund Husserl (1859–1938), pure phenomenology or phenomenological philosophy was the description of the contents of immediate experience from a certain point of view. This was the point of view of philosophy, and this program of systematic description was to be the cumulative task of philosophers engaged in this universal science, the "science of pure possibilities" which logically preceded the "science of real facts," the empirical sciences—although the possible derives from the real. This point of view of philosophy is the so-called "phenomenological reduction," by which attention is given only to essential structures or relations, not to particular facts, and by which the world and its questions are excluded and attention turns to the "pure" consciousness of the individual thinker, freed from all presuppositions—my own perceivings, rememberings, imaginings. This is "secondary" reflection, getting behind primary reflection, going back to "the things themselves," but in a different sense from Marcel's, for it describes the stream of consciousness in order to discern ultimate structures, a "scientific" concern, not in order to recover the unity of experience and to participate in existence, a "therapeutic" (or "existentialist") concern.

However, Heidegger, Husserl's successor, does not restrict himself to the rigorous discipline of pure phenomenology. He moves toward a concept of Being by way of an interpretation of human being in the world. He rejects traditional ontologies because they have forgotten the real question of Being and goes behind them to the pre-Socratics before this happened. But he thinks a "phenomenological ontology" is possible because the Being of entities discloses itself in phenomena uncovered by phenomenological research.

Jaspers, on the other hand, insists that there can be no ontology because Being cannot be the object of a science, even the "philosophical" science of pure phenomenology. The ancient and modern goals of philosophical thinking cannot be reached by science, and a philosophical science is a contradition in terms. In place of ontology he would put a "periechontology" which makes no assertions about what Being is and leads to no concept of Being but explores the modes in which we can encounter Being. Marcel, in principle, agrees with this refusal of an ontology.

Differences

What these differences amount to is arguable, and they can be played up or played down. What is certain is that there are deep differences among these thinkers, methodological, metaphysical, and in temper and concerns; and it is impossible to give a general account of existentialist thinking without blurring these differences or speaking now in the voice of one, now in the voice of another, when each speaks solely for himself. And they are critics of one another.

Marcel, like Buber, stands for a metaphysic of *we are* as opposed to a metaphysic of *I think*. Intersubjectivity, he says, a whole which is togetherness, relationship with, is the starting point and ground for inquiry into Being. This is a criticism of Sartre, of whom he says: "The fundamental opposition between *pour soi* and *en soi* makes impossible by definition intersubjectivity in the precise sense I have given to the word, or makes it impossible to be open to the other, to welcome him in the deepest sense of the word, and to become at the same time more accessible to oneself." Indeed, Sartre's account of interpersonal relations—his descriptions of attempts to reduce the other or to reduce oneself to a thing, or to possess or to eliminate the other as a subject, all doomed to frustration—is certainly not a metaphysic of *we are*. For, he contends, the experience of *we are* is strictly and merely empirical and fugitive, in no sense a solution of the essential conflict that subsists between subjects as such. Here the difference is sharp, and it is metaphysical, nothing less than the recognition, on the one side, of *we are* as the ground for an acknowledgment of and response to an absolute *Thou* or transcendental ground of Being, and, on the other, the rejection of this as being invalid. In fact there is here reproduced within existentialism what would seem to be the deepest division in the whole tradition of philosophy, between "the perennial philosophy," the metaphysic which acknowledges a divine reality, and those naturalist or humanist philosophies whose acknowledgment stops at human reality. This major opposition is there in the beginning with Kierkegaard and Nietzsche. What, then, it may be asked, is the value of existentialist thinking if it does not lead to any decisive answer on what is perhaps the main question which thinking mankind wants to have resolved?

This demand that philosophy shall take sides on the large issues of life and give the common man the reassurance he needs, or at least some definite answers, is not necessarily acknowledged as legitimate by philosophers. A proponent of "scientific" philosophy will deplore all the "isms" and think it scandalously inappropriate to call for vote-casting in his discipline. Philosophers may, perhaps must, take sides, but this comes afterward and is strictly nonphilosophical. The existentialist cannot go along with a philosopher of this kind, because for him philosophy cannot be a science and because for him the thinker is in a situation which requires him to decide, to act, to take sides, and his thinking enables him to do so with more light and to better purpose. However, the philosopher cannot "give the answer," not because it is not his business, but because it cannot be done.

Kierkegaard is a man of faith, but he does nothing to reduce the risks of this position for others. On the contrary, his whole insistence is on the inescapable risk: he himself, and all others like him, are forever out "over seventy thousand fathoms of water." His decision is public, but it does not help another; it does not even help himself tomorrow. His public witness is not to the truth of his belief, but to the inescapable hazard of his response, a total commitment to what is wholly Other. Similar is Nietzsche, who assumes that God is dead. He is not in any state of agony about whether this assumption is justified or not, but he continues to live with the consequences: he is alternately thrilled and overcome with vertigo at the thought of man as pure possibility, totally responsible for all values, for his own essence. His public witness is not to the nonexistence of God, but to the responsibility demanded by the consequences of this disbelief: he is not asserting or denying a proposition, but calling to a task. Both men are concerned with the same situation in the same way, although the difference in what they assume or believe is total. Existentialist thinking sharpens this difference to the utmost. At the same time, it brings together those on both sides of the division who recognize that it is the condition of man to live with enduring, irresolvable tensions, against those whose thinking establishes a harmony which does not and cannot exist. This difference in philosophy (Heraclitus versus Pythagoras) is more ultimate in this thinking than the great division that separates the tradition of the "perennial" philosophy from that of the naturalist and humanist philosophies.

The metaphysical difference is linked with a difference in temper and concerns. If existentialism is thought of as a movement, it should be recognized that it has a left wing and a right wing, a political pole as well as a religious pole. Sartre and Merleau-Ponty were cofounders of *Les Temps Modernes* in 1945; their preoccupation is with Marxist politics, not with God or transcendence. At the same time, both wings, in the midst of these seemingly opposite concerns, are equally devoted to the rescue of human reality, not by trying t[illegible]onserve human values in a world hostile on all fronts, [illegible]by demonstrating that this human reality is in its constit[illegible]a transcendent, free, responsible.

Influence

Probably it is true to say, and natural to expect, that the influence of existentialist thinking has been an influence on practice rather than on thought—in religion, in politics, and in psychiatry.

Kierkegaard concentrated upon the task of translating completely into terms of reflection what it means to become a Christian. Marcel's concern is to open the way again from reflection (by this transformation of thought) to the possibility of becoming a Christian. Similarly, Rudolf Bultmann uses Heidegger's analysis of human existence to enable modern man to hear again the message of the Gospels. "Demythologizing" does away with the objectivity of the message, but its objectivity, so it is claimed, stands in the way of its truth and of its acceptance. The diffusion of existentialist thinking has been the main influence in producing in Protestant circles a modern Christian radicalism which has outpaced an older "modernism" that was rationalist in character. The concessions of this modernism to rationalism are regarded as being mistaken in principle, since rationalism itself is radically mistaken.

In politics, Sartre and his colleagues, formed by experiences in the oven of the Resistance, have decisively influenced a generation of French-speaking intellectuals. In this Sartre is consciously reversing the influence of an earlier humanism in which, he says, three generations of Frenchmen were bred. This humanism valued above everything the discursive disinterested intelligence, eager to resolve everything in "understanding"—and therefore unable to recognize evil (e.g., Nazism) and take a stand against it. Sartre has done his best to bring home to everybody that personal involvement and responsibility, decision-making and "engagement" are inescapable since they constitute the nature and situation of human beings. "Commitment" and "meeting" or "encounter" are not merely religious words, although they have been exploited in contemporary religious discussion; they belong to the vocabulary of the phenomenological description of human being.

The influence on psychiatry has been perhaps the most beneficial and creative influence of existentialist thinking. The analyst trained in a particular school is liable to be "blinded by science," to see only what he has been schooled to recognize, whereas the existentialist refuses to see in the "other" an object of knowledge and is ready to "encounter" and "meet" a person even in a patient. Further, since the existentialist thinks of the individual as becoming a person only in interpersonal relations, as analyst he is concerned with restoring the possibility of interpersonal relations to one whose disability is largely an incapacity for interpersonal relations. The clinical approach is in any case different from the approach of the behavioral scientist, but existentialist thinking provides theoretical justification and direction for the clinical approach in psychological medicine. Indeed, it is not too much to say that existentialism (like stoicism) is itself a therapeutic view of man and comes into its own in psychiatric practice.

Criticism

An introduction to existentialist thinking is not the place for making nor for dealing with criticism. Perhaps it may be said, however, that the most interesting general criticism comes from the Thomist side and the Marxist side, both heirs to the classical ontology to which existentialists are most opposed. For a Thomist, existentialism is the inevitable *débacle* in philosophy which must follow from an acceptance of Kantian agnosticism. If Protestant theologians have rejoiced in their freedom, they will continue to do so only so long as they are on easy terms with intellectual chaos and moral anarchy.

The distinguished Hungarian critic Georg Lukacs, like other Marxists, has seen existentialism as the last redoubt of bourgeois philosophy, trying to establish a third way between or beyond idealism and materialism. This, he tries to show, is an eclecticism which makes the worst of both worlds, for there is no third way possible, and existentialism is either an enfeebled idealism, substituting intuition for reason, or an ineffectual materialism which will not come to terms with the real determinants at work, or a plain nihilism which finds in death the only reality and the final meaning of life. A philosophy which has abandoned a rational universe, which insists that the world cannot be thought, must be preoccupied with the suprarational or with the irrational, the absurd. It is a philosoph[illegible]ithout criterion or program. And a philosophy which refu[illegible] bound by its own thoughts and a morality which refuses to be bound by its own acts hypostasize and falsify the moment of choice. Liberty is marginal, not central.

Is this an illuminating criticism? What is idealism? Existentialism, far from being a third alternative, is a protest against the formulation of issues in terms of such abstractions; perhaps it is a symptom of the disintegration of this kind of philosophy. At the same time, existentialist philosophers are not refusing issues that have been posed in these terms (idealism, materialism); they are not confining philosophy to general analysis, a critique of concepts, a body of techniques. On the contrary, they speak in dramatic tones, they use gestures; in their return from the abstract to the concrete, they seem to want to abandon philosophy for literature. To refuse all reductions and abstractions, to distrust clear and distinct ideas and prefer a certain uneasiness of life, to find that problems after all are not problems to be solved, to insist on the limits of reason, and on the virtues of ambiguity, paradox, discontinuity, "mystery," and on the insecurity of all standards and values, as well as ideas and programs: this, surely, amounts to intellectual defeatism. Is existentialist thinking a campaign against philosophy itself?

The existentialist thinker certainly could not agree that he is voting to abolish thinking in favor of existence. On the contrary, he stands as a condemnation of that prevalent form of "seriousness" which abdicates personal existence in favor of the reality of the world. He simply asks for the frank recognition that thought, as abstraction and reduction, necessarily is in tension with existence and can neither overshadow it nor take its place. This tension between thought and existence which has to be lived and can never be resolved, which makes the human condition and is the source of human reality, is neither futile nor fatal. On the contrary, it is the established philosophies that are futile and fatal, because they establish themselves in the world—and in place of the world. Insofar as a thinker identifies himself with any of them, he forfeits his own independent reality and loses touch with the otherness of the other and the aseity of things. Existentialist thinking establishes this reality and these contacts by achieving interrelations that are not simply "given."

If existentialism is not an established philosophy, it nevertheless is a body of teaching about "human reality" and about the role of thinking. As such, it must undergo scrutiny on the dissecting table of the professional philosopher, and it remains to be tested like everything else by the sober experience of mankind. Perhaps it may be left with the remark that a return to the pre-Socratics may be less loudly derided if it is recalled that Socrates, the great father of rationalism, had no use for fields and trees and poets because they could not teach him anything.

SÖREN KIERKEGAARD

(1813–1855)

At the outset, the editor is made culpable. For Kierkegaard insists that existentialist writing is not ordinary direct communication: existentialist thinking has no results which can be summarized or sampled. Existentialist thought is essentially secretive, and its communication is a work of art. The most that can be done is to induce in the reader a certain subjective condition—which is not the same as handing over a subjective opinion and is not achieved by passing on any agreed or objectively supported truth.

Kierkegaard's own voluminous writings, consecrated to "the task of translating completely into terms of reflection what Christianity is, what it means to become a Christian," signified "his own education in Christianity" and constituted a complete dialectical structure, of which the several parts are whole works. This systematic achievement was not a system. Indeed, it was an elaborate attack upon "the System" (Hegel's) and aimed at the conviction of all systems, past and future, not because of their errors but for the original sin of being conceived. To tamper with the system of the system-breaker is as bad as to confuse his system with theirs.

To take Kierkegaard seriously in this, however, would be to limit his public (but he speaks only to individuals) to the few whom he addressed in the situation of his own time and place and who took the trouble to study his carefully planned output, his "complete dialectical structure," his system. To make him for his own sake even more esoteric than "the System" would be the unkindest cut of all. The only alternative would also offend, but it cannot be helped: it is to take him seriously "to a certain extent," to take him seriously up to a point, to the point of publishing and underlining his warning, but not to the point of presenting everything or nothing.

Following his own clue, and also because all these selections are drawn from the philosophical writings of the existentialists, and none from their other literary productions, the passages have been chosen from his main philosophical work,

Concluding Unscientific Postscript (1846), which followed his other philosophical work, *Philosophical Fragments, or a Fragment of Philosophy* (1844), a slim preface to the *Postscript.* He calls this work the "turning point of the whole authorship, which states the 'Problem' and at the same time, by indirect attack and Socratic dialectic, inflicts upon the System a mortal wound—from behind, fighting the System and Speculation in order to show that 'the way' is not from the Simple to the System and Speculation, but from the System and Speculation back again to the simple thing of becoming a Christian, fighting for this cause and vigorously slashing through to find the way back."

The reader of these philosophical extracts should be warned that no one can fully understand Kierkegaard who has not also read and understood his devotional works or religious writings, particularly, perhaps, *The Sickness Unto Death* (1849), a reflection on existentialist despair over what it means to be a human being—so different from philosophical doubt.

EXTRACTS

Concluding Unscientific Postscript. Trans. by David F. Swenson and Walter Lowrie. Princeton University Press, 1941.
Book Two, Part One, Chapter II, Section 4.B. "An existential system is impossible."
Book Two, Part Two, Chapter II, "Truth is Subjectivity."
Book Two, Part Two, Chapter III, "The Subjective Thinker."
Book Two, Part Two, Chapter V, Conclusion: "Objective Christianity," "Subjective Christianity."

from *Concluding Unscientific Postscript*

AN EXISTENTIAL SYSTEM IS IMPOSSIBLE

Respecting the impossibility of an existential system, let us then ask quite simply, as a Greek youth might have asked his teacher (and if the superlative wisdom can explain everything, but cannot answer a simple question, it is clear that the world is out of joint): "Who is to write or complete such a system?" Surely a human being; unless we propose again to begin using the strange mode of speech which assumes that a human being becomes speculative philosophy in the abstract, or becomes the identity of subject and object. So then, a human being—and surely a living human being, i.e. an existing individual. Or if the speculative thought which brings the systems to light is the joint effort of different thinkers: in what last concluding thought does this fellowship finally realize itself, how does it reach the light of day? Surely through some human being? And how are the individual participants related to the joint effort, what are the categories which mediate between the individual and world-process, and who is it again who strings them all together on the systematic thread? Is he a human being, or is he speculative philosophy in the abstract? But if he is a human being, then he is also an existing individual. Two ways, in general, are open for an existing individual: *Either* he can do his utmost to forget that he is an existing individual, by which he becomes a comic figure, since existence has the remarkable trait of compelling an existing individual to exist whether he wills it or not. . . . *Or* he can concentrate his entire energy upon the fact that he is an existing individual. It is from this side, in the first instance, that objection must be made to modern philosophy; not that it has a mistaken presupposition, but that it has a comical presupposition, occasioned by its having forgotten, in a sort of world-historical absent-mindedness, what it means to be a human being. Not indeed, what it means to be a human being in general; for this is the sort of thing that one might even induce a speculative philosopher to agree to; but what it means that you and I and he are human beings, each one for himself.

. . . The existing individual who forgets that he is an existing individual, will become more and more absent-minded; and as people sometimes embody the fruits of their leisure moments in books, so we may venture to expect as the fruit of his absent-mindedness the expected existential system—well, perhaps not all of us, but only those who are almost as absent-minded as he is. While the Hegelian philosophy goes on and becomes an existential system in sheer distraction of mind, and what is more, is finished—without having an Ethics (where existence properly belongs), the more simple philosophy which is propounded by an existing individual for existing individuals, will more especially emphasize the ethical.

As soon as it is remembered that philosophizing does not consist in addressing fantastic beings in fantastic language, but that those to whom the philosopher addresses himself are human beings; so that we have not to determine fantastically *in abstracto* whether a persistent striving is something lower than the systematic finality, or *vice versa,* but that the question is what existing human beings, in so far as they are existing beings, must needs be content with: then it will be evident that the ideal of a persistent striving is the only view of life that does not carry with it an inevitable disillusionment. Even if a man has attained to the highest, the repetition by which life receives content (if one is to escape retrogression or avoid becoming fantastic) will again constitute a persistent striving; because here again finality is moved further on, and postponed. It is with this view of life as it is with the Platonic interpretation of love [1] as a want; and the principle that not only he is in want who desires something he does not have, but also he who desires the continued possession of what he has. In a speculative-fantastic sense we have a positive finality in the System, and in an aesthetic-fantastic sense we have one in the fifth act of the drama. But this sort of finality is valid only for fantastic beings.

The ideal of a persistent striving expresses the existing subject's ethical view of life. It must therefore not be understood in a metaphysical sense, nor indeed is there any individual who exists metaphysically. One might thus by way of misunderstanding set up an antithesis between finality and the persistent striving for truth. But this is merely a misunderstanding in this sphere. In the ethical sense, on the contrary, the persistent striving represents the consciousness of being an existing individual; the constant learning is the expression for the incessant realization, in no moment complete as long as the subject is in existence; the subject is aware of this fact, and hence is not deceived. But Greek philosophy always had a relation to Ethics. Hence it was not imagined that the principle of always being a learner was a great discovery, or the enthusiastic enterprise of a particular distinguished individual; for it was neither more nor less than the realization that a human being is an existing individual, which it constitutes no great merit to be aware of, but which it is thoughtless to forget.

So-called pantheistic systems have often been characterized and challenged in the assertion that they abrogate the distinction between good and evil, and destroy freedom. Perhaps one would express oneself quite as definitely, if one said that every such system fantastically dissipates the concept *exist-*

1. In the *Symposium* [Ed.].

ence. But we ought to say this not merely of pantheistic systems; it would be more to the point to show that every system must be pantheistic precisely on account of its finality. Existence must be revoked in the eternal before the system can round itself out; there must be no existing remainder, not even such a little minikin as the existing Herr Professor who writes the system. But this is not the way in which the problem is usually dealt with. No, pantheistic systems are attacked, partly in tumultuous aphorisms which again and again promise a new system; and partly by way of scraping together something supposed to be a system, and inserting in it a special paragraph in which it is laid down that the concept *existence,* or actuality, is intended to be especially emphasized. That such a paragraph is a mockery of the entire system, that instead of being a paragraph in a system it is an absolute protest against the system, makes no difference to busy systematists. If the concept of existence is really to be stressed, this cannot be given a direct expression as a paragraph in a system; all direct swearing and oath-supported assurances serve only to make the topsy-turvy profession of the paragraph more and more ridiculous. An actual emphasis on existence must be expressed in an essential form; in view of the elusiveness of existence, such a form will have to be an indirect form, namely, the absence of a system. But this again must not degenerate into an asseverating formula, for the indirect character of the expression will constantly demand renewal and rejuvenation in the form. In the case of committee reports, it may be quite in order to incorporate in the report a dissenting opinion; but an existential system which includes the dissenting opinion as a paragraph in its own logical structure, is a curious monstrosity. What wonder that the System continues to sustain its life as a going concern. In general, objections are haughtily ignored; if a particular objection seems to attract a little attention, the systematic entrepreneurs engage a copyist to copy off the objection, which thereupon is incorporated in the System; and when the book is bound the System is complete.

The systematic Idea is the identity of subject and object, the unity of thought and being. Existence, on the other hand, is their separation. It does not by any means follow that existence is thoughtless; but it has brought about, and brings about, a separation between subject and object, thought and being. In the objective sense, thought is understood as being pure thought; this corresponds in an equally abstract-objective sense to its object, which object is therefore the thought itself, and the truth becomes the correspondence of thought with itself. This objective thought has no relation to the existing subject; and while we are always confronted with the difficult question of how the existing subject slips into this objectivity, where subjectivity is merely pure abstract subjectivity (which again is an objective determination, not signifying any existing human being), it is certain that the existing subjectivity tends more and more to evaporate. And finally, if it is possible for a human being to become anything of the sort, and it is merely something of which at most he becomes aware through the imagination, he becomes the pure abstract conscious participation in and knowledge of this pure relationship between thought and being, this pure identity; aye, this tautology, because this being which is ascribed to the thinker does not signify that he is, but only that he is engaged in thinking.

The existing subject, on the other hand, is engaged in existing, which is indeed the case with every human being. Let us therefore not deal unjustly with the objective tendency, by calling it an ungodly and pantheistic self-deification; but let us rather view it as an essay in the comical. For the notion that from now on until the end of the world nothing could be said except what proposed a further improvement in an almost completed system, is merely a systematic consequence for systematists.

By beginning at once to use ethical categories in criticism of the objective tendency, one does it an injustice, and fails to make contact with it, because one has nothing in common with what is under attack. But by remaining in the metaphysical sphere, one is enabled to use the comical, which also lies in the metaphysical, so as to bring such a transfigured professor to book. If a dancer could leap very high, we would admire him. But if he tried to give the impression that he could fly, let laughter single him out for suitable punishment; even though it might be true that he could leap as high as any dancer ever had done. Leaping is the accomplishment of a being essentially earthly, one who respects the earth's gravitational force, since the leaping is only momentary. But flying carries a suggestion of being emancipated from telluric conditions, a privilege reserved for winged creatures, and perhaps also shared by the inhabitants of the moon—and there perhaps the System will first find its true readers.

• • •

TRUTH IS SUBJECTIVITY

• • •

When the question of truth is raised in an objective manner, reflection is directed objectively to the truth, as an object to which the knower is related. Reflection is not focussed upon the relationship, however, but upon the question of whether it is the truth to which the knower is related. If only the object to which he is related is the truth, the subject is accounted to be in the truth. When the question of the truth is raised subjectively, reflection is directed subjectively to the nature of the individual's relationship; i[illegible] only the mode of this relationship is in the truth, the ind[illegible]al is in the trut[illegible] even if he should happen to be thus r[illegible]d to what is no[illegible] true.[2] Let us take as an example the k[illegible]ledge of God. Objectively, reflection is directed to the prob[illegible]m of whether this object is the true God; subjectively, reflection is directed to the question whether the individual is related to a something *in such a manner* that his relationship is in truth a God-relationship. On which side is the truth now to be found? Ah, may we not here resort to a mediation, and say: It is on neither side, but in the mediation of both? Excellently well said, provided we might have it explained how an existing individual manages to be in a state of mediation. For to be in a state of mediation is to be finished, while to exist is to become. Nor can an existing individual be in two places at the same time—he cannot be an identity of subject and object. When he is nearest to being in two places at the same time he is in passion; but passion is momentary, and passion is also the highest expression of subjectivity.

The existing individual who chooses to pursue the objective way enters upon the entire approximation-process by which it is proposed to bring God to light objectively. But this is in all eternity impossible, because God is a subject, and therefore exists only for subjectivity in inwardness. The existing individual who chooses the subjective way apprehends instantly the entire dialectical difficulty involved in having to use some time, perhaps a long time, in finding God objectively; and he feels this dialectical difficulty in all its painfulness, because every moment is wasted in which he does not

2. The reader will observe that the question here is about essential truth, or about the truth which is essentially related to existence, and that it is precisely for the sake of clarifying it as inwardness or as subjectivity that this contrast is drawn.

have God.[3] That very instant he has God, not by virtue of any objective deliberation, but by virtue of the infinite passion of inwardness. The objective inquirer, on the other hand, is not embarrassed by such dialectical difficulties as are involved in devoting an entire period of investigation to finding God—since it is possible that the inquirer may die tomorrow; and if he lives he can scarcely regard God as something to be taken along if convenient, since God is precisely that which one takes *à tout prix*, which in the understanding of passion constitutes the true inward relationship to God.

It is at this point, so difficult dialectically, that the way swings off for everyone who knows what it means to think, and to think existentially; which is something very different from sitting at a desk and writing about what one has never done, something very different from writing *de omnibus dubitandum* and at the same time being as credulous existentially as the most sensuous of men. Here is where the way swings off, and the change is marked by the fact that while objective knowledge rambles comfortably on by way of the long road of approximation without being impelled by the urge of passion, subjective knowledge counts every delay a deadly peril, and the decision so infinitely important and so instantly pressing that it is as if the opportunity had already passed.

• • •

When subjectivity is the truth, the conceptual determination of the truth must include an expression for the antithesis to objectivity, a memento of the fork in the road where the way swings off; this expression will at the same time serve as an indication of the tension of the subjective inwardness. Here is such a definition of truth: *An objective uncertainty held fast in an appropriation-process of the most passionate inwardness is the truth,* the highest truth attainable for an *existing* individual. At the point where the way swings off (and where this is cannot be specified objectively, since it is a matter of subjectivity), there objective knowledge is placed

3. In this manner God certainly becomes a postulate, but not in the otiose manner in which this word is commonly understood. It becomes clear rather that the only way in which an existing individual comes into relation with God, is when the dialectical contradiction brings his passion to the point of despair, and helps him to embrace God with the "category of despair" (faith). Then the postulate is so far from being arbitrary that it is precisely a life-necessity. It is then not so much that God is a postulate, as that the existing individual's postulation of God is a necessity.

in abeyance. Thus the subject merely has, objectively, the uncertainty; but it is this which precisely increases the tension of that infinite passion which constitutes his inwardness. The truth is precisely the venture which chooses an objective uncertainty with the passion of the infinite. I contemplate the order of nature in the hope of finding God, and I see omnipotence and wisdom; but I also see much else that disturbs my mind and excites anxiety. The sum of all this is an objective uncertainty. But it is for this very reason that the inwardness becomes as intense as it is, for it embraces this objective uncertainty with the entire passion of the infinite. In the case of a mathematical proposition the objectivity is given, but for this reason the truth of such a proposition is also an indifferent truth.

But the above definition of truth is an equivalent expression for faith. Without risk there is no faith. Faith is precisely the contradiction between the infinite passion of the individual's inwardness and the objective uncertainty. If I am capable of grasping God objectively, I do not believe, but precisely because I cannot do this I must believe. If I wish to preserve myself in faith I must constantly be intent upon holding fast the objective uncertainty, so as to remain out upon the deep, over seventy thousand fathoms of water, still preserving my faith.

In the principle that subjectivity, inwardness, is the truth, there is comprehended the Socratic wisdom, whose everlasting merit it was to have become aware of the essential significance of existence, of the fact that the knower is an existing individual. For this reason Socrates was in the truth by virtue of his ignorance, in the highest sense in which this was possible within paganism. To attain to an understanding of this, to comprehend that the misfortune of speculative philosophy is again and again to have forgotten that the knower is an existing individual, is in our objective age difficult enough. But to have made an advance upon Socrates without even having understood what he understood, is at any rate not "Socratic." . . .

. . .

When subjectivity, inwardness, is the truth, the truth becomes objectively a paradox; and the fact that the truth is objectively a paradox shows in its turn that subjectivity is the truth. For the objective situation is repellent; and the expression for the objective repulsion constitutes the tension and the measure of the corresponding inwardness. The paradoxical character of the truth is its objective uncertainty; this uncertainty is an expression for the passionate inwardness, and this passion is precisely the truth. So far the Socratic principle. The eternal and essential truth, the truth which has an essential relationship to an existing individual because it pertains essentially to existence (all other knowledge being from the Socratic point of view accidental, its scope and degree a matter of indifference), is a paradox. But the eternal essential truth is by no means in itself a paradox; but it becomes paradoxical by virtue of its relationship to an existing individual. The Socratic ignorance gives expression to the objective uncertainty attaching to the truth, while his inwardness in existing is the truth. To anticipate here what will be developed later, let me make the following remark. The Socratic ignorance is an analogue to the category of the absurd, only that there is still less of objective certainty in the absurd, and in the repellent effect that the absurd exercises. It is certain only that it is absurd, and precisely on that account it incites to an infinitely greater tension in the corresponding inwardness. The Socratic inwardness in existing is an analogue to faith; only that the inwardness of faith, corresponding as it does, not to the repulsion of the Socratic ignorance, but to the repulsion exerted by the absurd, is infinitely more profound.

Socratically the eternal essential truth is by no means in its own nature paradoxical, but only in its relationship to an existing individual. This finds expression in another Socratic proposition, namely, that all knowledge is recollection. This proposition is not for Socrates a cue to the speculative enterprise, and hence he does not follow it up; essentially it becomes a Platonic principle. Here the way swings off; Socrates concentrates essentially upon accentuating existence, while Plato forgets this and loses himself in speculation. Socrates' infinite merit is to have been an *existing* thinker, not a speculative philosopher who forgets what it means to exist. For Socrates therefore the principle that all knowledge is recollection has at the moment of his leave-taking and as the constantly rejected possibility of engaging in speculation, the following two-fold significance: (1) that the knower is essentially *integer*, and that with respect to the knowledge of the eternal truth he is confronted with no other difficulty than the circumstance that he exists; which difficulty, however, is so essential and decisive for him that it means that existing, the process of transformation to inwardness in and by existing, is the truth; (2) that existence in time does not have any decisive significance, because the possibility of taking oneself back into eternity through recollection is always there, though this possibility is constantly nullified by utilizing the time, not for speculation, but for the transformation to inwardness in existing.

The infinite merit of the Socratic position was precisely to accentuate the fact that the knower is an existing individual, and that the task of existing is his essential task. Making an advance upon Socrates by failing to understand this, is quite a mediocre achievement. This Socratic principle we must therefore bear in mind, and then inquire whether the formula may not be so altered as really to make an advance beyond the Socratic position.

Subjectivity, inwardness, has been posited as the truth; can any expression for the truth be found which has a still higher degree of inwardness? Aye, there is such an expression, provided the principle that subjectivity or inwardness is the truth begins by positing the opposite principle: that subjectivity is untruth. Let us not at this point succumb to such haste as to fail in making the necessary distinctions. Speculative philosophy also says that subjectivity is untruth, but says it in order to stimulate a movement in precisely the opposite direction, namely, in the direction of the principle that objectivity is the truth. Speculative philosophy determines subjectivity negatively as tending toward objectivity. This second determination of ours, however, places a hindrance in its own way while proposing to begin, which has the effect of making the inwardness far more intensive. Socratically speaking, subjectivity is untruth if it refuses to understand that subjectivity is truth, but, for example, desires to become objective. Here, on the other hand, subjectivity in beginning upon the task of becoming the truth through a subjectifying process, is in the difficulty that it is already untruth. Thus, the labor of the task is thrust backward, backward, that is, in inwardness. So far is it from being the case that the way tends in the direction of objectivity, that the beginning merely lies still deeper in subjectivity.

But the subject cannot be untruth eternally, or eternally be presupposed as having been untruth; it must have been brought to this condition in time, or here become untruth in time. The Socratic paradox consisted in the fact that the eternal was related to an existing individual, but now existence has stamped itself upon the existing individual a second time. There has taken place so essential an alteration in him that he cannot now possibly take himself back into the eternal by way of recollection. To do this is to speculate; to be able to do this, but to reject the possibility by apprehending the task of life as a realization of inwardness in existing, is the Socratic position. But now the difficulty is that what followed Socrates on his way as a rejected possibility, has become an impossibility. If engaging in speculation was a dubious merit even from the point of view of the Socratic, it is now neither more nor less than confusion.

The paradox emerges when the eternal truth and existence are placed in juxtaposition with one another; each time the stamp of existence is brought to bear, the paradox becomes more clearly evident. Viewed Socratically the knower was simply an existing individual, but now the existing individual bears the stamp of having been essentially altered by existence.

Let us now call the untruth of the individual *Sin*. Viewed eternally he cannot be sin, nor can he be eternally presupposed as having been in sin. By coming into existence therefore (for the beginning was that subjectivity is untruth), he becomes a sinner. He is not born as a sinner in the sense that he is presupposed as being a sinner before he is born, but he is born in sin and as a sinner. This we might call *Original Sin*. But if existence has in this manner acquired a power over him, he is prevented from taking himself back into the eternal by way of recollection. If it was paradoxical to posit the eternal truth in relationship to an existing individual, it is now absolutely paradoxical to posit it in relationship to such an individual as we have here defined. But the more difficult it is made for him to take himself out of existence by way of recollection, the more profound is the inwardness that his existence may have in existence; and when it is made impossible for him, when he is held so fast in existence that the back door of recollection is forever closed to him, then his inwardness will be the most profound possible. But let us never forget that the Socratic merit was to stress the fact that the knower is an existing individual; for the more difficult the matter becomes, the greater the temptation to hasten along the easy road of speculation, away from fearful dangers and crucial decisions, to the winning of renown and honors and property, and so forth. If even Socrates understood the dubiety of taking himself speculatively out of existence back into the eternal, although no other difficulty confronted the existing individual except that he existed, and that existing was his essential task, now it is impossible. Forward he must, backward he cannot go.

Subjectivity is the truth. By virtue of the relationship subsisting between the eternal truth and the existing individual, the paradox came into being. Let us now go further, let us suppose that the eternal essential truth is itself a paradox. How does the paradox come into being? By putting the eternal essential truth into juxtaposition with existence. Hence when we posit such a conjunction within the truth itself, the truth becomes a paradox. The eternal truth has come into being in time: this is the paradox. If in accordance with the determinations just posited, the subject is prevented by sin from taking himself back into the eternal, now he need not trouble himself about this; for now the eternal essential truth is not behind him but in front of him, through its being in existence or having existed, so that if the individual does not existentially and in existence lay hold of the truth, he will never lay hold of it.

Existence can never be more sharply accentuated than by means of these determinations. The evasion by which speculative philosophy attempts to recollect itself out of existence has been made impossible. With reference to this, there is nothing for speculation to do except to arrive at an understanding of this impossibility; every speculative attempt which insists on being speculative shows *eo ipso* that it has not understood it. The individual may thrust all this away from him, and take refuge in speculation; but it is impossible first to accept it, and then to revoke it by means of speculation, since it is definitely calculated to prevent speculation.

When the eternal truth is related to an existing individual it becomes a paradox. The paradox repels in the inwardness of the existing individual, through the objective uncertainty and the corresponding Socratic ignorance. But since the paradox is not in the first instance itself paradoxical (but only in its relationship to the existing individual), it does not repel with a sufficient intensive inwardness. For without risk there is no faith, and the greater the risk the greater the faith; the more objective security the less inwardness (for inwardness is precisely subjectivity), and the less objective security the more profound the possible inwardness. When the paradox is paradoxical in itself, it repels the individual by virtue of its absurdity, and the corresponding passion of inwardness is faith. But subjectivity, inwardness, is the truth; for otherwise we have forgotten what the merit of the Socratic position is. But there can be no stronger expression for inwardness than when the retreat out of existence into the eternal by way of recollection is impossible; and when, with truth confronting the individual as a paradox, gripped in the anguish and pain of sin, facing the tremendous risk of the objective insecurity, the individual believes. But without risk no faith, not even the Socratic form of faith, much less the form of which we here speak.

When Socrates believed that there was a God, he held fast to the objective uncertainty with the whole passion of his inwardness, and it is precisely in this contradiction and in this risk, that faith is rooted. Now it is otherwise. Instead of the objective uncertainty, there is here a certainty, namely, that objectively it is absurd; and this absurdity, held fast in the passion of inwardness, is faith. The Socratic ignorance is as a witty jest in comparison with the earnestness of facing the absurd; and the Socratic existential inwardness is as Greek light-mindedness in comparison with the grave strenuosity of faith.

What now is the absurd? The absurd is—that the eternal truth has come into being in time, that God has come into being, has been born, has grown up, and so forth, precisely like any other individual human being, quite indistinguishable from other individuals. For every assumption of immediate recognizability is pre-Socratic paganism, and from the Jewish point of view, idolatry; and every determination of what really makes an advance beyond the Socratic must essentially bear the stamp of having a relationship to God's having come into being; for faith *sensu strictissimo*, as was developed in the *Fragments*, refers to becoming. When Socrates believed that there was a God, he saw very well that where the way swings off there is also an objective way of approximation, for example by the contemplation of nature and human history, and so forth. His merit was precisely to shun this way, where the quantitative siren song enchants the mind and deceives the existing individual.

In relation to the absurd, the objective approximation-process is like the comedy, *Misunderstanding upon Misunderstanding*,[4] which is generally played by *Privatdocents* and speculative philosophers. The absurd is precisely by its objective repulsion the measure of the intensity of faith in

4. A comedy by Overskou [Ed.].

inwardness. Suppose a man who wishes to acquire faith; let the comedy begin. He wishes to have faith, but he wishes also to safeguard himself by means of an objective inquiry and its approximation-process. What happens? With the help of the approximation-process the absurd becomes something different; it becomes probable, it becomes increasingly probable, it becomes extremely and emphatically probable. Now he is ready to believe it, and he ventures to claim for himself that he does not believe as shoemakers and tailors and simple folk believe, but only after long deliberation. Now he is ready to believe it; and lo, now it has become precisely impossible to believe it. Anything that is almost probable, or probable, or extremely and emphatically probable, is something he can almost know, or as good as know, or extremely and emphatically almost *know*—but it is impossible to *believe*. For the absurd is the object of faith, and the only object that can be believed.

Or suppose a man who says that he has faith, but desires to make his faith clear to himself, so as to understand himself in his faith. Now the comedy again begins. The object of faith becomes almost probable, as good as probable, extremely and emphatically probable. He has completed his investigations, and he ventures to claim for himself that he does not believe as shoemakers and tailors and other simple folk believe, but that he has also understood himself in his believing. Strange understanding! On the contrary, he has in fact learned something else about faith than when he believed; and he has learned that he no longer believes, since he almost knows, or as good as knows, or extremely and emphatically almost knows.

In so far as the absurd comprehends within itself the factor of becoming, one way of approximation will be that which confuses the absurd fact of such a becoming (which is the object of faith) with a simple historical fact, and hence seeks historical certainty for that which is absurd, because it involves the contradiction that something which can become historical only in direct opposition to all human reason, has become historical. It is this contradiction which constitutes the absurd, and which can only be believed. If historical certainty with respect to it is assumed, the certainty attained is merely that the something which is thus assumed as certain is not the thing in question. A witness can testify that he has believed it, and hence that so far from being an historical certainty it is directly contrary to his own reason; but such a witness thrusts the individual away in precisely the same sense that the absurd itself does. And a witness who does not so repel is *eo ipso* a deceiver, or a man who talks about something quite different, and can help only to obtain certainty about something quite different. A hundred thousand individual witnesses, who are individual witnesses precisely on account of the peculiar character of their testimony (that they have believed the absurd), cannot *en masse* become anything else, so as to make the absurd less absurd—and why less absurd? Because a hundred thousand human beings have separately, each one for himself, believed that it was absurd? On the contrary, these hundred thousand witnesses again exercise a repellent influence in nearly the same way that the absurd itself exercises it.

• • •

I do not deny that it is a lordly thing to stand so high above Christianity. I do not deny that it is comfortable to be a Christian, and at the same time be exempted from the martyrdom which is always present, even if no persecution menaces from without, even if the Christian is as unnoticed in life as if he had not lived, and is spared the martyrdom of believing against the understanding, the peril of lying upon the deep, the seventy thousand fathoms, in order there to find God. The wader feels his way with his foot, lest he get beyond his depth; and so the shrewd and prudent man feels his way with the understanding in the realm of the probable, and finds God where the probabilities are favorable, and gives thanks on the great holidays of probability, when he has acquired a good livelihood, and there is probability besides for an early advancement; when he has got himself a pretty and attractive wife, and even Councillor Marcussen says that it will be a happy marriage, and that the young woman is of the type of beauty that will in all probability last a long time, and that her physique is such that she will in all probability give birth to strong and healthy children. To believe against the understanding is something different, and to believe with the understanding cannot be done at all; for he who believes with the understanding speaks only of livelihood and wife and fields and oxen and the like, which things are not the object of faith. Faith *always* gives thanks, is *always* in peril of life, in this collision of finite and infinite which is precisely a mortal danger for him who is a composite of both. The probable is therefore so little to the taste of a believer that he fears it most of all, since he well knows that when he clings to probabilities it is because he is beginning to lose his faith.

Faith has in fact two tasks: to take care in every moment to discover the improbable, the paradox; and then to hold it fast with the passion of inwardness. The common conception is that the improbable, the paradoxical, is something to which faith is related only passively; it must provisionally be content with this relationship, but little by little things will become better, as indeed seems probable. O miraculous creation of confusions in speaking about faith! One is to begin believing, in reliance upon the probability that things will soon become better. In this way probability is after all smuggled in, and one is prevented from believing; so that it is easy to understand that the fruit of having been for a long time a believer is, that one no longer believes, instead of, as one might think, that the fruit is a more intensive inwardness in faith. No, faith is self-active in its relation to the improbable and the paradoxical, self-active in the discovery, and self-active in every moment holding it fast—in order to believe. Merely to lay hold of the improbable requires all the passion of the infinite and its concentration in itself; for the improbable and the paradoxical are not to be reached by the understanding's quantitative calculation of the more and more difficult. Where the understanding despairs, faith is already present in order to make the despair properly decisive, in order that the movement of faith may not become a mere exchange within the bargaining sphere of the understanding. But to believe against the understanding is martyrdom; to begin to get the understanding a little in one's favor, is temptation and retrogression. This martyrdom is something that the speculative philosopher is free from. That he must pursue his studies, and especially that he must read many modern books, I admit is burdensome; but the martyrdom of faith is not the same thing. What I therefore fear and shrink from, more than I fear to die and to lose my sweetheart, is to say about Christianity that it is to a certain degree true. If I lived to be seventy years old, if I shortened the night's sleep and increased the day's work from year to year, inquiring into Christianity—how insignificant such a little period of study, viewed as entitling me to judge in so lofty a fashion about Christianity! For to be so embittered against Christianity after a casual acquaintance with it, that I declared it to be false: that would be far more pardonable, far more human. But this lordly superiority seems to me the true corruption, making every saving relationship impossible

—and it may possibly be the case, that Christianity is the truth.

• • •

. . . if inwardness is the truth, results are only rubbish with which we should not trouble each other. The communication of results is an unnatural form of intercourse between man and man, in so far as every man is a spiritual being, for whom the truth consists in nothing else than the self-activity of personal appropriation, which the communication of a result tends to prevent. Let a teacher in relation to the essential truth (for otherwise a direct relationship between teacher and pupil is quite in order) have, as we say, much inwardness of feeling, and be willing to publish his doctrines day in and day out; if he assumes the existence of a direct relationship between the learner and himself, his inwardness is not inwardness, but a direct outpouring of feeling; the respect for the learner which recognizes that he is in himself the inwardness of truth, is precisely the teacher's inwardness. Let a learner be enthusiastic, and publish his teacher's praises abroad in the strongest expressions, thus, as we say, giving evidence of his inwardness; this inwardness is not inwardness, but an immediate devotedness; the devout and silent accord, in which the learner by himself assimilates what he has learned, keeping the teacher at a distance because he turns his attention within himself, this is precisely inwardness. Pathos is indeed inwardness, but it is an immediate inwardness, when it is expressed; but pathos in a contrary form is an inwardness which remains with the maker of the communication in spite of being expressed, and cannot be directly appropriated by another except through that other's self-activity: the contrast of the form is the measure of the inwardness. The more complete the contrast of the form, the greater the inwardness, and the less contrast, up to the point of direct communication, the less the inwardness. It may be difficult enough for an enthusiastic genius, who would so gladly make all men happy and bring them to a knowledge of the truth, to learn in this manner to restrain himself, and to give heed to the *nota bene* of reduplication, the truth not being a circular with signatures affixed, but the *valore intrinseco* of inwardness; for an idler and frivolous person this understanding comes more easily. As soon as the truth, the essential truth, may be assumed to be known by everyone, the objective becomes appropriation and inwardness, and here only an indirect form is applicable. The position of an apostle is different, for he has to preach an unknown truth, whence a direct form of communication may in his case have provisional validity.

It is strange that while there is such universal insistence on the positive, and on the direct form of communication, it occurs to no one to register a complaint against God, who as the eternal spirit from whom all spirits are derived, might in communicating the truth, seem to be justified in sustaining a direct relationship to the derivative spirits, in quite a different sense from that in which the relationship is one between derived spirits, who having a common derivation from God, are *essentially* equal. For no anonymous author can more cunningly conceal himself, no practitioner of the maieutic art more carefully withdraw himself from the direct relationship, than God. He is in the creation, and present everywhere in it, but directly He is not there; and only when the individual turns to his inner self, and hence only in the inwardness of self-activity, does he have his attention aroused, and is enabled to see God.

The immediate relationship to God is paganism, and only after the breach has taken place can there be any question of a true God-relationship. But this breach is precisely the first act of inwardness in the direction of determining the truth as inwardness. Nature is, indeed, the work of God, but only the handiwork is directly present, not God. Is not this to behave, in His relationship to the individual, like an elusive author who nowhere sets down his result in large type, or gives it to the reader beforehand in a preface? And why is God elusive? Precisely because He is the truth, and by being elusive desires to keep men from error. The observer of nature does not have a result immediately set before him, but must by himself be at pains to find it, and thereby the direct relationship is broken. But this breach is precisely the act of self-activity, the irruption of inwardness, the first determination of the truth as inwardness.

Or is not God so unnoticeable, so secretly present in His works, that a man might very well live his entire life, be married, become known and respected as citizen, father, and captain of the hunt, without ever having discovered God in His works, and without ever having received any impression of the infinitude of the ethical, because he helped himself out with what constitutes an analogy to the speculative confusion of the ethical with the historical process, in that he helped himself out by having recourse to the customs and traditions prevailing in the town where he happened to live? As a mother admonishes her child when it sets off for a party: "Now be sure to behave yourself, and do as you see the other well-behaved children do,"—so he might manage to live by conducting himself as he sees others do. He would never do anything first, and he would never have any opinion which he did not first know that others had; for this "others" would be for him the first. Upon extraordinary occasions he would behave as when at a banquet a dish is served, and one does not know how it should be eaten: he would look around until he saw how the others did it, and so forth. Such a man might perhaps know many things, perhaps even know the System by rote; he might be an inhabitant of a Christian country, and bow his head whenever the name of God was mentioned; he would perhaps also see God in nature when in company with others who saw God; he would be a pleasant society man—and yet he would have been deceived by the direct nature of his relationship to the truth, to the ethical, and to God.

If one were to delineate such a man experimentally, he would be a satire upon the human. Essentially it is the God-relationship that makes a man a man, and yet he lacked this. No one would hesitate, however, to regard him as a real man (for the absence of inwardness is not directly apparent); in reality he would constitute a sort of marionette, very deceptively imitating everything human—even to the extent of having children by his wife. At the end of his life, one would have to say that one thing had escaped him: his consciousness had taken no note of God. If God could have permitted a direct relationship, he would doubtless have taken notice. If God, for example, had taken on the figure of a very rare and tremendously large green bird, with a red beak, sitting in a tree on the mound, and perhaps even whistling in an unheard of manner—then the society man would have been able to get his eyes open, and for the first time in his life would be first.

All paganism consists in this, that God is related to man directly, as the obviously extraordinary to the astonished observer. But the spiritual relationship to God in the truth, i.e. in inwardness, is conditioned by a prior irruption of inwardness, which corresponds to the divine elusiveness that God has absolutely nothing obvious about Him, that God is so far from being obvious that He is invisible. It cannot immediately occur to anyone that He exists, although His invisibility is again His omnipresence. An omnipresent person is one that is everywhere to be seen, like a policeman, for example: how deceptive then, that an omnipresent being should be recognizable precisely by being invisible,[5] only and alone recognizable by this trait, since his visibility would annul his omnipresence. The relationship between omnipresence and invisibility is like the relation between mystery and revelation. The mystery is the expression for the fact that the revelation is a revelation in the stricter sense, so that the mystery is the only trait by which it is known; for otherwise a revelation would be something very like a policeman's omnipresence.

• • •

THE SUBJECTIVE THINKER

Just as existence has combined thought and existence by making the existing individual a thinker, so there are two media: the medium of abstract thought, and the medium of reality. But pure thought is still a third medium, quite recently discovered. It therefore begins, as the saying is, after the most exhaustive abstraction. The relation which abstract thought still sustains to that from which it abstracts, is something which pure thought innocently or thoughtlessly ignores. Here is rest for every doubt, here is the eternal positive truth, and whatever else one may be pleased to say. That is, pure thought is a phantom. If the Hegelian philosophy has emancipated itself from every presupposition, it has won this freedom by means of one lunatic postulate: the initial transition to pure thought.

Existence constitutes the highest interest of the existing individual, and his interest in his existence constitutes his reality. What reality is, cannot be expressed in the language of abstraction. Reality is an *inter-esse* between the moments of that hypothetical unity of thought and being which abstract

5. To point out how deceptive the rhetorical can be, I shall here show how one might rhetorically perhaps produce an effect upon a listener, in spite of the fact that what was said was dialectically a regress. Let a pagan religious speaker say that here on earth, God's temples are really empty, but (and now begins the rhetorical) in heaven, where all is more perfect, where water is air and air is ether, there are also temples and sanctuaries for the gods, but the difference is that the gods really dwell in these temples: then we have here a dialectical regress in the proposition that God really dwells in the temple, for the fact that He does not so dwell is an expression for the spiritual relationship to the invisible. But rhetorically it produces an effect. I have as a matter of fact had in view a definite passage by a Greek author, whom I do not, however, wish to cite.

thought presupposes. Abstract thought considers both possibility and reality, but its concept of reality is a false reflection, since the medium within which the concept is thought is not reality, but possibility. Abstract thought can get hold of reality only by nullifying it, and this nullification of reality consists in transforming it into possibility. All that is said about reality in the language of abstraction and within the sphere of abstract thought, is really said within the sphere of the possible. The entire realm of abstract thought, speaking in the language of reality, sustains the relation of possibility to the realm of reality; but this latter reality is not one which is included within abstract thought and the realm of the possible. Reality or existence is the dialectical moment in a trilogy, whose beginning and whose end cannot be for the existing individual, since *qua* existing individual he is himself in the dialectical moment. Abstract thought closes up the trilogy. Just so. But how does it close the trilogy? Is abstract thought a mystic something, or is it not the act of the abstracting individual? But the abstracting individual is the existing individual, who is as such in the dialectical moment, which he cannot close or mediate, least of all absolutely, as long as he remains in existence. So that when he closes the trilogy, this closure must be related as a possibility to the reality or existence in which he remains. And he is bound to explain how he manages to do it, i.e. how he manages to do it as an existing individual; or else he must explain whether he ceases to be an existing individual, and whether he has any right to do this.

The moment we begin to ask this sort of question, we ask ethically, and assert the claim which the ethical has upon the existing individual. This claim is not that he should abstract from existence, but rather that he should exist; and this is at the same time his highest interest.

It is not possible for an existing individual, least of all *as* an existing individual, to hold fast absolutely a suspension of the dialectical moment, namely, existence. This would require another medium than existence, which is the dialectical moment. If an existing individual can become conscious of such a suspension, it can be only as a possibility. But this possibility cannot maintain itself when the existential interest is posited, for which reason the awareness of it can exist only in a state of disinterestedness. But the existing individual can never wholly attain this state *qua* existing individual; and ethically he is not justified even in trying to attain it *approximando*, since the ethical seeks contrariwise to make the existential interest infinite, so infinite that the principle of contradiction becomes absolutely valid.

Here again it appears, as was shown above, that the difficulty inherent in existence and confronting the existing individual is one which abstract thought does not recognize or treat. To think about the real in the medium of the possible does not involve the same difficulty as attempting to think it in the medium of existence, where existence and its process of becoming tend to prevent the individual from thinking, just as if existence could not be thought, although the existing individual is a thinker. In pure thought we are over our ears in profundity, and yet there is something rather absent-minded about it all, because the pure thinker is not clear about what it means to be a human being.

All knowledge about reality is possibility. The only reality to which an existing individual may have a relation that is more than cognitive, is his own reality, the fact that he exists; this reality constitutes his absolute interest. Abstract thought requires him to become disinterested in order to acquire knowledge; the ethical demand is that he become infinitely interested in existing.

The only reality that exists for an existing individual is his own ethical reality. To every other reality he stands in a cognitive relation; but true knowledge consists in translating the real into the possible.

The apparent trustworthiness of sense is an illusion. This was shown adequately as early as in Greek scepticism, and modern idealism has likewise demonstrated it. The trustworthiness claimed by a knowledge of the historical is also a deception, in so far as it assumes to be the very trustworthiness of reality; for the knower cannot know an historical reality until he has resolved it into a possibility. (On this point, more in what follows.) Abstract thought embraces the possible, either the preceding or the subsequent possibility; pure thought is a phantom.

The real subject is not the cognitive subject, since in knowing he moves in the sphere of the possible; the real subject is the ethically existing subject. An abstract thinker exists to be sure, but this fact is rather a satire on him than otherwise. For an abstract thinker to try to prove his existence by the fact that he thinks, is a curious contradiction; for in the degree that he thinks abstractly he abstracts from his own existence. In so far his existence is revealed as a presupposition from which he seeks emancipation; but the act of abstraction nevertheless becomes a strange sort of proof for his existence, since if it succeeded entirely his existence would cease. The Cartesian *cogito ergo sum* has often been repeated. If the "I" which is the subject of *cogito* means an individual human being, the proposition proves nothing: "I am thinking, *ergo* I am; but if I *am* thinking what wonder that I *am*:" the assertion has already been made, and the first proposition says even more than the second. But if the "I" in *cogito* is interpreted as meaning a particular existing human being, philosophy cries: "How silly; here there is no question of your self or my self, but solely of the pure ego." But this pure ego cannot very well have any other than a purely conceptual existence; what then does the *ergo* mean? There is no conclusion here, for the proposition is a tautology.

It has been said above that the abstract thinker, so far from proving his existence by his thought, rather makes it evident that his thought does not wholly succeed in proving the opposite. From this to draw the conclusion that an existing individual who really exists does not think at all, is an arbitrary misunderstanding. He certainly thinks, but he thinks everything in relation to himself, being infinitely interested in existing. Socrates was thus a man whose energies were devoted to thinking; but he reduced all other knowledge to indifference in that he infinitely accentuated ethical knowledge. This type of knowledge bears a relation to the existing subject who is infinitely interested in existing.

The attempt to infer existence from thought is thus a contradiction. For thought takes existence away from the real and thinks it by abrogating its actuality, by translating it into the sphere of the impossible. (Of this more in the following.) With respect to every reality other than the individual's own reality, the principle obtains that he can come to know it only by thinking it. With respect to his own reality, it is a question whether his thought can succeed in abstracting from it completely. This is what the abstract thinker aims at. But it avails him nothing, since he still exists; and this existential persistence, this sometimes pitiful professorial figure, is an epigram upon the abstract thinker, to say nothing of the insistent objection of the ethical.

In Greece, the philosopher was at any rate aware of what it means to exist. The so-called ataraxy of the sceptics was therefore an existential attempt to abstract from existence. In our time the process of abstracting from existence has been relegated to the printed page, just as the task of doubting everything is disposed of once for all on paper. One of the things that has given rise to so much confusion in modern philosophy is that the philosophers have so many brief sayings about infinite tasks, and respect this paper money among themselves, while it almost never occurs to anyone to try to realize the posited task. In this way everything is easily finished, and it becomes possible to begin without presuppositions. The presupposition of a universal doubt, for example, would require an entire human life; now, it is no sooner said than done.

• • •

In [illegible] day the ethical tends more and more to [illegible] ignored [illegible] had among other things the harmful co[illegible] quence th[illegible] and speculative thought have becon[illegible] unsettled, an[illegible] deserted the lofty disinterestedness of th[illegible] possible in order to reach out for reality. Instead of assigning to each sphere its own proper scale of values, a double confusion has been introduced. Poetry makes one attempt after the other to play the rôle of reality, which is entirely unpoetical. Speculative thought repeatedly attempts to reach reality within its own domain, assuring us that whatever is thought is real, that thought is not only capable of thinking reality but of bestowing it, while the truth is the direct opposite; and simultaneously a forgetfulness of what it means to exist, extends itself more and more. The age becomes increasingly unreal, and the people in it; hence these substitutes to make up for what is lacking. The ethical tends more and more to be abandoned; the life of the individual not only becomes poetic, but is unsettled by an abnormal historical consciousness that prevents him from existing ethically. It follows that reality must be provided in other ways. But this spurious reality resembles what would happen if a generation and its members had become prematurely old, and sought to obtain an artificial youth. Instead of recognizing that ethical existence is reality, the age has grown overwhelmingly contemplative, so that not only is everyone engrossed in contemplation, but this has finally become falsified as if it were reality. We smile at the life of the cloister, and yet no hermit ever lived so unreal a life as is common nowadays. For the hermit abstracted from the entire world, but he did not abstract from himself. We know how to describe the fantastic situation of the cloister, far from the haunts of men, in the solitude of the forest, in the distant blue of the horizon; but we take no notice of the fantastic situation of pure thought. And yet, the pathetic unreality of the hermit is far preferable to the comic unreality of the pure thinker; and the passionate forgetfulness of the hermit, which takes from him the entire world, is much to be preferred to the comical distraction of the philosopher engrossed in the contemplation of universal history, which leads him to forget himself.

Ethically regarded, reality is higher than possibility. The ethical proposes to do away with the disinterestedness of the [illegible]ossible, by making existence the infinite interest. It therefore [illegible]pposes every confusing attempt, like that of [illegible]roposing [illegible]thically to *contemplate* humanity and the world. Su[illegible]hical [illegible]ntemplation is impossible, since there is only on[illegible] of [illegible]hical contemplation, namely, self-contemplatio[illegible]ics closes immediately about the individual, and dema[illegible]at he exist ethically; it does not make a parade of millio[illegible] of generations of men; it does not take humanity in the [illegible]p, any more than the police arrest humanity at large. The [illegible]ical is concerned with particular human beings, and with each and every one of them by himself. If God knows how many hairs there are on a man's head, the ethical knows how many human beings there are; and its enumeration is not in the interest of a total sum, but for the sake of each individual. The ethical requirement is imposed upon each individual, and when it judges, it judges each individual by himself; only a tyrant or an impotent man is content to decimate. The ethical lays hold of each individual and demands that he refrain from all contemplation, especially of humanity and the world; for the ethical, as being the internal, cannot be observed by an outsider. It can be realized only by the individual subject, who alone can know what it is that moves within him. This ethical reality is the only reality which does not become a mere possibility through being known, and which can be known only through being thought; for it is the individual's own reality. Before it became a reality it was known by him in the form of a conceived reality, and hence as a possibility. But in the case of another person's reality he could have no knowledge about it until he conceived it in coming to know it, which means that he transformed it from a reality into a possibility.

With respect to every reality external to myself, I can get hold of it only through thinking it. In order to get hold of it really, I should have to be able to make myself into the other, the acting individual, and make the foreign reality my own reality, which is impossible. For if I make the foreign reality my own, this does not mean that I become the other through knowing his reality, but it means that I acquire a new reality, which belongs to me as opposed to him.

When I think something which I propose to do but have not yet done, the content of this conception, no matter how exact it may be, if it be ever so much entitled to be called a conceived reality, is a possibility. Conversely, when I think about something that another has done, and so conceive [illegible] reality, I lift this given reality out of the real and set it int[illegible] the possible; for a conceived reality is a possibility, and [illegible] higher than reality from the standpoint of thought, but n[illegible] from the standpoint of reality. This implies that there is n[illegible] immediate relationship, ethically, between subject and subject. When I understand another person, his reality is for me a possibility, and in its aspect of possibility this conceived reality is related to me precisely as the thought of something I have not done is related to the doing of it.

• • •

Precisely in the degree to which I understand a thinker I become indifferent to his reality; that is, to his existence as a particular individual, to his having really understood this or that so and so, to his actually having realized his teaching, and so forth. Aesthetic and speculative thought is quite justified in insisting on this point, and it is important not to lose sight of it. But this does not suffice for a defense of pure thought as a medium of communication between man and man. Because the reality of the teacher is properly indifferent to me as his pupil, and my reality conversely to him, it does not by any means follow that the teacher is justified in being indifferent to his own reality. His communication should bear the stamp of this consciousness, but not directly, since the ethical reality of an individual is not directly communicable (such a direct relationship is exemplified in the paradoxical relation of a believer to the object of his faith), and cannot be understood immediately, but must be understood indirectly through indirect signs.

When the different spheres are not decisively distinguished from one another, confusion reigns everywhere. When people are curious about a thinker's reality and find it interesting to know something about it, and so forth, this interest is intellectually reprehensible. The maximum of attainment in the sphere of the intellectual is to become altogether indifferent to the thinker's reality. But by being thus muddle-headed in the intellectual sphere, one acquires a certain resemblance to a believer. A believer is one who is infinitely interested in another's reality. This is a decisive criterion for faith, and the interest in question is not just a little curiosity, but an absolute dependence upon faith's object.

The object of faith is the reality of another, and the relationship is one of infinite interest. The object of faith is not a doctrine, for then the relationship would be intellectual, and it would be of importance not to botch it, but to realize the maximum intellectual relationship. The object of faith is not a teacher with a doctrine; for when a teacher has a doctrine, the doctrine is *eo ipso* more important than the teacher, and the relationship is again intellectual, and it again becomes important not to botch it, but to realize the maximum intellectual relationship. The object of faith is the reality of the teacher, that the teacher really exists. The answer of faith is therefore unconditionally yes or no. For it does not concern a doctrine, as to whether the doctrine is true or not; it is the answer to a question concerning a fact: "Do you or do you not suppose that he has really existed?" And the answer, it must be noted, is with infinite passion. In the case of a human being, it is thoughtlessness to lay so great and infinite a stress on the question whether he has existed or not. If the object of faith is a human being, therefore, the whole proposal is the vagary of a stupid person, who has not even understood the spirit of the intellectual and the aesthetic. The object of faith is hence the reality of the God-man in the sense of his existence. But existence involves first and foremost particularity, and this is why thought must abstract from existence, because the particular cannot be thought, but only the universal. The object of faith is thus God's reality in existence as a particular individual, the fact that God has existed as an individual human being.

Christianity is no doctrine concerning the unity of the divine and the human, or concerning the identity of subject and object; nor is it any other of the logical transcriptions of Christianity. If Christianity were a doctrine, the relationship to it would not be one of faith, for only an intellectual type of relationship can correspond to a doctrine. Christianity is therefore not a doctrine, but the fact that God has existed.

The realm of faith is thus not a class for numskulls in the sphere of the intellectual, or an asylum for the feeble-minded. Faith constitutes a sphere all by itself, and every misunderstanding of Christianity may at once be recognized by its transforming it into a doctrine, transferring it to the sphere of the intellectual. The maximum of attainment within the sphere of the intellectual, namely, to realize an entire indifference as to the reality of the teacher, is in the sphere of faith at the opposite end of the scale. The maximum of attainment within the sphere of faith is to become infinitely interested in the reality of the teacher.

The ethical reality of the individual is the only reality. That this should seem strange to many does not seem strange to me. To me it rather seems strange that the System, aye, even systems in the plural, have been completed without raising a question concerning the ethical. If we could only get the dialogue introduced again in the Greek manner, for the purpose of testing what we know and what we do not know, the entire ingenious affectation that clusters about recent philosophy, its artificiality and unnaturalness, would soon disappear. It is not by any means my opinion that Hegel should be asked to talk with a day-laborer, and that it would prove anything if the latter could not be made to understand him; though it will always remain a beautiful eulogy upon Socrates, these simple words of Diogenes,[6] that he philosophized in the workshops and in the market-place. But this is not what I mean, and my proposal does not in the slightest resemble an idler's attack on science. But let a philosopher of the Hegelian school or Hegel himself enter into conversation with a cultivated person, who has made himself competent dialectically through having existed, and from the very beginning all that is affected and chimerical will be frustrated. When a man writes or dictates paragraphs in a running stream, promising that everything will be made clear at the end, it becomes increasingly difficult to discover just where the confusion begins, and to find a fixed point of departure. By means of "Everything will be made clear at the end," and intermittently by means of the category, "This is not the proper place to discuss this question," the very cornerstone of the System, often used as ludicrously as if one were to cite under the heading of misprints a single example, and then add, "There

6. Diogenes Laertius: *Lives* [Ed.].

are indeed other misprints in the book, but this is not the proper place to deal with them,"—by means of these two phrases the reader is constantly defrauded, one of them cheating him definitely, the other intermediately. In the situation of the dialogue, however, this whole fantastic business of pure thought would lose all its plausibility. Instead of conceding the contention of Idealism, but in such a manner as to dismiss as a temptation the entire problem of a reality in the sense of a thing-in-itself eluding thought, which like other temptations cannot be vanquished by giving way to it; instead of putting an end to Kant's misleading reflection which brings reality into connection with thought; instead of relegating reality to the ethical—Hegel scored a veritable advance; for he became fantastic and vanquished idealistic scepticism by means of pure thought, which is merely an hypothesis, and even if it does not so declare itself, a fantastic hypothesis. The triumphant victory of pure thought, that in it being and thought are one, is something both to laugh at and to weep over, since in the realm of pure thought it is not even possible to distinguish them. That thought has validity was assumed by Greek philosophy without question. By reflecting over the matter one would have to arrive at the same result; but why confuse the validity of thought with reality? A valid thought is a possibility, and every further question as to whether it is real or not should be dismissed as irrelevant.

The questionableness of the "Method" becomes apparent already in Hegel's relation to Kant. A scepticism which attacks thought itself cannot be vanquished by thinking it through, since the very instrument by which this would have to be done is in revolt. There is only one thing to do with such a scepticism, and that is to break with it. To answer Kant within the fantastic shadow-play of pure thought is precisely not to answer him. The only thing-in-itself which cannot be thought is existence, and this does not come within the province of thought to think. But how could pure thought possibly vanquish this difficulty, when it is abstract? And what does pure thought abstract from? Why from existence, to be sure, and hence from that which it purports to explain.

When it is impossible to think existence, and the existing individual nevertheless thinks, what does this signify? It signifies that he thinks intermittently, that he thinks before and after. His thought cannot attain to absolute continuity. It is only in a fantastic sense that an existing individual can be constantly *sub specie aeterni.*

. . .

. . . Existence is always something particular, the abstract does not exist. From this to draw the conclusion that the abstract is without validity is a misunderstanding; but it is also a misunderstanding to confound discourse by even raising the question of existence, or of reality in the sense of existence, in connection with the abstract. When an existing individual raises the question of the relation between thought and being, thinking and existing, and philosophy explains that it is one of identity, the answer does not reply to the question because it does not reply to the questioner. Philosophy explains: "Thought and being are one; but not in connection with things that are what they are solely by virtue of existing, as for example a rose, which has no Idea within itself; and hence not in connection with things that make it most clearly evident what it means to exist, as opposed to what it means to think. But thought and being are one in connection with things whose existence is essentially indifferent, because they are so abstract as to have only conceptual existence." To answer the question in this manner is to evade it; for the question had reference to existence as a particular human being. An existence of this sort is of a different order from the existence of a potato, but neither is it the kind of existence that attaches to an Idea. Human existence has Idea in it, but it is not a purely ideal existence. Plato [7] placed the Idea in the second rank of existence, as intermediary between God and matter; an existing human being does indeed participate in the Idea, but he is not himself an Idea.

In Greece, as in the youth of philosophy generally, it was found difficult to win through to the abstract and to leave existence, which always gives the particular; in modern times, on the other hand, it has become difficult to reach existence. The process of abstraction is easy enough for us, but we also desert existence more and more, and the realm of pure thought is the extreme limit of such desertion.

In Greece, philosophizing was a mode of action, and the philosopher was therefore an existing individual. He may not have possessed a great amount of knowledge, but what he did know he knew to some profit, because he busied himself early and late with the same thing. But nowadays, just what

7. *The Republic* [Ed.].

is it to philosophize, and what does a philosopher really know? For of course I do not deny that he knows everything.

The philosophical principle of identity is precisely the opposite of what it seems to be; it is the expression for the fact that thought has deserted existence altogether, that it has emigrated to a sixth continent where it is wholly sufficient to itself in the absolute identity of thought and being. We may finally reach the stage of identifying existence with evil, taken in a certain emasculated metaphysical sense; in the humorous sense, existence will become an extremely long dragging out of things, a ludicrous delay. But even so there remains a possibility that the ethical may impose some restraint, since it accentuates existence, and abstract thought and humor still retain a relationship to existence. But pure thought has won through to a perfect victory, and has nothing, nothing to do with existence.

If thought could give reality in the sense of actuality, and not merely validity in the sense of possibility, it would also have the power to take away existence, and so to take away from the existing individual the only reality to which he sustains a real relationship, namely, his own. (To the reality of another he stands related only by way of thought, as was shown above.) That is to say, the individual would have to be able to think himself out of existence, so that he would really cease to be. I venture to think that no one will wish to accept this supposition, which would betray as superstitious a faith in the power of pure thought as is conversely illustrated by the remark of a lunatic in a comedy, that he proposed to go down in the depths of Dovrefjeld and blow up the entire world with a syllogism. A man may be absent-minded by nature, or may become absent-minded through continuous absorption in pure thought. But the success is never complete, or rather, the failure is complete; and one becomes, by way of the "sometimes pitiful professorial figure," what the Jews feared so much to become, namely, a proverb. I can abstract from myself; but the fact that I abstract from myself means precisely that I exist.

God does not think, He creates; God does not exist, He is eternal. Man thinks and exists, and existence separates thought and being, holding them apart from one another in succession.

What is abstract thought? It is thought without a thinker. Abstract thought ignores everything except the thought, and only the thought is, and is in its own medium. Existence is not devoid of thought, but in existence thought is in a foreign medium. What can it then mean to ask in the language of abstraction about reality in the sense of existence, seeing that abstract thought abstracts precisely from existence? What is concrete thought? It is thought with a relation to a thinker, and to a definite particular something which is thought, existence giving to the existing thinker thought, time, and place.

. . .

Objectively, What It Is To Become Or To Be A Christian Is Defined in the Following Way:

1. A Christian is one who accepts the doctrine of Christianity. But if it is the doctrine which is to decide in the last resort whether one is a Christian, then instantly attention is directed outward, in order to learn to know in the minutest detail what the doctrine of Christianity is, because this indeed is to decide, not what Christianity is, but whether I am a Christian. That same instant begins the erudite, the anxious, the timorous effort at approximation. Approximation can be protracted as long as you please, and in the end the decision whereby one becomes a Christian is relegated to oblivion.

This incongruity has been remedied by the assumption that everyone in Christendom is a Christian, we are all of us what one in a way calls Christians. With this assumption things go better with the objective theories. We are all Christians. The Bible-theory has now to investigate quite objectively what Christianity is (and yet we are in fact Christians, and the objective information is assumed to make us Christians, the objective information which we who are Christians shall now for the first time learn to know—for if we are not Christians, the road here taken will never lead us to become such). The Church theory assumes that we are Christians, but now we have to be assured in a purely objective way what Christianity is, in order that we may defend ourselves against the Turk and the Russian and the Roman yoke, and gallantly fight out the battle of Christianity so that we may make our age, as it were, a bridge to the peerless future which already is glimpsed. This is sheer aesthetics. Christianity is an existence-communication, the task is to become a Christian and continue to be such, and the most dangerous of all illusions is to be so sure of being such that one has to defend the whole of Christendom against the Turk—instead of being alert to defend our own faith against the illusion about the Turk.

2. One says, No, not every acceptance of the Christian doctrine makes one a Christian; what it principally depends upon is appropriation, that one appropriates and holds fast this doctrine quite differently from anything else, that one is ready to live in it and to die in it, to venture one's life for it, etc. This seems as if it were something. However, the category "quite differently" is a mediocre category, and the whole formula, which makes an attempt to define more subjectively what it is to be a Christian, is neither one thing nor the other; in a way it avoids the difficulty involved in the distraction and deceit of approximation, but it lacks categorical definition. The pathos of approximation which is talked of here is that of immanence; one can just as well say that an enthusiastic lover is so related to his love: he holds fast to it and appropriates it quite differently from anything else, he is ready to live in it and die in it, he will venture everything for it. To this extent there is no difference between a lover and a Christian with respect to inwardness, and one must again recur to the *what,* which is the doctrine—and with that we again come under No. 1.

The pathos of appropriation needs to be so defined that it cannot be confused with any other pathos. The more subjective interpretation is right in insisting that it is appropriation which decides the matter, but it is wrong in its definition of appropriation, which does not distinguish it from every other immediate pathos.

Neither is this distinction made when one defines appropriation as faith, but at once imparts to faith headway and direction towards reaching an understanding, so that faith becomes a provisional function whereby one holds what essentially is to be an object for understanding, a provisional function wherewith poor people and stupid men have to be content, whereas *Privatdocents* and clever heads go further. The mark of being a Christian (i.e. faith) is appropriated, but in such a way that it is not specifically different from other intellectual appropriation where a preliminary assumption serves as a provisional function looking forward to understanding. Faith is not in this case the specific mark of the relationship to Christianity, and again it will be the *what* of faith which decides whether one is a Christian or not. But therewith the thing is again brought back under No. 1.

That is to say, the appropriation by which a Christian is a

Christian must be so specific that it cannot be confused with anything else.

3. One defines the thing of becoming and being a Christian, not objectively by the *what* of the doctrine, nor subjectively by appropriation, not by what has gone on in the individual, but by what the individual has undergone: that he was baptized. Though one adjoins to baptism the assumption of a confession of faith, nothing decisive will be gained, but the definition will waver between accentuating the *what* (the path of approximation) and talking indefinitely about acceptance and acceptance and appropriation, etc., without any specific determination.

If being baptized is to be the definition, attention will instantly turn outward towards the reflection, whether I have really been baptized. Then begins the approximation with respect to a historical fact.

If, on the other hand, one were to say that he did indeed receive the Spirit in baptism and by the witness it bears together with his spirit, he knows that he was baptized—then the inference is inverted; he argues from the witness of the Spirit within him to the fact that he was baptized, not from the fact of being baptized to the possession of the Spirit. But if the inference is to be drawn in this way, baptism is quite rightly not regarded as the mark of the Christian, but inwardness is, and so here in turn there is needed a specific definition of inwardness and appropriation whereby the witness of the Spirit in the individual is distinguished from all other (universally defined) activity of spirit in man.

It is noteworthy moreover that the orthodoxy which especially has made baptism the decisive mark is continually complaining that among the baptized there are so few Christians, that almost all, except for an immortal little band, are spiritless baptized pagans—which seems to indicate that baptism cannot be the decisive factor with respect to becoming a Christian, not even according to the latter view of those who in the first form insist upon it as decisive with respect to becoming a Christian.

Subjectively, What It Is To Become a Christian Is Defined Thus:

The decision lies in the subject. The appropriation is the paradoxical inwardness which is specifically different from all other inwardness. The thing of being a Christian is not determined by the *what* of Christianity but by the *how* of the Christian. This *how* can only correspond with one thing, the absolute paradox. There is therefore no vague talk to the effect that being a Christian is to accept, and to accept, and to accept quite differently, to appropriate, to believe, to appropriate by faith quite differently (all of them purely rhetorical and fictitious definitions); but *to believe* is specifically different from all other appropriation and inwardness. Faith is the objective uncertainty due to the repulsion of the absurd held fast by the passion of inwardness, which in this instance is intensified to the utmost degree. This formula fits only the believer, no one else, not a lover, not an enthusiast, not a thinker, but simply and solely the believer who is related to the absolute paradox.

Faith therefore cannot be any sort of provisional function. He who from the vantage point of a higher knowledge would know his faith as a factor resolved in a higher idea has *eo ipso* ceased to believe. Faith *must* not *rest content* with unintelligibility; for precisely the relation to or the repulsion from the unintelligible, the absurd, is the expression for the passion of faith.

This definition of what it is to be a Christian prevents the erudite or anxious deliberation of approximation from enticing the individual into byways so that he becomes erudite instead of becoming a Christian, and in most cases a smatterer instead of becoming a Christian; for the decision lies in the subject. But inwardness has again found its specific mark whereby it is differentiated from all other inwardness and is not disposed of by the chatty category "quite differently" which fits the case of every passion at the moment of passion.

The psychologist generally regards it as a sure sign that a man is beginning to give up a passion when he wishes to treat the object of it objectively. Passion and reflection are generally exclusive of one another. Becoming objective in this way is always retrogression, for passion is man's perdition, but it is his exaltation as well. In case dialectic and reflection are not used to intensify passion, it is a retrogression to become objective; and even he who is lost through passion has not lost so much as he who lost passion, for the former had the possibility.

BIBLIOGRAPHY

Together, the Princeton University Press and the Oxford University Press have made available in English most of

Kierkegaard's works, chiefly translated by David F. Swenson and Walter Lowrie during the past twenty years. The Princeton translations by Walter Lowrie include:

Repetition (1941; reissued by Harper Torchbooks, 1964)
Fear and Trembling (1941; reissued by Doubleday Anchor Books, 1954)
The Concept of Dread (1944)
Stages on Life's Way (1940)
The Sickness Unto Death (1941; reissued by Doubleday Anchor Books, 1954)
The Attack Upon "Christendom" (1944; reissued by Beacon Press Paperbacks, 1956)

The Princeton translations by David F. Swenson include:

Philosophical Fragments (1936; reissued, with revisions, 1963)
Works of Love (with Lillian M. Swenson, 1946)

The following Princeton translations were begun by Professor and Mrs. Swenson and completed or edited by Dr. Lowrie:

Either/Or (1944; reissued, with revisions by Howard A. Johnson, by Doubleday Anchor Books, 1959)
Concluding Unscientific Postscript (1941)

The Oxford translations by Walter Lowrie include:

The Point of View for My Work as an Author (1939)
Training in Christianity (1941)
For Self-Examination (1941)
Judge For Yourselves! (1941)
The Present Age (with Alexander Dru, 1940; reissued by Harper Torchbooks, 1962)
Christian Discourses (1940; reissued as a Galaxy Book, 1961)

Harper Torchbooks has published a selection from *The Journals of Kierkegaard*, translated by Alexander Dru (1959; London, Fontana Books, 1959) and a selection from the *Edifying Discourses* (1958) made by Paul L. Holmer from the four volumes originally translated by David and Lillian Swenson (Minneapolis, Augsburg Publishing House, 1943-

1946). Also available as a Torchbook is the Swensons' translation of *Purity of Heart is to Will One Thing* (1956) with an introductory essay by Douglas V. Steere, first published by Harper in 1938.

Other translations include:

Johannes Climacus; or De omnibus dubitandum est, translated with an assessment by T. H. Croxall (Stanford University Press, 1958)
The Gospel of Suffering, translated by David and Lillian Swenson (Minneapolis, Augsburg Publishing House, 1948)
Thoughts on Crucial Situations in Human Life and *Three Discourses on Imagined Situations,* translated by David Swenson (Minneapolis, Augsburg Publishing House, 1941)
The Prayers of Kierkegaard, translated and edited by Perry D. LeFevre (University of Chicago Press, 1956)

Three volumes of selections should be mentioned:

A Kierkegaard Anthology, edited by Robert Bretall (Princeton and Oxford, 1946; reissued by Modern Library, 1961). Substantial selections from eighteen works with introductions and a bibliography.
Selections from the Writings of Kierkegaard, translated by Lee M. Hollander (Doubleday Anchor Books, 1960). This revised reprint of one of the earliest translations of Kierkegaard into English (1923) includes selections from five works and provides an introduction to Kierkegaard and a comprehensive bibliography.
The Living Thoughts of Kierkegaard, presented by W. H. Auden (New York, David McKay, 1952; reissued by Indiana University Press as a Midland Book, 1962)

Walter Lowrie has done a full-length biography, *Kierkegaard* (Oxford University Press, 1938; reissued by Harper Torchbooks, 1962), and *A Short Life of Kierkegaard* (Princeton University Press, 1942; reissued by Doubleday Anchor Books, 1962). David Swenson published *Søren Kierkegaard* (Menasha, Wisconsin, 1920). Peter Rohde's *Søren Kierkegaard,* translated by Alan Moray Williams (London, 1963), is an account of Kierkegaard's life and works in his own words, filled in with connecting narratives by a leading Danish critic.

FRIEDRICH WILHELM NIETZSCHE

(1844–1900)

Nietzsche is for the most part highly readable, but the student is liable to misread him, not because the author wants to hide himself to tease and test his reader, as perhaps Kierkegaard did, but simply because his thought is, to an exceptional degree, exploratory. He is thinking and rethinking aloud, improvising (as he did on the piano); and the gemlike aphoristic character of his writings is sheer virtuosity, not perpetual polish. When he said, "I have always put my whole body and life into my writings, I know nothing of purely intellectual problems" and "One must be willing to live the great problems," he was not using a rhetorical figure of speech. The ruthless destructiveness of his thinking is ruthless destruction of his own presuppositions, predispositions, predilections, an extirpation of the forgotten conditioning of his own feeling and thinking. He takes himself up by the roots. He reduces himself to despair. His solutions, his results, are not conclusions which bring a stormy and hazardous voyage to a safe harbor, for he remains liable to be seized by his "most abysmal thought," the eternal recurrence of the worthless. As Kierkegaard was pulled apart by his equal adherence to reason and to faith, so was Nietzsche torn between his Dionysian yea-saying, his exultation in the destructive-creative behavior of things, and his horror at their blind nonrationality. Neither the faith of the one nor the *amor fati* of the other could become faith and *amor fati* pure and simple.

Perhaps the best introduction is his early essay, "The Use and Abuse of History" (1874). Here is a straightforward thoughtful criticism of the prevailing "historicism" which made the climate of culture at the time, an attack on Hegel for the same reasons as Kierkegaard's. Supplemented by "Schopenhauer as Educator," of the same year, this essay represents Nietzsche's fundamental attitude and his conception of his task. Like Burke, and for similar reasons, he is against "modern ideas," the ideas of the Enlightenment; but he sees the Enlightenment as beginning with the Greek Enlightenment, with Socrates. The indictment of Plato is the clue to Nietzsche's thinking, a critique of European idealism and rationalism. Kant was a futile dam to a flood of consequences which followed from the death of God and the loss of the Logos. By circumscribing reason, Kant and Schopenhauer had halted the long error of human reason in its dream of a rational universe. Now that reason had at last learned to know its own source and the limits of its reach, the task remained to translate man back into nature. Not only was God dead, but also man as god; and the task was not merely to naturalize man, but equally to prevent his being denaturalized, turned into sand, grains of infinite sand, which was in effect the modern intention.

Nietzsche's part, opposed to Kierkegaard's but in the same drama, was to translate completely into terms of reflection what it means to become a non-Christian and what it means to become a modern pre-Socratic. Here, too, his attitude is under the tension of ambivalence, for he said of Socrates, "I confess that he is so close to me that I am nearly always struggling against him."

The substance of his philosophy is exemplified in the manner of his philosophizing, for abandonment of the quest for explanation becomes concentration on general description; the philosopher becomes psychologist; and he begins with the body.

The two volumes of *The Will to Power* contain notes for Nietzsche's *magnum opus*, to which the earlier works (aside from *Zarathustra*) are preliminary essays. The notes are often mere notes, lacking the finish of the earlier aphorisms, but this is hardly to be regretted in one who so intensely admired the *Pensées* of Pascal because they had the white-hot impetuous character of genuine thoughts. ("The will to power," it should be said, is neither political ambition nor Schopenhauer's metaphysical principle, but rather the *élan vital* of Bergson, a generalization of all behavior, the plastic vitality of things.) A fair sample of Nietzsche's work might be found in *The Will to Power*, vol. I, bk. 2, pt. iii and vol. II, bk. 3, pt. i, supplemented by "The Use and Abuse of History;" *The Joyful Wisdom*, bk. V; and *The Genealogy of Morals*, Third Essay.

EXTRACTS

All the extracts are taken from the English translation of Nietzsche's works in 18 volumes edited by Dr. Oscar Levy (London and Edinburgh, 1909–1913).

The Dawn of Day (1881), trans. by J. M. Kennedy
Book 2, Aphorisms 104, 105, 118, 164.
Book 3, Aphorism 174.
Book 4, Aphorisms 501, 552, 560.

The Joyful Wisdom (1883), trans. by Thomas Common
Book 3, Aphorisms 110–114, 124, 125.
Book 5, "We Fearless Ones," Aphorisms 343, 345–347, 370.

Beyond Good & Evil (1885–6), trans. by Helen Zimmern
Chapter i, "Prejudices of Philosophers," 23.
Chapter v, "The Natural History of Morals," 187, 188, 191.
Chapter vii, "Our Virtues," 230, 231.
Chapter ix, "What is Noble?" 268.

The Genealogy of Morals (1887), trans. by Horace B. Samuel
Third Essay, "What is the Meaning of Ascetic Ideals?" 12, 23, 24, 25, 27, 28.

The Twilight of the Idols (1889), trans. by A. M. Ludovici
"How the 'True World' Ultimately Became a Fable"

The Will to Power: An Attempted Transvaluation of all Values (1883–1889), trans. by A. M. Ludovici
vol. I, book 2 ("A Criticism of the Highest Values That Have Prevailed Hitherto"), part iii, "Criticism of Philosophy," 326, 409, 430, 432, 434, 436–439, 443–447, 452, 465.
vol. II, book 3 ("The Principles of a New Valuation"), part i, "The Will to Power in Science," 481, 487, 492, 521, 522, 524, 555–560, 567, 569, 612, 613; part ii, "The Will to Power in Nature," 659; book 4 ("Discipline and Breeding"), part ii, "Dionysus," 1041.

☙ from *The Dawn of Day*

104

Our Valuations.—All actions may be referred back to valuations, and all valuations are either one's own or adopted, the latter being by far the more numerous. Why do we adopt them? Through fear, *i.e.* we think it more advisable to pretend that they are our own, and so well do we accustom ourselves to do so that it at last becomes second nature to us. A valuation of our own, which is the appreciation of a thing in accordance with the pleasure or displeasure it causes us and no one else, is something very rare indeed!—But must not our valuation of our neighbour—which is prompted by the motive that we adopt his valuation in most cases—proceed from ourselves and by our own decision? Of course, but then we come to these decisions during our childhood, and seldom change them. We often remain during our whole lifetime the dupes of our childish and accustomed judgments in our manner of judging our fellowmen (their minds, rank, morality, character, and reprehensibility), and we find it necessary to subscribe to their valuations.

105

PSEUDO-EGOISM.—The great majority of people, whatever they may think and say about their "egoism," do nothing for their ego all their life long, but only for a phantom of this ego which has been formed in regard to them by their friends and communicated to them. As a consequence, they all live in a haze of impersonal and half-personal opinions and of arbitrary and, as it were, poetic valuations: the one always in the head of another, and this head, again, in the head of somebody else—a queer world of phantoms which manages to give itself a rational appearance! This haze of opinions and habits grows in extent and lives almost independently of the people it surrounds; it is it which gives rise to the immense effect of general judgments on "man"—all those men, who do not know themselves, believe in a bloodless abstraction which they call "man," *i.e.* in a fiction; and every change caused in this abstraction by the judgments of powerful individualities (such as princes and philosophers) produces an extraordinary and irrational effect on the great majority,—for the simple reason that not a single individual in this haze can oppose a real ego, an ego which is accessible to and fathomed by himself, to the universal pale fiction, which he could thereby destroy.

118

What is our Neighbour?—What do we conceive of our neighbour except his limits: I mean that whereby he, as it were, engraves and stamps himself in and upon us? We can understand nothing of him except the changes which take place upon our own person and of which he is the cause, what we know of him is like a hollow, modelled space. We impute to him the feelings which his acts arouse in us, and thus give him a wrong and inverted positivity. We form him after our knowledge of ourselves into a satellite of our own system, and if he shines upon us, or grows dark, and we in any case are the ultimate cause of his doing so, we nevertheless still believe the contrary! O world of phantoms in which we live! O world so perverted, topsy-turvy and empty, and yet dreamt of as full and upright!

164

Perhaps Premature.—It would seem at the present time that, under many different and misleading names, and often with a great want of clearness, those who do not feel themselves attached to morals and to established laws are taking the first initial steps to organise themselves, and thus to create a right for themselves; whilst hitherto, as criminals, free-thinkers, immoral men and miscreants, they have lived beyond the pale of the law, under the bane of outlawry and bad conscience, corrupted and corrupting. On the whole, we should consider this as right and proper, although it may result in insecurity for the coming century and compel every one to bear arms.—There is thereby a counterforce which continually reminds us that there is no exclusively moral-making morality, and that a morality which asserts itself to the exclusion of all other morality destroys too much sound strength and is too dearly bought by mankind. The non-conventional and deviating people, who are so often productive and inventive, must no longer be sacrificed: it must never again be considered as a disgrace to depart from morality either in actions or thought; many new experiments must be made upon life and society, and the world must be relieved from a huge weight of bad conscience. These general aims must be recognised and encouraged by all those upright people who are seeking truth.

174

THE MORAL FASHION OF A COMMERCIAL COMMUNITY.—Behind the principle of the present moral fashion: "Moral actions are actions performed out of sympathy for others," I see the social instinct of fear, which thus assumes an intellectual disguise: this instinct sets forth as its supreme, most important, and most immediate principle that life shall be relieved of all the dangerous characteristics which it possessed in former times, and that every one must help with all his strength towards the attainment of this end. It is for that reason that only those actions which keep in view the general security and the feeling of security of society are called "good." How little joy must men now have in themselves when such a tyranny of fear prescribes their supreme moral law, if they make no objection when commanded to turn their eyes from themselves and to look aside from themselves! And yet at the same time they have lynx eyes for all distress and suffering elsewhere! Are we not, then, with this gigantic intention of ours of smoothing down every sharp edge and corner in life, utilising the best means of turning mankind into sand! Small, soft, round, infinite sand! Is that your ideal, ye harbingers of the "sympathetic affections"? In the meantime even the question remains unanswered whether we are of more use to our neighbour in running immediately and continually to his help,—which for the most part can only be done in a very superficial way, as otherwise it would become a tyrannical meddling and changing,—or by transforming ourselves into something which our neighbour can look upon with pleasure, —something, for example, which may be compared to a beautiful, quiet, and secluded garden, protected by high walls against storms and the dust of the roads, but likewise with a hospitable gate.

501

MORTAL SOULS.—Where knowledge is concerned perhaps the most useful conquest that has ever been made is the abandonment of the belief in the immortality of the soul. Humanity is henceforth at liberty to wait: men need no longer be in a hurry to swallow badly-tested ideas as they had to do in former times. For in those times the salvation of this poor "immortal soul" depended upon the extent of the knowledge which could be acquired in the course of a short existence: decisions had to be reached from one day to another, and "knowledge" was a matter of dreadful importance!

Now we have acquired good courage for errors, experiments, and the provisional acceptance of ideas—all this is not so very important!—and for this very reason individuals and whole races may now face tasks so vast in extent that in former years they would have looked like madness, and defiance of heaven and hell. Now we have the right to experiment upon ourselves! Yes, men have the right to do so! the greatest sacrifices have not yet been offered up to knowledge —nay, in earlier periods it would have been sacrilege, and a sacrifice of our eternal salvation, even to surmise such ideas as now precede our actions.

552

Ideal Selfishness.—Is there a more sacred state than that of pregnancy? To perform every one of our actions in the silent conviction that in one way or another it will be to the benefit of that which is being generated within us—that it must augment its mysterious value, the very thought of which fills us with rapture? At such a time we refrain from many things without having to force ourselves to do so: we suppress the angry word, we grasp the hand forgivingly; our child must be born from all that is best and gentlest. We shun our own harshness and brusqueness in case it should instil a drop of unhappiness into the cup of the beloved unknown. Everything is veiled, ominous; we know nothing about what is going on, but simply wait and try to be prepared. During this time, too, we experience a pure and purifying feeling of profound irresponsibility, similar to that felt by a spectator before a drawn curtain; *it* is growing, *it* is coming to light; we have nothing to do with determining its value, or the hour of its arrival. We are thrown back altogether upon indirect, beneficent and defensive influences. "Something greater than we are is growing here"—such is our most secret hope; we prepare everything with a view to his birth and prosperity—not merely everything that is useful, but also the noblest gifts of our souls.

We should, and can, live under the influence of such a blessed inspiration! Whether what we are looking forward to is a thought or a deed, our relationship to every essential achievement is none other than that of pregnancy, and all our vainglorious boasting about "willing" and "creating" should be cast to the winds! True and ideal selfishness consists in always watching over and restraining the soul, so that our productiveness may come to a beautiful termination. Thus in this indirect manner we must provide for and watch over the good of all; and the frame of mind, the mood in which we live, is a kind of soothing oil which spreads far around us on the restless souls.—Still, these pregnant ones are funny people! let us therefore dare to be funny also, and not reproach others if they must be the same. And even when this phenomenon becomes dangerous and evil we must not show less respect to that which is generating within us or others than ordinary worldly justice, which does not allow the judge or the hangman to interfere with a pregnant woman.

560

What we are Free to do.—We can act as the gardeners of our impulses, and—which few people know—we may cultivate the seeds of anger, pity, vanity, or excessive brooding, and make these things fecund and productive, just as we can train a beautiful plant to grow along trellis-work. We may do this with the good or bad taste of a gardener, and as it were, in the French, English, Dutch, or Chinese style. We may let nature take its own course, only trimming and embellishing a little here and there; and finally, without any knowledge or consideration, we may even allow the plants to spring up in accordance with their own natural growth and limitations, and fight out their battle among themselves,—nay, we can even take delight in such chaos, though we may possibly have a hard time with it! All this is at our option: but how many know that it is? Do not the majority of people believe in themselves as complete and perfect facts? and have not the great philosophers set their seal on this prejudice through their doctrine of the unchangeability of character?

☙ from *The Joyful Wisdom*

110

Origin of Knowledge.—Throughout immense stretches of time the intellect has produced nothing but errors; some of them proved to be useful and preservative of the species: he who fell in with them, or inherited them, waged the battle for himself and his offspring with better success. Those erroneous articles of faith which were successively transmitted by inheritance, and have finally become almost the property and stock of the human species, are, for example, the following:—that there are enduring things, that there are equal things, that there are things, substances, and bodies, that a thing is what it appears, that our will is free, that what is good for me is also good absolutely. It was only very late that the deniers and doubters of such propositions came forward,—it was only very late that truth made its appearance as the most impotent form of knowledge. It seemed as if it were impossible to get along with truth, our organism was adapted for the very opposite; all its higher functions, the perceptions of the senses, and in general every kind of sensation co-operated with those primevally embodied, fundamental errors. Moreover, those propositions became the very standards of knowledge according to which the "true" and the "false" were determined—throughout the whole domain of pure logic. The *strength* of conceptions does not, therefore, depend on their degree of truth, but on their antiquity, their embodiment, their character as conditions of life. Where life and knowledge seemed to conflict, there has never been serious contention; denial and doubt have there been regarded as madness. The exceptional thinkers like the Eleatics, who, in spite of this, advanced and maintained the antitheses of the natural errors, believed that it was possible also *to live* these counterparts: it was they who devised the sage as the man of immutability, impersonality and universality of intuition, as one and all at the same time, with a special faculty for that reverse kind of knowledge; they were of the belief that their knowledge was at the same time the principle of *life*. To be able to affirm all this, however, they had to *deceive* themselves concerning their own condition: they had to attribute to themselves impersonality and unchanging permanence, they had to mistake the nature of the philosophic individual, deny the force of the impulses in cognition, and conceive of reason generally as an entirely free and self-originating activity; they kept their eyes shut to the fact that they also had reached their doctrines in contradiction to valid methods, or through their longing for repose or for exclusive possession or for domination. The subtler development of sincerity and of scepticism finally made these men impossible; their life also and their judgments turned out to be dependent on the primeval impulses and fundamental errors of all sentient being.—The subtler sincerity and scepticism arose whenever two antithetical maxims appeared to be *applicable* to life, because both of them were compatible with the fundamental errors; where, therefore, there could be contention concerning a higher or lower degree of *utility* for life; and likewise where new maxims proved to be, not in fact useful, but at least not injurious, as expressions of an intellectual impulse to play a game that was, like all games, innocent and happy. The human brain was gradually filled with such judgments and convictions; and in this tangled skein there arose ferment, strife and lust for power. Not only utility and delight, but every kind of impulse took part in the struggle for "truths": the intellectual struggle became a business, an attraction, a calling, a duty, an honour—: cognizing and striving for the true finally arranged themselves as needs among other needs. From that moment, not only belief and conviction, but also examination, denial, distrust and contradiction became *forces;* all "evil" instincts were subordinated to knowledge, were placed in its service, and acquired the prestige of the permitted, the honoured, the useful, and finally the appearance and innocence of the *good.* Knowledge thus became a portion of life itself, and as life it became a continually growing power: until finally the cognitions and those primeval, fundamental errors clashed with each other, both as life, both as power, both in the same man. The thinker is now the being in whom the impulse to truth and those life-preserving errors wage their first conflict, now that the impulse to truth has also *proved* itself to be a life-preserving power. In comparison with the importance of this conflict everything else is indifferent; the final question concerning the conditions of life is here raised, and the first attempt is here made to answer it by experiment. How far is truth susceptible of embodiment?—that is the question, that is the experiment.

111

Origin of the Logical.—Where has logic originated in men's heads? Undoubtedly out of the illogical, the domain of which must originally have been immense. But numberless beings who reasoned otherwise than we do at present, perished; albeit that they may have come nearer to truth than we! Whoever, for example, could not discern the "like" often enough with regard to food, and with regard to animals dangerous to him, whoever, therefore, deduced too slowly, or was too circumspect in his deductions, had smaller probability of survival than he who in all similar things immediately divined the equality. The preponderating inclination, however, to deal with the similar as the equal—an illogical inclination, for there is nothing equal in itself—first created the whole basis of logic. It was just so (in order that the conception of substance might originate, this being indispensable to logic, although in the strictest sense nothing actual corresponds to it) that for a long period the changing process in things had to be overlooked, and remain unperceived; the beings not seeing correctly had an advantage over those who saw everything "in flux." In itself every high degree of circumspection in conclusions, every sceptical inclination, is a great danger to life. No living being would have been preserved unless the contrary inclination—to affirm rather than suspend judgment, to mistake and fabricate rather than wait, to assent rather than deny, to decide rather than be in the right—had been cultivated with extraordinary assiduity.—The course of logical thought and reasoning in our modern brain corresponds to a process and struggle of impulses, which singly and in themselves are all very illogical and unjust; we experience usually only the result of the struggle, so rapidly and secretly does this primitive mechanism now operate in us.

112

CAUSE AND EFFECT.—We say it is "explanation"; but it is only in "description" that we are in advance of the older stages of knowledge and science. We describe better,—we explain just as little as our predecessors. We have discovered a manifold succession where the naïve man and investigator of older cultures saw only two things, "cause" and "effect," as it was said; we have perfected the conception of becoming, but have not got a knowledge of what is above and behind the conception. The series of "causes" stands before us much more complete in every case; we conclude that this and that must first precede in order that that other may follow—but we have not *grasped* anything thereby. The peculiarity, for example, in every chemical process seems a "miracle," the same as before, just like all locomotion; nobody has "explained" impulse. How could we ever explain! We operate only with things which do not exist, with lines, surfaces, bodies, atoms, divisible times, divisible spaces—how can explanation ever be possible when we first make everything a *conception*, our conception! It is sufficient to regard science as the exactest humanising of things that is possible; we always learn to describe ourselves more accurately by describing things and their successions. Cause and effect: there is probably never any such duality; in fact there is a *continuum* before us, from which we isolate a few portions;—just as we always observe a motion as isolated points, and therefore do not properly see it, but infer it. The abruptness with which many effects take place leads us into error; it is however only an abruptness for us. There is an infinite multitude of processes in that abrupt moment which escape us. An intellect which could see cause and effect as a *continuum*, which could see the flux of events not according to our mode of perception, as things arbitrarily separated and broken—would throw aside the conception of cause and effect, and would deny all conditionality.

113

The Theory of Poisons.—So many things have to be united in order that scientific thinking may arise, and all the necessary powers must have been devised, exercised, and fostered singly! In their isolation, however, they have very often had quite a different effect than at present, when they are confined within the limits of scientific thinking and kept mutually in check:—they have operated as poisons; for example, the doubting impulse, the denying impulse, the waiting impulse, the collecting impulse, the disintegrating impulse. Many hecatombs of men were sacrificed ere these impulses learned to understand their juxtaposition and regard themselves as functions of one organising force in one man! And how far are we still from the point at which the artistic powers and the practical wisdom of life shall co-operate with scientific thinking, so that a higher organic system may be formed, in relation to which the scholar, the physician, the artist, and the lawgiver, as we know them at present, will seem sorry antiquities!

114

The Extent of the Moral.—We construct a new picture, which we see immediately with the aid of all the old experiences which we have had, *always according to the degree* of our honesty and justice. The only events are moral events, even in the domain of sense-perception.

124

In the Horizon of the Infinite.—We have left the land and have gone aboard ship! We have broken down the bridge behind us,—nay, more, the land behind us! Well, little ship!

look out! Beside thee is the ocean; it is true it does not always roar, and sometimes it spreads out like silk and gold and a gentle reverie. But times will come when thou wilt feel that it is infinite, and that there is nothing more frightful than infinity. Oh, the poor bird that felt itself free, and now strikes against the walls of this cage! Alas, if homesickness for the land should attack thee, as if there had been more *freedom* there,—and there is no "land" any longer!

125

THE MADMAN.—Have you ever heard of the madman who on a bright morning lighted a lantern and ran to the market-place calling out unceasingly: "I seek God! I seek God!"—As there were many people standing about who did not believe in God, he caused a great deal of amusement. Why! is he lost? said one. Has he strayed away like a child? said another. Or does he keep himself hidden? Is he afraid of us? Has he taken a sea-voyage? Has he emigrated?—the people cried out laughingly, all in a hubbub. The insane man jumped into their midst and transfixed them with his glances. "Where is God gone?" he called out. "I mean to tell you! *We have killed him,* —you and I! We are all his murderers! But how have we done it? How were we able to drink up the sea? Who gave us the sponge to wipe away the whole horizon? What did we do when we loosened this earth from its sun? Whither does it now move? Whither do we move? Away from all suns? Do we not dash on unceasingly? Backwards, sideways, forewards, in all directions? Is there still an above and below? Do we not stray, as through infinite nothingness? Does not empty space breathe upon us? Has it not become colder? Does not night come on continually, darker and darker? Shall we not have to light lanterns in the morning? Do we not hear the noise of the grave-diggers who are burying God? Do we not smell the divine putrefaction?—for even Gods putrefy! God is dead! God remains dead! And we have killed him! How shall we console ourselves, the most murderous of all murderers? The holiest and the mightiest that the world has hitherto possessed, has bled to death under our knife,—who will wipe the blood from us? With what water could we cleanse ourselves? What lustrums, what sacred games shall we have to devise? Is not the magnitude of this deed too great for us? Shall we not ourselves have to become Gods, merely to seem worthy of it? There never was a greater event,—and on account of it, all who are born after us belong to a higher history than any history hitherto!"—Here the madman was silent and looked again at his hearers; they also were silent and looked at him in surprise. At last he threw his lantern on the ground, so that it broke in pieces and was extinguished. "I come too early," he then said, "I am not yet at the right time. This prodigious event is still on its way, and is travelling,—it has not yet reached men's ears. Lightning and thunder need time, the light of the stars needs time, deeds need time, even after they are done, to be seen and heard. This deed is as yet further from them than the furthest star,—*and yet they have done it!*" —It is further stated that the madman made his way into different churches on the same day, and there intoned his *Requiem aeternam deo.* When led out and called to account, he always gave the reply: "What are these churches now, if they are not the tombs and monuments of God?"—

WE FEARLESS ONES

343

WHAT OUR CHEERFULNESS SIGNIFIES.—The most important of more recent events—that "God is dead," that the belief in the Christian God has become unworthy of belief—already begins to cast its first shadows over Europe. To the few at least whose eye, whose *suspecting* glance, is strong enough and subtle enough for this drama, some sun seems to have set, some old, profound confidence seems to have changed into doubt: our old world must seem to them daily more darksome, distrustful, strange and "old." In the main, however, one may say that the event itself is far too great, too remote, too much beyond most people's power of apprehension, for one to suppose that so much as the report of it could have *reached* them; not to speak of many who already knew *what* had really taken place, and what must all collapse now that this belief had been undermined,—because so much was built upon it, so much rested on it, and had become one with it: for example, our entire European morality. This lengthy, vast and uninterrupted process of crumbling, destruction, ruin and overthrow which is now imminent: who has realised it sufficiently to-day to have to stand up as the teacher and herald of such a tremendous logic of terror, as the prophet of a period of gloom and eclipse, the like of which has probably never taken place on earth before? . . . Even we, the born riddle-readers, who wait as it were on the mountains posted 'twixt to-day and to-morrow, and engirt by their contradiction, we, the firstlings and premature children of the coming century, into whose sight especially the shadows which must forthwith envelop Europe *should* already have come—how is it that even we, without genuine sympathy for this period of gloom, contemplate its advent without any *personal* solicitude or fear? Are we still, perhaps, too much under the *immediate effects* of the event—and are these effects, especially as regards *ourselves,* perhaps the reverse of what was to be expected—not at all sad and depressing, but rather like a new and indescribable variety of light, happiness, relief, enlivenment, encouragement, and dawning day? . . . In fact, we philosophers and "free spirits" feel ourselves irradiated as by a new dawn by the report that the "old God is dead"; our hearts overflow with gratitude, astonishment, presentiment and expectation. At last the horizon seems open once more, granting even that it is not bright; our ships can at last put out to sea in face of every danger; every hazard is again permitted to the discerner; the sea, *our* sea, again lies open before us; perhaps never before did such an "open sea" exist.—

345

Morality as a Problem.—A defect in personality revenges itself everywhere: an enfeebled, lank, obliterated, self-disavowing and disowning personality is no longer fit for anything good—it is least of all fit for philosophy. "Selflessness" has no value either in heaven or on earth; the great problems all demand *great love,* and it is only the strong, well-rounded, secure spirits, those who have a solid basis, that are qualified for them. It makes the most material difference whether a thinker stands personally related to his problems, having his fate, his need, and even his highest happiness therein; or merely impersonally, that is to say, if he can only feel and grasp them with the tentacles of cold, prying thought. In the latter case I warrant that nothing comes of it: for the great problems, granting that they let themselves be grasped at all, do not let themselves be *held* by toads and weaklings: that has ever been their taste—a taste also which they share with all high-spirited women.—How is it that I have not yet met with any one, not even in books, who seems to have stood to morality in this position, as one who knew morality as a problem, and this problem as *his own* personal need, affliction, pleasure and passion? It is obvious that up to the present morality has not been a problem at all; it has rather been the very ground on which people have met, after all distrust, dissension, and contradiction, the hallowed place of peace, where thinkers could obtain rest even from themselves, could recover breath and revive. I see no one who has ventured to *criticise* the estimates of moral worth. I miss in this connection even the attempts of scientific curiosity, and the fastidious, groping imagination of psychologists and historians, which easily anticipates a problem and catches it on the wing, without rightly knowing what it catches. With difficulty I have discovered some scanty data for the purpose of furnishing a *history of the origin* of these feelings and estimates of value (which is something different from a criticism of them, and also something different from a history of ethical systems). In an individual case, I have done everything to encourage the inclination and talent for this kind of history—in vain, as it would seem to me at present. There is little to be learned from those historians of morality (especially Englishmen): they themselves are usually, quite unsuspiciously, under the influence of a definite morality, and act unwittingly as its armour-bearers and followers—perhaps still repeating sincerely the popular superstition of Christian Europe, that the characteristic of moral action consists in abnegation, self-denial, self-sacrifice, or in fellow-feeling and fellow-suffering. The usual error in their premises is their insistence on a certain *consensus* among human beings, at least among civilised human beings, with regard to certain propositions of morality, and from thence they conclude that these propositions are absolutely binding even upon you and me; or reversely, they come to the conclusion that *no* morality at all is binding, after the truth has dawned upon them that to different peoples moral valuations are *necessarily* different: both of which conclusions are equally childish follies. The error of the more subtle amongst them is that they discover and criticise the probably foolish opinions of a people about its own morality, or the opinions of mankind about human morality generally; they treat accordingly of its origin, its religious sanctions, the superstition of free will, and such matters; and they think that just by so doing they have criticised the morality itself. But the worth of a precept, "Thou shalt," is still fundamentally different from and independent of such opinions about it, and must be distinguished from the weeds of error with which it has perhaps been overgrown: just as the worth of a medicine to a sick person is altogether independent of the question whether he has a scientific opinion about medicine, or merely thinks about it as an old wife would do. A morality could even have grown *out of* an error: but with this knowledge the problem of its worth would not even be touched.—Thus, no one has hitherto tested the *value* of that most celebrated of all medicines, called morality: for which purpose it is first of all necessary for one—*to call it in question.* Well, that is just our work.—

346

Our Note of Interrogation.—But you don't understand it? As a matter of fact, an effort will be necessary in order to understand us. We seek for words; we seek perhaps also for ears. Who are we after all? If we wanted simply to call ourselves in older phraseology, atheists, unbelievers, or even immoralists, we should still be far from thinking ourselves designated thereby: we are all three in too late a phase for people generally to conceive, for *you,* my inquisitive friends, to be able to conceive, what is our state of mind under the circumstances. No! we have no longer the bitterness and passion of him who has broken loose, who has to make for himself a belief, a goal, and even a martyrdom out of his unbelief! We have become saturated with the conviction (and have grown cold and hard in it) that things are not at all divinely ordered in this world, nor even according to human standards do they go on rationally, mercifully, or justly: we know the fact that the world in which we live is ungodly, immoral, and "inhuman,"—we have far too long interpreted it to ourselves falsely and mendaciously, according to the wish and will of our veneration, that is to say, according to our *need.* For man is a venerating animal! But he is also a distrustful animal: and that the world is *not* worth what we have believed it to be worth is about the surest thing our distrust has at last managed to grasp. So much distrust, so much philosophy! We take good care not to say that the world is of *less* value: it seems to us at present absolutely ridiculous when man claims to devise values *to surpass* the values of the actual world,—it is precisely from that point that we have retraced our steps; as from an extravagant error of human conceit and irrationality, which for a long period has not been recognised as such. This error had its last expression in modern Pessimism; an older and stronger manifestation in the teaching of Buddha; but Christianity also contains it, more dubiously, to be sure, and more ambiguously, but none the less seductive on that account. The whole attitude of "man *versus* the world," man as world-denying principle, man as the standard of the value of things, as judge of the world, who in the end puts existence itself on his scales and finds it too light—the monstrous impertinence of this attitude has dawned upon us as such, and has disgusted us,—we now laugh when we find, "Man *and* World" placed beside one another, separated by the sublime presumption of the little word "and"! But how is it? Have we not in our very laughing just made a further step in despising mankind? And consequently also in Pessimism, in despising the existence cognisable *by us*? Have we not just thereby become liable to a suspicion of an opposition between the world in which we have hitherto been at home with our venerations —for the sake of which we perhaps *endure* life—and another world *which we ourselves are:* an inexorable, radical, most profound suspicion concerning ourselves, which is continually getting us Europeans more annoyingly into its power, and could easily face the coming generation with the terrible alternative: Either do away with your venerations, or—*with yourselves!*" The latter would be Nihilism—but would not the former also be Nihilism? This is *our* note of interrogation.

347

BELIEVERS AND THEIR NEED OF BELIEF.—How much *faith* a person requires in order to flourish, how much "fixed opinion" he requires which he does not wish to have shaken, because he *holds* himself thereby—is a measure of his power (or more plainly speaking, of his weakness). Most people in old Europe, as it seems to me, still need Christianity at present, and on that account it still finds belief. For such is man: a theological dogma might be refuted to him a thousand times,—provided, however, that he had need of it, he would again and again accept it as "true,"—according to the famous "proof of power" of which the Bible speaks. Some have still need of metaphysics; but also the impatient *longing for certainty* which at present discharges itself in scientific, positivist fashion among large numbers of the people, the longing by all means to get at something stable (while on account of the warmth of the longing the establishing of the certainty is more leisurely and negligently undertaken): even this is still the longing for a hold, a support; in short, the *instinct of weakness,* which, while not actually creating religions, metaphysics, and convictions of all kinds, nevertheless—preserves them. In fact, around all these positivist systems there fume the vapours of a certain pessimistic gloom, something of weariness, fatalism, disillusionment, and fear of new disillusionment—or else manifest animosity, ill-humour, anarchic exasperation, and whatever there is of symptom or masquerade of the feeling of weakness. Even the readiness with which our cleverest contemporaries get lost in wretched corners and alleys, for example, in Vaterländerei (so I designate Jingoism, called *chauvinisme* in France, and "*deutsch*" in Germany), or in petty æsthetic creeds in the manner of Parisian *naturalisme* (which only brings into prominence and uncovers *that* aspect of nature which excites simultaneously disgust and astonishment —they like at present to call this aspect *la vérité vraie*), or in Nihilism in the St Petersburg style (that is to say, in the *belief in unbelief*, even to martyrdom for it):—this shows always and above all the need of belief, support, backbone, and buttress. . . . Belief is always most desired, most pressingly needed where there is a lack of will: for the will, as emotion of command, is the distinguishing characteristic of sovereignty and power. That is to say, the less a person knows how to command, the more urgent is his desire for one who commands, who commands sternly,—a God, a prince, a caste, a physician, a confessor, a dogma, a party conscience. From whence perhaps it could be inferred that the two world-religions, Buddhism and Christianity, might well have had the cause of their rise, and especially of their rapid extension, in an extraordinary *malady of the will*. And in truth it has been so: both religions lighted upon a longing, monstrously exaggerated by malady of the will, for an imperative, a "Thou-shalt," a longing going the length of despair; both religions were teachers of fanaticism in times of slackness of will-power, and thereby offered to innumerable persons a support, a new possibility of exercising will, an enjoyment in willing. For in fact fanaticism is the sole "volitional strength" to which the weak and irresolute can be excited, as a sort of hypnotising of the entire sensory-intellectual system, in favour of the over-abundant nutrition (hypertrophy) of a particular point of view and a particular sentiment, which then dominates—the Christian calls it his *faith*. When a man arrives at the fundamental conviction that he *requires* to be commanded, he becomes "a believer." Reversely, one could imagine a delight and a power of self-determining, and a *freedom* of will whereby a spirit could bid farewell to every belief, to every wish for certainty, accustomed as it would be to support itself on slender cords and possibilities, and to dance even on the verge of abysses. Such a spirit would be the *free spirit par excellence.*

370

What is Romanticism?—It will be remembered perhaps, at least among my friends, that at first I assailed the modern world with some gross errors and exaggerations, but at any rate with *hope* in my heart. I recognised—who knows from what personal experiences?—the philosophical pessimism of the nineteenth century as the symptom of a higher power of thought, a more daring courage and a more triumphant *plenitude* of life than had been characteristic of the eighteenth century, the age of Hume, Kant, Condillac, and the sensualists: so that the tragic view of things seemed to me the peculiar *luxury* of our culture, its most precious, noble, and dangerous mode of prodigality; but nevertheless, in view of its overflowing wealth, a *justifiable* luxury. In the same way I interpreted for myself German music as the expression of a Dionysian power in the German soul: I thought I heard in it the earthquake by means of which a primeval force that had been imprisoned for ages was finally finding vent—indifferent as to whether all that usually calls itself culture was thereby made to totter. It is obvious that I then misunderstood what constitutes the veritable character both of philosophical pessimism and of German music,—namely, their *Romanticism.* What is Romanticism? Every art and every philosophy may be regarded as a healing and helping appliance in the service of growing, struggling life: they always presuppose suffering and sufferers. But there are two kinds of sufferers: on the one hand those that suffer from *overflowing vitality,* who need Dionysian art, and require a tragic view and insight into life; and on the other hand those who suffer from *reduced vitality,* who seek repose, quietness, calm seas, and deliverance from themselves through art or knowledge, or else intoxication, spasm, bewilderment and madness. All Romanticism in art and knowledge responds to the twofold craving of the *latter;* to them Schopenhauer as well as Wagner responded (and responds),—to name those most celebrated and decided romanticists who were then *misunderstood* by me (*not* however to their disadvantage, as may be reasonably conceded to me). The being richest in overflowing vitality, the Dionysian God and man, may not only allow himself the spectacle of the horrible and questionable, but even the fearful deed itself, and all the luxury of destruction, disorganisation and negation. With him evil, senselessness and ugliness seem as it were licensed, in consequence of the overflowing plenitude of procreative, fructifying power, which can convert every desert into a luxuriant orchard. Conversely, the greatest sufferer, the man poorest in vitality, would have most need of mildness, peace and kindliness in thought and action: he would need, if possible, a God who is specially the God of the sick, a "Saviour"; similarly he would have need of logic, the abstract intelligibility of existence—for logic soothes and gives confidence;—in short he would need a certain warm, fear-dispelling narrowness and imprisonment within optimistic horizons. In this manner I gradually began to understand Epicurus, the opposite of a Dionysian pessimist;—in a similar manner also the "Christian," who in fact is only a type of Epicurean, and like him essentially a romanticist:—and my vision has always become keener in tracing that most difficult and insidious of all forms of *retrospective inference,* in which most mistakes have been made—the inference from the work to its author, from the deed to its doer, from the ideal to him who *needs* it, from every mode of thinking and valuing to the imperative *want* behind it.—In regard to all æsthetic values I now avail myself of this radical distinction: I ask in every single case, "Has hunger or superfluity become creative here?" At the outset another distinction might seem to recommend itself more—it is far more conspicuous,—namely, to have in view whether the desire for rigidity, for perpetuation, for *being* is the cause of the creating, or the desire for destruction, for change, for the new, for the future—for *becoming.* But when looked at more carefully, both these kinds of desire prove themselves ambiguous, and are explicable precisely according to the before-mentioned and, as it seems to me, rightly preferred scheme. The desire for *destruction,* change and becoming, may be the expression of overflowing power, pregnant with futurity (my *terminus* for this is of course the word "Dionysian"); but it may also be the hatred of the ill-constituted, destitute and unfortunate, which destroys, and *must* destroy, because the enduring, yea, all that endures, in fact all being, excites and provokes it. To understand this emotion we have but to look closely at our anarchists. The will to *perpetuation* requires equally a double interpretation. It may on the one hand proceed from gratitude and love:—art of this origin will always be an art of apotheosis, perhaps dithyrambic, as with Rubens, mocking divinely, as with Hafiz, or clear and kind-hearted as with Goethe, and spreading a Homeric brightness and glory over everything (in this case I speak of *Apollonian* art). It may also, however, be the tyrannical will of a sorely-suffering, struggling or tortured being, who would like to stamp his most personal, individual and narrow characteristics, the very idiosyncrasy of his suffering, as an obligatory law and constraint on others; who, as it were, takes revenge on all things, in that he imprints, enforces and brands *his* image, the image of *his* torture, upon them. The latter is *romantic pessimism* in its most extreme form, whether it be as Schopenhauerian will-philosophy, or as Wagnerian music:—romantic pessimism, the last *great* event in the destiny of our civilisation. (That there *may be* quite a different kind of pessimism, a classical pessimism—this presentiment and vision belongs to me, as something inseparable from me, as my *proprium* and *ipsissimum;* only that the word "classical" is repugnant to my ears, it has become far too worn, too indefinite and indistinguishable. I call that pessimism of the future,—for it is coming! I see it coming!—*Dionysian* pessimism.)

☙ from *Beyond Good and Evil*

PREJUDICES OF PHILOSOPHERS

23

All psychology hitherto has run aground on moral prejudices and timidities, it has not dared to launch out into the depths. In so far as it is allowable to recognise in that which has hitherto been written, evidence of that which has hitherto been kept silent, it seems as if nobody had yet harboured the notion of psychology as the Morphology and *Development-doctrine of the Will to Power,* as I conceive of it. The power of moral prejudices has penetrated deeply into the most intellectual world, the world apparently most indifferent and unprejudiced, and has obviously operated in an injurious, obstructive, blinding, and distorting manner. A proper physio-psychology has to contend with unconscious antagonism in the heart of the investigator, it has "the heart" against it: even a doctrine of the reciprocal conditionalness of the "good" and the "bad" impulses, causes (as refined immorality) distress and aversion in a still strong and manly conscience—still more so, a doctrine of the derivation of all good impulses from bad ones. If, however, a person should regard even the emotions of hatred, envy, covetousness, and imperiousness as life-conditioning emotions, as factors which must be present, fundamentally and essentially, in the general economy of life (which must, therefore, be further developed if life is to be further developed), he will suffer from such a view of things as from sea-sickness. And yet this hypothesis is far from being the strangest and most painful in this immense and almost new domain of dangerous knowledge; and there are in fact a hundred good reasons why every one should keep away from it who *can* do so! On the other hand, if one has once drifted hither with one's bark, well! very good! now let us set our teeth firmly! let us open our eyes and keep our hand fast on the helm! We sail away right *over* morality, we crush out, we destroy perhaps the remains of our own morality by daring to make our voyage thither—but what do *we* matter! Never yet did a *profounder* world of insight reveal itself to daring travellers and adventurers, and the psychologist who thus "makes a sacrifice"—it is *not* the *sacrifizio dell' intelletto,* on the contrary!—will at least be entitled to demand in return that psychology shall once more be recognised as the queen of the sciences, for whose service and equipment the other sciences exist. For psychology is once more the path to the fundamental problems.

THE NATURAL HISTORY OF MORALS

187

Apart from the value of such assertions as "there is a categorical imperative in us," one can always ask: What does such an assertion indicate about him who makes it? There are systems of morals which are meant to justify their author in the eyes of other people; other systems of morals are meant to tranquillise him, and make him self-satisfied; with other systems he wants to crucify and humble himself; with others he wishes to take revenge; with others to conceal himself; with others to glorify himself and gain superiority and distinction;—this system of morals helps its author to forget, that system makes him, or something of him, forgotten; many a moralist would like to exercise power and creative arbitrariness over mankind; many another, perhaps, Kant especially, gives us to understand by his morals that "what is estimable in me, is that I know how to obey—and with you it *shall* not be otherwise than with me!" In short, systems of morals are only a *sign-language of the emotions.*

188

In contrast to *laisser-aller*, every system of morals is a sort of tyranny against "nature" and also against "reason"; that is, however, no objection, unless one should again decree by some system of morals, that all kinds of tyranny and unreasonableness are unlawful. What is essential and invaluable in every system of morals, is that it is a long constraint. In order to understand Stoicism, or Port-Royal, or Puritanism, one should remember the constraint under which every language has attained to strength and freedom—the metrical constraint, the tyranny of rhyme and rhythm. How much trouble have the poets and orators of every nation given themselves!—not excepting some of the prose writers of to-day, in whose ear dwells an inexorable conscientiousness—"for the sake of a folly," as utilitarian bunglers say, and thereby deem themselves wise—"from submission to arbitrary laws," as the anarchists say, and thereby fancy themselves "free," even free-spirited. The singular fact remains, however, that everything of the nature of freedom, elegance, boldness, dance, and masterly certainty, which exists or has existed, whether it be in thought itself, or in administration, or in speaking and persuading, in art just as in conduct, has only developed by means of the tyranny of such arbitrary law; and in all seriousness, it is not at all improbable that precisely this is "nature" and "natural"—and *not laisser-aller!* Every artist knows how different from the state of letting himself go, is his "most natural" condition, the free arranging, locating, disposing, and constructing in the moments of "inspiration"—and how strictly and delicately he then obeys a thousand laws, which, by their very rigidness and precision, defy all formulation by means of ideas (even the most stable idea has, in comparison therewith, something floating, manifold, and ambiguous in it). The essential thing "in heaven and in earth" is, apparently (to repeat it once more), that there should be long *obedience* in the same direction; there thereby results, and has always resulted in the long run, something which has made life worth living; for instance, virtue, art, music, dancing, reason, spirituality—anything whatever that is transfiguring, refined, foolish, or divine. The long bondage of the spirit, the distrustful constraint in the communicability of ideas, the discipline which the thinker imposed on himself to think in accordance with the rules of a church or a court, or conformable to Aristotelian premises, the persistent spiritual will to interpret everything that happened according to a Christian scheme, and in every occurrence to rediscover and justify the Christian God:—all this violence, arbitrariness, severity, dreadfulness, and unreasonableness, has proved itself the disciplinary means whereby the European spirit has attained its strength, its remorseless curiosity and subtle mobility; granted also that much irrecoverable strength and spirit had to be stifled, suffocated, and spoilt in the process (for here, as everywhere, "nature" shows herself as she is, in all her extravagant and *indifferent* magnificence, which is shocking, but nevertheless noble). That for centuries European thinkers only thought in order to prove something—nowadays, on the contrary, we are suspicious of every thinker who "wishes to prove something"—that it was always settled beforehand what *was to be* the result of their strictest thinking, as it was perhaps in the Asiatic astrology of former times, or as it is still at the present day in the innocent, Christian-moral explanation of immediate personal events "for the glory of God," or "for the good of the soul":—this tyranny, this arbitrariness, this severe and magnificent stupidity, has *educated* the spirit; slavery, both in the coarser and the finer sense, is apparently an indispensable means even of spiritual education and discipline. One may look at every system of morals in this light: it is "nature" therein which teaches to hate the *laisser-aller*, the too great freedom, and implants the need for limited horizons, for immediate duties—it teaches the *narrowing of perspectives*, and thus, in a certain sense, that stupidity is a condition of life and development. "Thou must obey some one, and for a long time; *otherwise* thou wilt come to grief, and lose all respect for thyself"—this seems to me to be the moral imperative of nature, which is certainly neither "categorical," as old Kant wished (consequently the "otherwise"), nor does it address itself to the individual (what does nature care for the individual!), but to nations, races, ages, and ranks, above all, however, to the animal "man" generally, to *mankind.*

191

The old theological problem of "Faith" and "Knowledge," or more plainly, of instinct and reason—the question whether, in respect to the valuation of things, instinct deserves more authority than rationality, which wants to appreciate and act according to motives, according to a "Why," that is to say, in conformity to purpose and utility—it is always the old moral problem that first appeared in the person of Socrates, and had divided men's minds long before Christianity. Socrates himself, following, of course, the taste of his talent—that of a surpassing dialectician—took first the side of reason; and, in fact, what did he do all his life but laugh at the awkward incapacity of the noble Athenians, who were men of instinct, like all noble men, and could never give satisfactory answers concerning the motives of their actions? In the end, however, though silently and secretly, he laughed also at himself: with his finer conscience and introspection, he found in himself the same difficulty and incapacity. "But why"—he said to himself —"should one on that account separate oneself from the instincts! One must set them right, and the reason *also*—one must follow the instincts, but at the same time persuade the reason to support them with good arguments." This was the real *falseness* of that great and mysterious ironist; he brought his conscience up to the point that he was satisfied with a kind of self-outwitting: in fact, he perceived the irrationality in the moral judgment.—Plato, more innocent in such matters, and without the craftiness of the plebeian, wished to prove to himself, at the expenditure of all his strength—the greatest strength a philosopher had ever expended—that reason and instinct lead spontaneously to one goal, to the good, to "God"; and since Plato, all theologians and philosophers have followed the same path—which means that in matters of morality, instinct (or as Christians call it, "Faith," or as I call it, "the herd") has hitherto triumphed. Unless one should make an exception in the case of Descartes, the father of rationalism (and consequently the grandfather of the Revolution), who recognised only the authority of reason: but reason is only a tool, and Descartes was superficial.

OUR VIRTUES

230

Perhaps what I have here said about a "fundamental will of the spirit" may not be understood without further details; I may be allowed a word of explanation.—That imperious something, which is popularly called "the spirit," wishes to be master internally and externally, and to feel itself master: it has the will of a multiplicity for a simplicity, a binding, taming, imperious, and essentially ruling will. Its requirements and capacities here, are the same as those assigned by physiologists to everything that lives, grows, and multiplies. The power of the spirit to appropriate foreign elements reveals itself in a strong tendency to assimilate the new to the old, to simplify the manifold, to overlook or repudiate the absolutely contradictory; just as it arbitrarily re-underlines, makes prominent, and falsifies for itself certain traits and lines in the foreign elements, in every portion of the "outside world." Its object thereby is the incorporation of new "experiences," the assortment of new things in the old arrangements —in short, growth; or more properly, the *feeling* of growth, the feeling of increased power—is its object. This same will has at its service an apparently opposed impulse of the spirit, a suddenly adopted preference of ignorance, of arbitrary shutting out, a closing of windows, an inner denial of this or that, a prohibition to approach, a sort of defensive attitude against much that is knowable, a contentment with obscurity, with the shutting-in horizon, an acceptance and approval of ignorance: as that which is all necessary according to the degree of its appropriating power, its "digestive power," to speak figuratively (and in fact "the spirit" resembles a stomach more than anything else). Here also belong an occasional propensity of the spirit to let itself be deceived (perhaps with a waggish suspicion that it is *not* so and so, but is only allowed to pass as such), a delight in uncertainty and ambiguity, an exulting enjoyment of arbitrary, out-of-the-way narrowness and mystery, of the too-near, of the foreground, of the magnified, the diminished, the misshapen, the beautified —an enjoyment of the arbitrariness of all these manifestations of power. Finally, in this connection, there is the not unscrupulous readiness of the spirit to deceive other spirits and dissemble before them—the constant pressing and straining of a creating, shaping, changeable power: the spirit enjoys therein its craftiness and its variety of disguises, it enjoys also its feeling of security therein—it is precisely by its Protean arts that it is best protected and concealed!—*Counter to this* propensity for appearance, for simplification, for a disguise, for a cloak, in short, for an outside—for every outside is a cloak— there operates the sublime tendency of the man of knowledge, which takes, and *insists* on taking things profoundly, variously, and thoroughly; as a kind of cruelty of the intellectual conscience and taste, which every courageous thinker will acknowledge in himself, provided, as it ought to be, that he has sharpened and hardened his eye sufficiently long for introspection, and is accustomed to severe discipline and even severe words. He will say: "There is something cruel in the tendency of my spirit": let the virtuous and amiable try to convince him that it is not so! In fact, it would sound nicer, if, instead of our cruelty, perhaps our "extravagant honesty" were talked about, whispered about and glorified—we free, *very* free spirits—and some day perhaps *such* will actually be [illegible]r—posthumous glory! Meanwhile—for there is plenty of time [illegible]n—we should be least inclined to deck ourselves out in [illegible]orid and fringed moral verbiage; our whole former work has just made us sick of this taste and its sprightly exuberance. They are beautiful, glistening, jingling, festive words: honesty, love of truth, love of wisdom, sacrifice for knowledge, heroism of the truthful—there is something in them that makes one's heart swell with pride. But we anchorites and marmots have long ago persuaded ourselves in all the secrecy of an anchorite's conscience, that this worthy parade of verbiage also belongs to the old false adornment, frippery, and gold-dust of unconscious human vanity, and that even under such flattering colour and repainting, the terrible original text *homo natura* must again be recognised. In effect, to translate man back again into nature; to master the many vain and visionary interpretations and subordinate meanings which have hitherto been scratched and daubed over the eternal original text, *homo natura;* to bring it about that man shall henceforth stand before man as he now, hardened by the discipline of science, stands before the *other* forms of nature, with fearless Œdipus-eyes, and stopped Ulysses-ears, deaf to the enticements of old metaphysical bird-catchers, who have piped to him far too long: "Thou art more! thou art higher! thou hast a different origin!"—this may be a strange and foolish task, but that it is a *task*, who can deny! Why did we choose it, this foolish task? Or, to put the question differently: "Why knowledge at all?" Every one will ask us about this. And thus pressed, we, who have asked ourselves the question a hundred times, have not found, and cannot find any better answer. . . .

231

Learning alters us, it does what all nourishment does that does not merely "conserve"—as the physiologist knows. But at the bottom of our souls, quite "down below," there is certainly something unteachable, a granite of spiritual fate, of predetermined decision and answer to predetermined, chosen questions. In each cardinal problem there speaks an unchangeable "I am this"; a thinker cannot learn anew about man and woman, for instance, but can only learn fully—he can only follow to the end what is "fixed" about them in himself. Occasionally we find certain solutions of problems which make strong beliefs for *us;* perhaps they are henceforth called "convictions." Later on—one sees in them only footsteps to self-knowledge, guide-posts to the problem which we ourselves *are*—or more correctly to the great stupidity which we embody, our spiritual fate, the *unteachable* in us, quite "down below."—In view of this liberal compliment which I have just paid myself, permission will perhaps be more readily allowed me to utter some truths about "woman as she is," provided that it is known at the outset how literally they are merely—*my* truths.

WHAT IS NOBLE?

268

What, after all, is ignobleness?—Words are vocal symbols for ideas; ideas, however, are more or less definite mental symbols for frequently returning and concurring sensations, for groups of sensations. It is not sufficient to use the same words in order to understand one another: we must also employ the same words for the same kind of internal experiences, we must in the end have experiences *in common.* On this account the people of one nation understand one another better than those belonging to different nations, even when they use the same language; or rather, when people have lived long together under similar conditions (of climate, soil, danger, requirement, toil) there *originates* therefrom an entity that "understands itself"—namely, a nation. In all souls a like number of frequently recurring experiences have gained the upper hand over those occurring more rarely: about these matters people understand one another rapidly and always more rapidly—the history of language is the history of a process of abbreviation; on the basis of this quick comprehension people always unite closer and closer. The greater the danger, the greater is the need of agreeing quickly and readily about what is necessary; not to misunderstand one another in danger—that is what cannot at all be dispensed with in intercourse. Also in all loves and friendships one has the experience that nothing of the kind continues when the discovery has been made that in using the same words, one of the two parties has feelings, thoughts, intuitions, wishes, or fears different from those of the other. (The fear of the "eternal misunderstanding": that is the good genius which so often keeps persons of different sexes from too hasty attachments, to which sense and heart prompt them—and *not* some Schopenhauerian "genius of the species"!) Whichever groups of sensations within a soul awaken most readily, begin to speak, and give the word of command—these decide as to the general order of rank of its values, and determine ultimately its list of desirable things. A man's estimates of value betray something of the *structure* of his soul, and wherein it sees its conditions of life, its intrinsic needs. Supposing now that necessity has from all time drawn together only such men as could express similar requirements and similar experiences by similar symbols, it results on the whole that the easy *communicability* of need, which implies ultimately the undergoing only of average and *common* experiences, must have been the most potent of all the forces which have hitherto operated upon mankind. The more similar, the more ordinary people, have always had and are still having the advantage; the more select, more refined, more unique, and difficultly comprehensible, are liable to stand alone; they succumb to accidents in their isolation, and seldom propagate themselves. One must appeal to immense opposing forces, in order to thwart this natural, all-too-natural *progressus in simile*, the evolution of man to the similar, the ordinary, the average, the gregarious—to the *ignoble!*—

☙§ from *The Genealogy of Morals*

WHAT IS THE MEANING OF ASCETIC IDEALS?

12

Granted that such an incarnate will for contradiction and unnaturalness is induced to *philosophise;* on what will it vent its pet caprice? On that which has been felt with the greatest certainty to be true, to be real; it will look for *error* in those very places where the life instinct fixes truth with the greatest positiveness. It will, for instance, after the example of the ascetics of the Vedanta Philosophy, reduce matter to an illusion, and similarly treat pain, multiplicity, the whole logical contrast of "*Subject*" and "*Object*"—errors, nothing but errors! To renounce the belief in one's own ego, to deny to one's self one's own "reality"—what a triumph! and here already we have a much higher kind of triumph, which is not merely a triumph over the senses, over the palpable, but an infliction of violence and cruelty on *reason;* and this ecstasy culminates in the ascetic self-contempt, the ascetic scorn of one's own reason making this decree: *there is* a domain of truth and of life, but reason is specially *excluded* therefrom. . . . By the bye, even in the Kantian idea of "the intellegible character of things" there remains a trace of that schism, so dear to the heart of the ascetic, that schism which likes to turn reason against reason; in fact, "intelligible character" means in Kant a kind of quality in things of which the intellect comprehends this much, that for it, the intellect, it is *absolutely incomprehensible.* After all, let us, in our character of knowers, not be ungrateful towards such determined reversals of the ordinary perspectives and values, with which the mind had for too long raged against itself with an apparently futile sacrilege! In the same way the very seeing of another vista, the very *wishing* to see another vista, is no little training and preparation of the intellect for its eternal "*Objectivity*"—objectivity being understood not as "contemplation without interest" (for that is inconceivable and nonsensical), but as the ability to have the pros and cons *in one's power* and to switch them on and off, so as to get to know how to utilise, for the advancement of knowledge, the *difference* in the perspective and in the emotional interpretations. But let us, forsooth, my philosophic colleagues, henceforward guard ourselves more carefully against this mythology of dangerous ancient ideas, which has set up a "pure, will-less, painless, timeless subject of knowledge"; let us guard ourselves from the tentacles of such contradictory ideas as "pure reason," "absolute spirituality," "knowledge-in-itself":—in these theories an eye that cannot be thought of is required to think, an eye which *ex hypothesi* has no direction at all, an eye in which the active and interpreting functions are cramped, are absent; those functions, I say, by means of which "abstract" seeing first became seeing something; in these theories consequently the absurd and the nonsensical is always demanded of the eye. There is only a seeing from a perspective, only a "knowing" from a perspective, and the *more* emotions we express over a thing, the *more* eyes, different eyes, we train on the same thing, the more complete will be our "idea" of that thing, our "objectivity." But the elimination of the will altogether, the switching off of the emotions all and sundry, granted that we could do so, what! would not that be called intellectual *castration?*

23

The ascetic ideal has corrupted not only health and taste, there are also third, fourth, fifth, and sixth things which it has corrupted—I shall take care not to go through the catalogue (when should I get to the end?). I have here to expose not what this ideal effected; but rather [illegible] what it *means*, on what it is based, what lies lurking beh[illegible] and under it, that of which it is the provisional expression, [illegible]n obscure expression bristling with queries and misunderstandings. And with *this* object only in view I presumed "not to spare" my readers a glance at the awfulness of its results, a glance at its fatal results; I did this to prepare them for the final and most awful aspect presented to me by the question of the significance of that ideal. What is the significance of the *power* of that ideal, the monstrousness of its power? Why is it given such an amount of scope? Why is not a better resistance offered against it? The ascetic ideal expresses one will: where is the opposition will, in which an *opposition ideal* expresses itself? The ascetic ideal has an aim—this goal is, putting it generally, that all the other interests of human life should, measured by its standard, appear petty and narrow; it explains epochs, nations, men, in reference to this one end; it forbids any other interpretation, any other end; it repudiates, denies, affirms, confirms, only in the sense of its own interpretation (and was there ever a more thoroughly elaborated system of interpretation?); it subjects itself to no power, rather does it believe in its own precedence over every power—it believes that nothing powerful exists in the world that has not first got to receive from "it" a meaning, a right to exist, a value, as being an instrument in its work, a way and means to its end, to one end. Where is the *counterpart* of this complete system of will, end, and interpretation? Why is the counterpart lacking? Where is the other "one aim"? But I am told it is not lacking, that not only has it fought a long and fortunate fight with that ideal, but that further it has already won the mastery over that ideal in all essentials: let our whole modern *science* attest this—that modern science, which, like the genuine reality-philosophy which it is, manifestly believes in itself alone, manifestly has the courage to be itself, the will to be itself, and has got on well enough without God, another world, and negative virtues.

With all their noisy agitator-babble, however, they effect nothing with me; these trumpeters of reality are bad musicians, their voices do not come from the deeps with sufficient audibility, they are *not* the mouthpiece for the abyss of scientific knowledge—for to-day scientific knowledge is an abyss—the word "science," in such trumpeter-mouths, is a prostitution, an abuse, an impertinence. The truth is just the opposite from what is maintained in the ascetic theory. Science has to-day absolutely *no* belief in itself, let alone in an ideal superior to itself, and wherever science still consists of passion, love, ardour, suffering, it is not the opposition to that ascetic ideal, but rather the *incarnation of its latest and noblest form.* Does that ring strange? There are enough brave and decent working people, even among the learned men of to-day, who like their little corner, and who, just because they are pleased so to do, become at times indecently loud with their demand, that people to-day should be quite content, especially in science—for in science there is so much useful work to do. I do not deny it—there is nothing I should like less than to spoil the delight of these honest workers in their handiwork; for I rejoice in their work. But the fact of science requiring hard work, the fact of its having contented workers, is absolutely no proof of science as a whole having to-day one end, one will, one ideal, one passion for a great faith; the contrary, as I have said, is the case. When science is not the latest manifestation of the ascetic ideal—but these are cases of such rarity, selectness, and exquisiteness, as to preclude the general judgment being affected thereby—science is a *hiding-place* for every kind of cowardice, disbelief, remorse, *despectio sui,* bad conscience—it is the very *anxiety* that springs from having no ideal, the suffering from the *lack* of a great love, the discontent with an enforced moderation. Oh, what does all science not cover to-day? How much, at any rate, does it not try to cover? The diligence of our best scholars, their senseless industry, their burning the candle of their brain at both ends—their very mastery in their handiwork—how often is the real meaning of all that to prevent themselves continuing to see a certain thing? Science is a self-anæsthetic: *do you know that?* You wound them—every one who consorts with scholars experiences this—you wound them sometimes to the quick through just a harmless word; when you think you are paying them a compliment you embitter them beyond all bounds, simply because you didn't have the *finesse* to infer the real kind of customers you had to tackle, the *sufferer* kind (who won't own up even to themselves what they really are), the dazed and unconscious kind who have only one fear—*coming to consciousness.*

24

And now look at the other side, at those rare cases, of which I spoke, the most supreme idealists to be found nowadays among philosophers and scholars. Have we, perchance, found in them the sought-for *opponents* of the ascetic ideal, its *anti-idealists?* In fact, they *believe* themselves to be such, these "unbelievers" (for they are all of them that): it seems that this idea is their last remnant of faith, the idea of being opponents of this ideal, so earnest are they on this subject, so passionate in word and gesture;—but does it follow that what they believe must necessarily be *true?* We "knowers" have grown by degrees suspicious of all kinds of believers, our suspicion has step by step habituated us to draw just the opposite conclusions to what people have drawn before; that is to say, wherever the strength of a belief is particularly prominent to draw the conclusion of the difficulty of proving what is believed, the conclusion of its actual *improbability.* We do not again deny that "faith produces salvation": *for that very reason* we do deny that faith *proves* anything,—a strong faith, which produces happiness, causes suspicion of the object of that faith, it does not establish its "truth," it does establish a certain probability of—*illusion.* What is now the position in these cases? These solitaries and deniers of to-day; these fanatics in one thing, in their claim to intellectual cleanness; these hard, stern, continent, heroic spirits, who constitute the glory of our time; all these pale atheists, anti-Christians, immoralists, Nihilists; these sceptics, "ephectics," and "hectics" of the intellect (in a certain sense they are the latter, both collectively and individually); these supreme idealists of knowledge, in whom alone nowadays the intellectual conscience dwells and is alive—in point of fact they believe themselves as far away as possible from the ascetic ideal, do these "free, very free spirits": and yet, if I may reveal what they themselves cannot see—for they stand too near themselves: this ideal is simply *their* ideal, they represent it nowadays and perhaps no one else, they themselves are its most spiritualised product, its most advanced picket of skirmishers and scouts, its most insidious delicate and elusive form of seduction.—If I am in any way a reader of riddles, then I will be one with this sentence: for some time past there have been no *free spirits; for they still believe in truth.* When the Christian Crusaders in the East came into collision with that invincible order of assassins, that order of free spirits *par excellence,* whose lowest grade lives in a state of discipline such as no order of monks has ever attained, then in some way or other they managed to get an inkling of that symbol and tally-word, that was reserved for the highest grade alone as their *secretum,* "Nothing is true, everything is allowed,"—in sooth, *that* was *freedom* of thought, thereby was *taking leave* of the very belief in truth. Has indeed any European, any Christian freethinker, ever yet wandered into this proposition and its labyrinthine *consequences?* Does he know *from experience* the Minotauros of this den?—I doubt it—nay, I know otherwise. Nothing is more really alien to these "monofanatics," these *so-called* "free spirits," than freedom and unfettering in that sense; in no respect are they more closely tied, the absolute fanaticism of their belief in truth is unparalleled. I know all this perhaps too much from experience at close quarters—that dignified philosophic abstinence to which a belief like that binds its adherents, that stoicism of the intellect, which eventually vetoes negation as rigidly as it does affirmation, that *wish* for standing still in front of the actual, the *factum brutum,* that fatalism in "*petits faits*" (*ce petit faitalism,* as I call it), in which French Science now attempts a kind of moral superiority over German, this renunciation of interpretation generally (that is, of forcing, doctoring, abridging, omitting, suppressing, inventing, falsifying, and all the other *essential* attributes of interpretation)—all this, considered broadly, expresses the asceticism of virtue, quite as efficiently as does any repudiation of the senses (it is at bottom only a *modus* of that repudiation). But what forces it into that unqualified will for truth is the faith *in the ascetic ideal itself,* even though it take the form of its unconscious imperatives, —make no mistake about it, it is the faith, I repeat, in a *metaphysical* value, an *intrinsic* value of truth, of a character which is only warranted and guaranteed in this ideal (it stands and falls with that ideal). Judged strictly, there does not exist a science without its "hypotheses," the thought of such a science is inconceivable, illogical: a philosophy, a faith, must always exist first to enable science to gain thereby a direction, a meaning, a limit and method, a *right* to existence. (He who holds a contrary opinion on the subject—he, for example, who takes it upon himself to establish philosophy "upon a strictly scientific basis"—has first got to "turn up-side-down" not only philosophy but also truth itself—the gravest insult which could possibly be offered to two such respectable females!) Yes, there is no doubt about it—and here I quote my *Joyful Wisdom*, cp. Book V. Aph. 344: "The man who is truthful in that daring and extreme fashion, which is the presupposition of the faith in science, *asserts thereby a different world* from that of life, nature, and history; and in so far as he asserts the existence of that different world, come, must he not similarly repudiate its counterpart, this world, *our* world? The belief on [illegible] our faith in science is based has remained to this day [illegible] metaphysical belief—even we knowers of to-day, we godless foes of metaphysics, we too take our fire from that conflagration which was kindled by a thousand-year-old faith, from that Christian belief, which was also Plato's belief, the belief that God is truth, that truth is *divine*. . . . But what if this belief becomes more and more incredible, what if nothing proves itself to be divine, unless it be error, blindness, lies—what if God Himself proved Himself to be our *oldest lie?*"—It is necessary to stop at this point and to consider the situation carefully. Science itself now *needs* a justification (which is not for a minute to say that there is such a justification). Turn in this context to the most ancient and the most modern philosophers: they all fail to realise the extent of the need of a justification on the part of the Will for Truth—here is a gap in every philosophy—what is it caused by? Because up to the present the ascetic ideal dominated all philosophy, because Truth was fixed as Being, as God, as the Supreme Court of Appeal, because Truth was not allowed to be a problem. Do you understand this "allowed"? From the minute that the belief in the God of the ascetic ideal is repudiated, there exists *a new problem:* the problem of the value of truth. The Will for Truth needed a critique—let us define by these words our own task—the value of truth is tentatively *to be called in question*. . . . (If this seems too laconically expressed, I recommend the reader to peruse again that passage from the *Joyful Wisdom* which bears the title, "How far we also are still pious," Aph. 344, and best of all the whole fifth book of that work, as well as the Preface to *The Dawn of Day*.)

25

No! You can't get round me with science, when I search for the natural antagonists of the ascetic ideal, when I put the question: "*Where* is the opposed will in which the *opponent ideal* expresses itself?" Science is not, by a long way, independent enough to fulfil this function; in every department science needs an ideal value, a power which creates values, and in whose *service* it *can believe* in itself—science itself never creates values. Its relation to the ascetic ideal is not in itself antagonistic; speaking roughly, it rather represents the progressive force in the inner evolution of that ideal. Tested more exactly, its opposition and antagonism are concerned not with the ideal itself, but only with that ideal's outworks, its outer garb, its masquerade, with its temporary hardening, stiffening, and dogmatising—it makes the life in the ideal free once more, while it repudiates its superficial elements. These two phenomena, science and the ascetic ideal, both rest on the same basis—I have already made this clear—the basis, I say, of the same over-appreciation of truth (more accurately the same belief in the *impossibility* of valuing and of criticising truth), and consequently they are *necessarily* allies, so that, in the event of their being attacked, they must always be attacked and called into question together. A valuation of the ascetic ideal inevitably entails a valuation of science as well; lose no time in seeing this clearly, and be sharp to catch it! (*Art,* I am speaking provisionally, for I will treat it on some other occasion in greater detail,—art, I repeat, in which lying is sanctified and the *will for deception* has good conscience on its side, is much more fundamentally opposed to the ascetic ideal than is science: Plato's instinct felt this—Plato, the greatest enemy of art which Europe has produced up to the present. Plato *versus* Homer, that is the complete, the true antagonism—on the one side, the whole-hearted "transcendental," the great defamer of life; on the other, its involuntary panegyrist, the *golden* nature. An artistic subservience to the service of the ascetic ideal is consequently the most absolute artistic *corruption* that there can be, though unfortunately it is one of the most frequent phases, for nothing is more corruptible than an artist.) Considered physiologically, moreover, science rests on the same basis as does the ascetic ideal: a certain *impoverishment of life* is the presupposition of the latter as of the former—add, frigidity of the emotions, slackening of the *tempo,* the substitution of dialectic for instinct, *seriousness* impressed on mien and gesture (seriousness, that most unmistakable sign of strenuous metabolism, of struggling, toiling life). Consider the periods in a nation in which the learned man comes into prominence; they are the periods of exhaustion, often of sunset, of decay—the effervescing strength, the confidence in life, the confidence in the future are no more. The preponderance of the mandarins never signifies any good, any more than does the advent of democracy, or arbitration instead of war, equal rights for women, the religion of pity, and all the other symptoms of declining life. (Science handled as a problem! what is the meaning of science?—upon this point the Preface to the *Birth of Tragedy*.) No! this "modern science"—mark you this well—is at times the *best* ally for the ascetic ideal, and for the very reason that it is the ally which is most unconscious, most automatic, most secret, and most subterranean! They have been playing into each other's hands up to the present, have these "poor in spirit" and the scientific opponents of that ideal (take care, by the bye, not to think that these opponents are the antithesis of this ideal, that they are the *rich* in spirit—that they are *not;* I have called them the *hectic* in spirit). As for these celebrated *victories* of science; there is no doubt that they are victories —but victories over what? There was not for a single minute any victory among their list over the ascetic ideal, rather was it made stronger, that is to say, more elusive, more abstract, more insidious, from the fact that a wall, an outwork, that had got built on to the main fortress and disfigured its appearance, should from time to time be ruthlessly destroyed and broken down by science. Does any one seriously suggest that the downfall of the theological astronomy signified the downfall of that ideal?—Has, perchance, man grown *less in need* of a transcendental solution of his riddle of existence, because since that time this existence has become more random, casual, and superfluous in the *visible* order of the universe? Has there not been since the time of Copernicus an unbroken progress in the self-belittling of man and his *will* for belittling himself? Alas, his belief in his dignity, his uniqueness, his irreplaceableness in the scheme of existence, is gone —he has become animal, literal, unqualified, and unmitigated animal, he who in his earlier belief was almost God ("child of God," "demi-God"). Since Copernicus man seems to have fallen on to a steep plane—he rolls faster and faster away from the centre—whither? into nothingness? *into the "thrilling sensation of his own nothingness"?*—Well! this would be the straight way—to the *old* ideal?—*All* science (and by no means only astronomy, with regard to the humiliating and deteriorating effect of which Kant has made a remarkable confession, "it annihilates my own importance"), all science, natural as much as *unnatural*—by unnatural I mean the self-critique of reason—nowadays sets out to talk man out of his present opinion of himself, as though that opinion had been nothing but a bizarre piece of conceit; you might go so far as to say that science finds its peculiar pride, its peculiar bitter form of stoical ataraxia, in preserving man's *contempt of himself*, that state which it took so much trouble to bring about, as man's final and most serious claim to self-appreciation (rightly so, in point of fact, for he who despises is always "one who has not forgotten how to appreciate"). But does all this involve any real effort to *counteract* the ascetic ideal? Is it really seriously suggested that Kant's *victory* over the theological dogmatism about "God," "Soul," "Freedom," "Immortality," has damaged that ideal in any way (as the theologians have imagined to be the case for a long time past)?—And in this connection it does not concern us for a single minute, if Kant himself intended any such consummation. It is certain that from the time of Kant every type of transcendentalist is playing a winning game—they are emancipated from the theologians; what luck!—he has revealed to them that secret art, by which they can now pursue their "heart's desire" on their own responsibility, and with all the respectability of science. Similarly, who can grumble at the agnostics, reverers, as they are, of the unknown and the absolute mystery, if they now worship *their very query* as God? (Xaver Doudan talks somewhere of the *ravages* which *l'habitude d'admirer l'intelligible au lieu de rester tout simplement dans l'inconnu* has produced —the ancients, he thinks, must have been exempt from those ravages.) Supposing that everything, "known" to man, fails to satisfy his desires, and on the contrary contradicts and horrifies them, what a divine way out of all this to be able to look for the responsibility, not in the "desiring" but in "knowing"!—"There is no knowledge. *Consequently*—there is a God"; what a novel *elegantia syllogismi!* what a triumph for the ascetic ideal!

27

Enough! enough! let us leave these curiosities and complexities of the modern spirit, which excite as much laughter as disgust. *Our* problem can certainly do without them, the problem of the *meaning* of the ascetic ideal—what has it got to do with yesterday or to-day? those things shall be handled by me more thoroughly and severely in another connection (under the title "A Contribution to the History of European Nihilism," I refer for this to a work which I am preparing: *The Will to Power, an Attempt at a Transvaluation of All Values*). The only reason why I come to allude to it here is this: the ascetic ideal has at times, even in the most intellectual sphere, only one real kind of enemies and *damagers:* these are the comedians of this ideal—for they awake mistrust. Everywhere otherwise, where the mind is at work seriously, powerfully, and without counterfeiting, it dispenses altogether now with an ideal (the popular expression for this abstinence is "Atheism")—*with the exception of the will for truth.* But this will, this *remnant* of an ideal, is, if you will believe me, that ideal itself in its severest and cleverest formulation, esoteric through and through, stripped of all outworks, and consequently not so much its remnant as its *kernel.* Unqualified honest atheism (and its air only do we breathe, we, the most intellectual men of this age) is *not* opposed to that ideal, to the extent that it appears to be; it is rather one of the final phases of its evolution, one of its syllogisms and pieces of inherent logic—it is the awe-inspiring *catastrophe* of a two-thousand-year training in truth, which finally forbids itself *the lie of the belief in God.* (The same course of development in India—quite independently, and consequently of some demonstrative value—the same ideal driving to the same conclusion, the decisive point reached five hundred years before the European era, or more precisely at the time of Buddha—it started in the Sankhyam philosophy, and then this was popularised through Buddha, and made into a religion.)

What, I put the question with all strictness, has really *triumphed* over the Christian God? The answer stands in my *Joyful Wisdom,* Aph. 357: "the Christian morality itself, the idea of truth, taken as it was with increasing seriousness, the confessor-subtlety of the Christian conscience translated and sublimated into the scientific conscience into intellectual cleanness at any price. Regarding Nature as though it were a proof of the goodness and guardianship of God; interpreting history in honour of a divine reason, as a constant proof of a moral order of the world and a moral teleology; explaining our own personal experiences, as pious men have for long enough explained them, as though every arrangement, every nod, every single thing were invented and sent out of love for the salvation of the soul; all this is now done away with, all this has the conscience *against* it, and is regarded by every subtler conscience as disreputable, dishonourable, as lying, feminism, weakness, cowardice—by means of this severity, if by means of anything at all, are we, in sooth, *good Europeans* and heirs of Europe's longest and bravest self-mastery.". . . All great things go to ruin by reason of themselves, by reason of an act of self-dissolution: so wills the law of life, the law of *necessary* "self-mastery" even in the essence of life—ever is the law-giver finally exposed to the cry, "*patere legem quam ipse tulisti*"; in thus wise did Christianity *go to ruin as a dogma,* through its own morality; in thus wise must Christianity go again to ruin to-day as a morality—we are standing on the threshold of this event. After Christian truthfulness has drawn one conclusion after the other, it finally draws its *strongest conclusion,* its conclusion *against* itself; this, however, happens, when it puts the question, "*what is the meaning of every will for truth?*" And here again do I touch on my problem, on our problem, my *unknown* friends (for as yet *I know* of no friends): what sense has our whole being, if it does not mean that in our own selves that will for truth has come to its own consciousness *as a problem?*—By reason of this attainment of self-consciousness on the part of the will for truth, morality from henceforward—there is no doubt about it—goes *to pieces:* this is that great hundred-act play that is reserved for the next two centuries of Europe, the most terrible, the most mysterious, and perhaps also the most hopeful of all plays.

28

If you except the ascetic ideal, man, the *animal* man had no meaning. His existence on earth contained no end; "What is the purpose of man at all?" was a question without an answer; the *will* for man and the world was lacking; behind every great human destiny rang as a refrain a still greater "Vanity!" The ascetic ideal simply means this: that something *was lacking,* that a tremendous *void* encircled man—he did not know how to justify himself, to explain himself, to affirm himself, he *suffered* from the problem of his own meaning. He suffered also in other ways, he was in the main a *diseased* animal; but his problem was not suffering itself, but the lack of an answer to that crying question, "*To what purpose* do we suffer?" Man, the bravest animal and the one most inured to suffering, does *not* repudiate suffering in itself: he *wills* it, he even seeks it out, provided that he is shown a meaning for it, a *purpose* of suffering. *Not* suffering, but the senselessness of suffering was the curse which till then lay spread over humanity—*and the ascetic ideal gave it a meaning!* It was up till then the only meaning; but any meaning is better than no meaning; the ascetic ideal was in that connection the "*faute de mieux*" *par excellence* that existed at that time. In that ideal suffering *found an explanation;* the tremendous gap seemed filled; the door to all suicidal Nihilism was closed. The explanation—there is no doubt about it—brought in its train new suffering, deeper, more penetrating, more venomous, gnawing more brutally into life: it brought all suffering under the perspective of *guilt;* but in spite of all that—man was *saved* thereby, he had a *meaning,* and from henceforth was no more like a leaf in the wind, a shuttlecock of chance, of nonsense, he could now "will" something—absolutely immaterial to what end, to what purpose, with what means he wished: *the will itself was saved.* It is absolutely impossible to disguise *what* in point of fact is made clear by every complete will that has taken its direction from the ascetic ideal: this hate of the human, and even more of the animal, and more still of the material, this horror of the senses, of reason itself, this fear of happiness and beauty, this desire to get right away from all illusion, change, growth, death, wishing and even desiring—all this means—let us have the courage to grasp it—a will for Nothingness, a will opposed to life, a repudiation of the most fundamental conditions of life, but it is and remains *a will!*—and to say at the end that which I said at the beginning—man will wish *Nothingness* rather than not wish *at all.*

◆§ from *The Twilight of the Idols*

HOW THE "TRUE WORLD" ULTIMATELY BECAME A FABLE

The History of an Error

1. The true world, attainable to the sage, the pious man and the man of virtue,—he lives in it, *he is it.*

(The most ancient form of the idea was relatively clever, simple, convincing. It was a paraphrase of the proposition "I, Plato, am the truth.")

2. The true world which is unattainable for the moment,

is promised to the sage, to the pious man and to the man of virtue ("to the sinner who repents").

(Progress of the idea: it becomes more subtle, more insidious, more evasive,—*it becomes a woman,* it becomes Christian.)

3. The true world is unattainable, it cannot be proved, it cannot promise anything; but even as a thought, alone, it is a comfort, an obligation, a command.

(At bottom this is still the old sun; but seen through mist and scepticism: the idea has become sublime, pale, northern, Königsbergian.[1])

4. The true world—is it unattainable? At all events it is unattained. And as unattained it is also *unknown.* Consequently it no longer comforts, nor saves, nor constrains: what could something unknown constrain us to?

([illegible] grey of dawn. Reason stretches itself and yawns for th[illegible]st time. The cock-crow of positivism.)

5. The "true world"—an idea that no longer serves any purpose, that no longer constrains one to anything,—a useless idea that has become quite superfluous, consequently an exploded idea: let us abolish it!

(Bright daylight; breakfast; the return of common sense and of cheerfulness; Plato blushes for shame and all freespirits kick up a shindy.)

6. We have suppressed the true world: what world survives? the apparent world perhaps? . . . Certainly not! *In abolishing the true world we have also abolished the world of appearance!*

(Noon; the moment of the shortest shadows; the end of the longest error; mankind's zenith; *Incipit Zarathustra.*)

❧ from *The Will to Power*

326

Virtues are as dangerous as vices, in so far as they are allowed to rule over one as authorities and laws coming from outside, and not as qualities one develops one's self. The latter

1. Kant was a native of Königsberg and lived there all his life. Did Nietzsche know that Kant was simply a Scotch Puritan, whose family settled in Germany under the name of Cant, and who, to prevent the mispronunciation of his name as *Zant* (Anglicé: Tsant), wrote it *Kant,*—a change which concealed from the Germans that which was at the very bottom of his creed —Cant? [Trans.]

is the only right way; they should be the most personal means of defence and most individual needs—the determining factors of precisely *our* existence and growth, which we recognise and acknowledge independently of the question whether others grow with us with the help of the same or of different principles. This view of the danger of the virtue which is understood as impersonal and *objective* also holds good of modesty: through modesty many of the choicest intellects perish. The morality of modesty is the worst possible softening influence for those souls for which it is pre-eminently necessary that they become *hard* betimes.

CRITICISM OF PHILOSOPHY

409

Philosophers have had (1) from times [illegible]morial a wonderful capacity for the *contradictio in adje*[illegible] (2) they have always trusted concepts as unconditionally [illegible] they have mistrusted the senses: it never seems to have occurred to them that notions and words are our inheritance of past ages in which thinking was neither very clear nor very exact.

What seems to dawn upon philosophers last of all: that they must no longer allow themselves to be presented with concepts already conceived, nor must they merely purify and polish up those concepts; but they must first *make* them, *create* them, themselves, and then present them and get people to accept them. Up to the present, people have trusted their concepts generally, as if they had been a wonderful *dowry* from some kind of wonderland: but they constitute the inheritance of our most remote, most foolish, and most intelligent forefathers. This *piety* towards that *which already exists in us* is perhaps related to the *moral element in science.* What we needed above all is absolute scepticism towards all traditional concepts (like that which a certain philosopher may already have possessed—and he was Plato, of course: for he taught *the reverse*).

430

The great reasonableness underlying all moral education lay in the fact that it always attempted to attain to *the certainty of an instinct:* so that neither good intentions nor good means, as such, first required to enter consciousness. Just as the soldier learns his exercises, so should man learn how to act in life. In truth this unconsciousness belongs to every kind of perfection: even the mathematician carries out his calculations unconsciously. . . .

What, then, does Socrates' *reaction* mean, which recommended dialectics as the way to virtue, and which was charmed when morality was unable to justify itself logically? But this is precisely what proves its *superiority*—without unconsciousness *it is worth nothing!*

In reality it means *the dissolution of Greek instincts,* when *demonstrability* is posited as the first condition of personal excellence in virtue. All these great "men of virtue" and of words are themselves types of dissolution.

In practice, it means that moral judgments have been torn from the conditions among which they grew and in which alone they had some sense, from their Greek and Græco-political soil, in order to be *denaturalised* under the cover of being *made sublime.* The great concepts "good" and "just" are divorced from the first principles of which they form a part, and, as "ideas" *become free,* degenerate into subjects for discussion. A certain truth is sought behind them; they are regarded as entities or as symbols of entities: a world is *invented* where they are "at home," and from which they are supposed to hail.

In short: the scandal reaches its apotheosis in Plato. . . . And then it was necessary to invent the *perfectly abstract* man also:—good, just, wise, and a dialectician to boot—in short, the *scarecrow* of the ancient philosopher: a plant without any soil whatsoever; a human race devoid of all definite ruling instincts; a virtue which "justifies" itself with reasons. The perfectly absurd "individual" *per se!* the highest form of *Artificiality.* . . .

Briefly, the denaturalisation of moral values resulted in the creation of a degenerate *type of man*—"the good man," "the happy man," "the wise man"—Socrates represents a moment of the most *profound perversity* in the history of values.

432

THE PROBLEM OF SOCRATES.—The two antitheses: the *tragic* and the *Socratic* spirits—measured according to the law of Life.

To what extent is the Socratic spirit a decadent phenomenon? to what extent are robust health and power still revealed by the whole attitude of the scientific man, his dialectics, his ability, and his severity? (the health of the *plebeian;* whose malice, *esprit frondeur,* whose astuteness, whose rascally depths, are held in check by his *cleverness;* the whole type is "ugly").

Uglification: self-derision, dialectical dryness, intelligence in the form of a *tyrant* against the "tyrant" (instinct). Everything in Socrates is exaggeration, eccentricity, caricature; he is a buffoon with the blood of Voltaire in his veins. He discovers a new form of *agon;* he is the first fencing-master in the superior classes of Athens; he stands for nothing else than the *highest form of cleverness:* he calls it "virtue" (he regarded it as a means of *salvation;* he did not choose to be *clever,* cleverness was *de rigueur*); the proper thing is to control one's self in suchwise that one enters into a struggle *not* with passions but with reasons as one's weapons (Spinoza's stratagem—the unravelment of the errors of passion);—it is desirable to discover how every one may be caught once he is goaded into a passion, and to know how illogically passion proceeds; self-mockery is practised in order to injure the very roots of the *feelings of resentment.*

It is my wish to understand which idiosyncratic states form a part of the Socratic problem: its association of reason, virtue, and happiness. With this absurd doctrine of the identity of these things it succeeded *in charming* the world: ancient philosophy could not rid itself of this doctrine. . . .

Absolute lack of objective interest: hatred of science: the idiosyncrasy of considering one's self a problem. Acoustic hallucinations in Socrates: morbid element. When the intellect is rich and independent, it most strongly resists preoccupying itself with morality. How is it that Socrates is a *moral-maniac?* —Every "practical" philosophy immediately steps into the foreground in times of distress. When morality and religion become the chief interests of a community, they are signs of a state of distress.

434

WHY EVERYTHING RESOLVED ITSELF INTO MUMMERY.—Rudimentary psychology, which only considered the *conscious* lapses of men (as causes), which regarded "consciousness" as an attribute of the soul, and which sought a will behind every action (*i.e.* an intention), could only answer "*Happiness*" to the question: "*What does man desire?*" (it was impossible to answer "Power," because that would have been *immoral*);—consequently behind all men's actions there is the intention of attaining to happiness by means of them. Secondly: if man as a matter of fact does not attain to happiness, why is it? Because he mistakes the means thereto.—*What is the unfailing means of acquiring happiness?* Answer: *virtue.*—Why virtue? Because virtue is supreme rationalness, and rationalness makes mistakes in the choice of means impossible: virtue in the form of *reason* is the way to happiness. Dialectics is the constant occupation of virtue, because it does away with passion and intellectual cloudiness.

As a matter of fact, man does *not* desire "happiness." Pleasure is a sensation of power: if the passions are excluded, those states of the mind are also excluded which afford the greatest sensation of power and therefore of pleasure. The highest rationalism is a state of cool clearness, which is very far from being able to bring about that feeling of power which every kind of *exaltation* involves. . . .

The ancient philosophers combat everything that intoxicates and exalts—everything that impairs the perfect coolness and impartiality of the mind. . . . They were consistent with their first false principle: that consciousness was the *highest,* the *supreme* state of mind, the prerequisite of perfection—whereas the reverse is true. . . .

Any kind of action is imperfect in proportion as it has been willed or conscious. The philosophers of antiquity *were the greatest duffers* in practice, because they condemned themselves theoretically to *dufferdom.* . . . In practice everything resolved itself into theatricalness: and he who saw through it, as Pyrrho did, for instance, thought as everybody did—that is to say, that in goodness and uprightness "paltry people" were far superior to philosophers.

All the deeper natures of antiquity were disgusted at the *philosophers of virtue;* all people saw in them was brawlers and actors. (This was the judgment passed on *Plato* by *Epicurus* and *Pyrrho.*)

Result: In practical life, in patience, goodness, and mutual assistance, paltry people were above them:—this is something like the judgment Dostoievsky or Tolstoy claims for his muzhiks: they are more philosophical in practice, they are more courageous in their way of dealing with the exigencies of life. . . .

436

To what extent do dialectics and the faith in reason rest upon *moral* prejudices? With Plato we are as the temporary inhabitants of an intelligible world of goodness, still in possession of a bequest from former times: divine dialectics taking its root in goodness leads to everything good (it follows, therefore, that it must lead "backwards"). Even Descartes had a notion of the fact that, according to a thoroughly Christian and moral attitude of mind, which includes a belief in a *good* God as the Creator of all things, the truthfulness of God *guarantees* the judgments of our senses for us. But for this religious sanction and warrant of our senses and our reason, whence should we obtain our right to trust in existence? That thinking must be a measure of reality,—that what cannot be the subject of thought, cannot *exist*,—is a coarse *non plus ultra* of a moral blind confidence (in the essential principle of truth at the root of all things); this in itself is a mad assumption which our experience contradicts every minute. We cannot think of anything precisely as it is. . . .

437

The real *philosophers of Greece* are those which came before Socrates (with Socrates something changes). They are all distinguished men, they take their stand away from the people and from usage; they have travelled; they are earnest to the point of sombreness, their eyes are calm, and they are not unacquainted with the business of state and diplomacy. They anticipated all the great concepts which coming sages were to have concerning things in general: they themselves represented these concepts, they made systems out of themselves. Nothing can give a higher idea of Greek intellect than this sudden fruitfulness in types, than this involuntary completeness in the drawing up of all the great possibilities of the philosophical ideal. I can see only one original figure in those that came afterwards: a late arrival, but necessarily the last—*Pyrrho* the nihilist. His instincts were opposed to the influences which had become ascendant in the meantime: the Socratic school, Plato, and the artistic optimism of Heraclitus. (Pyrrho goes back to Democritus *via* Protagoras. . . .)

Wise weariness: Pyrrho. To live humbly among the humble. Devoid of pride. To live in the vulgar way [illegible] honour and believe what every one believes. To be on o[illegible]s guard against science and intellect, and against everything that *puffs one out*. . . . To be simply patient in the extreme, careless and mild;—*ἀπάθεια*, or, better still, *πραΰτης*. A Buddhist for Greece, bred amid the tumult of the Schools; born after his time; weary; an example of the protest of weariness against the eagerness of dialecticians; the incredulity of the tired man in regard to the importance of everything. He had seen *Alexander;* he had seen the *Indian penitents.* To such late-arrivals and creatures of great subtlety, everything lowly, poor, and idiotic, is seductive. It narcoticises: it gives them relaxation (Pascal). On the other hand, they mix with the crowd, and get confounded with the rest. These weary creatures need warmth. . . . To overcome contradiction; to do away with contests; to have no will to excel in any way: to deny the *Greek* instincts. (Pyrrho lived with his sister, who was a midwife.) To rig out wisdom in such a way that it no longer distinguishes; to give it the ragged mantle of poverty; to perform the lowest offices, and to go to market and sell sucking-pigs. . . . Sweetness, clearness, indifference; no need of virtues that require attitudes; to be equal to all even in virtue: final conquest of one's self, final indifference.

Pyrrho and Epicurus:—two forms of Greek decadence: they are related in their hatred of dialectics and all *theatrical* virtues. These two things together were then called philosophy; Pyrrho and Epicurus intentionally held that which they loved in low esteem; they chose common and even contemptible names for it, and they represented a state in which one is neither ill, healthy, lively, nor dead. . . . Epicurus was more *naïf,* more idyllic, more grateful; Pyrrho had more experience of the world, had travelled more, and was more nihilistic. His life was a protest against the great *doctrine of Identity* (Happiness = Virtue = Knowledge). The proper way of living is not promoted by science: wisdom does not make "wise.". . . The proper way of living does not desire happiness, it turns away from happiness. . . .

438

The war against the "old faith," as Epicurus waged it, was, strictly speaking, a struggle against *pre-existing* Christianity—the struggle against a world then already gloomy, moralised, acidified throughout with feelings of guilt, and grown old and sick.

Not the "moral corruption" of antiquity, but precisely its *moral infectedness* was the prerequisite which enabled Christianity to become its master. Moral fanaticism (in short: Plato) destroyed paganism by transvaluing its values and poisoning its innocence. We ought at last to understand that what was then destroyed was *higher* than what prevailed! Christianity grew on the soil of psychological corruption, and could only take root in rotten ground.

439

SCIENCE: AS A DISCIPLINARY MEASURE OR AS AN INSTINCT.—I see a *decline of the instincts* in Greek philosophers: otherwise they could not have been guilty of the profound error of regarding the *conscious* state as the more *valuable* state. The *intensity of consciousness* stands in the *inverse* ratio to the ease and speed of cerebral transmission. Greek philosophy upheld the *opposite view,* which is always the sign of *weakened* instincts.

We must, in sooth, seek *perfect life* there where it is least conscious (that is to say, there where it is least aware of its logic, its reasons, its means, its intentions, and its *utility*). The return to the facts of *common sense,* the facts of the common man and of "paltry people." *Honesty and intelligence* stored up for generations by people who are quite unconscious of their principles, and who even have some fear of principles. It is not reasonable to desire a *reasoning virtue.* . . . A philosopher is compromised by such a desire.

443

At bottom, morality is *hostile* to science: Socrates was so already too—and the reason is, that science considers certain things important which have no relation whatsoever to "good" and "evil," and which therefore reduce the gravity of our feelings concerning "good" and "evil." What morality requires is that the whole of a man should serve it with all his power: it considers it waste on the part of a creature that *can ill afford waste,* when a man earnestly troubles his head about stars or plants. That is why science very quickly declined in Greece, once Socrates had inoculated scientific work with the disease of morality. The mental attitudes reached by a Democritus, a Hippocrates, and a Thucydides, have not been reached a second time.

444

The problem of the *philosopher* and of the *scientific* man.—The influence of age; depressing habits (sedentary study *à la* Kant; over-work; inadequate nourishment of the brain; reading). A more essential question still: is it not already perhaps a *symptom* of decadence when thinking tends to establish *generalities?*

Objectivity regarded as the disintegration of the will (to be able to remain as detached as possible . . .). This presupposes a tremendous adiaphora in regard to the strong passions: a kind of isolation, an exceptional position, opposition to the normal passions.

Type: desertion of *home-country;* emigrants go ever greater distances afield; growing exoticism; the voice of the old imperative dies away;—and the continual question "whither?" ("happiness") is a sign of *emancipation* from forms of organisation, a sign of breaking loose from everything.

Problem: is the man of *science* more of a decadent symptom than the philosopher?—as a *whole* the scientific man is not cut loose from everything, only a part of his being is consecrated exclusively to the service of knowledge and disciplined to maintain a special attitude and point of view; in his department he is in need of *all* the virtues of a strong race, of robust health, of great severity, manliness, and intelligence. He is rather a symptom of the great multiformity of culture than of the effeteness of the latter. The decadent scholar is a *bad* scholar. Whereas the decadent philosopher has always been reckoned hitherto as the typical philosopher.

445

Among philosophers, nothing is more rare than *intellectual uprightness:* they perhaps say the very reverse, and even believe it. But the prerequisite of all their work is, that they can only admit of certain truths; they know what they *have* to prove; and the fact that they must be agreed as to these "truths" is almost what makes them recognise one another as philosophers. There are, for instance, the truths of morality. But belief in morality is not a proof of morality: there are cases—and the philosopher's case is one in point—when a belief of this sort is simply a piece of *immorality.*

446

What is the Retrograde Factor in a Philosopher?—He teaches that the qualities which he happens to possess are the only qualities that exist, that they are indispensable to those who wish to attain to the "highest good" (for instance, dialectics with Plato). He would have all men raise themselves, *gradatim,* to *his* type as the highest. He despises what is generally esteemed—by him a gulf is cleft between the highest *priestly* values and the values of the *world*. He knows what is true, who God is, what every one's goal should be, and the way thereto. . . . The typical philosopher is thus an absolute dogmatist;—if he *requires* scepticism at all it is only in order to be able to speak dogmatically of his *principal purpose*.

447

When the philosopher is confronted with his rival—science, for instance, he becomes a sceptic; then he appropriates a *form of knowledge* which he denies to the man of science; he goes hand in hand with the priest so that he may not be suspected of atheism or materialism; he considers an attack made upon himself as an attack upon morals, religion, virtue, and order—he knows how to bring his opponents into ill repute by calling them "seducers" and "underminers": then he marches shoulder to shoulder with power.

The philosopher at war with other philosophers:—he does his best to compel them to appear like anarchists, disbelievers, opponents of authority. In short, when he fights, he fights exactly like a priest and like the priesthood.

452

Error and ignorance are fatal.—The assumption that *truth has been found* and that ignorance and error are at an end, constitutes one of the most seductive thoughts in the world. Granted that it be generally accepted, it paralyses the will to test, to investigate, to be cautious, and to gather experience: it may even be regarded as criminal—that is to say, as a *doubt* concerning truth. . . .

"Truth" is therefore more fatal than error and ignorance, because it paralyses the forces which lead to enlightenment and knowledge. The passion for *idleness* now stands up for "truth" ("Thought is pain and misery!"), as also do order, rule, the joy of possession, the pride of wisdom—in fact, *vanity:* —it is easier to *obey* than to *examine;* it is more gratifying to think "I possess the truth," than to see only darkness in all directions; . . . but, above all, it is reassuring, it lends confidence, and alleviates life—it "improves" the character inasmuch as it *reduces mistrust*. "Spiritual peace," "a quiet conscience"—these things are inventions which are only possible provided *"Truth be found."*—"By their fruits ye shall know them.". . ."Truth" is the truth because it makes men *better*.

. . . The process goes on: all goodness and all success is placed to the credit of "truth."

This is the *proof by success:* the happiness, contentment, and the welfare of a community or of an individual, are now understood to be the *result of the belief in morality.* . . . Conversely: *failure* is ascribed to a *lack* of faith.

465

Under "Spiritual freedom" I understand something very definite: it is a state in which one is a hundred times superior to philosophers and other disciples of "truth" in one's severity towards one's self, in one's uprightness, in one's courage, and in one's absolute will to say nay even when it is dangerous to say nay. I regard the philosophers that have appeared heretofore as *contemptible libertines* hiding behind the petticoats of the female "Truth."

THE WILL TO POWER IN SCIENCE

481

In opposition to Positivism, which halts at phenomena and says, "These are only *facts* and nothing more," I would say: No, facts are precisely what is lacking, all that exists consists of *interpretations.* We cannot establish any fact "in itself": it may even be nonsense to desire to do such a thing. "Everything is *subjective,*" ye say: but that in itself is *interpretation.* The "subject" is nothing given, but something superimposed by fancy, something introduced behind.—Is it necessary to set an interpreter behind the interpretation already to hand? Even that would be fantasy, hypothesis.

To the extent to which knowledge has any sense at all, the world is knowable: but it may be interpreted *differently,* it has not one sense behind it, but hundreds of senses.—"Perspectivity."

It is our needs that *interpret the world;* our instincts and their impulses for and against. Every instinct is a sort of thirst for power; each has its point of view, which it would fain impose upon all the other instincts as their norm.

487

Should not all philosophy ultimately disclose the first principles on which the reasoning processes depend?—that is to say, our *belief* in the "ego" as a substance, as the only reality according to which, alone, we are able to ascribe reality to things? The oldest realism at length comes to light, simultaneously with man's recognition of the fact that his whole religious history is no more than a history of soul-superstitions. *Here there is a barrier:* our very thinking, itself, involves that belief (with its distinctions—substance, accident, action, agent, etc.); to abandon it would mean to cease from being able to think.

But that a belief, however useful it may be for the preservation of a species, has nothing to do with the truth[illegible]y be seen from the fact that we *must* believe in time, space, and motion, without feeling ourselves compelled to regard them as absolute realities.

492

The body and physiology the starting-point: why?—We obtain a correct image of the nature of our subject-entity, that is to say, as a number of regents at the head of a community (not as "souls" or as "life-forces"), as also of the dependence of these regents upon their subjects, and upon the conditions of a hierarchy, and of the division of labour, as the means ensuring the existence of the part and the whole. We also obtain a correct image of the way in which the living entities continually come into being and expire, and we see how eternity cannot belong to the "subject"; we realise that the struggle finds expression in obeying as well as in commanding, and that a fluctuating definition of the limits of power is a factor of life. The comparative *ignorance* in which the ruler is kept, of the individual performances and even disturbances taking place in the community, also belong to the conditions under which government may be carried on. In short, we obtain a valuation even of *want-of-knowledge,* of seeing-things-generally-as-a-whole, of simplification, of falsification, and of perspective. What is most important, however, is, that we regard the ruler and his subjects as of the *same kind,* all feeling, willing, thinking—and that wherever we see or suspect movement in a body, we conclude that there is co-operative-subjective and invisible life. Movement as a symbol for the eye; it denotes that something has been felt, willed, thought.

The danger of directly questioning the subject *concerning* the subject, and all spiritual self-reflection, consists in this, that it might be a necessary condition of its activity to interpret itself *erroneously.* That is why we appeal to the body and lay the evidence of sharpened senses aside: or we try and see whether the subjects themselves cannot enter into communication with us.

521

CONCERNING "LOGICAL APPEARANCE."—The concept "individual" and the concept "species" are equally false and only apparent. "*Species*" only expresses the fact that an abundance of similar creatures come forth at the same time, and that the speed of their further growth and of their further transformation has been made almost imperceptible for a long time: so that the actual and trivial changes and increase of growth are of no account at all (—a stage of evolution in which the process of evolving is not visible, so that, not only does a state of equilibrium *seem* to have been reached, but the road is also made clear for the error of supposing *that an actual goal has been reached*—and that evolution had a goal . . .).

The form seems to be something enduring, and therefore valuable; but the form was invented merely by ourselves; and however often "the same form is attained," it does not signify that it *is the same form,—because something new always appears;* and we alone, who compare, reckon the new with the old, in so far as it resembles the latter, and embody the two in the unity of "form." As if a *type* had to be reached and were actually intended by the formative processes.

Form, species, law, idea, purpose—the same fault is made in respect of all these concepts, namely, that of giving a false realism to a piece of fiction: as if all phenomena were infused with some sort of obedient spirit—an artificial distinction is here made between that *which* acts and that *which* guides action (but both these things are only fixed in order to agree with our metaphysico-logical dogma: they are not "facts").

We should not interpret this *constraint* in ourselves, to imagine concepts, species, forms, purposes, and laws ("*a world of identical cases*") as if we were in a position to construct a *real world;* but as a constraint to adjust a world by means of which *our existence* will be ensured: we thereby create a world which is determinable, simplified, comprehensible, etc., for us.

The very same constraint is active in *the functions of the senses* which support the reason—by means of simplification, coarsening, accentuation, and interpretation; whereon all "recognition," all the ability of making one's self intelligible rests. Our *needs* have made our senses so precise, that the "same world of appearance" always returns, and has thus acquired the semblance of *reality.*

Our subjective constraint to have faith in logic, is expressive only of the fact that long before logic itself became conscious in us, we did nothing *save introduce its postulates into the nature of things:* now we find ourselves in their presence,—we can no longer help it,—and now we would fain believe that this constraint is a guarantee of "truth." We it was who created the "thing," the "same thing," the subject, the attribute, the action, the object, the substance, and the form, after we had carried the process of equalising, coarsening, and simplifying as far as possible. The world *seems* logical to us, because we have already made it logical.

522

FUNDAMENTAL SOLUTION.—We believe in reason: this is, however, the philosophy of colourless *concepts.* Language is built upon the most *naïf* prejudices.

Now we read discord and problems into things, because we are able to *think only* in the form of language—we also believe in the "eternal truth" of "wisdom" (for instance, subject, attribute, etc.).

We cease from thinking if we do not wish to think under the control of language; the most we can do is to attain to an attitude of doubt concerning the question whether the boundary here really is a boundary.

Rational thought is a process of interpreting according to a scheme which we cannot reject.

524

THE PART "CONSCIOUSNESS" PLAYS.—It is essential that one should not mistake the part that "consciousness" plays: it is our *relation to the outer world; it was the outer world that developed it.* On the other hand, the *direction*—that is to say, the care and cautiousness which is concerned with the interrelation of the bodily functions, does *not* enter into our consciousness any more than does the *storing activity* of the intellect: that there is a superior controlling force at work in these things cannot be doubted—a sort of directing committee, in which the various *leading desires* make their votes and their power felt. "Pleasure" and "pain" are indications which reach us from this sphere: as are also *acts of will* and *ideas.*

In short: That which becomes conscious has causal relations which are completely and absolutely concealed from our knowledge—the sequence of thoughts, feelings, and ideas, in consciousness, does not signify that the order in which they come is a causal order: it is *so apparently,* however, in the highest degree. We have *based* the whole of our notion of *intellect, reason, logic,* etc., upon this *apparent truth* (all these things do not exist: they are imaginary syntheses and entities), and we then projected the latter into and *behind* all things!

As a rule *consciousness* itself is understood to be the general sensorium and highest ruling centre; albeit, it is only a *means of communication:* it was developed by intercourse, and with a view to the interests of intercourse. . . . "Intercourse" is understood, here, as "relation," and is intended to cover the action of the outer world upon us and our necessary response to it, as also our actual influence *upon* the outer world. It is *not* the conducting force, but an *organ of the latter.*

555

The greatest of all fables is the one relating to knowledge. People would like to know how things-in-themselves are constituted: but behold, there are no things-in-themselves! But even supposing there *were* an "in-itself," an unconditional thing, it could on that very account *not be known!* Something unconditioned cannot be known: otherwise it would not be unconditioned! Knowing, however, is always a process of "coming into relation with something"; the knowledge-seeker, on this principle, wants the thing, which he would know, to be nothing to him, and to be nothing to anybody at all: and from this there results a contradiction,—in the first place, between this *will* to know, and this desire that the thing to be known *should* be nothing to him (wherefore know at all then?); and secondly, because something which is nothing to anybody, does not even *exist,* and therefore cannot be known. Knowing means: "to place one's self in relation with something," to feel one's self conditioned by something and one's self conditioning it—under all circumstances, then, it is a process of *making stable or fixed,* of *defining,* of *making conditions conscious* (not a process of *sounding* things, creatures, or objects "in-themselves").

556

A "thing-in-itself" is just as absurd as a "sense-in-itself," a "meaning-in-itself." There is no such thing as a "fact-in-itself," *for a meaning must always be given to it before it can become a fact.*

The answer to the question, "What is that?" is a process of *fixing a meaning* from a different standpoint. The "*essence,*" the "*essential factor,*" is something which is only seen as a whole in perspective, and which presupposes a basis which is mutifarious. Fundamentally the question is "What is that for me?" (for us, for everything that lives, etc. etc.).

A thing would be defined when all creatures had asked and answered this question, "What is that?" concerning it. Supposing that one single creature, with its own relations and standpoint in regard to all things, were lacking, that thing would still remain undefined.

In short: the essence of a thing is really only an *opinion* concerning that "thing." Or, better still; "*it is worth*" is actually what is meant by "*it is,*" or by "that is."

One may not ask: "*Who* interprets, then?" for the act of interpreting *itself,* as a form of the Will to Power, manifests itself (not as "Being," but as a *process,* as *Becoming*) as a passion.

The origin of "things" is wholly the work of the idealising, thinking, willing, and feeling subject. The concept "thing" as well as all its attributes.—Even "the subject" is a creation of this order, a "thing" like all others: a simplification, aiming at a definition of the *power* that fixes, invents, and thinks, as such, as distinct from all isolated fixing, inventing, and thinking. Thus a capacity defined or distinct from all other individual capacities: at bottom action conceived collectively in regard to all the action which has yet to come (action and the probability of similar action).

557

The qualities of a thing are its effects upon other "things."

If one imagines other "things" to be non-existent, a thing has no qualities.

That is to say: *there is nothing without other things.*

That is to say: there is no "thing-in-itself."

558

The thing-in-itself is nonsense. If I think all the "relations," all the "qualities," all the "activities" of a thing, away, the thing itself does *not* remain: for "thingness" was only *invented fancifully* by us to meet certain logical needs—that is to say, for the purposes of definition and comprehension (in order to correlate that multitude of relations, qualities, and activities).

559

"Things which have a nature *in themselves*"—a dogmatic idea, which must be absolutely abandoned.

560

That things should have a *nature in themselves,* quite apart from interpretation and subjectivity, *is a perfectly idle hypothesis:* it would presuppose that *interpretation* and the *act of being subjective* are not essential, that a thing divorced from all its relations can still be a thing.

Or, the other way round: the apparent *objective* character of things; might it not be merely the result of a *difference of degree* within the subject perceiving?—could not that which changes slowly strike us as being "objective," lasting, Being, "in-itself"?—could not the objective view be only a false way of conceiving things and a contrast *within* the perceiving subject?

567

The world of appearance, *i.e.* a world regarded in the light of values; ordered, selected according to values—that is to say, in this case, according to the standpoint of utility in regard to the preservation and the increase of power of a certain species of animals.

It is *the point of view,* then, which accounts for the character of "appearance." As if a world could remain over, when the point of view is cancelled! By such means *relativity* would also be cancelled!

Every centre of energy has its *point of view* of the whole of the *remainder* of the world—that is to say, its perfectly definite *valuation,* its mode of action, its mode of resistance. The "world of appearance" is thus reduced to a specific kind of action on the world proceeding from a centre.

But there is no other kind of action: and the "world" is only a word for the collective play of these actions. *Reality* consists precisely in this particular action and reaction of every isolated factor against the whole.

There no longer remains a shadow of a *right* to speak here of "appearance." . . .

The *specific way of reacting* is the only way of reacting; we do not know how many kinds and what sort of kinds there are.

But there is no "*other*," no "real," no essential being,—for thus a world *without* action and reaction would be expressed. . . .

The antithesis: world of appearance and real world, is thus reduced to the antithesis "world" and "nonentity."

569

The nature of our psychology is determined by the fact—

(1) That *communication* is necessary, and that for communication to be possible something must be stable, simplified, and capable of being stated precisely (above all, in the so-called *identical case*). In order that it may be communicable, it must be felt as something *adjusted*, as "*recognisable*." The material of the senses, arranged by the senses, reduced to coarse leading features, made similar to other things, and classified with its like. Thus: the indefiniteness and the chaos of sense-impressions are, as it were, *made logical*.

(2) The *phenomenal* world is the adjusted world which *we believe to be real*. Its "reality" lies in the constant return of similar, familiar, and related things, in their *rationalised character*, and in the belief that we are here able to reckon and determine.

(3) The opposite of this phenomenal world is not "the real world," but the amorphous and unadjustable world consisting of the chaos of sensations—that is to say, *another kind* of phenomenal world, a world which to us is "unknowable."

(4) The question how "things-in-themselves" are constituted must be answered, quite apart from our sense-receptivity and from the activity of our understanding, by the further question: how were we able to know *that things existed?* "Thingness" is one of our own inventions. The question is whether there are not a good many more ways of creating such a world of appearance—and whether this creating, rationalising, adjusting, and falsifying be not the best-guaranteed *reality* itself: in short, whether that which "fixes the meaning of things" is not the only reality: and whether the "effect of environment upon us" be not merely the result of such will-exercising subjects. . . . The other "creatures" act upon us; our *adjusted* world of appearance is an arrangement and an *overpowering* of its activities: a sort of *defensive* measure. *The subject alone is demonstrable;* the *hypothesis*

might be advanced *that subjects are all that exist*,—that "object" is only a form of action of subject upon subject . . . a *modus of the subject.*

612

The right to great passion must be reclaimed for the investigator, after self-effacement and the cult of "objectivity" have created a false order of rank in this sphere. Error reached its zenith when Schopenhauer taught: *passion was got rid of*, in will alone lay the road to "truth," to knowledge; the intellect freed from will *could not help* regarding truth as the actual essence of things.

The same error in art: as if everything became *beautiful* the moment it was regarded without will.

613

The contest for supremacy among the passions, and the dominion of one of the passions over the intellect.

THE WILL TO POWER IN NATURE

659

WITH THE BODY AS CLUE.—Granting that the "*soul*" was only an attractive and mysterious thought, from which philosophers rightly, but reluctantly, separated themselves—that which they have since learnt to put in its place is perhaps even more attractive and even more mysterious. The human *body*, in which the whole of the most distant and most recent past of all organic life once more becomes living and corporal, seems to flow through this past and right over it like a huge and inaudible torrent: the body is a more wonderful thought than the old "soul." In all ages the body, as our actual property, as our most certain being, in short, as our ego, has been more earnestly believed in than the spirit (or the "soul," or the subject, as the school jargon now calls it). It has never occurred to any one to regard his stomach as a strange or a divine stomach; but that there is a tendency and a predilection in man to regard all his thoughts as "inspired," all his values as "imparted to him by a God," all his instincts as dawning activities—this is proved by the evidence of every age in man's history. Even now, especially among artists, there may very often be noticed a sort of wonder, and a deferential hesitation to decide, when the question occurs to them, by what means they achieved their happiest work, and from which world the creative thought came down to them: when they question in this way, they are possessed by a feeling of guilelessness and childish shyness. They dare not say: "That came from me; it was my hand which threw that die." Conversely, even those philosophers and theologians, who in their logic and piety found the most imperative reasons for regarding their body as a deception (and even as a deception overcome and disposed of), could not help recognising the foolish fact that the body still remained: and the most unexpected proofs of this are to be found partly in Pauline and partly in Vedantic philosophy. But what does *strength of faith* ultimately mean? Nothing!—A strong faith might also be a foolish faith!—There is food for reflection.

And supposing the faith in the body were ultimately but the result of a conclusion; supposing it were a false conclusion, as idealists declare it is, would it not then involve some doubt concerning the trustworthiness of the spirit itself which thus causes us to draw wrong conclusions?

Supposing the plurality of things, and space, and time, and motion (and whatever the other first principles of a belief in the body may be) were errors—what suspicions would not then be roused against the spirit which led us to form such first principles? Let it suffice that the belief in the body is, at any rate for the present, a much stronger belief than the belief in the spirit, and he who would fain undermine it assails the authority of the spirit most thoroughly in so doing!

DIONYSUS

1041

My New Road to an Affirmative Attitude.—Philosophy, as I have understood it and lived it up to the present, is the voluntary quest of the repulsive and atrocious aspects of existence. From the long experience derived from such wandering over ice and desert, I learnt to regard quite differently everything that had been philosophised hitherto: the *concealed* history of philosophy, the psychology of its great names came into the light for me. "How much truth can a spirit *endure;* for how much truth is it *daring* enough?"—this for me was the real measure of value. Error is a piece of *cowardice* . . . every victory on the part of knowledge, is the *result* of courage, of hardness towards one's self, of cleanliness towards one's self. . . . The kind of *experimental philosophy* which I am living, even anticipates the possibility of the most fundamental Nihilism, on principle: but by this I do not mean that it remains standing at a negation, at a *no*, or at a will to negation. It would rather attain to the very reverse—to a *Dionysian affirmation* of the world, as it is, without subtraction, exception, or choice—it would have eternal circular motion: the same things, the same reasoning, and the same illogical concatenation. The highest state to which a philosopher can attain: to maintain a Dionysian attitude to Life —my formula for this is *amor fati.*

To this end we must not only consider those aspects of life which have been denied hitherto, as *necessary*, but as desirable in respect to those aspects which have been affirmed hitherto (as complements or first prerequisites, so to speak); but for their own sake, as the more powerful, more terrible, and more *veritable* aspects of life, in which the latter's will expresses itself most clearly.

To this end, we must also value that aspect of existence which alone has been affirmed until now; we must understand whence this valuation arises, and to how slight an extent it has to do with a Dionysian valuation of Life: I selected and understood that which in this respect says "yea" (on the one hand, the instinct of the sufferer; on the other, the gregarious instinct; and thirdly, the *instinct of the greater number* against the exceptions).

Thus I divined to what extent a stronger kind of man must necessarily imagine—the elevation and enhancement of man in another direction: *higher creatures,* beyond good and evil, beyond those values which bear the stamp of their origin in the sphere of suffering, of the herd, and of the greater number—I searched for the data of this topsy-turvy formation of ideals in history (the concepts "pagan," "classical," "noble," have been discovered afresh and brought forward).

BIBLIOGRAPHY

The standard German edition was published in sixteen volumes by C. G. Naumann (Leipzig).

The English translation, edited by Oscar Levy (London, 1909–1913), includes: *The Birth of Tragedy; The Use and Abuse of History; The Case of Wagner; Thus Spake Zarathustra; Beyond Good and Evil; The Genealogy of Morals; The Will to Power; The Antichrist;* and *Ecce Homo.*

Selected Letters, translated by A. M. Ludovici and edited by Oscar Levy, was published in London (1921).

The Portable Nietzsche, edited by Walter Kaufmann (New York, Viking Press; London, Mayflower Books, 1954), is a group of newly translated selections with a critical introduction.

Paperback editions include:

The Birth of Tragedy and *The Genealogy of Morals,* translated by Francis Golffing (Doubleday Anchor Books, 1956) *Joyful Wisdom* (New York, Frederick Ungar; London, Constable) *Thus Spake Zarathustra* (London, Penguin Books)

Biographical studies include:

Nietzsche: Philosopher, Psychologist, Antichrist, by Walter Kaufmann (Princeton University Press, 1950; reissued by Meridian Books, 1956)

The Tragic Philosopher: A Study of Friedrich Nietzsche, by Frank A. Lea (London, 1957)

KARL JASPERS

(BORN 1893)

"My book on the *Psychologie der Weltanschauungen* [1919] appears, in historical retrospect, as the earliest writing in the later so-called modern Existentialism." Jaspers' previous work, *Allgemeine Psychopathologie* (1913), expressed his rooted concern with the individual human being and with the human being in extreme situations, and also his concern with the problem of method and of conceptual knowledge in attempting to grasp such phenomena and to communicate experience of them for scientific purposes.

Here, quite early, he derived his clues and insights from Kant and from Kierkegaard: from Kierkegaard, the notion of *Existenz*, the subject or self, which is never an object and is not merely consciousness-as-such, which springs from relation with Transcendence, and from which issues authentic thinking and acting; from Kant, the modern concept of "reason" as not only the rational but also an understanding of the rational and its limits, and thereby an illumination of the transcendental. The other major influences on the development of Jaspers' philosophizing were Nietzsche, with whom he faces the extreme possibility of modern nihilism, and Max Weber, whose grandeur touched him in person and whose profound concern with the ideals and limits of modern science and scholarship was exemplary. Kierkegaard and Nietzsche, Jaspers puts together as the disturbing influence which has changed the course of philosophy.

More than any other existentialist thinker, Jaspers is rooted in science and history. He is not alienated from them by modern "scientism" and "historicism"; rather, the philosopher is for him the scientist or the historian aware of himself and of his instrument and its limitations, so that he is master of his thought, instead of unconsciously identified with forms and trains of thought. He speaks of his philosophic faith as a third way between ecclesiastical religion and nihilism, but it is also a third way between theology and positivism, which treats science as a sufficient and final account of things in principle. Jaspers does not offer an ontology on the traditional model, as the ultimate structure of the world for science (Kant was the end of all that); he uses science as the sole reliable form of knowledge, but goes on to use his head beyond science to encounter and decipher Being by means of science and otherwise. He raises the question of the relation between science and philosophy as of central importance to both and to man.

His answer to this question leads him into his two main preoccupations—the method of philosophizing, or philosophical logic, and the world history of philosophy. In this connection he wishes to study the continuity and communication of human thinking.

As with the others, the dialectical development of his thinking makes it difficult to represent him adequately by selections. He has given his own introduction to his way of thinking in the radio lectures translated (by Ralph Manheim) as *Way to Wisdom* (Yale paperbound, 1960), a volume which also reprints from the *Partisan Review* a valuable statement, "Philosophy and Science." The central content of the philosophy can be studied in the three central chapters of *Reason and Existenz*, "Basic Ideas for the Clarification of Reason and Existenz," and in the short concluding section from *Von der Warheit*, the first and only volume of his philosophical logic, translated as *Truth and Symbol* (Vision Press, 1959) by Jean T. Wilde, William Kluback, and William Kimmel.

Jaspers has been included in The Library of Living Philosophers, edited by Paul Arthur Schilpp. His "Philosophical Autobiography" in that volume should be read, as should also Section 7, "The Idea of the Encompassing" (pp. 790–800) in his "Reply to My Critics" at the end. Attention is called to the following articles in the volume, together with Jaspers' comments on them in his "Reply": Edwin Latzel's "The Concept of 'Ultimate Situation' in Jaspers' Philosophy" ("Reply," p. 853); "Max Weber's Influence on Jaspers" by Ernst Moritz Manasse ("Reply," p. 854); "Jaspers' Relation to Nietzsche" by Walter Kaufmann ("Reply," pp. 857–863); "Anthropology in the Philosophy of Karl Jaspers" by William Earle ("Reply," pp. 817–820). Finally, there is in small compass a comprehensive, informed, and appreciative review of Jaspers in the front-page article of The Times Literary Supplement of April 12, 1963 (No. 3,189), "Karl Jaspers, a Philosopher of Humanity."

EXTRACTS

Reason and Existenz (five lectures delivered at the University of Groningen in 1935) trans. by William Earle. (Routledge & Kegan Paul and Noonday Press, 1956.)
The Origin of the Contemporary Philosophical Situation. First Lecture, "The historical meaning of Kierkegaard and Nietzsche."

"Philosophy and Science," reprinted from the *Partisan Review* in *Way to Wisdom*, trans. by Ralph Manheim. (London, 1951; Yale paperbound, 1960.)

☙§ from *Reason and Existenz*

FIRST LECTURE: THE ORIGIN OF THE CONTEMPORARY PHILOSOPHICAL SITUATION

The historical meaning of Kierkegaard and Nietzsche

I. Historical Reflections; The Contemporary Situation

The rational is not thinkable without its other, the non-rational, and it never appears in reality without it. The only question is, in what form the other appears, how it remains in spite of all, and how it is to be grasped.

It is appropriate for philosophizing to strive to absorb the non-rational and counter-rational, to form it through reason, to change it into a form of reason, indeed, finally to show it as identical with reason; all Being should become law and order.

But both the defiant will and honest mind turn against this. They recognize and assert the unconquerable non-rational.

For knowing, this non-rational is found in the opacity of the here and now; in matter, it is what is only enveloped but never consumed by rational form; it is in actual empirical existence which is just as it is and not otherwise, which is subsumed under just those regularities we experience and not others; it is in the contents of faith for religious revelation. All philosophizing which would like to dissolve Being into pure rationality retains in spite of itself the non-rational; this may be reduced to a residue of indifferent matter, some primordial fact, an impulse, or an accident.

The will utilizes these possibilities in knowledge to its own advantage. A battle arises for and against reason. Opposed to pure, transparent reason's drive toward rest within the conceivable, stands a drive to destroy reason, not only to indicate its limits, but to enslave it. We want to subordinate ourselves to an inconceivable supersensible, which however appears in the world through human utterances and makes demands. We wish to subordinate ourselves to the natural character of impulses and passions, to the immediacy of what is now present. These drives are now translated by the philosophy which adheres to them into a knowledge of the non-rational: philosophy expresses its falling into the non-rational, the counter-rational, and the super-rational as a knowledge about them. Yet, even in the most radical defiance of reason, there remains a minimum of rationality.

To show how the many-fold distinction between reason and non-reason appears at the bases of all thinking would require an analysis of the history of philosophy out of its own actual principles. Let us recall a few selected points.

To the Greeks this problem of Being was already present in myth. The clarity of the Greek gods was surrounded by the sublime incomprehensibility of Fate, limiting their knowledge and power.

Most of the philosophers touched incidentally, although in important ways, upon what was inaccessible to reason.

Socrates listened to the forbidding voice of the uncomprehended daimon. Plato recognized madness, which if pathological is less than reason, but if divinely begotten, more; only through madness can poets, lovers, and philosophers come to a vision of Being. To be sure, according to Aristotle, in human affairs, happiness was the result of rational deliberation, but not totally; happiness could appear without and even opposed to deliberation. For Aristotle, there were men, the *alogoi,* who had a better principle than deliberative reason; their affairs succeeded without and even counter to reason.

These examples stand alongside the general form of Greek thought, which opposed appearance to Being (Parmenides), the void to things (Democritus), non-Being to genuine Being (Plato), and matter to form (Aristotle).

In Christianity, the opposition between reason and non-reason developed as a struggle between reason and faith within each man; what was inaccessible to reason was no longer regarded simply as other than reason, but was a revelation of something higher. In the observations of the world, the non-rational was no longer mere chance, or blind chaos, or some astonishing principle surpassing reason, but was taken comprehensively as Providence. All the fundamental ideas of a rationally unintelligible faith could only be expressed in irrational antinomies. Every rational, literal interpretation of faith became a heresy.

In the succeeding centuries, on the other hand, Descartes and his followers attempted a radical grounding of reason upon itself alone—at least in the philosophical excogitation of Being which the individual accomplished by himself. Although Descartes left society, state, and church intact, the attitude of the Enlightenment arose as a consequence; with what I validly think and can empirically investigate, I can achieve the right organization of the world. Rational thought, in the sense of presuppositionless universality, is a sufficient basis for human life in general. From the beginning, however, a counter-movement worked against this philosophy of reason, whether it be called rationalism or empiricism. This counter-movement was led by men who, although in complete possession of rationality themselves, at the same time saw its limits: that other which was important before any reason, which made reason possible, and restrained it. Over against Descartes, stands Pascal; over against Descartes, Hobbes, and Grotius, stands Vico; over against Locke, Leibnitz, and Spinoza, stands Bayle.

The philosophy of the seventeenth and eighteenth centuries seems to work itself out in these great antitheses. But the thinkers were irreconcilable, and their ideas were mutually exclusive.

In contrast to this world of thought, the philosophers of German idealism made an astonishing attempt to create a reconciliation, seeing in reason more than reason itself. German philosophy in its great period went beyond all previous possibilities and developed a concept of reason which was historically independent. In Kant, a new beginning was created. This concept of reason got lost in the fantastic construction of Hegel but broke through again in Fichte and Schelling.

When one looks over the thought of centuries, the same thing always seems to happen: in whatever form this Other to reason appears, in the course of rational understanding it is either changed back into reason, or sometimes it is recognized as a limit in its place; but then in its consequences it is circumscribed and delimited by reason itself, or sometimes it is seen and developed as the source of a new and better reason.

It is as though at the bottom of this thought, even in all its unrest, there always lay the quiet of a reason which was never wholly and radically questioned. All awareness of Being grounded itself finally in reason or in God. All questioning was circumscribed by unquestioned assumptions; or else there were merely individual and historically inefficacious pioneers who never achieved a thorough understanding of themselves. The counter-movements against rationality were like a distant thunder announcing storms which could be released, but which were not yet.

Thus the great history of Western philosophy from Parmenides and Heraclitus through Hegel can be seen as a thorough-going and completed unity. Its great forms are even today preserved in the tradition, and are rediscovered as the true salvation from the destruction of philosophy. For a century we have seen individual philosophers become objects of special studies, and have seen restorations of their doctrines. We know the totality of past teachings in the sense of "doctrines" perhaps better than any of the earlier great philosophers. But the consciousness of a change into mere knowing about doctrines and about history, of separation from life itself and from actually believed truth, has made us question the ultimate sense of this tradition, great as it is and despite all the satisfaction it has provided and provides today. We question whether the truth of philosophizing has been grasped or even if it can be grasped in this tradition.

Quietly, something enormous has happened in the reality of Western man: a destruction of all authority, a radical disillusionment in an overconfident reason, and a dissolution of bonds have made anything, absolutely anything, seem possible. Work with the old words can appear as a mere veil which hid the preparing powers of chaos from our anxious eyes. This work seemed to have no other power than that of a long continued deception. The passionate revivifying of these words and doctrines, though done with good intentions, appears as without real effect, an impotent call to hold fast. Philosophizing to be authentic must grow out of our new reality, and there take its stand.

II. Kierkegaard and Nietzsche.

The contemporary philosophical situation is determined by the fact that two philosophers, Kierkegaard and Nietzsche, who did not count in their times and, for a long time, remained without influence in the history of philosophy, have continually grown in significance. Philosophers after Hegel have increasingly returned to face them, and they stand today unquestioned as the authentically great thinkers of their age. Both their influence and the opposition to them prove it. Why then can these philosophers no longer be ignored, in our time?

In the situation of philosophizing, as well as in the real life of men, Kierkegaard and Nietzsche appear as the expression of destinies, destinies which nobody noticed then, with the exception of some ephemeral and immediately forgotten presentiments, but which they themselves already comprehended.

As to what this destiny really is, the question remains open even today. It is not answered by any comparison of the two thinkers, but it is clarified and made more urgent. This comparison is all the more important since there could have been no influence of one upon the other, and because their very differences make their common features so much more impressive. Their affinity is so compelling, from the whole course of their lives down to the individual details of their thought, that their nature seems to have been elicited by the necessities of the spiritual situation of their times. With them a shock occurred to Western philosophizing whose final meaning can not yet be underestimated.

Common to both of them is a type of thought and humanity which was indissolubly connected with a moment of this epoch, and so understood by them. We shall, therefore, discuss their affinity: first, in their thought; second, in their actual thinking Existenz; and third, in the way in which they understood themselves.

A. What is common to their thought: the questioning of reason.

Their thinking created a new atmosphere. They passed beyond all of the limits then regarded as obvious. It is as if they no longer shrank back from anything in thought. Everything permanent was as if consumed in a dizzying suction: with Kierkegaard by an otherworldly Christianity which is like Nothingness and shows itself only in negation (the absurd, martyrdom) and in negative resolution; with Nietzsche, a vacuum out of which, with despairing violence, a new reality was to be born (the eternal return, and the corresponding dogmatics of Nietzsche).

Both questioned reason from the depths of Existenz. Never on such a high level of thought had there been such a thorough-going and radical opposition to mere reason. This questioning is never simply hostility to reason; rather both sought to appropriate limitlessly all modes of rationality. It was no philosophy of feeling, for both pushed unremittingly toward the concept for expression. It is certainly not dogmatic scepticism; rather their whole thought strove toward the genuine truth.

In a magnificent way, penetrating a whole life with the earnestness of philosophizing, they brought forth not some doctrines, not any basic position, not some picture of the world, but rather a new total intellectual attitude for men. This attitude was in the medium of infinite reflection, a reflection which is conscious of being unable to attain any real ground by itself. No single thing characterizes their nature; no fixed doctrine or requirement is to be drawn out of them as something independent and permanent.

1. SUSPICION OF SCIENTIFIC MEN. Out of the consciousness of their truth, both suspect truth in the naive form of scientific knowledge. They do not doubt the methodological correctness of scientific insight. But Kierkegaard was astonished at the learned professors; they live for the most part with science and die with the idea that it will continue, and would like to live longer that they might, in a line of direct progress, always understand more and more. They do not experience the maturity of that critical point where everything turns upside down, where one understands more and more that there is something which one cannot understand. Kierkegaard thought the most frightful way to live was to bewitch the whole world through one's discoveries and cleverness—to explain the whole of nature and not understand oneself. Nietzsche is inexhaustible in destructive analyses of types of scholars, who have no genuine sense of their own activity, who can not be themselves, and who, with their ultimately futile knowledge, aspire to grasp Being itself.

2. AGAINST THE SYSTEM. The questioning of every self-enclosed rationality which tries to make the whole truth communicable made both radical opponents of the "system," that

is, the form which philosophy had had for centuries and which had achieved its final polish in German idealism. The system is for them a detour from reality and is, therefore, lies and deception. Kierkegaard granted that empirical existence could be a system for God, but never for an existing spirit; system corresponds with what is closed and settled, but existence is precisely the contrary. The philosopher of systems is, as a man, like someone who builds a castle, but lives next door in a shanty. Such a fantastical being does not himself live within what he thinks; but the thought of a man must be the house in which he lives or it will become perverted. The basic question of philosophy, what it itself is, and what science is, is posed in a new and unavoidable form. Nietzsche wanted to doubt better than Descartes, and saw in Hegel's miscarried attempt to make reason evolve nothing but Gothic heaven-storming. The will-to-system is for him a lack of honesty.

3. BEING AS INTERPRETATION. What authentic knowing is, was expressed by both in the same way. It is, for them, nothing but interpretation. They also understood their own thought as interpretation.

Interpretation, however, reaches no end. Existence, for Nietzsche, is capable of infinite interpretation. What has happened and what was done, is for Kierkegaard always capable of being understood in a new way. As it is interpreted anew, it becomes a new reality which yet is hidden; temporal life can therefore never be correctly understood by men; no man can absolutely penetrate through his own consciousness.

Both apply the image of interpretation to knowledge of Being, but in such a fashion that Being is as if deciphered in the interpretation of the interpretation. Nietzsche wanted to uncover the basic text, *homo natura*, from its overpaintings and read it in its reality. Kierkegaard gave his own writings no other meaning than that they should read again the original text of individual, human existential relations.

4. MASKS. With this basic idea is connected the fact that both, the most open and candid of thinkers, had a misleading aptitude for concealment and masks. For them masks necessarily belong to the truth. Indirect communication becomes for them the sole way of communicating genuine truth; indirect communication, as expression, is appropriate to the ambiguity of genuine truth in temporal existence, in which process it must be grasped through sources in every Existenz.

5. BEING ITSELF. Both, in their thinking, push toward that basis which would be Being itself in man. In opposition to

the philosophy which from Parmenides through Descartes to Hegel said, Thought is Being, Kierkegaard asserted the proposition, as you believe, so are you: Faith is Being. Nietzsche saw the Will to Power. But Faith and Will to Power are mere *signa*, which do not directly connote what is meant but are themselves capable of endless explication.

6. HONESTY. With both there is a decisive drive toward honesty. This word for them both is the expression of the ultimate virtue to which they subject themselves. It remains for them the minimum of the absolute which is still possible although everything else becomes involved in a bewildering questioning. It becomes for them also the dizzying demand for a veracity which, however, brings even itself into question, and which is the opposite of that violence which would like to grasp the truth in a literal and barbaric certitude.

7. THEIR READERS. One can question whether in general anything is said in such thought. In fact, both Kierkegaard and Nietzsche were aware that the comprehension of their thought was not possible to the man who only thinks. It is important who it is that understands.

They turn to the individuals who must bring with them and bring forth from themselves what can only be said indirectly. The epigram of Lichtenberg applies to Kierkegaard, and he himself cites it: such works are like mirrors; if an ape peeks in, no apostle will look out. Nietzsche says one must have earned for oneself the distinction necessary to understand him. He held it impossible to teach the truth where the mode of thought is base. Both seek the reader who belongs to them.

B. Their thinking Existenz in its actual setting: the age.

Such thinking is grounded in the Existenz of Kierkegaard and Nietzsche insofar as it belonged to their age in a distinctive way. That no single idea, no system, no requirement is decisive for them follows from the fact that neither thinker expressed his epoch at its peak, that they constructed no world, nor any image of a passing world. They did not feel themselves to be a positive expression of their times; they rather expressed what it was negatively through their very being: an age absolutely rejected by them and seen through in its ruin. Their problem appeared to be to experience this epoch to the end in their own natures, to be it completely in order to overcome it. This happened at first involuntarily, but then consciously through the fact that they were not representatives of their epoch, but needling and scandalous *exceptions*. Let us look at this a little closer.

1. THEIR PROBLEM. Both had become aware of their *problem* by the end of their youth, even if unclearly. A decision which gripped the entire man, which sometimes was silent and no longer conscious, but which would return to force itself upon them, pushed them into a radical loneliness. Although without position, marriage, without any effective role in existence, they nevertheless appear as the great realists, who had an authentic feeling for the depths of reality.

2. PERCEPTION OF SUBSTANTIAL CHANGE IN ESSENCE OF MEN. They touched this reality in their fundamental experience of their epoch as ruins; looking back over centuries, back to the beginnings in Greek antiquity, they felt the end of this whole history. At the crucial point, they called attention to this moment, without wanting to survey the meaning and course of history as a whole.

Men have tried to understand this epoch in economic, technological, historico-political, and sociological terms. Kierkegaard and Nietzsche, on the other hand, thought they saw a change in the very substance of man.

Kierkegaard looked upon the whole of Christianity as it is today as upon an enormous deception in which God is held to be a fool. Such Christianity has nothing to do with that of the New Testament. There are only two ways: either to maintain the deception through tricks and conceal the real conditions, and then everything comes to nothing; or honestly to confess the misery that in truth, today, not one single individual is born who can pass for a Christian in the sense of the New Testament. Not one of us is a Christian, but rather we live in a pious softening of Christianity. The confession will show if there is anything true left in this honesty, if it has the approval of Providence. If not, then everything must again be broken so that in this horror individuals can arise again who can support the Christianity of the New Testament.

Nietzsche expressed the historical situation of the epoch in one phrase: God is dead.

Thus, common to both, is an historical judgment on the very substance of their times. They saw before them Nothingness; both knew the substance of what had been lost, but neither willed Nothingness. If Kierkegaard presupposed the truth, or the possibility of the truth of Christianity, and Nietzsche, on the other hand, found in atheism not simply a loss but rather the greatest opportunity—still, what is common to both is a will toward the substance of Being, toward the nobility and value of man. They had no political program for reform, no program at all; they directed their attention to no single detail, but rather wanted to effect something through their thought which they foresaw in no clear detail. For Nietzsche, this indeterminateness was his "larger politics" at long range; for Kierkegaard, it was becoming Christian in the new way of indifference to all worldly being. Both in their relation to their epoch were possessed by the question of what will become of man.

3. MODERNITY OVERCOME. They are modernity itself in a somersaulting form. They ran it to the ground, and overcame it by living it through to the end. We can see how both experienced the distress of the epoch, not passively, but suicidally through totally doing what most only half did: first of all, in their endless reflection; and then, in opposition to this, in their drive toward the basic; and finally, in the way in which, as they sank into the bottomless, they grasped hold upon the Transcendent.

(i) *Unlimited Reflection.* The age of reflection has, since Fichte, been characterized as reasoning without restraint, as the dissolving of all authority, as the surrender of content which gives to thinking its measure, purpose, and meaning, so that from now on, without hindrance and as an indifferent play of the intellect, it can fill the world with noise and dust.

Kierkegaard and Nietzsche did not oppose reflection in order to annihilate it, but rather in order to overcome it by limitlessly engaging in it and mastering it. Man cannot sink back into an unreflective immediacy without losing himself; but he can go this way to the end, not destroying reflection, but rather coming to the basis in himself in the medium of reflection.

Their "infinite reflection" has, therefore, a twofold character. It can lead to a complete ruin just as well as it can become the condition of authentic Existenz. Both express this, perhaps Kierkegaard is the clearer of the two:

Reflection cannot exhaust or stop itself. It is faithless, since it hinders every decision. It is never finished and, in the end, can become "dialectical twaddle"; in this respect, he called it the poison of reflection. But that it is possible, indeed necessary, lies grounded in the endless ambiguity of all existence and action for us: anything can mean something else for reflection. This situation makes possible on one side a sophistry of existence, enables the Existenz-less esthete to profit, who merely wants to savor everything as an interesting novelty. Even if he should take the most decisive step, still he always holds before himself the possibility of reinterpreting everything, so that, in one blow, it is all changed. But on the other hand, this situation can be truly grasped by the knowledge that insofar as we are honest we live in a "sea of reflection where no one can call to another, where all buoys are dialectical."

Without infinite reflection we should fall into the quiet of the settled and established which, as something permanent in the world, would become absolute; that is, we should become superstitious. An atmosphere of bondage arises with such a settlement. Infinite reflection, therefore, is, precisely through its endlessly active dialectic, the condition of freedom. It breaks out of every prison of the finite. Only in its medium is there any possibility of an infinite passion arising out of immediate feeling which, because it is unquestioning, is still unfree. In infinite passion the immediate feeling, which is held fast and genuinely true throughout the questioning, is grasped as free.

But in order to prevent this freedom from becoming nothing through vacuous reflection, in order for it to fulfill itself, infinite reflection must strand itself. Then, for the first time, does it issue out of something real, or exhaust itself in the decision of faith and resolution. As untrue as the arbitrary and forced arrest of reflection is, so true is that basis by which reflection is mastered in the encounter of Existenz. Here Existenz is given to itself for the first time, so that it becomes master of infinite reflection through totally surrendering to it.

Reflection, which can just as well dissolve into nothing as become the condition of Existenz, is described as such and in the same way by both Kierkegaard and Nietzsche. Out of it, they have imparted an almost immeasurable wealth of thought in their works. This thinking, according to its own meaning, is possibility: it can indicate and prepare the way for the shipwreck, but cannot accomplish it.

Thus, in their thinking about the possibilities of man, both thinkers were aware of what they themselves were not in their thought. The awareness of possibilities, in analogy to poetry, is not a false, but rather a questioning and awakening reflection. Possibility is the form in which I permit myself to know about what I am not yet, and a preparation for being it.

Kierkegaard called his method most frequently, "an experimental psychology"; Nietzsche called his thought, "seductive."

Thus they left what they themselves were and what they ultimately thought concealed to the point of unrecognizability and, in its appearance, sunk into the incomprehensible. Kierkegaard's pseudonym writes: "The something which I am . . . is precisely a nothing." It gave him a high satisfaction to hold his "Existenz at that critical zero . . . between something and nothing, a mere perhaps." And Nietzsche willingly called himself a "philosopher of the dangerous perhaps."

Reflection is for both pre-eminently self-reflection. For them, the way to truth is through understanding oneself. But they both experienced how one's own substance can disappear this way, how the free, creative self-understanding can be replaced by a slavish rotation about one's own empirical existence. Kierkegaard knew the horror "of everything disappearing before a sick brooding over the tale of one's own miserable self." He sought for the way "between this devouring of oneself in observations as though one were the only man who had ever been, and the sorry comfort of a universal human shipwreck." He knew the "unhappy relativity in everything, the unending question about what I am." Nietzsche expressed it:

> Among a hundred mirrors
> before yourself false . . .
> strangled in your own net
> Self-knower!
> Self-executioner!
> crammed between two nothings,
> a question mark . . .

(ii) *Drive Toward the Basic.* The age which could no longer find its way amidst the multiplicity of its reflections and rationalizing words pushed out of reflection toward bases. Kierkegaard and Nietzsche here too seem to be forerunners. Later generations sought the basic in general in articulateness, in the esthetic charm of the immediately striking, in a general simplification, in unreflective experience, in the existence of the things closest to us. To them, Kierkegaard and Nietzsche seem useful; for both lived consciously with a passionate love for the sources of human communicability.

They were creative in language to the degree that their works belong to the peaks of the literatures of their countries; and they knew it. They were creative in the thrilling way which made them among the most widely read authors, even though the content was of the same weight and their genuine comprehension of the same difficulty as that of any of the great philosophers. But both also knew the tendency of the verbal to become autonomous, and they despised the literary world.

Both were moved by music to the point of intoxication; but both warned of its seduction, and along with Plato and Augustine belonged to those who suspected it existentially.

Everywhere they created formulas of striking simplicity. But both were full of concern before that simplicity which, in order to give some deceptive support to the weak and mediocre, offered flat, spiritless simplifications in place of the genuine simplicity which was the result of the most complicated personal development, which, like Being itself, never had a single rational meaning. They warned, as no thinker before had, against taking their words too simply, words which seemed to stand there apodictically.

In fact, they went by the most radical way to the basic, but in such a fashion that the dialectical movement never stopped. Their seriousness was absorbed neither into an illusion of the dogmatic fixedness of some supposed basis, nor into the purposes of language, esthetic charm, and simplicity.

(iii) *Arrest in Transcendence.* Both pursued a path which, for them, could not end short of a transcendental stop, for their reflections were not, like the usual reflections of modernity, stopped by the obvious limits of vital needs and interests. They, for whom it was a question of all or nothing, dared limitlessness. But this they could do only because from the very beginning onwards they were rooted in what was at the same time hidden from them: both, in their youth, spoke of an *unknown God.* Kierkegaard, even when twenty-five years old, wrote: "In spite of the fact that I am very far from understanding myself, I have . . . revered the unknown God." And Nietzsche at twenty years of age created his first unforgettable poem, "To the Unknown God":

> I would know Thee, Unknown,
> Thou who grips deep in my soul,
> wandering through my life like a storm,
> Thou inconceivable, my kin!
> I would know Thee, even serve Thee.

Never in their limitless reflection could they remain within the finite, conceivable, and therefore trivial; but just as little could they hold to reflection itself. Precisely because he had been thoroughly penetrated by reflection, Kierkegaard thought:

"The religious understanding of myself has deserted me; I feel like an insect with which children are playing, so pitilessly does existence handle me." In his terrible loneliness, understood by and really bound to absolutely no one, he called to God: "God in heaven, if there were not some most inward center in a man where all this could be forgotten, who could hold out?"

Nietzsche was always conscious of moving on the sea of the infinite, of having given up land once and for all. He knew that, perhaps, neither Dante nor Spinoza knew his loneliness; somehow, they had God for company. But Nietzsche, empty in his loneliness, without men and without the ancient God, envisaged Zarathustra and meditated upon the eternal return, thoughts which left him as horrified as happy. He lived continually like someone mortally wounded. He suffered his problems. His thought is a self-arousal: "If I only had the courage to think all that I know." But, in this limitless reflecting, a deeply satisfying content was revealed which was in fact transcendent.

Thus both leaped toward Transcendence, but to a form of transcendence where practically no one could follow. Kierkegaard leaped to a Christianity which was conceived as an absurd paradox, as decision for utter world negation and martyrdom. Nietzsche leaped to the eternal return and supermen.

Thus the ideas, which were for Nietzsche himself the very deepest, can look empty to us; Kierkegaard's faith can look like a sinister alienation. If one takes the symbols of Nietzsche's religion literally, there is no longer any transcendental content in their will toward immanence: aside from the eternal cycle of things, there is the will to power, the affirmation of Being, the pleasure which "wills deep, deep eternity." Only with circumspection and by taking pains does a more essential content emerge. With Kierkegaard, who revivified the profound formulas of theology, it can seem like the peculiar art of perhaps a nonbeliever, forcing himself to believe.

The similarity of their thought is ever so much more striking precisely because of their apparent differences: the Christian belief of the one, and the atheism emphasized by the other. In an epoch of reflection, where what had really passed away seemed still to endure, but which actually lived in an absence of faith—rejecting faith and forcing oneself to believe belong together. The godless can appear to be a believer; the believer can appear as godless; both stand in the same dialectic.

What they brought forth in their existential thinking would not have been possible without a complete possession of tradition. Both were brought up with a classical education. Both were nurtured in Christian piety. Their tendencies are unthinkable without Christian origins. If they passionately opposed the stream of this tradition in the form which it had come to assume through the centuries, they also found an historical and, for them, indestructible arrest in these origins. They bound themselves to a basis which fulfilled their own belief: Kierkegaard to a Christianity of the New Testament as he understood it, and Nietzsche to a pre-Socratic Hellenism.

But nowhere is there any final stop for them, neither in finitude, nor in an explicitly grasped basis, nor in a determinately grasped Transcendence, nor in an historical tradition. It is as though their very being, experiencing the abandonment of the age to the end, shattered and, in the shattering itself, manifested a truth which otherwise would never have come to expression. If they won an unheard-of mastery over their own selves, they also were condemned to a worldless loneliness; they were as though pushed out.

4. THEIR BEING AS EXCEPTIONS. They were exceptions in every sense. Physically, their development was in retard of their character. Their faces disconcert one because of their relative unobtrusiveness. They do not impress one as types of human greatness. It is as if they both lacked something in sheer vitality. Or as though they were eternally young spirits, wandering through the world, without reality because without any real connection with the world.

Those who knew them felt attracted in an enigmatic way by their presence, as though elevated for a moment to a higher mode of being; but no one really loved them.

In the circumstances of their lives, one finds astonishing and alien features. They have been called simply insane. They would be in fact objects for a psychiatric analysis, if that were not to the prejudice of the singular height of their thought and the nobility of their natures. Indeed, then they would first come to light. But any typical diagnosis or classification would certainly fail.

They cannot be classed under any earlier type (poet, philosopher, prophet, savior, genius). With them, a new form of human reality appears in history. They are, so to speak, representative destinies, sacrifices whose way out of the world leads to experiences for others. They are by the total staking of their whole natures like modern martyrs, which, however, they precisely denied being. Through their character as exceptions, they solved their problem.

Both are irreplaceable, as having dared to be shipwrecked. We orient ourselves by them. Through them we have intimations of something we could never have perceived without such sacrifices, of something that seems essential which even today we cannot adequately grasp. It is as if the Truth itself spoke, bringing an unrest into the depths of our consciousness of being.

Even in the external circumstances of their lives we find astonishing similarities. Both came to a sudden end in their forties. Shortly before, without knowledge of their approaching end, they both made public and passionate attacks: Kierkegaard on church Christianity and on dishonesty, Nietzsche on Christendom itself.

Both made literary reputations in their first publications; but then their new books followed unceasingly, and they had to print what they wrote at their own expense.

They also both had the fate of finding a response which however was without understanding. They were merely sensations in an age when nothing opposed them. The beauty and sparkle of language, the literary and poetic qualities, the aggressiveness of their matter all misled readers from their genuine intentions. Both, toward the end, were almost idolized by those with whom they had the least in common. The age that wanted to surpass itself could, so to speak, wear itself out in ideas casually selected out of them.

The modern world has nourished itself on them precisely in its negligence. Out of their reflection, instead of remaining in the seriousness of endless reflection, it made an instrument for sophistry in irresponsible talk. Their words, like their whole lives, were savored for their great esthetic charm. They dissolved what remained of connections among men, not to lead to the bases of true seriousness, but in order to prepare a free path for caprice. Thus their influence became utterly destructive, contrary to the meaning of their thought and being.

C. *The ways in which they understood themselves: against interchangeability.*

Their problem became clearer to them from their youth onward through a continually accompanying reflection. Both of them, at the end and in retrospect, gave us an indication of how they understood themselves through a total interpretation of their work. This interpretation remained convincing to the extent that we, today, in fact understand them as they wished to be understood. All their thought takes on a new sense beyond what is immediately comprehensible in it. This picture itself is inseparable from their work, for the fashion in which they understood themselves is not an accidental addition, but an essential feature of their total thought.

One of the motives in common for the comprehensive expression of their self-understanding is the will not to be mistaken for someone else. This was, they said, one of their deepest concerns, and out of it not only were they always seeking new forms of communication, but also they directly announced the total meaning as it appeared to them at the end. They always worked by all possible means to prepare a correct understanding of their work through the ambiguity of what they said.

1. THEIR SELF-CONSCIOUSNESS. They both had a clear perception of their epoch, seeing what was going on before them down to the smallest detail with a certitude that was overmastering: it was the end of a mode of life that had hung together for centuries. But they also perceived that no one else saw it, that they had an awareness of their epoch which no one else yet had, but which presently others, and finally all, would have. Thus they necessarily passed into an unprecedented intensity of *self-consciousness*. Their Existenz was in a very special state of affairs. It was not just a simple spiritual superiority which they must have noticed—Kierkegaard over everybody who encountered him, Nietzsche over most—but rather something monstrous which they made themselves into: unique, solitary world-historical destinies.

2. THEIR CONSCIOUSNESS OF FAILURE, OF EXCEPTIONALITY, OF LONELINESS. But this well-grounded self-consciousness, momentarily expressed and then suppressed again, is always with Kierkegaard moderated through the humility of his Christian attitude and, with both, is tempered by the psychological knowledge of their human failure. The astonishing thing with them again is that the precise mode of their failure is itself the condition of their distinctive greatness. For this greatness is not absolute greatness, but something that uniquely belongs to the situation of the epoch.

It is noteworthy how they both came to the same metaphors for this side of their natures. Nietzsche compared himself to the "scratchings which an unknown power makes on paper, in order to test a new pen." The positive value of his illness is his standing problem. Kierkegaard thought he indeed "would be erased by God's mighty hand, extinguished as an unsuccessful experiment." He felt like a sardine squashed against the sides of a can. The idea came to him that, "in every generation there are two or three who are sacrificed for the others, who discover in frightful suffering what others shall profit by." He felt like an "interjection in speaking, without influence upon the sentence," like a "letter which is printed upside down in the line." He compared himself with the paper notes in the financial crises of 1813, the year in which he was born. "There is something in me which might have been great, but due to the unfavorable market, I'm only worth a little."

Both were conscious of being exceptions. Kierkegaard developed a theory of the exception, through which he understood himself: he loved the universal, the human in men, but as something other, something denied to him. Nietzsche knew himself to be an exception, spoke "in favor of the exception, so long as it never becomes the rule." He required of philosophers "that they take care of the rule, since he is the exception."

Thus the last thing either wished was to become exemplary. Kierkegaard looked upon himself as "a sort of trial man." "In the human sense no one can imitate me. . . . I am a man as he could become in a crisis, an experimental rabbit, so to speak, for existence." Nietzsche turned away those who would follow him: "Follow not me, but you!"

This exceptionality, which was as excruciating to them as it was the unique requirement of their problem, they characterized—and here again they agree—as pure mentality, as though they were deprived of any authentic life. Kierkegaard said that he was "in almost every physical respect deprived of the conditions for being a whole man." He had never lived except as mind. He had never been a man: at very most, child and youth. He lacked "the animal side of humanity." His melancholy carried him almost to the "edge of imbecility" and was "something that he could conceal as long as he was independent, but made him useless for any service where he could not himself determine everything." Nietzsche experienced his own pure mentality as "through excess of light, through his radiance, condemned to be, not to love." He expressed it convulsively in the "Nightsong" of Zarathustra: "Light I am; ah! would that I were Night! . . . I live in my own light. . . ."

A terrible loneliness, bound up with their exceptionality, was common to both. Kierkegaard knew that he could have no friends. Nietzsche suffered his own growing loneliness in full consciousness to the limit where he felt he could endure it no longer. Again, the same image comes to both: Nietzsche compared himself to a fir tree on the heights overlooking an abyss: "Lonely! Who dares to be a guest here? Perhaps a bird of prey, gloating in the hair of the branches. . . ." And Kierkegaard: "Like a lonely fir tree, egoistically isolated, looking toward something higher, I stand there, throwing no shadow, only the wood dove building its nest in my branches."

3. PROVIDENCE AND CHANCE. In great contrast to the abandonment, failure, and contingency of their existence was the growing consciousness in the course of their lives of the meaning, sense, and necessity of all that happened to them.

Kierkegaard called it Providence. He recognized the divine in it: "That everything that happens, is said, goes on, and so forth, is portentous: the factual continually changes itself to mean something far higher." The factual for him is not something to abstract oneself from, but rather something to be penetrated until God himself gives the meaning. Even what he himself did became clear only later. It was "the extra which I do not owe to myself but to Providence. It shows itself continually in such a fashion that even what I do out of the greatest possible conviction, afterwards I understand far better."

Nietzsche called it chance. And he was concerned to use chance. For him "sublime chance" ruled existence. "The man of highest spirituality and power feels himself grown for every chance, but also inside a snowfall of contingencies." But this contingency increasingly took on for Nietzsche a remarkable meaning: "What you call chance—you yourself are that which befalls and astonishes you." Throughout his life, he found intimations of how chance events which were of the greatest importance to him carried a secret meaning, and in the end he wrote: "There is no more chance."

4. DANCING. At the limits of life's possibilities came not any heavy seriousness, but rather a complete lightness as the expression of their knowledge, and both used the image of the dance. In the last decade of his life Nietzsche, in ever-changing forms, used the dance as a metaphor for his thought, where it is original. And Kierkegaard said, "I have trained myself . . . always to be able to dance in the service of thought. . . . My life begins as soon as a difficulty shows up. Then dancing is easy. The thought of death is a nimble dancer. Everybody is too serious for me." Nietzsche saw his archenemy

in the "spirit of seriousness"—in morals, science, purposefulness, etc. But to conquer seriousness meant not to reject it for the thoughtlessness of arbitrary caprice, but rather to pass through the most serious to an authentic soaring, the triumph of which is the free dance.

5. NO PROPHECY. The knowledge that they were exceptions prevented either from stepping forth as prophets. To be sure, they seem like those prophets who speak to us out of inaccessible depths but who speak in a contemporary way. Kierkegaard compared himself to a bird which foretells rain: "When in a generation, a thunderstorm begins to threaten, individuals like me appear." They are prophets who must conceal themselves as prophets. They were aware of their problem in a continual return from the extremities of their demands to a rejection of any idea which would make them models or ways of life. Kierkegaard repeated innumerable times that he was not an authority, or a prophet, apostle, or reformer, nor did he have the authority of position. His problem was to awaken men. He had a certain police talent, to be a spy in the service of the divinity. He uncovered, but he did not assert what should be done. Nietzsche wanted to "awaken the highest suspicion against himself," explaining that "to the humanity of a teacher belongs the duty of warning his students against himself." What he wanted he let Zarathustra say who left his disciples with: "Go away from me, and turn yourselves against me." And, even in *Ecce Homo,* Nietzsche says: "And finally, there is nothing in me of the founder of a religion. . . . I want no believers. . . . I have a terrible anxiety that some day, they will speak reverently of me. I will not be a saint, rather a Punch. Maybe I am Punch."

6. THE DEED. There is in both a confusing polarity between the appearance of an absolute and definite demand and, at the same time, shyness, withdrawal, the appearance of not betting anything. The Seductive, the Perhaps, the Possible is the manner of their discourse; an unreadiness to be a leader was their own attitude. But both lived in secret longing to bring salvation if they could, and if it could be done in human honesty. Accordingly, both toward the end of their lives became daring, desperate, and then, in utter calm, rose to public attack. From then on, the reticence of merely envisaging possibilities was given up for a will to act. Both made a similar attack: Kierkegaard attacked the Christianity of the church; Nietzsche attacked Christendom as such. Both acted with sudden force and merciless resolution. Both attacks were purely negative

actions: deeds from truthfulness, not for the construction of a world.

III. Meaning of the Philosophical Situation Produced by Kierkegaard and Nietzsche

The significance of Kierkegaard and Nietzsche first becomes clear through what followed in consequence. The effect of both is immeasurably great, even greater in general thinking than in technical philosophy, but it is always ambiguous. What Kierkegaard really meant is clear neither in theology, nor in philosophy. Modern Protestant theology in Germany, when it is genuine, seems to stand under either a direct or indirect influence of Kierkegaard. But Kierkegaard with regard to practical consequences of his thought wrote in May, 1855, a pamphlet with the motto, "But at midnight there is a cry" (Matthew 25:6), where he says: "By ceasing to take part in the official worship of God as it now is . . . thou hast one guilt less, . . . thou dost not participate in treating God as a fool, calling it the Christianity of the New Testament, which it is not."

A. *Ambiguity of both.*

In modern philosophy several decisive themes have been developed through Kierkegaard. The most essential basic categories of contemporary philosophizing, at least in Germany, go back to Kierkegaard–Kierkegaard whose whole thought however appeared to dissolve all previous systematic philosophy, to reject speculation, and who, when he recognized philosophy, said at most: "Philosophy can pay attention to but cannot nourish us."

It might be that theology, like philosophy, when it follows Kierkegaard is masking something essential in order to use his ideas and formulas for its own totally different purposes.

It might be that within theology there is an unbelief which employs the refined Kierkegaardian intellectual techniques of dialectical paradox to set forth a kind of creed which can be understood, and which believes itself the genuine Christian faith.

It might be that philosophizing in the fashion of Kierkegaard secretly nourishes itself on the substance of Christianity, which it ignores in words.

The significance of Nietzsche is no clearer. His effect in

Germany was like that of no other philosopher. But it seems as though every attitude, every world-view, every conviction claims him as authority. It might be that none of us really knows what this thought includes and does.

B. *Their disordering influence.*

The problem, therefore, for everyone who allows Kierkegaard and Nietzsche to influence him, is to become honest about how he really comes to terms with them, what they are to him, what he can make out of them.

Their common effect, to enchant and then to disillusion, to seize and then leave one standing unsatisfied as though one's hands and heart were left empty—such is only a clear expression of their own intention: that everything depends upon what their reader by his own inner action makes out of their communication, where there is no specific content as in the special sciences, works of art, philosophical systems, or some accepted prophecy. They deny every satisfaction.

C. *The problem of philosophizing in relation to both.*

In fact, they are exceptions and not models for followers. Whenever anyone has tried to imitate Kierkegaard or Nietzsche, if only in style, he has become ridiculous. What they did themselves at moments approaches the limit where the sublime passes into the ridiculous. What they did was only possible once. To be sure, everything great is unique, and can never be repeated identically. But there is something essentially different in our relation to this uniqueness: and this whether we live through them, and, by making them our own, revive them, or see them through the distance of an orientation which changes us but makes them more remote.

They abandon us without giving us any final goals and without posing any definite problems. Through them, each one can only become what he himself is. What their consequences are is not yet decided even today. The question is: how those of us shall live who are not exceptions but who are seeking our inner way in the light of these exceptions.

We are in that cultural situation where the application of this knowledge already contains the kernel of dishonesty. It is as though through them we were forced out of a certain thoughtlessness, which without them would have remained even in the study of great philosophers. We can no longer tranquilly proceed in the continuity of a traditional, intellectual education. For through Kierkegaard and Nietzsche a mode of existential experience has become effective, whose consequences on all sides have not yet come to light. They posed a question which is not yet clear but which one can feel; this question is still open. Through them we have become aware that for us there is no longer any self-evident foundation. There is no longer any secure background for our thought.

For the individual working with them, there are two equally great dangers: really to encounter them and not to take them seriously at all. Unavoidably, one's attitude toward them is ambivalent. Neither constructed a world, and both seemed to have destroyed everything; yet both were positive spirits. We must achieve a distinctively new relation to the creative thinker if we are really to approach them otherwise than we would any great man.

D. *The question: What now?*

With respect to our epoch and the thought of Kierkegaard and Nietzsche, if we pose the question, what now? then Kierkegaard points in the direction of an absurd Christianity before which the world sinks away, and Nietzsche points to the distance, the indeterminate, which does not appear to be a substance out of which we can live. Nobody has accepted their answers; they are not ours. It is for us to see what will become of us through ourselves as we look upon them. This is, however, in no way to sketch out or establish anything in advance.

Thus we would err if we thought we could deduce what must now happen from a world-historical survey of the development of the human spirit. We do not stand outside like a god who can survey the whole at a glance. For us, the present cannot be replaced by some supposed world history out of which our situation and problems would emerge. And this lecture has no intention of surveying the whole, but rather of making the present situation perceptible by reflecting upon the past. Nobody knows where man and his thinking are going. Since existence, man, and his world are not at an end, a completed philosophy is as little possible as an anticipation of the whole. We men have plans with finite ends, but something else always comes out which no one willed. In the same way, philosophizing is an act which works upon the inwardness of man, but whose final meaning he cannot know. Thus the contemporary problem is not to be deduced from some a priori whole; rather it is to be brought to consciousness out of a basis which is now experienced and out of a content still unclearly willed. Philosophy as thought is always a consciousness of Being which is complete for this moment, but which knows it has no final permanence in its form of expression.

E. *The problem we have abstracted from the situation: Reason and Existenz.*

Instead of some supposed total view of the actual and cultural situation, rather we philosophize in consciousness of a situation which again leads to the final limits and bases of the human reality. Today, no one can completely and clearly develop the intellectual problems that grow out of such a situation. We live, so to speak, in a seething cauldron of possibilities, continually threatened by confusion, but always ready in spite of everything to rise up again. In philosophizing, we must always be ready, out of the present questioning, to elicit those ideas which bring forth what is real to us: that is, our humanity. These ideas are possible when the horizon remains unlimited, the realities clear, and the real questions manifest. Out of such problems which force themselves upon thought, I have selected one for the next three lectures. The ancient philosophical problem, which appears in the relation of the rational to the non-rational, must be seen in a new light through an appropriation of the tradition with our eyes upon Kierkegaard and Nietzsche.

We formulate this fundamental problem as that of reason and Existenz. This abbreviated formula signifies no antithesis: rather a connection which at the same time points beyond itself.

The words "reason" and "Existenz" are chosen because for us they express in the most penetrating and pure form the problem of the clarification of the dark, the grasping of the bases out of which we live, presupposing no transparency, but demanding the maximum of rationality.

The word "reason" has here its Kantian scope, clarity and truth. The word "Existenz" through Kierkegaard has taken on a sense through which we look into infinite depths at what defies all determinate knowledge. The word is not to be taken in its worn-out sense as one of the many synonyms for "being"; it either means nothing, or is to be taken with its Kierkegaardian claims.

What we shall undertake in the next three lectures may seem to move around other themes. But in common, they shall strive to grasp in the form of logically conceived questions the meaning of what is closest to life. Philosophy, wherever it is successful, consists of those unique ideas in which logical abstractness and the actual present become, so to speak, identical. The basic drives of living philosophy can express themselves truly only in purely formal thought. There are intellectual operations which through comprehension and cooperation can bring about an inner act of the entire man: the bringing forth of oneself out of possibilities in thought so as to apprehend Being in empirical existence.

If my lectures do not come even close to satisfying these high demands, it is still essential that the ideal of one's concerns be recognized. One can take courage to try to do that which passes beyond his strength from the fact that it is a human problem, and man is that creature which poses problems beyond his powers. And also from this, that whoever even once thought he heard softly the authentic philosophic note can never tire of trying to communicate it.

The Fifth Lecture shall take up again the theme of this one. It will in reference to the previously developed ideas take up the problems of contemporary philosophy in a situation decisively determined by Kierkegaard and Nietzsche.

Philosophy and Science

Philosophy has from its very beginnings looked upon itself as science, indeed as science par excellence. To achieve the highest and most certain knowledge is the goal that has always animated its devotees.

How its scientific character came to be questioned can be understood only in the light of the development of the specifically modern sciences. These sciences made their greatest strides in the nineteenth century, largely outside philosophy, often in opposition to philosophy, and finally in an atmosphere of indifference to it. If philosophy was still expected to be a science, it was in a different sense than before; it was now expected to be a science in the same sense as those modern sciences that convince by virtue of their accomplishments. If it were unable to do so, it was argued, it had become pointless and might just as well die out.

Some decades ago the opinion was widespread that philosophy had had its place up to the moment when all the sciences had become independent of it, the original universal science. Now that all possible fields of research have been marked off, the days of philosophy are over. Now that we know how science obtains its universal validity, it has become evident that philosophy cannot stand up against judgment by these criteria. It deals in empty ideas because it sets up undemonstrable hypotheses, it disregards experience, it seduces by illusions, it takes possession of energies needed for genuine investigation and squanders them in empty talk about the whole.

This was the picture of philosophy as seen against science conceived as methodical, cogent, universally valid insight. Under such circumstances could any philosophy legitimately claim to be scientific? To this situation philosophy reacted in two ways:

1) The attack was regarded as justified. Philosophers withdrew to limited tasks. If philosophy is at an end because the sciences have taken over all its subject matter, there remains nevertheless the knowledge of its history, first as a factor in the history of the sciences themselves, then as a phenomenon in the history of thought, the history of the errors, the anticipated insights, the process of liberation by which philosophy has made itself superfluous. Finally, the history of philosophy must preserve the knowledge of the philosophical texts, if only for their aesthetic interest. Although these texts do not make any serious contribution to scientific truth, they are nevertheless worth reading for the sake of their style and the intellectual attitude they reflect.

Others paid tribute to the modern scientific trend by rejecting all previous philosophy and striving to give philosophy an exact scientific foundation. They seized upon questions which, they claimed, were reserved for philosophy because they concern all the sciences; namely, logic, epistemology, phenomenology. In an effort to refurbish its reputation, philosophy became a servile imitator, a handmaiden to the sciences. It proceeded to establish in theory the validity of scientific knowledge, which was not questioned anyhow. But in the field of logic it developed a specialized science which because of the universality of its purpose, i.e., to define the form of all true thinking, to provide a *mathesis universalis*, seemed capable of replacing all previous philosophy. Today many thinkers regard symbolic logic as the whole of philosophy.

This first reaction seems today to have given rise to the view that philosophy is a science among other sciences, a discipline among other disciplines. And like the others, it is carried on by specialists, it has its narrow circle of experts, its congresses, and its learned periodicals.

2) In opposition to this infatuation with science there has been a second reaction. Philosophy attempted to save itself from destruction by dropping its claim to scientific knowledge. Philosophy—according to this view—is not a science at all. It is based on feeling and intuition, on imagination and genius. It is conceptual magic, not knowledge. It is *élan vital* or resolute acceptance of death. Indeed, some went further and said: It does not behoove philosophy to concern itself with science since it is aware that all scientific truth is questionable. The modern sciences are altogether in error, witness the ruinous consequences for the soul and for life in general of the rational attitude. Philosophy itself is not a science, and for that very reason its element is authentic truth.

Both reactions—submission to science and rejection of science conceived as cogent, methodical, and universally valid knowledge—seem to spell the end of philosophy. Whether it is the slave of science or whether it denies all science, it has in either case ceased to be philosophy.

The seeming triumph of the sciences over philosophy has for some decades created a situation in which philosophers go back to various sources in search of true philosophy. If such a thing is found, the question of the relation between philosophy and science will be answered, both in a theoretical and in a concrete sense. It is a practical question of the utmost urgency.

We shall appreciate the full weight of this problem if we consider its historical origin. It developed from three complexly intertwined factors. These are a) the spirit of modern science; b) the ancient and ever recurrent attempt to achieve universal philosophical knowledge; c) the philosophical concept of truth, as it was first and for all time elucidated in Plato.

Ad a) The modern sciences, developed only in the last few centuries, have brought into the world a new scientific attitude which existed neither in Asia nor in antiquity nor in the Middle Ages.

Even the Greeks, to be sure, conceived of science as methodical, cogently certain, and universally valid knowledge. But the modern sciences not only have brought out these basic attributes of science with greater purity (a task which has not yet been completed), they have also given new form and new foundation to the purpose, scope, and unity of their fields of inquiry. I shall indicate certain of their fundamental characteristics:

1) To modern science *nothing is indifferent*. In its eyes every fact, even the smallest and ugliest, the most distant and most alien, is a legitimate object of inquiry for the very reason that it exists. Science has become truly universal. There is nothing that can evade it. Nothing must be hidden or passed over in silence; nothing must remain a mystery.

2) Modern science is by definition unfinished, because it progresses toward the infinite, whereas ancient science in every one of its forms presented itself as finished; its actual development was in every case short lived, and it never set its own development as its conscious goal. Modern scientists have understood that an all-embracing world-system, which deduces everything that exists from one or a few principles, is impossible. A world-system has other sources and can only claim universal validity if scientific critique is relaxed and particulars are mistaken for absolutes. Such unprecedented systematizations as those achieved by modern physics cover only one aspect of reality. Through them reality as a whole has become more split up and deprived of foundations than it ever before seemed to the human mind. Hence the incompleteness of the modern world as compared to the Greek cosmos.

3) The ancient sciences remained *scattered*, unrelated to one another. They did not aim at constituting an all-embracing body of specific knowledge, whereas the modern sciences strive to be integrated into a universal frame of reference. Though a true world-system is no longer possible for them, a cosmos of the sciences is still conceivable. Our sense of the inadequacy of each special branch of knowledge demands that each science be connected with knowledge as a whole.

4) The modern sciences attach little value to the *possibilities* of thought; they recognize the idea only in definite and concrete knowledge, after it has proved its worth as an instrument of discovery and been subjected to infinite modifications in the process of investigation. True, there is a certain similarity between ancient and modern atomic theory, in so far as the general pattern is concerned. But the ancient theory was merely an intrinsically finished interpretation of possibilities, based on plausible explanations of available experience, while the modern theory, in constant association with

experience, undergoes perpetual change by confirmation and disproof and is itself an implement of investigation.

5) Today a scientific attitude has become possible, an attitude of inquiry toward all phenomena; today the scientist can know certain things clearly and definitely, he can distinguish between what he knows and what he does not know; and he has amassed an unprecedented abundance of knowledge (how very little the Greek physician or the Greek technician knew by comparison!). The moral imperative of modern science is to search for reliable knowledge on the basis of unprejudiced inquiry and critique, without any preconceived ideas. When we enter into its sphere, we have the sensation of breathing clean air, of leaving behind us all vague talk, all plausible opinions, all stubborn prejudice and blind faith.

Ad b) Modern science shares the age-old striving for total philosophical knowledge. Philosophy had from the first set itself up as the science that knows the whole—not as infinitely progressing, factual knowledge but as self-contained doctrine. Now modern philosophy since Descartes has identified itself with modern science but in such a way that it still retained the philosophical concept of a total knowledge. It can be shown, however, that for this very reason Descartes did not understand modern science, the investigations of Galileo for example, and that his own work had in spirit little to do with modern science, although as a creative mathematician he helped to advance this science. The ensuing philosophers, even to a certain extent Kant, were still caught in this totalist conception of science. Hegel once again believed that he was achieving the construction of an authentic total science and that he possessed all the sciences in his cosmos of the mind.

This identification of modern science and modern philosophy with their old aspiration to total knowledge was catastrophic for both of them. The modern sciences which, by a self-deception common to all of them, looked on those great philosophies of the seventeenth century and on some later philosophies as pillars of their own edifice were tainted by their aspirations to absolute knowledge. Modern philosophy has done its greatest work only "in spite of" all this, or one might say, by a constant misunderstanding.

Ad c) Neither the modern concept of science nor science in the sense of a total philosophical system coincides with the strictly philosophical conception of science which Plato formulated in a way that has never been surpassed. How far removed is the truth, the knowledge of which Plato interprets in his parable of the cave and touches on in his dialectic, this truth that applies to being and to that which is above all being—how fundamentally different it is from the truth of the sciences, which move only amid the manifestations of being without ever attaining to being itself, and how different from the truth of the dogmatic system which holds itself to be in possession of the whole of being. What a distance between the truth which can nowhere be set down in writing but which, according to Plato's seventh epistle, though it can only be attained by thought, is kindled in a favourable moment of communication among men of understanding, and the truth which is written, universally cogent and intelligible, distinct and available to all thinking creatures!

Three so different conceptions of scientific knowledge—the first patterned on the method of modern science, the second derived from the idea of a total philosophical system, and the third related to faith in a truth which is directly apprehended by the intellect (Plato's truth being an example)—all contribute to the present confusion. An example:

Its inquiries and investigations in the economic field have made Marxism an important force in scientific development. But this it shares with many other trends, and its scientific contribution does not account for its influence. Marxism also represents a philosophical thesis regarding the dialectical course of history as a total process which it purports to understand. Thus it constitutes a philosophical doctrine but one with a claim to universal scientific validity. It has the same epistemological basis as Hegel's philosophy, whose dialectical method remains its implement. The difference is only that for Hegel the core of the historical process lies in what he calls the "idea," while for Marx it lies in the mode of production of man who, unlike the animals, obtains his sustenance through systematic labour. Both Hegel and Marx derive all phenomena from what they regard as the core. Marx therefore rightly claims to have stood Hegel on his head; that however is only in content, for he did not depart from Hegel's method of constructing reality by the dialectic of the concept.

Now this identification of economic knowledge, which is gained by scientific method, hence inductively, and which by its very nature is subject to constant modifications, with the dialectical knowledge of the total process, which passes for essentially definitive knowledge, is the source of the fallacy committed by Hegel and in a different form by the type of modern philosophy that began with Descartes and was repeated by Marx. Marx's absolute, exclusive claim therefore originates in a conception of philosophy as total, systematic knowledge; but at the same time, his doctrine is presented as a result of modern science, from which it does not at all follow.

In addition to the conceptions patterned on modern science and total philosophy, there operates in Marxism also a third conception, reflecting the lofty idea of an absolute truth that fulfills man's will and aspirations, analogous to the Platonic idea of truth, although entirely different in character. Marxism conceives of itself as the true consciousness of the classless man. This quasi-religious postulate is the source of a new kind of fanaticism which invokes not faith but modern science, which charges its opponents with stupidity, malice, or inability to overcome class prejudice and contrasts these with its own universal human truth that is free from class bondage and hence absolute.

Similar intellectual tendencies, which uncritically hypostatize a field of investigation that is meaningful within its limits into a total science and infuse it with a religious attitude, have been manifested in the domains of racial theory and psychoanalysis and in many other fields.

The false confusion of heterogeneous elements produces here, on a large scale, results that are so familiar on a small scale in everyday life—an attitude of never being at a loss for an answer, satisfaction with mere plausibility, stubbornly uncritical statements and affirmations, inability to explore in a genuine sense, to listen, analyse, test, and reflect on principles.

The infuriating part of it is that science is invoked to defend something that runs directly counter to the scientific spirit. For science leads us to the understanding of the principles, limitations, and meaning of our knowledge. It teaches us to know, in full consciousness of the methods by which each stage of knowledge is achieved. It produces a certainty whose relativity, i.e., dependence on presuppositions and methods of investigation, is its crucial characteristic.

Thus we are today confronted with an ambivalent concept of science. Genuine science can, as has always been the case, appear to be occult; it is in the nature of a public secret. It is public because it is accessible to everyone; it is a secret because it is far from being truly understood by everyone. All the more brightly shines the genuine, unswerving, never-failing scientific attitude, whose very critical awareness of its limits leaves room for every other source of truth in man.

In addition there is a wonderful virtue in science itself. In the course of scientific development only what is truly known is permanently preserved, the rest is eliminated through critique. So long as free discussion prevails, a body of knowledge forms that is more than the men who are its vehicle, a body of knowledge that no individual can encompass in all its scope.

At a time when confusion prevails regarding the meaning of science, three tasks are imperative, corresponding to the three tendencies discussed above.

First, the idea that total philosophical knowledge is scientific knowledge must be exposed as false. The sciences themselves critically explode this false total knowledge. It is here that the opposition to philosophy has its root, and in this respect contempt of it is justifiable.

Second, the sciences must be made pure. This can be accomplished through constant struggle and awareness in the course of our scientific activity itself. By and large, the need for basic clarity concerning science and its limits is readily admitted even by those who sin against such clarity in practice. But the essential is to achieve this purity within the specific sciences. This must be done largely through the critical work of the scientists themselves. But the philosopher who wishes to test the truth-meaning of scientific knowledge, to auscultate it, so to speak, must participate in the actual work of these scientists.

Third, a pure philosophy must be worked out in the new conditions that have been created by the modern sciences. This is indispensable for the sake of the sciences themselves. For philosophy is always alive in the sciences and so inseparable from them that the purity of both can be achieved only jointly. The rejection of philosophy usually leads to the unwitting development of a bad philosophy. The concrete work of the scientist is guided by his conscious or unconscious philosophy, and this philosophy cannot be the object of scientific method.

For example: It is impossible to prove scientifically that there should be such a thing as science. Or: The choice of an object of science that is made from among an infinite number of existing objects on the basis of this object itself is a choice that cannot be justified scientifically. Or: The ideas that guide us are tested in the systematic process of investigation, but they themselves do not become an object of direct investigation.

Science left to itself as mere science becomes homeless. The intellect is a whore, said Nicholas of Cusa, for it can prostitute itself to anything. Science is a whore, said Lenin, for it sells itself to any class interest. For Nicholas of Cusa it is Reason, and ultimately the knowledge of God, that gives meaning, certainty, and truth to intellectual knowledge; for Lenin, it is the classless society that promotes pure science. Be that as it may, awareness of all this is the business of philosophical reflection. Philosophy is inherent in the actual sciences themselves; it is their inner meaning that provides the scientist with sustenance and guides his methodical work. He who consolidates this guidance through reflection and becomes conscious of it has reached the stage of explicit philosophizing. If this guidance fails, science falls into gratuitous convention, meaningless correctness, aimless busy-ness, and spineless servitude.

A pure science requires a pure philosophy.

But how can philosophy be pure? Has it not always striven to be science? Our answer is: It is "science" but science of such a sort that in the sense of modern scientific inquiry it is both less and more than science.

Philosophy can be called science in so far as it presupposes the sciences. There is no tenable philosophy outside the sciences. Although conscious of its distinct character, philosophy is inseparable from science. It refuses to transgress against universally binding insight. Anyone who philosophizes must be familiar with scientific method.

Any philosopher who is not trained in a scientific discipline and who fails to keep his scientific interests constantly alive will inevitably bungle and stumble and mistake uncritical rough drafts for definitive knowledge. Unless an idea is submitted to the coldly dispassionate test of scientific inquiry, it is rapidly consumed in the fire of emotions and passions, or else it withers into a dry and narrow fanaticism.

Moreover, anyone who philosophizes strives for scientific knowledge, for it is the only way to genuine nonknowledge, it is as though the most magnificent insights could be achieved only through man's quest for the limit at which cognition runs aground, not seemingly and temporarily but genuinely and definitively, not with a sense of loss and despair but with a sense of genuine internal evidence. Only definitive knowledge can make definitive nonknowledge possible; it alone can achieve the authentic failure which opens up a vista, not merely upon the discoverable existent but upon being itself.

In accomplishing the great task of dispelling all magical conceptions, modern science enters upon the path that leads to the intuition of the true depth, the authentic mystery, which becomes present only through the most resolute knowledge in the consummation of nonknowledge.

Consequently philosophy turns against those who despise the sciences, against the sham prophets who deprecate scientific inquiry, who mistake the errors of science for science itself, and who would even hold science, "modern science," responsible for the evils and the inhumanity of our era.

Rejecting superstitious belief in science as well as contempt of science, philosophy grants its unconditional recognition to modern science. In its eyes science is a marvellous thing which can be relied upon more than anything else, the most significant achievement of man in his history, an achievement that is the source of great dangers but of even greater opportunities and that from now on must be regarded as a prerequisite of all human dignity. Without science, the philosopher knows, his own pursuits eventuate in nothing.

These pursuits can continue to be called scientific because philosophy proceeds methodically and because it is conscious of its methods. But these methods differ from those of science in that they have no object of inquiry. Any specific object is the object of a particular science. Were I to say that the object of philosophy is the whole, the world, being, philosophical critique would answer that such terms do not denote genuine objects. The methods of philosophy are methods of transcending the object. To philosophize is to transcend. But since our thinking is inseparable from objects, the history of philosophy is an account of how the progress of human thought has succeeded in transcending the objects of philosophy. These objects, the great creations of philosophy, function as road signs, indicating the direction of philosophical transcending. Thus there is no substitute for the profound discourse of the metaphysician, which speaks to us from the centuries; to assimilate it from its source in the history of philosophy is not only to know something that once was but to make it come to life.

The mass of sham philosophical knowledge taught in the schools originates in the hypostatization of entities that have served for a time as the signpost of philosophy but are always being transcended by it. Such hypostatized entities are nothing but the *capita mortua,* the ossuaries of the great metaphysical systems. To imagine that they confer knowledge is a philosophical perversion. In philosophizing we must not fall under the spell of the object that we use as a means of transcendence. We must remain masters of our thoughts and not be subjugated by them.

Yet in this intellectual transcendence, which is proper to philosophy and which is analogous to scientific forms, philosophy is less than science. For it does not gain any tangible results or any intellectually binding insight. There is no overlooking the simple fact that while scientific cognition is identical throughout the world, philosophy, despite its claim to universality, is not actually universal in any shape or form. This fact is the outward characteristic of the peculiar nature of philosophical truth. Although scientific truth is universally valid, it remains relative to method and assumptions; philosophical truth is absolute for him who conquers it in historical actuality, but its statements are not universally valid. Scientific truth is one and the same for all—philosophical truth wears multiple historical cloaks; each of these is the manifestation of a unique reality, each has its justification, but they are not identically transmissible.

The one philosophy is the *philosophia perennis* around which all philosophies revolve, which no one possesses, in which every genuine philosopher shares, and which nevertheless can never achieve the form of an intellectual edifice valid for all and exclusively true.

Thus philosophy is not only less but also more than science, namely, as the source of a truth that is inaccessible to scientifically binding knowledge. It is this philosophy that is meant in such definitions as: To philosophize is to learn how to die or to rise to godhead—or to know being qua being. The meaning of such definitions is: Philosophical thought is inward action; it appeals to freedom; it is a summons to transcendence. Or the same thing can be formulated differently: Philosophy is the act of becoming conscious of genuine being—or is the thinking of a faith in man that must be infinitely elucidated—or is the way of man's self-assertion through thinking.

But none of these propositions is properly speaking a definition. There is no definition of philosophy, because philosophy cannot be determined by something outside it. There is no genus above philosophy, under which it can be subsumed as a species. Philosophy defines itself, relates itself directly to godhead, and does not justify itself by any kind of utility. It grows out of the primal source in which man is given to himself.

To sum up: The sciences do not encompass all of the truth but only the exact knowledge that is binding to the intellect and universally valid. Truth has a greater scope, and part of it can reveal itself only to philosophical reason. Throughout the centuries since the early Middle Ages, philosophical works have been written under the title "On the Truth"; today the same task still remains urgent, i.e., to gain insight into the essence of truth in its full scope under the present conditions of scientific knowledge and historical experience.

The foregoing considerations also apply to the relation between science and philosophy. Only if the two are strictly distinguished can the inseparable connection between them remain pure and truthful.

Through research and study the university strives to achieve the great practical unity of the sciences and philosophy. At the university a philosophical view of the world has always been made manifest through scientific method.

The university is the meeting place of all sciences. In so far as these remain an aggregate, the university resembles an intellectual warehouse; but in so far as they strive toward unity of knowledge, it resembles a never-finished temple.

A century and a half ago this was still self-evident: the philosophical ideas that were assumed by the scientists in the various disciplines were brought to the highest light of consciousness by the philosophers. But the situation has changed. The sciences have become fragmented by specialization. It has come to be believed that scientific cognition, marked by the neatness of universally valid particular knowledge, could break away from philosophy.

Is the present dispersion of the sciences the ultimate and necessary stage? One might wish for a philosophy that would encompass and assimilate the whole tradition, that would be equal to the intellectual situation of our time, that would express the contents common to all of us, and this both in sublime intellectual constructions and in simple propositions capable of finding resonance in every man. Today we have no such philosophy.

Old university seals dating from the fifteenth century reveal figures wrought in gold which represent Christ distributing their tasks to the faculties. Even where such seals are still in use they no longer express the modern reality; yet they still bear witness to the task of unifying the whole.

Today neither theology nor philosophy creates a whole. Does the university still have a common spirit? As regards its organization, it still seems to constitute an ever-changing plan without symmetry or logic, never definitive, constantly in process of enlargement, a plan in which everything that achieves scientific status has its place. The most disparate elements meet. Not related by a knowledge of the whole, everyone is nevertheless compelled to see in this meeting something previously unknown, everyone learns to come into contact with highly unfamiliar things. Hence arises the intellectual life, the striving for greater expanse and freedom of thought. Thus a common spirit is no longer found in a faith binding to all but only in critical inquiry as such, in the recognition of the logically or empirically unascertainable, in the resolute refusal to perpetrate the *sacrificium intellectus*, in open-mindedness, in unlimited questioning, in integrity.

This spirit is the product of the last few centuries. Will the university content itself with this spirit forever? For philosophy this situation seems to offer extraordinary possibilities. But it would be absurd to draw up a programme for a task that can be carried out only by an intellectual world operating with a true sense of community, not by an individual.

So long as the philosopher retains his integrity, he is modestly aware of the limits of his knowledge. This must not be confused with another kind of modesty needed today, that of the *teacher* of philosophy. The best philosophers today are not perhaps to be found among those charged explicitly with the teaching of philosophy. For the philosophy *in* the sciences, which preserves us from dissipating our energies on things that are not worth knowing and which animates scientific inquiry, is the concrete philosophy that is embodied in the totality of a specific science. This philosophy thus becomes in a sense the spokesman for knowledge in general, provided that constant care is taken to see this particular domain in relation to all the knowable and thereby to anchor it in depth.

The teacher of philosophy in the service of such efforts is not a leader who lays down the law but an attentive and patient listener, eager to find meaning in the broadest interrelations.

The teacher of philosophy reveres the individual great philosophers, who are not specimens of a type but creators (such do not exist today), but he rejects the idolization of men, which began even in the academy of Plato, for even the greatest are men and err, and no one is an authority who must be obeyed by right.

And the teacher of philosophy has respect for each science whose insights are binding—but he condemns the scientific pride which imagines that everything can be known in its ultimate foundation or even goes so far as to suppose that it is known.

His ideal is that of a rational being coexisting with other rational beings. He wants to doubt, he thirsts for objections and attacks, he strives to become capable of playing his part in the dialogue of ever-deepening communication, which is the prerequisite of all truth and without which there is no truth.

His hope is that in the same measure as he becomes a rational being he may acquire the profound contents which can sustain man, that his will, in so far as his striving is honest, may become good through the direct help of the transcendent, without any human mediation.

As a teacher of philosophy, however, he feels that it is his duty not to let his students forget the great minds of the past, to preserve the various philosophical methods as an object of instruction, and to see to it that the sciences influence philosophical thinking; to elucidate the present age and at the same time to join his students in conquering a view of the eternal.

BIBLIOGRAPHY

(following Jaspers' classification in an appendix to the radio lectures in which he introduced his approach to philosophy)

Principal philosophic works:

Philosophie (three volumes, 1932; second edition, 1948)

Von der Wahrheit (Munich, 1947); a section, translated by William Kluback, Jean T. Wilde, and William Kimmel, published as *Truth and Symbol* (London, 1959)

Short works treating in greater detail the subject matter of the radio talks published as *Einführung in die Philosophie* (1950); translated by Ralph Manheim as *Way to Wisdom* (London, 1951; New Haven, Yale University Press, 1960):

Der philosophische Glaube (1948); translated by Ralph Manheim as *The Perennial Scope of Philosophy* (London, 1950)
Vernunft und Existenz (1935; second edition, 1947); translated by William Earle as *Reason and Existenz* (New York, 1955; London, 1956)
Philosophie und Wissenschaft (1948)

On contemporary philosophy:

Die geistige Situation der Zeit (1931; seventh edition, 1949); translated by Eden and Cedar Paul as *Man in the Modern Age* (London, 1934)
Von Ursprung und Ziel der Geschichte (1949); translated by Michael Bullock as *The Origin and Goal of History* (London, 1953)
Vom Europäischen Geist (1947); translated by Ronald Gregor Smith as *The European Spirit* (London, 1948)
Vernunft und Widervernunft in unserer Zeit (1950)

Works devoted to individual philosophers:

Descartes und die Philosophie (1937; second edition, 1947)
Nietzsche (1936; third edition, 1949)
Nietzsche und das Christentum (1946)
Max Weber (1921; second edition, 1947)
Lionardo als Philosoph (1953)
Schelling: Grösse und Verhängniss (1955)

On philosophy as manifested in the concrete sciences:

Allgemeine Psychopathologie (1913; sixth edition, 1953); translated by J. Hoenig and Marian W. Hamilton as *General Psychopathology* (Manchester, 1963)
Strindberg und Van Gogh (1922; third edition, 1949)
Wesen und Kritik der Psychotherapie (1955)

On questions of the day:

Die Schüldfrage (1956); translated by E. B. Ashton as *The Question of German Guilt* (New York, 1947)
Die Atombombe und die Zukunft des Menschen (1958); translated and edited by E. B. Ashton as *The Future of Mankind* (Chicago, 1961)

Die Idee der Universität (1923; new interpretation, 1946)
Die Frage der Entmythologisierung (discussion with Rudolf Bultmann, 1954); translated as *Myth and Christianity* (New York, 1958)

Collected Papers:

Rechenschaft und Ausblick (1951)
Philosophie und Welt (1958)

Jaspers' main project during recent years has been an interpretation of the history of philosophy, *Die grossen Philosophen*, of which the first volume (1957) has been translated by Ralph Manheim and edited by Hannah Arendt as *The Great Philosophers: The Foundations* (New York and London, 1963).

Selected essays and lectures, translated by E. B. Ashton, are available in *Philosophy and the World* (Chicago, 1963).

Studies of Jaspers include:

Karl Jaspers, edited by P. A. Schilpp (Library of Living Philosophers, Chicago, 1957)
"Karl Jaspers, A Philosopher of Humanity," *The Times Literary Supplement*, No. 3189, April 12, 1963.

GABRIEL MARCEL

(BORN 1889)

Gabriel Marcel records in his *Journal Métaphysique* (1913–1923) the independent movement of his thinking through and out of the dominant idealism to a concrete philosophizing—thought in the grip (or, rather, in the light or in the presence) of reality, thought grasping and remodeling itself in order to escape from its own images and ideas into responsiveness and participation. His philosophizing has a recognized resemblance to that of Jaspers in intent. Jaspers strives to attain and to maintain a philosophic faith; Marcel explores the approaches to a metaphysic of hope, which has a religious faith as its intelligible frame of reference. Both look down into the modern abyss of nihilism and set their faces toward a return route to a homeland. For Marcel, this is definitively the Christian faith. His metaphysic of hope, setting out from a broken world, would restore the possibility of Christian faith, although in his philosophizing he insistently remains this side of dogmatic theology. Both speak of the intent of their philosophy as an attempt to purify the air breathed in reflection upon what concerns us. Marcel calls this reflection "secondary," the tool of philosophic research, a reflection upon the habitual analytical results of "primary" reflection. The function of this secondary reflection proper to philosophy is to restore the spontaneous unity and openness of experience and thereby to bring back its lost possibilities, its readiness to be infused with the presence of Being, which gives its "ontological weight." Both think of communication or "intersubjectivity" (Marcel) as a reflectively attained level of conversation with oneself and with the other and as the clue to the experience of Being. Both think of their philosophy as a call, an appeal, an incitement, not as a doctrine.

Marcel's exposition is a winding exploration, unfolding and abandoning metaphors, following through descriptions of experience, advancing little by little, working a way up from life to thought and down from thought to life again. He speaks of the drama (he has written more than twenty plays) as having forced itself on him as a mode of expression and as intimately linked with his philosophical writings. The use of examples, he says, in his concrete philosophical approach is an essential method: it is not merely an exemplification of a pre-existing idea; rather, it provides for the development of the idea, as the soil for the seed. He is the artist developing his ideas and ideals in and through his medium. Marcel composes, and he frequently uses musical analogies. His winding interfusion of description and meditation on his themes is like a fugue. Musical improvisation is perhaps for him a metaphor for living, and therefore for thinking, which is inseparable from the experience to which it belongs. For his is not a metaphysic of "I think," but a metaphysic of "we are."

The affinity with Jaspers and with Buber (not forgetting the final sharp difference in Marcel's full communion with the Christian Church) is weighted by a notable lack of sympathy with Heidegger and, especially, with Sartre. A critique of Sartre's main philosophical work is included in *Homo Viator* (translated by Emma Crauford, London, 1951), and a survey of Sartre's philosophy written two years later is included in a small collection of his papers published as *The Philosophy of Existence* in 1948 in a translation by Manya Harari. This most useful concise collection is the best introduction to Marcel for the English reader. It reprints an autobiographical essay written in 1947 which is essential to an understanding of the inner springs of Marcel's thought, being a translation into reflection of his own formative experiences.

Marcel gave two series of Gifford Lectures, published in translation in 1950 and 1951 as *The Mystery of Being* (vol. I, *Reflection and Mystery;* vol. II, *Faith and Reality*). In these lectures he resumes, reponders, and develops together his main themes; but the continuity and system of this exposition in series do not suit Marcel's habit of mind, and the Gifford Lectures do not supersede the previously published collections of his papers. They can be read with advantage as a commentary on his own writings and a redeployment of his main themes, but the exposition in earlier papers of his fundamental notions of "creative fidelity" and "creative witness" should be read first.

EXTRACTS

Final part of "An Essay in Autobiography," first contributed to *Existentialisme Chrétien: Gabriel Marcel,* essays in honor of Marcel edited by Étienne Gilson

(Paris, 1947). The essay, translated by Manya Harari, was included with three other papers of Marcel in *The Philosophy of Existence* (London, 1948).

Outline of an essay read to the Society of Philosophical Studies, at Marseilles, on January 21, 1933, on "The Position of the Ontological Mystery and the Concrete Approaches to It," printed in the first section, "Journal métaphysique," of the first part of *Être et Avoir* (Paris, 1935), translated by Katharine Farrer as *Being and Having* (London, 1949).

Lecture given to the Scolasticat de Fourvière in 1942, "Sketch of a Phenomenology and a Metaphysic of Hope," printed in *Homo Viator* (Paris, 1945), translated by Emma Crauford (London and New York, 1951).

from *An Essay in Autobiography*

Whatever its ultimate meaning, the universe into which we have been thrown cannot satisfy our reason, let us have the courage to admit it once and for all. To deny it is not only scandalous, but in some ways truly sinful; and indeed I am convinced that this is precisely the besetting sin of the philosopher, the sin of Leibnitz and, less obviously, the sin of Hegel. The supreme mission of the philosopher cannot consist in proclaiming a certain number of official truths liable to rally votes at international congresses. In the last analysis, such truths inevitably turn out to be sheer platitudes. The imperishable glory of a Kierkegaard or a Nietzsche consists perhaps mainly in this, that they have proved, not only by their arguments, but by their trials and by their whole life, that a philosopher worthy of the name cannot be a man of congresses, and that he deviates from his path every time that he allows himself to be torn from the solitude which is his calling. It is only by clinging to this solitude that he remains at the disposal of those who await from him, if not a lead, at least a stimulation. Here again the satisfactory must be put aside; after all it is no more than a scholastic category. A candidate's answer to an examiner is or is not satisfactory; but then in an examination there are clearly formulated rules and the stage has been set in advance, whereas in the real world, which is, or should be, that of the philosopher, there is nothing of the kind. The stage always remains to be set; in a sense everything always starts from zero, and a philosopher is not worthy of the name unless he not only accepts but wills this harsh necessity. Whereas the temptation for a congress man is always to refer to an earlier congress where it was established that. . . . This perpetual beginning again, which may seem scandalous to the scientist or the technician, is an inevitable part of all genuinely philosophical work; and perhaps it reflects in its own order the fresh start of every new awakening and of every birth. Does not the very structure of duration and of life show that philosophical thought is unfaithful to reality whenever it attempts to proceed from conclusion to conclusion towards a *Summa* which, in the end, needs only to be expounded and memorised paragraph by paragraph? The conviction that reality cannot be "summed up," that this is indeed the last way in which it can be apprehended, came to me very early, partly as a result of reading Bradley. It seemed to me from then on that there was a danger of making an illicit use of the idea of integration, and that the more one relied on the richest and most concrete data of experience, the less this idea appeared to be applicable to reality. From this point of view, I think I can now say that, without ever regarding pluralism as a tenable metaphysical doctrine, I have always been inclined to believe that it had, at least, a negative value—the value of a refusal, of a necessary protest; though my own tendency has been rather to deny the ontological importance which metaphysicians, from the school of Aelia to the time of Hegel, have assigned to the opposition between the one and the many.

What started me on the way to denying the idea of an intelligible whole which is at the same time the motive principle and the end of dialectics, was, I think, primarily the consideration of action as something other than a mere content of thought. Is it that I was particularly receptive to the idea of action as a break, to what we would now call its revolutionary character? I would say rather—although this is only a *nuance*—that I have always been struck by its originality, or even by the singularity of the perspective by which it is inevitably governed. This is why I was attracted by monadism; and I might even have adopted this doctrine for good if the thesis of the incommunicability of monads had not seemed to me a challenge to experience and to common sense, while the notion of a pre-established harmony struck me as a pure invention as ingenious as it was artificial. To act was, to my mind, primarily equivalent to taking up a position, and it was only by a pure fiction that reality could be made to integrate the act whereby I took up my position in regard to it. Looking back on it now, I see that I was trying to establish a concrete and dramatic type of relationship in place of the abstract relationships of inherence or of exteriority between which traditional philosophies claimed to make me choose.

Strange as it may seem, I do not think that my concern with maintaining the primacy of action has ever expressed itself, as it has with others, in a philosophy of liberty. The traditional problem of liberty has never worried me to any great extent: I have always held that man could not but have the liberty which he required, and that, consequently, there was no real problem. So that this was never the centre of my philosophical anxiety. Granted the traditional distinction between philosophies of being and philosophies of liberty, I would say that my spontaneous tendency was towards the former. Not that I was conscious of it; indeed, in so far as I still followed in the footsteps of the criticists and even of Bergson, I was inclined to regard philosophies of being as philosophies of *das Ding* and to mistrust them accordingly. My effort can be best described as an attempt to establish a concept which precludes all equation of being with *Ding* while upholding the ontological without going back to the category of substance which I regarded with profound mistrust. It was in the light of this major preoccupation that I reflected upon faith and later upon fidelity: in particular, I think that the expression in *Être et Avoir*, "being as the place of fidelity," gives the clue to my previous inquiries and at the same time heralds a new stage. The same could be said of many expressions in *Homo Viator* and especially in *Phénoménologie de l'Espérance*. Perhaps I can best explain my continual and central metaphysical preoccupation by saying that my aim was to discover how a subject, in his actual capacity as subject, is related to a reality which cannot in this context be regarded as objective, yet which is persistently required and recognised as real. Such inquiries could not be carried out without going beyond the kind of psychology which limits itself to defining attitudes without taking their bearing and concrete intention into account. This is what accounts for the convergence of the metaphysical and the religious which became apparent in my earliest writings. Perhaps I should again note the manner in which this convergence was justified from the point of view which I held as far back as my first *Journal*. What this point of view tended ultimately to exclude was the idea that the mind can, as it were, objectively define the structure of reality and then regard itself as qualified to legislate for it. My own idea was, on the contrary, that the undertaking had to be pursued within reality itself, to which the philosopher can never stand in the relationship of an on-looker to a picture. Thus my inquiry anticipated the conception of mystery as I later defined it in my paper, *On the Ontological Mystery*. This leads me to believe that the development of my thought was largely an explicitation. It all seems to me to have happened as though I only gradually succeeded in treating as material for thought what had been an immediate experience, an experience less realised than assumed, rather like the blind groping in an unchartered cave; it is only later that the prospector can understand and retrace the way travelled in this first period of discovery. Moreover, I am convinced that I can be creative as a philosopher only for so long as my experience still contains unexploited and unchartered zones. And this explains at last what I said earlier on about experience being like a promised land: it has to become, as it were, its own beyond, inasmuch as it has to transmute itself and make its own conquest. After all, the error of empiricism consists only in ignoring the part of invention and even of creative initiative involved in any genuine experience. It might also be said that its error is to take experience for granted and to ignore its mystery; whereas what is amazing and miraculous is that there should be experience at all. Does not the deepening of metaphysical knowledge consist essentially in the steps whereby experience, instead of evolving technics, turns inwards towards the realisation of itself?

◆§ *Outline of an Essay on the Position of the Ontological Mystery and the Concrete Approaches to It*

Read to the Society of Philosophical Studies at Marseilles, on January 21st, 1933.

(*A*) If we consider the present position of philosophical thought, as expressed in the depths of a consciousness which is trying to fathom its own needs, we are led, I think, to make the following observations:

(1) The traditional terms in which some people are today

still trying to state the problem of being, commonly arouse a mistrust which is hard to overcome. Its source lies not so much in the adherence, whether explicit or implicit, to Kantian or simply idealist theories, as in the fact that people's minds are soaked in the results of Bergsonian criticism. One sees this even in those minds which would not stand by Bergsonianism in its metaphysical aspects.

(2) On the other hand, the complete withdrawal from the problem of being which characterises so many contemporary philosophical systems is in the last analysis an attitude which cannot be maintained. It can either be reduced to a kind of sitting on the fence, hardly defensible and generally due to laziness or timidity: or else—and this is what generally happens—it really comes down to a more or less explicit denial of Being, which disguises the refusal of a hearing to the essential needs of our being. Ours is a being whose concrete essence is to be in every way *involved*, and therefore to find itself at grips with a fate which it must not only undergo, but must also make its own by somehow re-creating it from within. The denial of Being could not really be the empirical *demonstration* of an absence or lack. We can only make the denial because we choose to make it, and we can therefore just as well choose not to make it.

(*B*) It is also worth noticing that I who ask questions about Being do not in the first place know either *if* I am nor *a fortiori what* I am. I do not even clearly know the meaning of the question "what am I?" though I am obsessed by it. *So we see the problem of Being here encroaching upon its own data,* and being studied actually inside the subject who states it. In the process, it is denied (or transcended) as problem, and becomes metamorphosed to mystery.

(*C*) In fact, it seems very likely that there is this essential difference between a problem and a mystery. A problem is something which I meet, which I find complete before me, but which I can therefore lay siege to and reduce. But a mystery is something in which I am myself involved, and it can therefore only be thought of as *a sphere where the distinction between what is in me and what is before me loses its meaning and its initial validity.* A genuine problem is subject to an appropriate technique by the exercise of which it is defined: whereas a mystery, by definition, transcends every conceivable technique. It is, no doubt, always possible (logically and psychologically) to degrade a mystery so as to turn it into a problem. But this is a fundamentally vicious proceeding, whose springs might perhaps be discovered in a kind of corruption of the intelligence. The problem of evil, as the philosophers have called it, supplies us with a particularly instructive example of this degradation.

(*D*) Just because it is of the essence of mystery to be recognised or capable of recognition, it may also be ignored and actively denied. It then becomes reduced to something I have "heard talked about," but which I refuse as only being *for other people;* and that in virtue of an illusion which these "others" are deceived by, but which I myself claim to have detected.

We must carefully avoid all confusion between the mysterious and the unknowable. The unknowable is in fact only the limiting case of the problematic, which cannot be actualised without contradiction. The recognition of mystery, on the contrary, is an essentially positive act of the mind, the supremely positive act in virtue of which all positivity may perhaps be strictly defined. In this sphere everything seems to go on as if I found myself acting on an intuition which I possess without immediately knowing myself to possess it—an intuition which cannot be, strictly speaking, self-conscious and which can grasp itself only through the modes of experience in which its image is reflected, and which it lights up by being thus reflected in them. The essential metaphysical step would then consist in a reflection upon this reflection (in a reflection "squared"). By means of this, thought *stretches out* towards the recovery of an intuition which otherwise loses itself in proportion as it is exercised.

Recollection, the actual possibility of which may be regarded as the most revealing ontological index we possess, is the real place in whose centre this recovery can be made.

(*E*) The "problem of being," then, will only be the translation into inadequate language of a mystery which cannot be given except to a creature capable of recollection—a creature whose central characteristic is perhaps that he is not simply identical with his own life. We can find the proof or confirmation of this non-identity in the fact that I more or less explicitly evaluate my life. It is in my power not only to condemn it by an abstract verdict, but to set an effective term to it. If I cannot set an effective term to my life considered in its ultimate depths, which may escape from my grasp, I at least have power over the finite and material expression to which *I am at liberty to believe* that this life is reduced. The fact that suicide is possible is, in this sense, an essential point of reference for all genuine metaphysical thought. And not only suicide: despair *in all its forms,* betrayal *in all its aspects,* in so far as they appear to us as active denials of being, and in so far as the soul which despairs shuts itself up against the central and mysterious assurance in which we believe we have found the principle of all positivity.

(*F*) It is not enough to say that we live in a world where betrayal is possible *at every moment, in every degree,* and in every form. It seems that the very constitution of our world recommends us, if it does not force us, to betrayal. The spectacle of death as exhibited by the world can, from one point of view, be regarded as a perpetual provocation to denial and to absolute desertion. It could also be added that space and time, regarded as paired modes of absence, tend, by throwing us back upon ourselves, to drive us into the beggarly instantaneity of pleasure. But it seems that at the same time, and correlatively, it is of the essence of despair, of betrayal, and even of death itself, that they can be refused and denied. If the word transcendence has a meaning, it means just this denial; or more exactly, this overpassing. (*Überwindung* rather than *Aufhebung.*) For the essence of the world is perhaps betrayal, or, more accurately, there is not a single thing in the world about which we can be certain that its spell could hold against the attacks of a fearless critical reflection.

(*G*) If this is so, the concrete approaches to the ontological mystery should not be sought in the scale of logical thought, the objective reference of which gives rise to a prior question. They should rather be sought in the elucidation of certain data which are spiritual in their own right, such as fidelity, hope and love, where we may see man at grips with the temptations of denial, introversion, and hard-heartedness. Here the pure metaphysician has no power to decide whether the principle of these temptations lies in man's very nature, in the intrinsic and invariable characteristics of that nature, or whether it lies rather in the corruption of that same nature as the result of a catastrophe which gave birth to history and was not merely an incident in history.

Perhaps on the ontological level it is fidelity which matters most. It is in fact the recognition—not a theoretical or verbal, but an actual recognition—of an ontological permanency; a permanency which endures and by reference to which we endure, a permanency which implies or demands a history, unlike the inert or formal permanency of a pure *validity,* a law for example. It is the perpetuation of a witness which could at any moment be wiped out or denied. It is an attestation which is creative as well as perpetual, and more creative in proportion as the ontological worth of what it attests is more outstanding.

(*H*) An ontology with this orientation is plainly open to a revelation, which, however, it could not of course either demand or presuppose or absorb, or even absolutely speaking understand, but the acceptance of which it can in some degree prepare for. To tell the truth, this ontology *may* only be capable of development *in fact* on a ground previously prepared by revelation. But on reflection we can see that there is nothing to surprise us, still less to scandalise us, in this. A metaphysic can only grow up within a certain situation which stimulates it. And in the situation which is ours, the existence of a Christian datum is an essential factor. It surely behoves us to renounce, once for all, the naively rationalist idea that you can have a system of affirmation valid for thought *in general*, or for *any consciousness whatsoever*. Such thought as this is the subject of scientific knowledge, a subject which is an idea but nothing else. Whereas the ontological order can only be recognised personally by the whole of a being, involved in a drama which is his own, though it overflows him infinitely in all directions—a being to whom the strange power has been imparted of asserting or denying himself. He asserts himself in so far as he asserts Being and opens himself to it: or he denies himself by denying Being and thereby closing himself to It. In this dilemma lies the very essence of his freedom.

☙ *Sketch of a Phenomenology and a Metaphysic of Hope* [1]

TO HENRI POURRAT

In a study such as the one I am here undertaking there can be no question of starting from a particular definition and endeavouring to explain its content progressively. I propose rather to appeal to a special experience which it must be supposed you have. This experience, which is that of "I hope . . . ," must, like the fundamental experience of faith, "I believe . . . ," be purified; or, more exactly, we must pass

1. Lecture given to the *Scolasticat de Fourvière* in February, 1942.

from this experience in its diluted or diffused state to the same experience, touched—I do not say absolutely conceived—at its highest tension or again at its point of complete saturation.

You must not therefore be surprised to find me starting from an "I hope" of a very low order which will constitute a negative point of departure.

"I hope that James will arrive in time for lunch to-morrow and not just in the afternoon." This, of course, means that I hope so because I should like to have James with me for as long as possible; *and* I have reason to think that what I want will come about: I know that he does not intend to return to his office and could therefore catch an early train, etc.

We can already detect two elements here which are always found together: there is a wish and a certain belief. I am, however, right in calling this a diluted condition, because in such a case I am near to what we can term the point of indifference. After all, it is not very important if James only arrives at five o'clock; there is nothing there for me to *take to heart*—notice this expression which we shall need to remember. Moreover, I observe that the reasons for hoping are here exterior to myself, they are outside my being, far from having their roots in the very depths of what I am. In reality it is merely a calculation concerning certain chances I am considering, a practical little problem of probabilities. Moreover, if I find James boring or his visit is inconvenient, I might quite easily say: "I am afraid he will arrive in time for lunch."

Now let us suppose, on the contrary, that I am going through a time of trial, either in my private affairs or in those of the group to which I belong. I long for some deliverance which would bring the trial to an end. The "I hope" in all its strength is directed towards salvation. It really is a matter of my coming out of a darkness in which I am at present plunged, and which may be the darkness of illness, of separation, exile or slavery. It is obviously impossible in such cases to separate the "I hope" from a certain type of situation of which it is really a part. Hope is situated within the framework of the trial, not only corresponding to it, but constituting our being's veritable *response*. I have used the metaphorical term of darkness, but this metaphor has nothing accidental about it. It is, indeed, true that throughout a trial of the kind I have in mind, I find I am deprived for an indefinite period of a certain light for which I long. In fact, I should say that every trial of this order can be considered as a form of captivity.

Let us try to get a closer view of the meaning of the word captivity, or rather let us examine the characteristics of any state which can be described as "being a captive or prisoner." A special kind of endurance is, of course, involved, but what are the conditions under which endurance becomes part of the experience of captivity? Here we must emphasise the part played by duration. I should consider myself a captive if I found myself not merely precipitated into, but as it were pledged by external constraint to a compulsory mode of existence involving restrictions of every kind touching my personal actions. In addition, that which characterises all the situations we are evoking at the moment, is that they invariably imply the impossibility, not necessarily of moving or even of acting in a manner which is relatively free, but *of rising to a certain fullness of life, which may be in the realms of sensation or even of thought in the strict sense of the word.* It is quite clear, for instance, that the artist or the writer who suffers from a prolonged sterility has literally a sense of being in prison, or, if you prefer, in exile, as though he had really been taken out of the light in which he normally has his being. We can, therefore, say that all captivity partakes of the nature of alienation. It may be in reality that, in tearing me out of myself, it gives me an opportunity of realising far more acutely than I should have done without it, the nature of that lost integrity which I now long to regain. This is illustrated in the case of the invalid for whom the word health arouses a wealth of associations generally unsuspected by those who are well. Yet, at the same time, we must determine not only what is positive but what is illusory in this idea of health which the sick man cherishes. A similar problem is presented when the beloved being whose disappearance I deplore seems to me more real and distinct now he is no longer with me than when I was able to enjoy a mutual and direct relationship with him.

I will not elaborate the details of the discussion which would take us away from our subject. I will merely remark that this method of reasoning does not seem to open the way for hope to us: quite on the contrary it is likely to land us in an anguish whence there is no escape, to make us prisoners of an experience which tears our hearts, where *fact* and *memory* are endlessly opposed and, far from merging together, are bound to contradict each other unrelentingly. All that we can say is that this form of reasoning brings into stronger relief the fundamental situation to which it is hope's mission to reply as to a signal of distress. But, it may be objected, are not some situations, where the tragic element seems to be absent, of such a nature as nevertheless to encourage or even to invite the exercise of hope? The woman who is expecting a baby, for instance, is literally inhabited by hope. It seems to me, however, that such examples, and I would even include that of the adolescent who anxiously awaits the coming of love, only seem to confirm what was said above. As a matter of fact, the soul always turns towards a light which it does not yet perceive, a light yet to be born, in the hope of being delivered from its present darkness, the darkness of waiting, a darkness which cannot be prolonged without dragging it in some way towards an organic dissolution. And might we not say in passing that it is from this point of view that such peculiarities as the aberrations frequent in adolescents and expectant mothers are to be explained?

In reality, we should probably go a step further in this direction and, interpreting the phenomena somewhat differently from Plato and the leaders of traditional spiritualism, recognise that there is quite a general aspect under which human existence appears as a captivity and that, precisely when it takes on this form, it becomes so to speak subject to hope. It would actually be easy to show, and as we proceed we shall probably realise more fully, that there is also an ever-present possibility of degrading this same existence to a state in which it would gradually lose all capacity for hope. By a paradox which need surprise only the very superficial thinker, *the less life is experienced as a captivity the less the soul will be able to see the shining of that veiled, mysterious light,* which, we feel sure without any analysis, illumines the very centre of hope's dwelling-place. It is incontestable, for instance, that free-thought impregnated with naturalism, however it may struggle, alas with increasing success, to obliterate certain great contrasts and to flood the world with the harsh light of the lecture hall, however it may at the same time advertise what I have elsewhere styled the category of the *perfectly natural*—it is, I repeat, incontestable that such a dogmatically standardised free-thought eventually runs the risk of depriving souls of the very rudiments of secular hope.

But with what kind of hope are we really concerned? What exactly is its object?

It seems very important to me to stress here, in connection with what I have just said about existence in general being a captivity, that hope, by a *nisus* which is peculiar to it, tends inevitably to transcend the particular objects to which it at first seems to be attached. Later on we shall have to recognise clearly the metaphysical implications of this remark. But even now it is possible to appreciate the distinction in tone between "I hope . . .," the absolute statement, and "I hope that . . .". This distinction clearly runs parallel to that which obtains in all religious philosophy and which opposes "I believe" to "I believe that."

The philosopher must also consider another point of an equally decisive nature. It bears on the fundamental characteristics of the subject in "I hope . . .". This subject is indeed in no way identical with the "I myself . . .", who is nevertheless present, or at any rate is likely to come to the surface whenever there is a question not of hope but of certainty or even doubt. Here I must refer back to a group of ideas which I worked out a little while ago on the subject of the *Ego and Its Relation to Others*. The *ego*, I said, very often, in fact almost invariably, needs to refer to some other person felt or conceived of as an opponent or a witness, or again merely summoned or imagined as an echo or a rectifier. "You have your doubts, because you are ill-informed or because you lack inner stability, or for any other reason; as for me, I am sure—and (be it understood) I am proud of the fact." Or, on the contrary, "You are quite sure of this because you are simple, or badly informed, or for any other reason; as for me, on the other hand, I have a more critical sense than you, therefore I am in doubt."

Naturally, I do not mean that *I am sure* or *I doubt* inevitably implies a position accentuated in this way; but what is certain is that the underlying meaning which animates the *I am sure* or *I doubt* is not really distorted, it does not lose its actual nature through such an accentuation. The case is quite different with *I hope*. Here there is not, and there cannot be the note of defiance or of provocation which, on the contrary, so easily becomes essential to *I doubt* and *I am sure*. What is the cause of this difference? It is surely due to the fact that "I hope" is not orientated in the same way: there is no statement directed towards, and at the same time against, some other person either present or imagined. Of course there is nothing to prevent me from saying in certain cases, "For my part, I hope, whilst you do not." But there would be none of that suggestion of aggressive self-complacency which, on the contrary, so often characterises "I am sure" or "I doubt."

This will be elucidated, I think, if we take the trouble to

examine the difference between hope and optimism. It is a difference which may seem to be more of a musical than a logical order and which accordingly is easy enough to misunderstand. Its importance, however, should not be overlooked.

The optimist is he who has a firm conviction, or in certain cases just a vague feeling, that things tend to "turn out for the best." This may concern some definite situation, some precise difficulty: it may have to do with difficulties, conflict and contradictions in general. It goes without saying that optimism can take very different forms. There is a purely sentimental optimism and an optimism with pretensions to reason (which to tell the truth is perhaps merely a camouflaged sentimentality). There are some kinds of optimism which maintain that they are based on practical experience; others, on the contrary, claim to rest on metaphysical or even religious arguments. I am inclined to think, however, that these differences are far less weighty than one might be tempted to believe at first. It is by no means certain that optimism does not always indicate the same disposition, the same *habitus*. Perhaps such a thing as deep optimism does not exist. The metaphysics of Leibnitz are deep, no doubt, but not in so far as they are optimistic, in so far as they are presented as a theodicy. When we come down to a final analysis, the optimist, as such, always relies upon an experience which is not drawn from the most intimate and living part of himself, but, on the contrary, is *considered from a sufficient distance* to allow certain contradictions to become alternated or fused into a general harmony. The optimist does not hesitate to extrapolate the conclusions which we are led to if only we are willing to "consider things" thoroughly, from a sufficient distance and over a wide enough stretch. "It always comes out right in the end . . ."; "We shall be bound to see . . ."; "If only we don't allow ourselves to stop too soon . . ." such are the formulæ which constantly recur in the speeches of optimists. Notice that the word "speeches" is important here. The optimist is essentially a maker of speeches. There is in the natural and favourably directed development to which he so complacently clings something which readily lends itself to oratorical sequences and written expression. In parentheses we note that there is a pessimism which is the exact counterpart of such optimism. It is oratorical in the same way, and there is no fundamental distinction between them. They are like the inside and outside of the same garment.

To go on from what has already been stated, we should say that this optimism (or, for the matter of that, this pessimism which does not really differ from it) remains strictly in the province of the "I myself." The optimist introduces himself indeed as a spectator with particularly keen sight. "If your vision is as good as mine, you are bound to see . . ."; "As your eyes are not as perfect as mine, do not hesitate to trust to my testimony and to my clear-sightedness. . . ." To be sure, the fact must be recognised that in the case of a given individual (seen in concrete reality and not through the writings of a theorist, be he economist or metaphysician), optimism cannot always be separated from an indistinct faith which cannot be shared by the spectator as such: but what is important for us here is optimism in its essence, that is to say precisely in so far as it does not include the intervention of faith, or even the direct participation, the engagement, which comes into being as soon as life is regarded as something other than purely external. But we have already seen, and we recognise more and more clearly, that he who hopes, inasmuch as his hope is real and not to be reduced to a mere platonic wish, seems to himself to be involved in some kind of a process; and it is only from this point of view that it is possible to realise what is specific, and, I should add super-rational, perhaps also super-relational, in hope. For, to use once again the expression I have so often employed, hope is a mystery and not a problem. We might point out from the same point of view that hope is very difficult to describe. Indeed, when I try to represent it to myself I am almost inevitably led to alter its true nature and to consider it as presumption. It is thus that we come to substitute "to flatter myself" for "to hope." But in reality if we succeed in learning its meaning more accurately or, which comes to the same thing, in imagining vividly enough what hoping amounts to in one of the situations described further back, we shall recognise that "I hope" cannot ever be taken to imply: "I am in on the secret, I know the purpose of God or of the gods, whilst you are a profane outsider; and moreover it is because I have the benefit of special enlightenment that I say what I do." Such an interpretation is as unfair and inaccurate as it is possible to be, it does not take into account all that there is of humility, of timidity, of *chastity* in the true character of hope. The difficult task of the philosopher is precisely to react strongly against such an interpretation, and at the same time to understand why it is so difficult to avoid making it. How can we fail to see that humility, modesty or chastity, by their essence, can never consent to be defined, that is to say they will never deliver their secret to the mercy of rationalistic investigation? Hence the fundamental insufficiency, the clumsy inadequacy of the interpretations we generally have to fall back upon in seeking to understand what I term the mystery of hope. For instance, adopting the realistic point of view, people are ready enough to say, "Does not the hope of the invalid, the prisoner or the exile boil down in the end to a sort of organic refusal to accept an intolerable situation as final? The amount of vitality which the individual retains can be measured by this refusal, and do we not find that, if he has been worn down to a certain point of exhaustion, he will become incapable of exercising the hope which supported him in the first stages of his trial?"

It must be acknowledged that the notion of vitality here referred to is vague enough in itself. But what is extremely characteristic is the tendency of the argument to belittle hope: "Let us have no illusions, hope is not anything but . . ., etc." In this way its specific nature is disputed. It is a matter for reflection to discover the origin of this anxiety to depreciate. We shall return to this point further on. But at the same time it is to be noted that without any doubt the soul can be in a state of drowsiness which tends to paralyse every kind of reaction; it is quite clear, for instance, that cold or hunger can reduce me to a state in which I cannot concentrate my attention on any idea, or *a fortiori* use my powers of reflection; it would be no less absurd to draw materialistic conclusions from this as to the nature of attention or thought. As it happens, experience seems to establish that hope is able to survive an almost total ruin of the organism; if then it is vitality in some sense, it is very difficult to determine what that sense is, for it has nothing in common with the meaning we attribute to the word in speaking of the vitality of a healthy body. At any rate, the principle must be laid down that any physical theory of hope is absurd and, according to all appearances, contradictory; perhaps we might be justified in maintaining that hope coincides with the spiritual principle itself. Thus we must be careful not to think that we can understand it by psychological suppositions; these as a matter of fact are always imagined *a posteriori*, to explain something which is an abiding mystery by its nature. To convince ourselves of this it is enough to observe that we are quite unable to tell before an ordeal what that ordeal will do to us and what resources we shall find we possess with which to face it.

The truth is that there can strictly speaking be no hope except when the temptation to despair exists. Hope is the act by which this temptation is actively or victoriously overcome. The victory may not invariably involve any sense of effort: I should even be quite ready to go so far as to say that such a feeling is not compatible with hope in its purest form.

What then does it mean to despair? We will not stop short here with symptoms and signs. What is the essence of the act of despair? It seems as though it were always capitulation before a certain *fatum* laid down by our judgment. But the difference between capitulation and non-capitulation, though certain, is hard to define. Let us suppose that I develop some incurable illness and that my condition shows no improvement. It may be that I say of myself, "I cannot be cured," or that it is the doctors who tell me, with or without tact, that there is no possible prospect of my recovery (they are, for instance, warning me in order to spare me from disappointments which would wear me out to no purpose). In the first case it seems as though I decide and defy any real or possible contradictions. "You, who claim to know something about it, say that I can get better; but I myself, who know how I feel and who have inner experience of all my symptoms, I tell you that you are mistaken and that I cannot recover." In this way, I pronounce my own sentence, and at the same time my relations and my doctor will no doubt feel that I have made conditions as unfavourable as possible for my constitution to put up an effective resistance. Is there not now every chance that, discouraged by this sentence, it will feel obliged to confirm it? So it comes about that, far from merely foreseeing my own destiny, I shall really have precipitated it. Strangely enough, things may very well happen quite differently in the second case we are considering. It may be that the verdict communicated to me, coming from outside, will arouse in me not merely the strength to deny it, but to prove it to be wrong in fact. At least we can say that in this second case I do not appear in principle to be furthering my non-recovery, unless I ratify and thus make my own the sentence which has been communicated to me. But it remains true that a certain margin is left me, a certain possibility of contradiction, precisely because it was someone else and not I who declared my recovery to be impossible.

However, it is still necessary here to distinguish between two inner attitudes which are very different and which help to decide the event itself. To capitulate, in the strongest sense of the word, is not only, perhaps is not at all, to accept the given sentence or even to recognise the inevitable as such, it is to go to pieces under this sentence, to disarm before the inevitable. It is at bottom to renounce the idea of remaining oneself, it is to be fascinated by the idea of one's own destruction to the point of anticipating this very destruction itself. To accept, on the contrary, can mean to hold on and to keep a firm hold of oneself, that is to say to safeguard one's integrity. Because I am condemned never to recover from this illness, or not to come out of this prison I do not mean to give up, I do not consent, from this very moment, to be the useless creature which my illness or my captivity may finally make of me; I will counter the fascination which the idea of this creature might have for me with the firm determination to remain what I am. It may thus come about that by accepting an inevitable destiny which I refuse with all my strength to anticipate, I will find a way of inward consolidation, of proving my reality to myself, and at the same time I shall rise infinitely above this *fatum* to which I have never allowed myself to shut my eyes. Herein without any doubt lies the power and greatness of stoicism, but, at the same time, it must be recognised that the stoic is always imprisoned within himself. He strengthens himself, no doubt, but he does not radiate. I would go as far as to say that he affords us the highest expression, the greatest degree of sublimation of the "I myself." He bears himself—and that means that above all he controls his interior life—as though he had no neighbours, as though he were concerned only with himself and had no responsibility towards anyone else.

It is obvious that in hope there is something which goes infinitely further than acceptance, or one might say more exactly that it is a non-acceptance, but positive and hence distinguishable from revolt. Non-acceptance can indeed be a mere stiffening or contraction. When it is this it is powerless and can be, in the same way as its opposite, abdication, a manner of working out one's own defeat, of relinquishing control. The important question for us is to know how it can take on the positive character. How, if I do not accept can I avoid tightening myself up, and, instead, relax in my very non-acceptance? We might compare this with the supple movements of the swimmer or the practised skier. But our difficulty is that it is very hard to conceive how there can be a suppleness and grace in something which, on the face of it, appears to be negation. We can begin to see the solution of this strange problem by reflecting that tightening up or stiffening, on whatever physical or spiritual level we may be considering it, always suggests the presence of the same physical factor, which, if not exactly fear, is at any rate of the same order, a concentration of the self on the self, the essence of which is probably a certain impatience. If we introduce the element of patience into non-acceptance we at once come very much nearer to hope. It seems then that there exists a secret and rarely discovered connection between the way in which the *ego* is either centred or not centred in itself, and its reaction to the duration of time, or more precisely to the temporal order, that is to say to the fact that change is possible in reality. A simple expression borrowed from everyday language is a help here: *to take one's time*. He who stiffens and rebels does not know how to take his time. What exactly do these words, so foreign to the vocabulary of technical philosophy, mean? "Take your time," an examiner would say, for example, to a flurried candidate. That means, do not force the personal rhythm, the proper cadence of your reflection, or even of your memory, for if you do you will spoil your chances, you will be likely to say at random the first words which come into your head. It may seem that we have wandered very far from hope in the strict sense of the word. I do not think so, and this is how I am going to try to explain the analogy, or more exactly, perhaps, the secret affinity between hope and relaxation. Does not he who hopes, and, as we have seen, has to contend with a certain trial comparable to a form of captivity, tend to treat this trial and to proceed in regard to it as he who is patient towards himself treats his inexperienced young *ego*, the *ego* which needs educating and controlling? Above all he never lets it contract but, on the other hand, he does not allow it to kick over the traces or take control prematurely or unwarrantably. From this point of view, hope means first accepting the trial as an integral part of the self, but while so doing it considers it as destined to be absorbed and transmuted by the inner workings of a certain creative process.

Further back I spoke of patience with oneself; perhaps it is still more instructive now to consider patience with others. This most certainly consists in never hustling or being rough with another person, more exactly, in never trying to substitute our own rhythm for his by violence. Neither should the other person be treated as though he lacked an autonomous rhythm, and could accordingly be forced or bent to suit us. Let us say positively this time that it consists in placing our confidence in a certain process of growth and development. To give one's confidence does not merely mean that one makes an act of theoretical acceptance with no idea of intervention, for that would, in fact, be to abandon the other purely and simply to himself. No, to have confidence here seems to mean to embrace this process, in a sense, so that we promote it from within. Patience seems, then, to suggest a certain temporal pluralism, a certain pluralisation of the self in time. It is radically opposed to the act by which I despair of the other person, declaring that he is good for nothing, or that he will never understand anything, or that he is incurable. That is, of course, the same despair which makes me proclaim that I shall never be cured, that I shall never see the end of my captivity, etc. It seems, strangely enough, that, in hoping, I develop in connection with the event, and perhaps above all through what it makes of me, a type of relationship, a kind of intimacy comparable to that which I have with the other person when I am patient with him. Perhaps we might go so far as to speak here of a certain *domesticating* of circumstances, which might otherwise, if we allowed them to get the better of us, frighten us into accepting them as a *fatum*. If we look no further than its etymological meaning, patience appears to be just a simple letting things alone, or allowing them to take their course, but if we take the analysis a little further we find that such non-interference is of a higher order than indifference and implies a subtle respect for the other person's need of time to preserve his vital rhythm, so that it tends to exercise a transforming influence upon him which is comparable to that which sometimes rewards love. It should moreover be shown how here and there pure causality is utterly left behind. Of course patience can easily be degraded; it can become mere weakness, or mere complacency, precisely in so far as it betrays the principle of charity which should animate it. But can it be overlooked that hope likewise is liable to degradations of the same order, when, for instance, it is found in the mere spectator who, without being in the least involved in the game or race at which he is present, hopes that one or other of the competitors will succeed, and at the same time, in a confused sort of way, congratulates himself that he is running no risk and has no direct part to play in the struggle.

To tell the truth, I have no doubt that the comparison I

have suggested will appear paradoxical and absurd. In the case of patience there is question of a being, but here we are not dealing with a being but a situation which in its essence has nothing personal about it. On reflection, however, the gap tends to narrow, perhaps because I can hope or not hope in the being of whom I am in a sense in charge, and we shall have to ask ourselves if "I place my hope in you" is not really the most authentic form of "I hope." But it is not everything; the trial affects me, it attacks my being so that I am likely to be permanently altered by it. Thus there is a risk that illness will make of me that deformed creature, a catalogued and professionalised invalid, who thinks of himself as such and contracts in all respects the *habitus* of illness. It is the same with captivity or exile, etc., and, I should say, with every sort of misfortune. In so far as I hope, I detach myself from this inner determinism which is rather like a cramp, threatening, when the trial is upon me, to change me into one of those degraded, abnormal, and in the end perhaps hypnotised expressions of human personality produced by despair, because it is above all things a fascination.

We come here, I think, to one of the vital centres of our subject. But immediately an objection presents itself which must be squarely faced. It does not seem possible to consider hope purely and simply as an inner action of defence by which I should be able to safeguard my integrity when it is threatened by an obsession: or more exactly, it is not the actual safeguard which we are aiming at; if this is secured by hope, it can only be indirectly. Everything goes to show that hope does not bear upon what is in me, upon the region of my interior life, but much more on what arises independently of my possible action, and particularly of my action on myself: I hope—for the return of someone who is absent, for the defeat of the enemy, for peace, which will give back to my country the liberties of which disaster has robbed it. If it is permissible to say, as I already implied above, that hope has the power of making things fluid, it remains to be seen exactly how and upon what this power is exercised.

Let us again this time make use of an example. For a long time a father has been without news of his son. The boy had gone on a mission to a distant country, telling his relations not to worry if he did not write for some time, but his silence is unduly prolonged and gives rise to the worst fears. Yet the father persists in hoping. Each day he awaits the letter which would bring his anxiety to an end. To despair would be to say, "I have been disappointed so many times there is every reason to expect that I shall be again to-day"; it would be to declare this wound incurable, this wound which not only is inflicted by separation but which *is* separation. "I shall never again be anything but the wounded, mutilated creature I am to-day. Death alone can end my trouble; and it will only do so by ending me myself. That is all destiny is able to do for me—destiny, that strange doctor which can only cure the disease by killing the sufferer." The despairing man not only contemplates and sets before himself the dismal repetition, the eternalisation of a situation in which he is caught like a ship in a sea of ice. By a paradox which is difficult to conceive, he anticipates this repetition. He sees it at the moment, and simultaneously he has the bitter certainty that this anticipation will not spare him from living through the same trial day by day until the extinction which, to tell the truth, he anticipates likewise, not seeing it as a remedy but as a supreme outrage to the departed for whom his mourning does at least ensure the shadow of survival. Despair here appears as an enchantment, or more exactly as a kind of witchcraft, whose evil action has a bearing on all which goes to form the very substance of a person's life.

Let us be still more precise. Each instant, my impressions, in the very general sense which Hume gives this word, stand out against a certain "background" in which reflection alone is able to discern, somewhat imperfectly perhaps, what belongs to the past or the future or what is only a horizon of floating possibilities. Contrary to what one is often tempted to admit, it is not true to argue that this "background" contrasts with given facts, as though it were merely imagined; it is also "given" in another form, that for instance in which we anticipate the future, and rejoice, grow sad or worry about a certain prospect. It is precisely because we place ourselves unwarrantably on the "ground of facts" that we are led to formulate the principle that the future is not given—and can therefore only be imagined. It would be much nearer the truth to say that in anticipating I receive, I pocket in advance, I take a certain advance percentage, on a given fact which is to come, and is quite literally credited to me. Actually it does not greatly matter here if these advances are different from the rest which we shall effectively realise one day. What I just called the substance of life can now be separated from the act, almost impossible to describe, by which I am aware of this substance at a given moment as one is aware of the quality of a wine or the water of a precious stone. Reflective analysis will no doubt here suggest the idea of a relationship between the immediate, the anticipated and also the remembered which we might say backs the operation. If we kept to the idea of this relationship we should easily come to speak of a triangulation which each of us is making at every moment of his existence. That, however, would only be a very imperfect approximation, for by this triangulation I could never determine anything but my position at a given moment. Now, the appreciation which is here under discussion is something quite different from a simple registration, indeed it tends at each moment to convert itself into a global judgment, valid *ubique et semper* and thereby infinitely transcending everything which is limited to the *hic et nunc*.

The truth is that it is impossible to rest satisfied here with an interpretation expressed in terms of relationships. An amateur psychologist, whose name I have unfortunately forgotten, brought out in a paper, which I believe is still unpublished, the importance of what he very aptly called "*L'entrain à la vie* (enthusiasm for living)." The appreciation, or *a fortiori* the triangulation, of which I mentioned the possibility just now, is in reality nothing but the intellectualised and inadequate expression of that which is dynamically known to us as enthusiasm or ardour for life. This term of ardour, unphilosophical as it may be, has the merit of retaining and as it were incarnating a metaphor which we cannot reduce to abstract terms without thereby condemning ourselves to miss the essential and inescapable connection which exists between life and a flame. In passing, how can we help noticing like Dr. Minkowski, that certain metaphors furnish us with settings for the human experience "to exist" to such a point that we have the right to regard them as veritable concrete categories. It is on this flame, which is life, that the malevolent action of despair is exercised. We might say to put it in another way that ardour renders soluble or volatile what without it would at every moment tend to prevent existence. It is turned towards a certain matter in the personal *becoming* which it is its function to consume. Where, however, "the evil spell" exists, this flame turns away from the matter which is its natural food, to devour itself. This is what we express admirably when we say of a being "he preys on himself." [2] From this point of view, despair can be compared to a certain spiritual autophagy. We must notice here, and keep in mind

2. *"Il se consume."*

for all that follows, the part played by the *self*, that action which consists not only of reflecting but of making the self the centre.

Do these indications throw any light on our problem? In the example we were considering—that of the son of whom there is no news—it is clear that the disappointing fact, the arrival of the postman who does not bring the longed-for letter, illustrates what I was speaking of as something to be consumed or dissolved. The term of liquefaction expresses the same process. But we must not forget the criticism to which we have previously subjected the confused notion of vitality. We might say that a natural optimism exists, which reflects before everything else the perfect functioning of the organism, but which may also correspond to a thoroughly egoistical desire to husband one's forces, to save oneself useless anxiety for as long as possible; it goes without saying that this natural optimism is not to be confused any more than theoretical optimism with hope. The latter appears to us as inspired by love, or perhaps more exactly by a combination of scenes which this love conjures up and irradiates. But an objection at once arises which we must now face squarely and which seems likely to ruin any metaphysical theory of hope.

The objection consists of questioning the value of the belief implied in hope. If I wish ardently for a certain thing, it will be said, I shall represent it to myself very distinctly, I shall realise it in my imagination and immediately, by the same process, I shall believe it is actually going to happen. If this be so, must we not admit that hope implies an illusion of which critical reflection at once exposes the mechanism? This is exactly the illusion which makes us take our wishes for realities—our wishes or our fears: the mechanism is obviously the same in both cases.

We must now ask ourselves under what conditions it is possible to save hope, that is to say to recognise a value in it which such criticism cannot diminish, pertinent as it may be in a great number of particular cases.

It is here no doubt that we must remember the distinction made above between "to hope" and "to hope that." The more hope tends to reduce itself to a matter of dwelling on, or of becoming hypnotised over, something one has represented to oneself, the more the objection we have just formulated will be irrefutable. On the contrary, the more hope transcends imagination, so that I do not allow myself to imagine what I hope for, the more this objection seems to disappear.

It might, however, be asked whether that is not just an evasion. Indeed, from the very moment that I am called upon to endure some trial such as illness or exile, what all my wishes are bent upon is my liberation. I may represent more or less precisely the exact way in which it will happen, but in any case I realise it intensely, and by that very fact I tend to believe in it: it seems then that the psychological mechanism functions in the same way even where my consciousness is not hypnotised by a certain precise image.

But it must be answered that in reasoning thus we arbitrarily simplify an interior situation which includes, as has been expressly stated, the essential element of temptation to despair. The stifling conditions which surround and as it were hedge us in, tend to appear unchangeable to us. We feel that there is no reason to suppose that a *miracle* will transform them into conformity with our desires. Notice that here another psychological mechanism is working in a precisely opposite direction from that which was shown to bring about the illusion exposed at the heart of hope. It must then be recognised that, in the situation and trials we have in mind, consciousness has to contend with two mechanisms which tend to work in opposite directions and this observation, coming at the end of what we have already noticed, leads us to recognise the secret connection between hope and liberty. Both take for granted the overruling action of the judgment.

Let us, for example, consider the example of the invalid; it is obvious that he has set his mind upon recovering by the end of a definite period; he is likely to despair if he is not cured at the appointed time. Here it would be the special function of the judgment to suggest that even if the time has passed without the expected recovery taking place, there is, all the same, plenty of room for hope. Here hope appears to be bound up with the use of a method of surmounting, by which thought rises above the imaginings and formulations upon which it had at first been tempted to depend. But, in this example, it depends no doubt on more than a question of dates. The very idea of recovery is capable, at any rate in a certain spiritual register, of being purified and transformed. "Everything is lost for me if I do not get well," the invalid is at first tempted to exclaim, naïvely identifying recovery with salvation. From the moment when he will have not only recognised in an abstract manner, but understood in the depths of his being, that is to say *seen*, that everything is not necessarily lost if there is no cure, it is more than likely that his inner attitude towards recovery or non-recovery will be radically changed; he will have regained the liberty, the faculty of relaxing to which we referred at length further back.

It really seems to be from this point of view that the distinction between believer and unbeliever stands out in its true meaning. The believer is he who will meet with no insurmountable obstacle on his way towards transcendence. Let us say again, to fix the meaning of the word obstacle more precisely, that in so far as I make my hope conditional I myself put up limits to the process by which I could triumph over all successive disappointments. Still more, I give a part of myself over to anguish; indeed I own implicitly that if my expectations are not fulfilled in some particular point, I shall have no possibility of escaping from the despair into which I must inevitably sink. We can, on the other hand, conceive, at least theoretically, of the inner disposition of one who, setting no condition or limit and abandoning himself in absolute confidence, would thus transcend all possible disappointment and would experience a security of his being, or in his being, which is contrary to the radical insecurity of *Having*.

This is what determines the ontological position of hope—absolute hope, inseparable from a faith which is likewise absolute, transcending all laying down of conditions, and for this very reason every kind of representation whatever it might be. The only possible source from which this absolute hope springs must once more be stressed. It appears as a response of the creature to the infinite Being to whom it is conscious of owing everything that it has and upon whom it cannot impose any condition whatsoever without scandal. From the moment that I abase myself in some sense before the absolute Thou who in his infinite condescension has brought me forth out of nothingness, it seems as though I forbid myself ever again to despair, or, more exactly, that I implicitly accept the possibility of despair as an indication of treason, so that I could not give way to it without pronouncing my own condemnation. Indeed, seen in this perspective, what is the meaning of despair if not a declaration that God has withdrawn himself from me? In addition to the fact that such an accusation is incompatible with the nature of the absolute Thou, it is to be observed that in advancing it I am unwarrantably attributing to myself a distinct reality which I do not possess.

It would however be vain to try to hide the difficulties, from the human point of view, of this position of which no one would dream of contesting the metaphysical and religious purity. Does not this invincible hope arise from the ruins of all human and limited hopes? Must not the true believer be ready to accept the death and ruin of his dear ones, the temporal destruction of his country, as possibilities against which it is forbidden to rebel? To go further: if these things come about, must he not be ready to adore the divine will in them? We cannot be enough on our guard against the softening processes to which some people have recourse in order to reassure those whose faith might fail in the presence of such terrible happenings. I have in mind particularly the allegations of those who claim to calm us by observing that God, being infinitely good, cannot tempt us beyond our strength by driving us to despair which he has actually forbidden us. I am afraid that these are no more than verbal tricks; we know neither the real extent of our powers nor the ultimate designs of God; and, if the arguments were really possible to accept, it would in the long run amount to an implicit and as it were hypocritical way of laying down conditions which would bring hope once more within the limits of the relative. But then must it not be agreed that the absolute hope to which we are invited tends to become identified with despair itself —with a despair however which it is no longer even permitted for us to indulge in, and which is perhaps no more than an infinite apathy?

On the other hand, it is to be wondered whether, in claiming to establish himself beyond the reach of any possible disappointment in a zone of utter metaphysical security, man does not become guilty of what might well be called treason from above. Does he not tend to violate in this way the fundamental conditions under which he is introduced into the world? To tell the truth, in falling back upon the idea of what I have called absolute hope, it seems that I elude my problems far more than I solve them and that I am juggling with the given facts.

But are we not then losing our way again in the inextricable? Here I take the example once more of the patriot who refuses to despair of the liberation of his native land which is provisionally conquered. In what, or in whom, does he place his hope? Does he not conditionalise his hope in the way which just now we decided was unwarrantable? Even if he recognises that there is no chance that he will himself witness the hoped-for liberation, he carries beyond his own existence the fulfilment of his desires, he refuses with all his being to admit that the darkness which has fallen upon his country can be enduring, he affirms that it is only an eclipse. Still more: it is not enough to say that he cannot believe in the death of his country, the truth is much more that he does not even consider he has the right to believe in it, and that it would seem to him that he was committing a real act of treason in admitting this possibility; and this is true whether he is a believer or not. In every case he has made a judgment, which lies outside all his power of reflection, that to despair would be disloyal, it would be to go over to the enemy. This judgment rests on a postulate which is actually very likely to remain implicit but which we must examine. It consists in the affirmation that in hoping for liberation I really help to prepare the way for it, and that, inversely, in raising a doubt about its possibility I reduce the chance of it to some degree. It is not that strictly speaking I impute a causal efficacy to the fact of hoping or not hoping. The truth is much rather that I am conscious that when I hope I strengthen, and when I despair, or simply doubt, I weaken or let go of, a certain bond which unites me to the matter in question. This bond shows every evidence of being religious in essence.

Here we come up, however, against a difficulty. Where the matter in question is strictly speaking my own fate, can we speak of a bond or indeed of religion? It is probably necessary here to introduce a distinction which we have previously had occasion to bring out. When I tremble for my own existence, it may be that I am giving way to the simple instinct of self-preservation: it is very doubtful if one can legitimately designate by the word "hope" the kind of organic attachment to myself which makes me imagine final liberation in the midst of danger, even where the future seems most threatening. It is different when piety towards oneself intervenes. By this I mean a reference to a certain spiritual interconnection at the heart of which my existence can preserve its meaning and its value. We are not dealing here with an abstraction, an impersonal order: if I inspire another being with love which I value and to which I respond, that will be enough to create this spiritual interconnection. The fact of the reciprocal love, the communion, will be enough to bring about a deep transformation in the nature of the bond which unites me to myself. Where the matter concerns me alone, or more exactly when I consider myself as though I were the only one concerned, the question of knowing what is going to happen to me may strike me as practically without interest or importance. This, however, will not prevent the instinct of self-preservation from remaining active in me with all that it entails. It is obviously not the same if I know that he whom I love is in some way dependent on me, and that what happens to me will affect him vitally. We might say in the manner of Hegel that my relationship to myself is mediated by the presence of the other person, by what he is for me and what I am for him. But it is of capital importance for our subject that we see at the same time that this spiritual interconnection of which I have only examined the simplest example here, invariably appears as veiled in mystery to him who is conscious of having a part in it. Here again, let us be as concrete as possible. To love anybody is to expect something from him, something which can neither be defined nor foreseen; it is at the same time in some way to make it possible for him to fulfil this expectation. Yes, paradoxical as it may seem, to expect is in some way to give: but the opposite is none the less true; no longer to expect is to strike with sterility the being from whom no more is expected; it is then in some way to deprive him or take from him in advance what is surely a certain possibility of inventing or creating. Everything looks as though we can only speak of hope where the interaction exists between him who gives and him who receives, where there is that exchange which is the mark of all spiritual life.

But perhaps, without sinning through excessive subtlety, it might be pointed out that this delicate interplay of relationships can exist internally wherever there is genuine creation. In that case we need only put outside the category of hope the blind attachment which impels us simply to go on living, carrying out day by day the functions, organic or otherwise, which are exercised for ourselves alone without any superior object in view, be it intellectual, moral or aesthetic. If this is so, the ancient distinction of the Stoics upon which any critical examination of hope is invariably founded, the distinction between things which depend, and do not depend, upon ourselves, will lose a great deal of its significance: Further, how can we fail to recall the connection established above between hope and liberty? Not only does voluntary action not presuppose an objective judgment already formed by which I should see in advance what was in my power to do and what was beyond it, but it must on the contrary be maintained that the authentic formula of willing is *I will*, therefore *I can;* in other words, I decide that it is in my power to do a certain thing, to obtain a certain result precisely because it is my will (or because it is necessary) that this thing should be done and this result obtained. Actually we only have to remember that to act freely is always to innovate, in order to see that there would be a contradiction in admitting that I should be obliged in my willing to depend simply on the knowledge of what I had done before. It is, however, only by starting from such knowledge that I could proceed to an objective setting of limits between what is in my power and what is beyond it.

It is not difficult to see how a positive philosophy of hope can be arrived at from these observations. We are actually going to find that all our foregoing remarks will come together as into a sheaf. When we said that hope was the very opposite of pretension or defiance, we were ready to recognise that it is essentially silent and modest, that it bears the mark of inviolable timidity except where it develops in the department of the *us*, that is to say in fellowship. We talk to each other of our common hope but hate to express it before those who do not share it, as if it were really—and perhaps indeed it is—a secret. If hope is not a defiance, perhaps it is nevertheless conscious of appearing defiant or provocative in the eyes of those who claim that they are established on the firm rock of experience: "It has always been seen that . . ." or, on the contrary "It has never been found that . . .". Hope with scandalously carefree grace undertakes to prove these assertions false; by what right?

It seems as though hope is linked to a certain candour, a certain virginity untouched by experience. It belongs to those who have not been hardened by life. We are impelled to introduce a notion here which, from the point of view of objective knowledge, will appear to be devoid of sense: it is that of a sullying or withering which is connected with experience. The notion of experience itself is ambiguous. On the one hand there is an established and catalogued experience in the name of which judgments are pronounced by the pronoun "one." On the other hand there is an experience in the making which is only possible precisely when all the other kind of experience has been set on one side, even if finally and after having been duly desiccated, it is given a place in the herbarium of universal wisdom. It is quite evident that hope is intimately bound up with experience in the second sense and perhaps it might be claimed that hope is its spring.

In the name of accepted experience people claim to trace some kind of circle of Popilius round us; "There is no way out"—that is the formula to which the experts of established experience fly. But postulated at the very basis of hope is the non-validity of such assertions, the truth that the more the real is real the less does it lend itself to a calculation of possibilities on the basis of accepted experience. Hope quite simply does not take any heed of this sum total. It might be said that in a sense hope is not interested in the *how:* and this fact shows how fundamentally untechnical it is, for technical thought, by definition, never separates the consideration of ends and means. An end does not exist for the technician, if he does not see approximately how to achieve it. This, however, is not true for the inventor or the discoverer who says, "There must be a way" and who adds: "I am going to find it." He who hopes says simply: "It will be found." In hoping, I do not create in the strict sense of the word, but I appeal to the existence of a certain creative power in the world, or rather to the actual resources at the disposal of this creative power. Where, on the other hand, my spirit has been as it were tarnished by catalogued experience, I refuse to appeal to this creative power, I deny its existence; all outside me, and perhaps within me also (if I am logical) appears to me as simple repetition.

We have arrived then at the important conclusion that what is specific in hope is lost sight of if the attempt is made to judge and condemn it from the point of view of *established experience*. It misunderstands the teaching of such experience with insolent ingenuity, though it is actually definite enough. The truth is much more that hope is engaged in the weaving of experience now in process, or in other words in an adventure now going forward. This does not run counter to an authentic empiricism but to a certain dogmatism which, while claiming to be experience, fundamentally misunderstands its nature, just as a cult of the scientific may stand in the way of living science in its creative development.

It is not difficult to see that hope thus understood involves a fundamental relationship of consciousness to time which we must now try to analyse.

If we accept the perspective of established experience, we are led to suppose that time will bring nothing new beyond an illustration or an added confirmation, actually superfluous, of the pronouncements engraved on the tables of universal wisdom or merely of common sense. It is as much as to say that we are here in a world where time no longer *passes*, or, which comes to the same thing, where time merely passes without bringing anything, empty of any material which could serve to establish a new truth or inspire a new being. How can we help remembering here the impression, rightly termed *hopeless*, which every child and adolescent has received when his elders pronounce one or other of those axioms which claim to express *truths which are indisputable* and duly established. Such axioms seem to strike out of existence all the dreams, all the confused aspirations of him who not having had *his own* experience refuses to accept a so-called proof with which he is in no way associated. We actually have grounds for wondering by what strange optical illusion the axiom which appears as hopeless and discouraging to him who is supposed to be instructed by it, causes such vanity and self-satisfaction in those who give it out. The reason is surely to be found in the sense of superiority which, rightly or wrongly, fills those people who imagine that they represent universal wisdom to youngsters whose wild presumption needs to be mortified as much as possible. We see the antagonism between the older and younger as an antagonism between someone who is trying to feel his way in life as we feel our way along a road, and who only has a flickering light to guide him, and someone who claims to be at the other side of this same life (and of his own life as well) and to be able to give out, from some abstract spot, truths acquired at a great price. It goes without saying that this conflict is at the heart of what is often called the problem of the generations and that no truly logical or rational solution can be found for it, because the antagonists are on different levels in time, because they have no real communion with each other and neither of them discusses with the other, but with a certain idea, a certain *eidôlon* of the other.

All then prepares us to recognise that despair is in a certain sense the consciousness of time as closed or, more exactly still, of time as a prison—whilst hope appears as piercing through time; everything happens as though time, instead of hedging consciousness round, allowed something to pass through it. It was from this point of view that I previously drew attention to the prophetic character of hope. Of course one cannot say that hope sees what is going to happen; but it affirms as *if* it saw. One might say that it draws its authority from a hidden vision of which it is allowed to take account without enjoying it.

We might say again that if time is in its essence a separation and as it were a perpetual splitting up of the self in relation to itself, hope on the contrary aims at reunion, at recollection, at reconciliation: in that way, and in that way alone, it might be called a memory of the future.

One cannot however disguise the impatience, one might say the uneasiness, which such glimpses give rise to in spirits dominated by an anxiety for truth: "Is there to be nothing in these explanations," it may be asked, "which enables us to discern if hope is anything but an illusion, if it is in any possible degree a light thrown upon a certain subsoil of things? And yet is not this, when we come down to the final analysis, the only question which matters?"

To reply to such a challenge, it will be well, I think, to introduce the idea of a certain human condition which we cannot hope to transcend by thought, for reflection shows that in trying to rise above it we make it unreal and impoverish it. The unpardonable mistake of a certain rationalism has consisted precisely in sacrificing the human as such, without anything to take its place, to certain *ideas,* whose regulative value we certainly should not think of questioning, but which lose all their meaning if we attempt to make of them a world existing by itself where "the human as such" will be counted as nothing but dross and rubbish. This general remark seems to me likely to throw light on the debate, which arises between those who want to save hope and those who on the contrary seek to banish it to the world of mirages.

The term "condition" is one which needs very careful definition. Perhaps we should see in the human condition a certain vital and spiritual order which we cannot violate without exposing ourselves to the loss not only of our equilibrium, but even of our integrity. As, however, the term condition may also be taken sometimes in a slightly different sense which is very nearly that of nature, we must recognise that it is a characteristic of man's condition in the second sense that he is able to fall short of his condition in the first sense. The condition-order implies a joint working which is always precarious between our nature and an acquired wisdom, infused into our will—a wisdom actually in no way bound to be explicitly conscious of itself. Again we must of course be careful not to confuse this wisdom with the dogmatic empiricism of which I have already pointed out the sterilising effect. Perhaps the human condition is characterised not only by the risks which go with it and which after

mistrust—mistrust not only of others, but of life itself—not tend to make the human soul less and less a possible dwelling place for hope, or indeed for joy? We seem here to touch the metaphysical roots of a denaturalisation which seems almost as though it were coextensive with a certain type of civilisation. It may be said in passing that the very fact that a certain belief in progress, far from arresting this evolution, has, on the contrary, helped to precipitate it, suffices to show how far such a belief is opposed to true hope, in spite of the fact that in its far distant origin it may have been a confusedly rationalised derivative of it.

We should not however hide from ourselves that all these considerations would not yet be enough to convince those who, under the influence of a stoicism or a more or less distorted form of the philosophy of Spinoza, persist in refusing to allow that hope has any metaphysical value. "Do you not," they say, "merely arrive at the very insignificant conclusion, for which it is really superfluous to use such complicated arguments, that hope is a tendency which constitutes the inner spring of human enterprises because it is calculated to stimulate usefully those who engage wholeheartedly in them?" This is as much as to say that in the last resort hope is only a subjective tendency, that by itself it would never be able to throw any light upon the inner meaning of things, and brings with it no guarantee that it will be realised.

But it must be replied that it is precisely such an opposition as we have here imagined that we have to repudiate or to transcend. Certainly there is no question of denying that this opposition has a meaning where an enterprise with some material aim is under consideration; the building of a port, or a pyramid; the hollowing out of a tunnel, or the damming of a river. Just because it is simply a question of producing certain material results, the inner disposition of the agent—or it would be better to say the instrument—can and should be regarded as a contingent fact in relation to the result to be produced. This in reality seems as though it could well be arrived at by pitiless masters driving a multitude of terrorised slaves with whips. But let us remember that such results do not in reality involve any genuine creation, any love of the thing created. Now it is precisely where such love exists, and only where it exists, that we can speak of hope, this love taking shape in a reality which without it would not be what it is. When this has come about it is untrue to claim that hope is merely a subjective stimulant; it is, on the contrary, a vital aspect of the very process by which an act of creation is accomplished.

"But," they will say again, "the hope we are discussing here is surely strangely different from that which was previously defined as a response to a situation which entailed captivity?" It may be taken that, in spite of appearances, this difference conceals a fundamental identity. Do not let us forget that, as a matter of fact, the general condition of man, even when his life appears to be quite normal, is always that of a captive, by reason of the enslavements of all kinds which he is called upon to endure, if only on account of the body, and more deeply still because of the night which shrouds his beginning and his end. We can be certain that all creative activity, whatever it may be, is bound up with this condition, in the double meaning which we have given to the word, and that it is in reality the only means given us of causing light to shine forth in our prison. It may be asked whether this is not to make of creation a diversion as Pascal would have understood it. I do not think so really, for the notion of Pascal involves the idea of the utter solitude of the creature struggling with the agony of his destiny, whereas we have seen, and we must return to it again, that hope is always associated with a communion, no matter how interior it may be. This is actually so true that one wonders if despair and solitude are not at bottom necessarily identical.

From this point of view the essential problem to which we are seeking to find the solution would be whether solitude is the last word, whether man is really condemned to live and to die alone, and whether it is only through the effect of a vivid illusion that he manages to conceal from himself the fact that such is indeed his fate. It is not possible to sit in judgment on the case of hope without at the same time trying the case of love.

It is curious to notice that a purely objective philosophy, in the name of which it is claimed to denounce the mirage of hope, is so near as to become identified with the radical subjectivity of a Proust, for whom love is a mis-knowing and resolves itself into nothing but illusions of perspective. There is every reason to think that it is by one and the same action that it is possible to free ourselves from these two philosophies which are only opposed outwardly, that is to say in the formula given to them, but which agree in their negative aims. For the rest, Proust himself puts us on the way of truths to which he becomes more and more blind as his work develops and as he comes to propose to himself an image of life which is at the same time more systematic and impoverished. The subjective conception of love, with the justification it confers upon despair (since only the pure artist possesses the key of salvation) appears all the more unimpeachable as the being becomes increasingly the prisoner of an obsession of which the other being is less the object than the excuse, since he evades the grasp not only of intuition but of all knowledge worthy of the name. I *see* a being so much the less the more I am obsessed by him, for my obsession tends to substitute itself for him. It must be added that this obsession itself becomes all the more tyrannical the more I claim to possess him, to monopolise him, the more obstinately I set my mind to break all the bonds which unite him to other beings, in the hope of making him totally mine. This is the illusion of Arnolphe, and it is to be wondered whether Molière did not forestall and surpass Proust. One of two things must happen. Faced with this determination to monopolise him, the other person either makes his escape by flight or lying, or else he loses his own nature and becomes a nonentity. In either case it follows inexorably that, because love has thus failed in its mission and become perverted, it consummates its own loss.

But it is to be asked whether a logical process of the same kind, though far less clearly and easily discernible, is not working itself out wherever the fundamental relationship uniting the human soul and the mysterious reality which surrounds and at the same time confronts it becomes perverted. This relationship, when grasped in its truth, is a participation. This means that we do not only become guilty of an usurpation but that, in spite of all appearances, we become strangers to ourselves, in so far as we treat the reality as something which can be won and placed at our disposal. We might say again that this reality thus referred and enslaved to selfish ends loses its true nature also, and becomes a sham and an idol. But shams and idols always appear, to those who view them with enough penetration, as milestones, marking the road to despair.

Perhaps we can now feel authorised to formulate a few general propositions which will sum up most of the observations we have been able to make in the course of our all too winding journey.

In face of the particular trial, whatever it may be, which confronts me and which must always be but a specimen of the trial of humanity in general, I shall always be exposed to the temptation of shutting the door which encloses me within myself and at the same time encloses me within time, as though the future, drained of its substance and its mystery, were no longer to be anything but a place of pure repetition, as though some unspecifiable disordered mechanism were to go on working ceaselessly, undirected by any intelligent motivisation. But a future thus devitalised, no longer being a future for me or anybody else, would be rather a prospect of vacancy.

A systematised empiricism, crystallised into impersonal and permanent formulæ, would confer upon what is in truth only a movement of the soul, a retraction, an inward disloyalty, the theoretical (and fallacious) justification which such a step needs in order to establish itself in its own eyes.

Against this combination of temptations there is only one remedy, and it has two aspects: it is the remedy of communion, the remedy of hope. If it is true that man's trial is infinite in its varieties and can assume the innumerable forms under which we know privation, exile, or captivity, it is no less certain that by a symmetrical but inverted process, each one of us can rise by his own special path from the humble forms of communion which experience offers the most despised, to a communion which is both more intimate and more abundant, of which hope can be equally regarded as the foreshadowing or the outcome.

"I hope in thee for us"; such is perhaps the most adequate and the most elaborate expression of the act which the verb "to hope" suggests in a way which is still confused and ambiguous. "In thee—for us": between this "thou" and this "us" which only the most persistent reflection can finally discover in the act of hope, what is the vital link? Must we not reply that "Thou" is in some way the guarantee of the union which holds us together, myself to myself, or the one to the other, or these beings to those other beings? More than a guarantee which secures or confirms from outside a union which already exists, it is the very cement which binds the whole into one. If this is the case, to despair of myself, or to despair of us, is essentially to despair of the Thou. Avowedly, it is conceivable that there is some difficulty in admitting that I form with myself a real community, an *us:* it is, however, only on this condition that I have my active share as a centre of intelligence, of love and of creation. This absolute Thou in whom I must hope but whom I also have always the possibility of denying, not only in theory but in practice, is at the heart of the city which I form with myself and which, as experience has given tragic proof, retains the power of reducing itself to ashes. It must be added that this city is not a monad and that it cannot establish itself as a distinct and isolated centre, without working for its own destruction, but that on the contrary it draws the elements of its life from what is brought to it along canals, often very badly marked out, from friendly cities, of which however it often scarcely knows the name or the situation. It is to a consciousness of these reciprocities, of this mysterious and incessant circulation, that I open my soul when I hope—a prophetic consciousness, as we have said, but vague and in danger of becoming obliterated to the extent that it seeks to pass itself off as second sight. If this is so, it must be said that to hope, as we have already hinted, is to live in hope instead of anxiously concentrating our attention on the poor little counters spread out in front of us which we feverishly reckon up over and over again without respite, tormented by the fear of being foiled or ruined. The more we allow ourselves to be the servants of Having, the more we shall let ourselves fall a prey to the gnawing anxiety which Having involves, the more we shall tend to lose not only the aptitude for hope, but even I should say the very belief, indistinct as it may be, of its possible reality. In this sense it is no doubt true that, strictly speaking, only those beings who are entirely free from the shackles of ownership in all its forms are able to know the divine light-heartedness of life in hope. But, as far as we can judge, this liberation, this exemption, must remain the privilege of a very small number of chosen souls. The vast majority of men are, as far as we can see, destined to remain entangled in the inextricable meshes of Having, and there are actually the gravest reasons for thinking that it is on this condition, burdensome as it may be, that humanity is able to discharge, well or badly as the case may be, the tasks, often so thankless and obscure, which have been assigned to it. A final condemnation of Having would amount basically to the rashest repudiation of finite existence by finite man himself. Such could not be uttered without an excessive humility which would look so much like the most inordinate and blasphemous pride as to be confused with it. What, however, we might perhaps dare to say is that if, however feebly, we remain penetrated by hope, it can only be through the cracks and openings which are to be found in the armour of Having which covers us: the armour of our possessions, our attainments, our experience and our virtues, perhaps even more than our vices. Thus, and only thus, can the breathing of the soul be maintained, but under conditions, alas, of irregular action and a dangerous uncertainty often on the increase so that it is always in danger of being blocked like the lungs or the bowels.

But in expressing ourselves thus, are we not led to make hope appear too much as a natural faculty? To go still deeper, what position should we adopt on the question as to whether it depends upon us or whether, on the contrary, it is either the fruit of an innate disposition, or a pure grace, and in final analysis the result of supernatural help? I will take care here not to venture upon theological ground. In the region of philosophic reflection, however, it seems as though it is equally true, and consequently equally false, to say that hope depends or does not depend upon me.

The meaning of this question does indeed become more obscure when it bears upon that which is most intimately myself. Does it depend upon me whether I am in love or whether I possess a certain creative faculty? Certainly not, but precisely because it does not depend upon me to be or not to be such as I am. Let us admit, on the contrary, without troubling about the philosophical controversies on free will with which we are not concerned, that it depends upon me whether I take a certain step, or make a certain journey, visit, gesture, etc., which anyone else in my place could equally well do. We are then led to the paradoxical conclusion that what depends upon me is the very thing which does not form part of me, which remains in a sense exterior (or indifferent) to me. It must however be added that a gift, whatever it may be, is never purely and simply *received* by a subject who has nothing to do but make a place for it in himself. The truth is much rather that the gift is a call to which we have to make response; it is as though a harvest of possibilities had to be gathered from us, among which we had to choose, or more exactly it is as though we had to actualise those which accorded best with the urgency interiorly felt which is, in reality, only mediation between us and ourselves.

It is from this general observation that we must start if we would recognise that it is both true and false to say that it depends on us whether we hope or not. At the root of hope there is something which is literally offered to us: but we can refuse hope just as we can refuse love. Moreover, we can no doubt deny hope, just as we can deny or degrade our love.

Both here and there the rôle of *Kaïros* seems to be to give our liberty an opportunity of exercising and spreading itself as it could never do if it were left to itself—a hypothesis which is probably contradictory, anyway.

We see from this why it is legitimate to consider hope as a virtue; the truth is that all virtue is the particularisation of a certain interior force, and that to live in hope is to obtain from oneself that one should remain faithful in the hour of darkness to that which in its origin was perhaps only an inspiration, an exaltation, a transport. But there is no doubt that this faithfulness cannot be put into practice except by virtue of a co-operation, whose principle will always remain a mystery, between the goodwill which is after all the only positive contribution of which we are capable and certain promptings whose centre remains beyond our reach, in those realms where values are divine gifts.

Perhaps, if we would elucidate the nature of hope more completely, at least, as far as such elucidation is possible, we should now tackle directly the question of the relationship connecting hope with our reasons for hoping. It may be best to state the problem in its most extreme form: can one hope when the reasons for so doing are insufficient or even completely lacking?

Let us notice first of all that this question must inevitably be asked by anyone who treats hope as an external phenomenon and wonders under what conditions it can appear. I will call such a one the observer in what is to follow.

Reflection soon shows us, however, that thinking in these terms of hope is the very way to stifle it.

First of all, the meaning of the word *can* is ambiguous.

(*a*) Can it in fact happen that anyone hopes without any reasons for hoping? Or on the other hand—

(*b*) Is it permissible to hope where the reasons are insufficient or lacking?

Let us notice first that in both cases we admit implicitly that the proposition "there is no reason, or at least no sufficient reason, for hope," has some meaning. We must not however be taken in by words; we cannot speak of the non-existence or existence of such reasons as of the non-existence or existence of something which could form part of anyone's experience. Here "there is" or "there is not" is necessarily related to a definite subject. We mean that in the eyes of X there is or there is not good enough reason for hope. But in the statement of our problem what subject is implied? Let us consider in particular question (*a*). Do we mean "Can it in fact happen that someone hopes under conditions which, for me who am asking the question, afford no grounds for hope?" or "under conditions which *for the subject himself* afford no grounds for it?"

We must obviously answer the first question in the affirmative: it is quite clear that the other can keep on hoping where the observer considers that reasons for hope do not exist, that is to say where they are invisible to him. This first question then is insignificant and idle.

Has the second a more precise meaning? Can anyone, in fact, hope where he himself admits that the reasons are insufficient or lacking? But, if he truly recognises in all sincerity that these reasons are non-existent or insufficient, he himself admits that he does not really hope (unless, of course, he has succumbed to human respect by granting to some interlocutor what he does not believe in his own heart; but such a case is outside our hypothesis). Moreover, the use of the word "sufficient" implies a contradiction, for, if the subject hopes, it would surely seem that the reasons for hoping are sufficient for him, whatever the observer may think about them.

But in reality the question which the subject is supposed to ask himself, and in this particular case to answer in the negative, does not arise for him unless he detaches himself in some degree from his hope. Actually, it comes into a different register and springs from a calculating faculty of the reason which, with the very approximate means at its disposal, proceeds to carry out a regular balancing up of chances. Without any doubt it may happen that, on consideration, hope gives in for a variable space of time to those calculations of the reason; above all if the subject is engaged in a discussion with someone whom he wants to convince: It is none the less true, however, that hope and the calculating faculty of reason are essentially distinct and everything will be lost if we try to combine them. On the other hand, in the statement (*b*), when we bring in the idea of a right to hope we are entering precisely upon this very process of reasoning by computation which at bottom means a calculation of probabilities. It is as though to hope were to argue in a certain way and as though there were a possibility of enquiring into the validity of the arguments. Looked at from this point of view, the answer to the question is obvious. It is absurd to claim that it can be legitimate to hope without sufficient reasons for hope. But we must repeat once more that here the meaning of the word hope has been completely distorted.

It seems as though we shall thus be led to an utterly negative conclusion and that we shall have to deny that the words "reasons for hoping" have any meaning whatsoever. If so, in this matter we shall have to subscribe to an irrationalism or a radical fideism. But faced with the facts of experience, such a thesis appears nothing short of absurd.

Take, for instance, a mother who persists in hoping that she will see her son again although his death has been certified in the most definite manner by witnesses who found his body, buried it, etc. Is not the observer justified in saying that there are no reasons for hoping that this son is still alive?

However subtle and irritating in certain respects the distinction I am going to introduce here may appear, perhaps we should reply to the objection in the following way: In so far as the hope of the mother is expressed as an objective judgment, "It is possible that John will come back," we have the right to say: "No, objectively speaking, the return must be considered as impossible." But at the root of the mother's objective judgment, which, as such, cannot be accepted, she has within her a loving thought which repudiates or transcends the facts, and it seems as though there was something absurd or even scandalous in disputing her right to hope, that is to say to love, against all hope. More exactly, what is absurd is the very idea of a right which we can recognise or dispute.

We are not at the end of our difficulties, however. Common sense will retort that it is not permissible to identify hope and love here. "Whatever may be the love which I feel for a certain individual, it cannot be admitted that in virtue of this love, I can assume the right to exceed the limits of logic." It is a mere sophism to say, "I cannot bear the idea that he will not come back, therefore it is possible that he will." But here again, hope is considered from outside and entered in a register where it does not belong. What hope gives us is the simple affirmation, "You are coming back." And this "you are coming back" is beyond the reach of objective criticism. Such criticism could only deal with it legitimately if it were translated into the language of prevision or of a judgment based on probabilities.

It cannot be denied that each of us is exposed to the temptation of carrying out such a substitution on our own account. We have already seen how hope loses its true nature by the very fact that it tends to offer itself for the approbation of the subject himself and also of other people. In this way it loses its essential elasticity, but it only loses it because it denies its own nature and this denial is a fall.

This, which at first appears very paradoxical, seems to me to be elucidated if we keep in mind the fundamental distinction between hope and desire and if we recall the observations which were made further back. We might say that hope only escapes from a particular metaphysical ruling on condition that it transcends desire—that is to say, that it does not remain centred upon the subject himself. Once again we are led to draw attention to the indissoluble connection which binds together hope and love. The more egoistical love is, the more the alluringly prophetic declarations it inspires should be regarded with caution as likely to be literally contradicted by experience; on the other hand, the nearer it approaches to true charity, the more the meaning of its declarations is inflected and tends to become full of an unconditional quality which is the very sign of a presence. This presence is incarnated in the "us" for whom "I hope in Thee," that is to say in a communion of which I proclaim the indestructibility. No doubt, as always, critical thought will immediately take up its position against this assertion. It will invoke the evidence of experience, and of the spectacle of endless visible destruction which it presents to us. But this evidence itself can only be challenged in the name of a certitude which we have already seen is not based on established experience—the certitude that all such arguments are only true in a very fleeting sense, and that the incessant changes to which critical pessimism claims to give so much importance, cannot touch the only authentic reality. This assertion is precisely what we discover when we reach the intelligible core of hope; what characterises it is *the very movement by which it challenges the evidence upon which men claim to challenge it itself*. We must add that this conception of hope is both symbolised and supported by all experiences of renewal, not considered in their philosophical or even physical processes, but in the infinite echo which they awaken in those who are called upon either to live through them directly, or to share sympathetically in the blessings they bring. So what we said above about the relationship which hope establishes between the soul and time is elucidated and completed. Might we not say that hope always implies the superlogical connection between a return (*nostos*) and something completely new (*Kaïnon ti*)? Following from this it is to be wondered whether preservation or restoration, on the one hand, and revolution or renewal on the other, are not the two movements, the two abstractly dissociated aspects of one and the same unity, which dwells in hope and is beyond the reach of all our faculties of reasoning or of conceptual formulation. This aspiration can be approximately expressed in the simple but contradictory words: *as before, but differently and better than before*. Here we undoubtedly come once again upon the theme of liberation, for it is never a simple return to the *status quo*, a simple return to our being; it is that and much more, and even the contrary of that: an undreamed-of promotion, a transfiguration.

Perhaps after these considerations we might at last attempt to give the definition which we would not allow ourselves to place at the beginning of our analysis: we might say that hope is essentially the availability of a soul which has entered intimately enough into the experience of communion to accomplish in the teeth of will and knowledge the transcendent act—the act establishing the vital regeneration of which this experience affords both the pledge and the first-fruits.

LE PEUCH.
January, 1942.

BIBLIOGRAPHY

Philosophy:

Journal Métaphysique, 1913–1923 (Paris, Gallimard, 1927); translated by Bernard Wall as *Metaphysical Journal* (London, Rockliffe, 1952)

Être et Avoir (Paris, Aubin, 1935); translated by Katharine Farrer as *Being and Having* (London, Dacre Press, and New York, Harper & Row, 1949)

Du Refus à l'invocation (Paris, Gallimard, 1940); translated by Robert Rosthal as *Creative Fidelity* (New York, Farrar, Straus and Company, 1964)

Homo Viator (Paris, Aubier, 1945); translated by Emma Crauford (London, Gollancz, 1951; Chicago, Regnery, 1951; reissued by Harper Torchbooks, 1962)

La Métaphysique de Josiah Royce (Paris, Aubier, 1947)

Position et approches concrètes du mystère ontologique (Paris, Vrin, 1949)

Le Mystère de l'être (Gifford Lectures, 1949–1950);

translated by G. S. Fraser as *The Mystery of Being*, volume I, *Reflection and Mystery* (London, The Harvill Press, 1950; Chicago, Regnery Gateway, 1960); volume II, *Faith and Reality* (London, The Harvill Press, 1951; Chicago, Regnery Gateway, 1960)

The Influence of Psychic Phenomena on My Philosophy (F. W. H. Myers Lecture, 1956)

Existentialisme chrétien: Gabriel Marcel. Presentation de Étienne Gilson (Paris, Plon, 1947). Essays in honor of Marcel, with an acknowledgment by Marcel in the form of an autobiographical sketch of great interest, translated by Manya Harari, with other useful papers, in *The Philosophy of Existence* (London, The Harvill Press, 1948; under the title *The Philosophy of Existentialism*, New York, Philosophical Library, 1956; reissued by Citadel Press, 1961)

The Existential Background of Human Dignity (William James Lectures, 1961–1962; Harvard University Press, 1964)

Plays:

La Grâce (1911)
Le Seuil invisible (1913)
Le Palais de sable (1914)
Le Coeur des autres (1921)
L'Iconoclaste (1923)
Le Quatuor en fa dièze (1925)
Un Homme de Dieu (1925); translated by Marjorie Gabain as *A Man of God*
Le Regard neuf (1931)
Le Mort de demain (1931)
La Chapelle ardente (1931); translated by Rosalind Heywood as *The Funeral Pyre*
Le Monde cassé (1933)
Le Chemin de crête (1936); translated by Rosalind Heywood as *Ariadne*
Le Dard (1936)
Le Fanal (1936)
La Soif (1938); published under the title *Les Coeurs avides* (1952)
L'Horizon (1945)
Colombyre, ou le brasier de la paix (1947)
La Double Expertise (1947)

Les Points sur les I (1947)
Le Divertissement posthume (1947)
L'Emissaire (1949)
Le Signe de la croix (1949)
La Fin des temps (1950)
Rome n'est plus dans Rome (1951)
Mon temps n'est pas le votre (1955)
Croissez et multipliez (1955)

MARTIN BUBER

(BORN 1878)

Martin Buber has brought to existentialist thinking a distinctively Jewish contribution. It is not simply that he came to Kierkegaard and Nietzsche (and Dostoevsky) from a Jewish background: he was and remains a Jewish thinker. As a young man, he withdrew to spend five years in the study of Hasidic texts; as an old man, he has devoted himself to a translation of the Bible into German and to Biblical exegesis; in his prime, he exercised perhaps the most formative influence upon German Jewry, upon Zionism, and upon world Jewry. He has introduced into Western culture the literature of modern Jewish mysticism and has revived Jewish culture with an infusion of vital thinking, giving it a modern philosophy of Judaism. The "life of dialogue" is at once a characteristic existentialist theme and Buber's own characteristic Biblical contribution to existentialist thinking. *I and Thou* (1923) is the classical moment in the development of his authorship. Since then, his work has been a consolidation of this statement and an application of it to education, to psychiatry, to politics, to theology, to "philosophical anthropology," and latterly and not least to his interpretation of the Bible.

"Encounter," "communication," the "I-thou" relationship are essential existentialist themes and they occur in some form in all these writers, but none has dealt more fully and philosophically than Buber with the ontological reality of the "sphere of the between" in the meeting of persons and with the subtle and perpetual interconnection and interpenetration (not mere contrast) of *I-Thou* and *I-It*. This exposition has been as much misunderstood as it has been influential. It has been said by a leading Christian (for the Jewish thinker has profoundly influenced Christian theology) that *I and Thou* is a book to be read over and over again and allowed slowly to remold one's thought.

Buber is accessible in English in Gregor Smith's translation of *Ich und Du* (1937), supplemented by his translation of an essential collection of papers published as *Between Man and*

Man (1947). This includes "The Question of the Single One," an important text for any study of identity and difference within existentialist thinking. Buber here acknowledges Kierkegaard as providing the impulse to a new philosophy and a new theology, and underlines the character of Kierkegaard's faith as responsibility; he goes on to show the difference of his own thinking about the self, the other, God, and the "crowd." His independent closeness to Marcel is remarkable, not only in his will to hallow the everyday world, but also in his treatment of openness, response, and fidelity as the existentialist answers to the question about Being which has to take the place of "the ontological problem" and in his patient translation of his experience into reflective terms.

EXTRACTS

I and Thou, trans. by Ronald Gregor Smith (Edinburgh, 1937)

Selected passages.

Between Man and Man, trans. by Ronald Gregor Smith (London, 1947)

"Dialogue" (1929), Section One: Description, "The Signs"; "Responsibility." Section Two: Limitation, "Of Thinking."

"What is Man?" (1938), Section Two: Modern Attempts, IV, "Prospect."

☙ from *I and Thou*

The fundamental difference between the two primary words comes to light in the spiritual history of primitive man. Already in the original relational event he speaks the primary word *I-Thou* in a natural way that precedes what may be termed visualisation of forms—that is, before he has recognised himself as *I*. The primary word *I-It*, on the other hand, is made possible at all only by means of this recognition—by means, that is, of the separation of the *I*.

The first primary word can be resolved, certainly, into *I* and *Thou*, but it did not arise from their being set together; by its nature it precedes *I*. The second word arose from the setting together of *I* and *It*; by nature it comes after *I*.

In the primitive relational event, in virtue of its exclusiveness, the *I* is included. While, that is to say, there are in it, in accordance with its being, only the two partners, the man and that which confronts him, in their full actuality, and while the world becomes in it a dual system, the man, without yet perceiving the *I* itself, is already aware of that cosmic pathos of the *I*.

On the other hand the *I* is not yet included in the natural, actual event which is to pass over into the primary word *I-It*, into the experience with its relation to *I*. This actual event is the separation of the human body, as the bearer of perceptions, from the world round about it. The body comes to know and to differentiate itself in its peculiarities; the differentiation, however, remains one of pure juxtaposition, and hence cannot have the character of the state in which *I* is implied.

But when the *I* of the relation has stepped forth and taken on separate existence, it also moves, strangely tenuous and reduced to merely functional activity, into the natural, actual event of the separation of the body from the world round about it, and awakens there the state in which *I* is properly active. Only now can the conscious act of the *I* take place. This act is the first form of the primary word *I-It*, of the experience in its relation to *I*. The *I* which stepped forth declares itself to be the bearer, and the world round about to be the object, of the perceptions. Of course, this happens in a "primitive" form and not in the form of a "theory of knowledge." But whenever the sentence "I see the tree" is so uttered that it no longer tells of a relation between the man—*I*—and the tree—*Thou*—, but establishes the perception of the tree as object by the human consciousness, the barrier between subject and object has been set up. The primary word *I-It*, the word of separation, has been spoken.

• • •

To man the world is twofold, in accordance with his twofold attitude.

He perceives what exists round about him—simply things, and beings as things; and what happens round about him—simply events, and actions as events; things consisting of qualities, events of moments; things entered in the graph of place, events in that of time; things and events bounded by other things and events, measured by them, comparable with them: he perceives an ordered and detached world. It is to some extent a reliable world, having density and duration. Its organisation can be surveyed and brought out again and again; gone over with closed eyes, and verified with open eyes. It is always there, next to your skin, if you look on it that way, cowering in your soul, if you prefer it so. It is your object, remains it as long as you wish, and remains a total stranger, within you and without. You peceive it, take it to yourself as the "truth," and it lets itself be taken; but it does not give itself to you. Only concerning it may you make yourself "understood" with others; it is ready, though attached to everyone in a different way, to be an object common to you all. But you cannot meet others in it. You cannot hold on to life without it, its reliability sustains you; but should you die in it, your grave would be in nothingness.

Or on the other hand, man meets what exists and becomes as what is over against him, always simply a *single* being and each thing simply as being. What exists is opened to him in happenings, and what happens affects him as what is. Nothing is present for him except this one being, but it implicates the whole world. Measure and comparison have disappeared; it lies with yourself how much of the immeasurable becomes reality for you. These meetings are not organised to make the world, but each is a sign of the world-order. They are not linked up with one another, but each assures you of your solidarity with the world. The world which appears to you in this way is unreliable, for it takes on a continually new appearance; you cannot hold it to its word. It has no density, for everything in it penetrates everything else; no duration, for it comes even when it is not summoned, and vanishes even when it is tightly held. It cannot be surveyed, and if you wish to make it capable of survey you lose it. It comes, and comes to bring *you* out; if it does not reach you, meet you, then it vanishes; but it comes back in another form. It is not outside you, it stirs in the depth of you; if you say "Soul of my soul" you have not said too much. But guard against wishing to remove it into your soul—for then you annihilate it. It is your present; only while you have it do you have the present. You can make it into an object for yourself, to experience and to use; you must continually do this—and as you do it you have no more present. Between you and it there is mutual giving: you say *Thou* to it and give yourself to it; it says *Thou* to you and gives itself to you. You cannot make yourself understood with others concerning it, you are alone with it. But it teaches you to meet others, and to hold your ground when you meet them. Through the graciousness of its comings and the solemn sadness of its goings it leads you away to the *Thou* in which the parallel lines of relations meet. It does not help to sustain you in life, it only helps you to glimpse eternity.

The world of *It* is set in the context of space and time.

The world of *Thou* is not set in the context of either of these.

The particular *Thou*, after the relational event has run its course, *is bound* to become an *It*.

The particular *It*, by entering the relational event, *may* become a *Thou*.

These are the two basic privileges of the world of *It*. They move man to look on the world of *It* as the world in which he has to live, and in which it is comfortable to live, as the world, indeed, which offers him all manner of incitements and excitements, activity and knowledge. In this chronicle of solid benefits the moments of the *Thou* appear as strange lyric and dramatic episodes, seductive and magical, but tearing us away to dangerous extremes, loosening the well-tried context, leaving more questions than satisfaction behind them, shattering security—in short, uncanny moments we can well dispense with. For since we are bound to leave them and go back into the "world," why not remain in it? Why not call to order what is over against us, and send it packing into the realm of objects? Why, if we find ourselves on occasion with no choice but to say *Thou* to father, wife, or comrade, not say *Thou* and mean *It*? To utter the sound *Thou* with the vocal organs is by no means the same as saying the uncanny primary word; more, it is harmless to whisper with the soul an amorous *Thou*, so long as nothing else in a serious way is meant but *experience* and *make use of*.

It is not possible to live in the bare present. Life would be quite consumed if precautions were not taken to subdue the present speedily and thoroughly. But it is possible to live in the bare past, indeed only in it may a life be organised. We only need to fill each moment with experiencing and using, and it ceases to burn.

And in all the seriousness of truth, hear this: without *It* man cannot live. But he who lives with *It* alone is not a man.

• • •

—It is understandable that the world of *It*, given over to itself, that is, not brought into contact with and melted down by the *Thou* as it comes into being, takes on the alien form of an incubus. But how is it that (as you say) the *I* of man is emptied of reality? Surely, whether living in or out of relation, the *I* is assured of itself through its self-consciousness, that strong golden thread on which the many-coloured circumstances are strung. If now I say, "I see you," or, "I see the tree," perhaps the seeing is not real in the same way in both, but the *I* in both is real in the same way.

—Let us make trial if this is so. The form of the words proves nothing. If many a spoken *Thou* indicates fundamentally an *It*, addressed as *Thou* only from habit and obtuseness, and many a spoken *It* fundamentally a *Thou*, its presentness remembered as it were remotely with the whole being, so are countless *I's* only indispensable pronouns, necessary abbreviations for "This man here who is speaking." You speak of self-consciousness? If in the one sentence the *Thou* of relation is truly meant and in the other the *It* of an experience, that is, if the *I* in both is truly meant, is it the same *I* out of whose self-consciousness both are spoken?

The *I* of the primary word *I-Thou* is a different *I* from that of the primary word *I-It*.

The *I* of the primary word *I-It* makes its appearance as individuality and becomes conscious of itself as subject (of experiencing and using).

The *I* of the primary word *I-Thou* makes its appearance as person and becomes conscious of itself as subjectivity (without a dependent genitive).

Individuality makes its appearance by being differentiated from other individualities.

A person makes his appearance by entering into relation with other persons.

The one is the spiritual form of natural detachment, the other the spiritual form of natural solidarity of connexion.

The aim of self-differentiation is to experience and to use, and the aim of these is "life," that is, dying that lasts the span of a man's life.

The aim of relation is relation's own being, that is, contact with the *Thou*. For through contact with every *Thou* we are stirred with a breath of the *Thou*, that is, of eternal life.

He who takes his stand in relation shares in a reality, that is, in a being that neither merely belongs to him nor merely lies outside him. All reality is an activity in which I share without being able to appropriate for myself. Where there is no sharing there is no reality. Where there is self-appropriation there is no reality. The more direct the contact with the *Thou*, the fuller is the sharing.

The *I* is real in virtue of its sharing in reality. The fuller its sharing the more real it becomes.

But the *I* that steps out of the relational event into separation and consciousness of separation, does not lose its reality. Its sharing is preserved in it in a living way. In other words, as is said of the supreme relation and may be used of all, "the seed remains in it." This is the province of subjectivity in which the *I* is aware with a single awareness of its solidarity of connexion and of its separation. Genuine subjectivity can only be dynamically understood, as the swinging of the *I* in its lonely truth. Here, too, is the place where the desire is formed and heightened for ever higher, more unconditioned relation, for the full sharing in being. In subjectivity the spiritual substance of the person matures.

The person becomes conscious of himself as sharing in being, as co-existing, and thus as being. Individuality becomes conscious of itself as being such-and-such and nothing else. The person says, "I am," the individual says, "I am such-and-such." "Know thyself," means for the person "know thyself to have being," for the individual it means "know thy particular kind of being." Individuality in differentiating itself from others is rendered remote from true being.

We do not mean by this that the person in any way "gives up" his special being, his being different—only that this being is not his observation-point, but simply there, the necessary and significant conception of being. Individuality, on the other hand, revels in its special being or, rather, mostly in the fiction of its special being which it has made up for itself. For to know itself means basically for it (for the most part) to establish an authoritative apparent self, capable of deceiving it ever more and more fundamentally, and to procure for itself, in looking to and honouring this apparent self, the semblance of knowledge of its own being as it really is. Real knowledge of its being would lead it to self-destruction—or to rebirth.

The person looks on his Self, individuality is concerned with its My—my kind, my race, my creation, my genius.

Individuality neither shares in nor obtains any reality. It differentiates itself from the other, and seeks through experiencing and using to appropriate as much of it as it can. This is *its* dynamic, self-differentiation and appropriation, each exercised on the *It* within the unreal. The subject, as it thinks itself to be, may make as much as it likes into its own; in virtue of this it acquires no substance, but remains a functional point, experiencing and using, no more. None of its extensive and manifold defined being and none of its zealous "individuality" can help it to win substance.

There are not two kinds of man, but two poles of humanity.

No man is pure person and no man pure individuality. None is wholly real, and none wholly unreal. Every man lives in the twofold *I*. But there are men so defined by person that they may be called persons, and men so defined by individuality that they may be called individuals. True history is decided in the field between these two poles.

The more a man, humanity, is mastered by individuality, the deeper does the *I* sink into unreality. In such times the person in man and in humanity leads a hidden subterranean and as it were cancelled existence—till it is recalled.

• • •

At times the man, shuddering at the alienation between the *I* and the world, comes to reflect that something is to be done. As when in the grave night-hour you lie, racked by waking dream—bulwarks have fallen away and the abyss is screaming—and note amid your torment: there is still life, if only I got through to it—but how, how?; so is this man in the hours of reflection, shuddering, and aimlessly considering this and that. And perhaps, away in the unloved knowledge of the depths within him, he really knows the direction of reversal, leading through sacrifice. But he spurns this knowledge; "mysticism" cannot resist the sun of electric light. He calls thought, in which he rightly has great confidence, to his aid; it shall make good everything for him again. It is, in truth, the high art of thought to paint a reliable picture of the world that is even worthy of belief. So this man says to his thought, "You see this thing stretched out here with the cruel eyes—was it not my playfellow once? You know how it laughed at me then with these very eyes, and they had good in them then? And you see my wretched *I*—I will confess to you, it is empty, and whatever I do in myself, as a result of experiencing and using, does not fathom its emptiness. Will you make it up between me and it, so that it leaves off and I recover?" And thought, ready with its service and its art, paints with its well-known speed one—no, two rows of pictures, on the right wall and on the left. On the one there is (or rather, there takes place, for the world-pictures of thought are reliable cinematography) the universe. The tiny earth plunges from the whirling stars, tiny man from the teeming earth, and now history bears him further through the ages, to rebuild persistently the ant-hill of the cultures which history crushes underfoot. Beneath the row of pictures is written: "One and all." On the other wall there takes place the soul. A spinner is spinning the orbits of all stars and the life of all creation and the history of the universe; everything is woven on one thread, and is no longer called stars and creation and universe, but sensations and imaginings, or even experiences, and conditions of the soul. And beneath the row of pictures is written: "One and all."

Thenceforth, if ever the man shudders at the alienation, and the world strikes terror in his heart, he looks up (to right or left, just as it may chance) and sees a picture. There he sees that the *I* is embedded in the world and that there is really no *I* at all—so the world can do nothing to the *I*, and he is put at ease; or he sees that the world is embedded in the *I*, and that there is really no world at all—so the world can do nothing to the *I*, and he is put at ease. Another time, if the man shudders at the alienation, and the *I* strikes terror in his heart, he looks up and sees a picture; which picture he sees does not matter, the empty *I* is stuffed full with the world or the stream of the world flows over it, and he is put at ease.

But a moment comes, and it is near, when the shuddering man looks up and sees both pictures in a flash together. And a deeper shudder seizes him.

• • •

Every real relation with a being or life in the world is exclusive. Its *Thou* is freed, steps forth, is single, and confronts you. It fills the heavens. This does not mean that nothing else exists; but all else lives in *its* light. As long as the presence of the relation continues, this its cosmic range is inviolable. But as soon as a *Thou* becomes *It*, the cosmic range of the relation appears as an offence to the world, its exclusiveness as an exclusion of the universe.

In the relation with God unconditional exclusiveness and unconditional inclusiveness are one. He who enters on the absolute relation is concerned with nothing isolated any more, neither things nor beings, neither earth nor heaven; but everything is gathered up in the relation. For to step into pure relation is not to disregard everything but to see everything in the *Thou*, not to renounce the world but to establish it on its true basis. To look away from the world, or to stare at it, does not help a man to reach God; but he who sees the world in Him stands in His presence. "Here world, there God" is the language of *It;* "God in the world" is another language of *It;*

but to eliminate or leave behind nothing at all, to include the whole world in the *Thou*, to give the world its due and its truth, to include nothing beside God but everything in Him—this is full and complete relation.

Men do not find God if they stay in the world. They do not find Him if they leave the world. He who goes out with his whole being to meet his *Thou* and carries to it all being that is in the world, finds Him who cannot be sought.

Of course God is the "wholly Other"; but He is also the wholly Same, the wholly Present. Of course He is the *Mysterium Tremendum* that appears and overthrows; but He is also the mystery of the self-evident, nearer to me than my *I*.

If you explore the life of things and of conditioned being you come to the unfathomable, if you deny the life of things and of conditioned being you stand before nothingness, if you hallow this life you meet the living God.

Man's sense of *Thou*, which experiences in the relations with every particular *Thou* the disappointment of the change to *It*, strives out but not away from them all to its eternal *Thou;* but not as something is sought: actually there is no such thing as seeking God, for there is nothing in which He could not be found. How foolish and hopeless would be the man who turned aside from the course of his life in order to seek God; even though he won all the wisdom of solitude and all the power of concentrated being he would miss God. Rather is it as when a man goes his way and simply wishes that it might be the way: in the strength of his wish his striving is expressed. Every relational event is a stage that affords him a glimpse into the consummating event. So in each event he does not partake, but also (for he is waiting) does partake, of the one event. Waiting, not seeking, he goes his way; hence he is composed before all things, and makes contact with them which helps them. But when he has *found*, his heart is not turned from them, though everything now meets him in the one event. He blesses every cell that sheltered him, and every cell into which he will yet turn. For this finding is not the end, but only the eternal middle, of the way.

It is a finding without seeking, a discovering of the primal, of origin. His sense of *Thou*, which cannot be satiated till he finds the endless *Thou*, had the *Thou* present to it from the beginning; the presence had only to become wholly real to him in the reality of the hallowed life of the world.

God cannot be inferred in anything—in nature, say, as its

author, or in history as its master, or in the subject as the self that is thought in it. Something else is not "given" and God then elicited from it; but God is the Being that is directly, most nearly, and lastingly, over against us, that may properly only be addressed, not expressed.

• • •

Man's religious situation, his *being there* in the Presence, is characterised by its essential and indissoluble antinomy. The nature of its being determines that this antinomy is indissoluble. He who accepts the thesis and rejects the antithesis does injury to the significance of the situation. He who tries to think out a synthesis destroys the significance of the situation. He who strives to make the antinomy into a relative matter abolishes the significance of the situation. He who wishes to carry through the conflict of the antinomy other than with his life transgresses the significance of the situation. The significance of the situation is that it is lived, and nothing but lived, continually, ever anew, without foresight, without forethought, without prescription, in the totality of its antinomy.

Comparison of the religious with the philosophical antinomy will make this clear. Kant may make the philosophical conflict between necessity and freedom into a relative matter by assigning the former to the world of appearances and the latter to the world of being, so that in their two settings they are no longer really opposed, but rather reconciled—just as the worlds for which they are valid are reconciled. But if I consider necessity and freedom not in worlds of thought but in the reality of my standing before God, if I know that "I am given over for disposal" and know at the same time that "It depends on myself," then I cannot try to escape the paradox that has to be lived by assigning the irreconcilable propositions to two separate realms of validity; nor can I be helped to an ideal reconciliation by any theological device: but I am compelled to take both to myself, to be lived together, and in being lived they are one.

• • •

What is the eternal, primal phenomenon, present here and now, of that which we term revelation? It is the phenomenon that a man does not pass, from the moment of the supreme meeting, the same being as he entered into it. The moment of meeting is not an "experience" that stirs in the receptive soul and grows to perfect blessedness; rather, in that moment something happens to the man. At times it is like a light breath, at times like a wrestling-bout, but always—it *happens*. The man who emerges from the act of pure relation that so involves his being has now in his being something more that has grown in him, of which he did not know before and whose origin he is not rightly able to indicate. However the source of this new thing is classified in scientific orientation of the world, with its authorised efforts to establish an unbroken causality, we, whose concern is real consideration of the real, cannot have our purpose served with subconsciousness or any other apparatus of the soul. The reality is that we receive what we did not hitherto have, and receive it in such a way that we know it has been given to us. In the language of the Bible, "Those who wait upon the Lord shall renew their strength." In the language of Nietzsche, who in his account remains loyal to reality, "We take and do not ask who it is there that gives."

Man receives, and he receives not a specific "content" but a Presence, a Presence as power. This Presence and this power include three things, undivided, yet in such a way that we may consider them separately. First, there is the whole fulness of real mutual action, of the being raised and bound up in relation: the man can give no account at all of how the binding in relation is brought about, nor does it in any way lighten his life—it makes life heavier, but heavy with meaning. Secondly, there is the inexpressible confirmation of meaning. Meaning is assured. Nothing can any longer be meaningless. The question about the meaning of life is no longer there. But were it there, it would not have to be answered. You do not know how to exhibit and define the meaning of life, you have no formula or picture for it, and yet it has more certitude for you than the perceptions of your senses. What does the revealed and concealed meaning purpose with us, desire from us? It does not wish to be explained (nor are we able to do that) but only to be done by us. Thirdly, this meaning is not that of "another life," but that of this life of ours, not one of a world "yonder" but that of this world of ours, and it desires its confirmation in this life and in relation with this world. This meaning can be received, but not experienced; it cannot be experienced but it can be done, and this is its purpose with us. The assurance I have of it does not wish to be sealed within me, but it wishes to be born by me into the world. But just as the meaning itself does not permit itself to be transmitted and made into knowledge generally current and admissible, so confirmation of it cannot be transmitted as a valid

Ought; it is not prescribed, it is not specified on any tablet, to be raised above all men's heads. The meaning that has been received can be proved true by each man only in the singleness of his being and the singleness of his life. As no prescription can lead us to the meeting, so none leads from it. As only acceptance of the Presence is necessary for the approach to the meeting, so in a new sense is it so when we emerge from it. As we reach the meeting with the simple *Thou* on our lips, so with the *Thou* on our lips we leave it and return to the world.

That before which, in which, out of which, and into which we live, even the mystery, has remained what it was. It has become present to us and in its presentnesss has proclaimed itself to us as salvation; we have "known" it, but we acquire no knowledge from it which might lessen or moderate its mysteriousness. We have come near to God, but not nearer to unveiling being or solving its riddle. We have felt release, but not discovered a "solution." We cannot approach others with what we have received, and say "You must know this, you must do this." We can only go, and confirm its truth. And this, too, is no "ought," but we can, we *must*.

This is the eternal revelation that is present here and now. I know of no revelation and believe in none whose primal phenomenon is not precisely this. I do not believe in a self-naming of God, a self-definition of God before men. The Word of revelation is *I am that I am.* That which reveals is that which reveals. That which is *is,* and nothing more. The eternal source of strength streams, the eternal contact persists, the eternal voice sounds forth, and nothing more.

☙ *Dialogue*

THE SIGNS

Each of us is encased in an armour whose task is to ward off signs. Signs happen to us without respite, living means being addressed, we would need only to present ourselves and to perceive. But the risk is too dangerous for us, the soundless thunderings seem to threaten us with annihilation, and from generation to generation we perfect the defence apparatus. All our knowledge assures us, "Be calm, everything happens as it must happen, but nothing is directed at you, you are not meant; it is just 'the world,' you can experience it as you like, but whatever you make of it in yourself proceeds from you alone, nothing is required of you, you are not addressed, all is quiet."

Each of us is encased in an armour which we soon, out of familiarity, no longer notice. There are only moments which penetrate it and stir the soul to sensibility. And when such a moment has imposed itself on us and we then take notice and ask ourselves, "Has anything particular taken place? Was it not of the kind I meet every day?" then we may reply to ourselves, "Nothing particular, indeed, it is like this every day, only we are not there every day."

The signs of address are not something extraordinary, something that steps out of the order of things, they are just what goes on time and again, just what goes on in any case, nothing is added by the address. The waves of the æther roar on always, but for most of the time we have turned off our receivers.

What occurs to me addresses me. In what occurs to me the world-happening addresses me. Only by sterilizing it, removing the seed of address from it, can I take what occurs to me as a part of the world-happening which does not refer to me. The interlocking sterilized system into which all this only needs to be dovetailed is man's titanic work. Mankind has pressed speech too into the service of this work.

From out of this tower of the ages the objection will be levelled against me, if some of its doorkeepers should pay any attention to such trains of thought, that it is nothing but a variety of primitive superstition to hold that cosmic and telluric happenings have for the life of the human person a direct meaning that can be grasped. For instead of understanding an event physically, biologically, sociologically (for which I, inclined as I always have been to admire genuine acts of research, think a great deal, when those who carry them out only know what they are doing and do not lose sight of the limits of the realm in which they are moving), these keepers say, an attempt is being made to get behind the event's alleged significance, and for this there is no place in a reasonable world continuum of space and time.

Thus, then, unexpectedly I seem to have fallen into the company of the augurs, of whom, as is well-known, there are remarkable modern varieties.

But whether they haruspicate or cast a horoscope their signs have this peculiarity that they are in a dictionary, even if not necessarily a written one. It does not matter how esoteric the information that is handed down: he who searches out the signs is *well up in* what life's juncture this or that sign means. Nor does it matter that special difficulties of separation and combination are created by the meeting of several signs of different kinds. For you can "look it up in the dictionary." The common signature of all this business is that it is for all time: things remain the same, they are discovered once for all; rules, laws, and analogical conclusions may be employed throughout. What is commonly termed superstition, that is, perverse faith, appears to me rather as perverse knowledge. From "superstition" about the number 13 an unbroken ladder leads into the dizziest heights of gnosis. This is not even the aping of a real faith.

Real faith—if I may so term presenting ourselves and perceiving—begins when the dictionary is put down, when you are done with it. What occurs to me says something to me, but what it says to me cannot be revealed by any esoteric information; for it has never been said before nor is it composed of sounds that have ever been said. It can neither be interpreted nor translated, I can have it neither explained nor displayed; it is not a *what* at all, it is said into my very life; it is no experience that can be remembered independently of the situation, it remains the address of that moment and cannot be isolated, it remains the question of a questioner and will have its answer.

(It remains the question. For that is the other great contrast between all the business of interpreting signs and the speech of signs which I mean here: this speech never gives information or appeasement.)

Faith stands in the stream of "happening but once" which is spanned by knowledge. All the emergency structures of analogy and typology are indispensable for the work of the human spirit, but to step on them when the question of the questioner steps up to you, to me, would be running away. Lived life is tested and fulfilled in the stream alone.

With all deference to the world continuum of space and time I know as a living truth only concrete world reality which is constantly, in every moment, reached out to me. I can separate it into its component parts, I can compare them and distribute them into groups of similar phenomena, I can derive them from earlier and reduce them to simpler phenomena; and when I have done all this I have not touched my concrete world reality. Inseparable, incomparable, irreducible, now, happening once only, it gazes upon me with a horrifying look. So in Stravinsky's ballet the director of the wandering marionette show wants to point out to the people at the annual fair that a pierrot who terrified them is nothing but a wisp of straw in clothes: he tears it asunder—and collapses, gibbering, for on the roof of the booth the *living* Petrouchka sits and laughs at him.

The true name of concrete reality is the creation which is entrusted to me and to every man. In it the signs of address are given to us.

RESPONSIBILITY

The idea of responsibility is to be brought back from the province of specialized ethics, of an "ought" that swings free in the air, into that of lived life. Genuine responsibility exists only where there is real responding.

Responding to what?

To what happens to one, to what is to be seen and heard and felt. Each concrete hour allotted to the person, with its content drawn from the world and from destiny, is speech for the man who is attentive. Attentive, for no more than that is needed in order to make a beginning with the reading of the signs that are given to you. For that very reason, as I have already indicated, the whole apparatus of our civilization is necessary to preserve men from this attentiveness and its consequences. For the attentive man would no longer, as his custom is, "master" the situation the very moment after it stepped up to him: it would be laid upon him to go up to and into it. Moreover, nothing that he believed he possessed as always available would help him, no knowledge and no technique, no system and no programme; for now he would have to do with what cannot be classified, with concretion itself. This speech has no alphabet, each of its sounds is a new creation and only to be grasped as such.

It will, then, be expected of the attentive man that he faces creation as it happens. It happens as speech, and not as speech rushing out over his head but as speech directed precisely at him. And if one were to ask another if he too heard and he said he did, they would have agreed only about an experiencing and not about something experienced.

But the sounds of which the speech consists—I repeat it in order to remove the misunderstanding, which is perhaps still possible, that I referred to something extraordinary and larger than life—are the events of the personal everyday life. In them, as they now are, "great" or "small," we are addressed, and those which count as great, yield no greater signs than the others.

Our attitude, however, is not yet decided through our becoming aware of the signs. We can still wrap silence about us —a reply characteristic of a significant type of the age—or we can step aside into the accustomed way; although both times we carry away a wound that is not to be forgotten in any productivity or any narcotism. Yet it can happen that we venture to respond, stammering perhaps—the soul is but rarely able to attain to surer articulation—but it is an honest stammering, as when sense and throat are united about what is to be said, but the throat is too horrified at it to utter purely the already composed sense. The words of our response are spoken in the speech, untranslatable like the address, of doing and letting—whereby the doing may behave like a letting and the letting like a doing. What we say in this way with the being is our entering upon the situation, into the situation, which has at this moment stepped up to us, whose appearance we did not and could not know, for its like has not yet been.

Nor are we now finished with it, we have to give up that expectation: a situation of which we have become aware is never finished with, but we subdue it into the substance of lived life. Only then, true to the moment, do we experience a life that is something other than a sum of moments. We respond to the moment, but at the same time we respond on its behalf, we answer for it. A newly-created concrete reality has been laid in our arms; we answer for it. A dog has looked at you, you answer for its glance, a child has clutched your hand, you answer for its touch, a host of men moves about you, you answer for their need.[1]

• • •

1. The significance of *responsibility* (and the point of the whole section, indeed of the whole of *Dialogue*) is brought out more acutely in the German than in the English. *Wort, Antwort, antworten, verantworten,* etc., are part of a closely interrelated situation in which speech and response, answering for and being responsible for, and so on, are more intimately connected than the English version can hope to show. If the reader will remember that "responsibility" carries in itself the root sense of being "answerable," then the significance of the "word" in actual life will not be lost. Buber's teaching about the "word" always carries a strict reference to "lived life," and is very far from being an abstraction, theological or other. [Trans.]

OF THINKING

To all unprejudiced reflection it is clear that all *art* is from its origin essentially of the nature of dialogue. All music calls to an ear not the musician's own, all sculpture to an eye not the sculptor's, architecture in addition calls to the step as it walks in the building. They all say, to him who receives them, something (not a "feeling" but a perceived mystery) that can be said only in this one language. But there seems to cling to *thought* something of the life of monologue to which communication takes a second, secondary place. Thought seems to arise in monologue. Is it so? Is there here—where, as the philosophers say, pure subject separates itself from the concrete person in order to establish and stabilize a world for itself—a citadel which rises towering over the life of dialogue, inaccessible to it, in which man-with-himself, the single one, suffers and triumphs in glorious solitude?

Plato has repeatedly called thinking a voiceless colloquy of the soul with itself. Everyone who has really thought knows that within this remarkable process there is a stage at which an "inner" court is questioned and replies. But that is not the arising of the thought but the first trying and testing of what has arisen. The arising of the thought does not take place in colloquy with oneself. The character of monologue does not belong to the insight into a basic relation with which cognitive thought begins; nor to the grasping, limiting and compressing of the insight; nor to its moulding into the independent conceptual form; nor to the reception of this form, with the bestowal of relations, the dovetailing and soldering, into an order of conceptual forms; nor, finally, to the expression and clarification in language (which till now had only a technical and reserved symbolic function). Rather are elements of dialogue to be discovered here. It is not himself that the thinker addresses in the stages of the thought's growth, in their answerings, but as it were the basic relation in face of which he has to answer for his insight, or the order in face of which he has to answer for the newly arrived conceptual form. And it is a misunderstanding of the dynamic of the event of thought to suppose that these apostrophizings of a being existing in nature or in ideas are "really" colloquies with the self.

But also the first trying and testing of the thought, when it is provisionally completed, before the "inner" court, in the platonic sense the stage of monologue, has besides the familiar form of its appearance another form in which dialogue plays a great part, well-known to Plato if to anyone. There he who is approached for judgment is not the empirical self but the *genius*, the spirit I am intended to become, the image-self, before which the new thought is borne for approval, that is, for taking up into its own consummating thinking.

And now from another dimension which even this lease of power does not satisfy there appears the longing for a trying and testing in the sphere of pure dialogue. Here the function of receiving is no longer given over to the *Thou-I* but to a genuine *Thou* which either remains one that is thought and yet is felt as supremely living and "other," or else is embodied in an intimate person. "Man," says Wilhelm von Humboldt in his significant treatise on *The Dual Number* (1827), "longs even for the sake of his mere thinking for a *Thou* corresponding to the *I*. The conception appears to him to reach its definiteness and certainty only when it reflects from another power of thought. It is produced by being torn away from the moving mass of representation and shaped in face of the subject into the object. But the objectivity appears in a still more complete form if this separation does not go on in the subject alone, if he really sees the thought outside himself; and this is possible only in another being, representing and thinking like himself. And between one power of thought and another there is no other mediator but speech." This reference, simplified to an aphorism, recurs with Ludwig Feuerbach in 1843: "True dialectic is not a monologue of the solitary thinker with himself, it is a dialogue between *I* and *Thou*."

But this saying points beyond that "reflecting" to the fact that even in the original stage of the proper act of thought the inner action might take place in relation to a genuine and not merely an "inward" (Novalis) *Thou*. And where modern philosophy is most earnest in the desire to ask its questions on the basis of human existence, situation and present, in some modifications an important further step is taken. Here it is certainly no longer just that the *Thou* is ready to receive and disposed to philosophize along with the *I*. Rather, and preeminently, we have the *Thou* in opposition because we truly have the other who thinks other things in another way. So, too, it is not a matter of a game of draughts in the tower of a castle in the air, but of the binding business of life on the hard earth, in which one is inexorably aware of the otherness of the other but does not at all contest it without realizing it; one takes up its nature into one's own thinking, thinks in relation to it, addresses it in thought.

This man of modern philosophy, however, who in this way no longer thinks in the untouchable province of pure ideation, but thinks in reality—does he think in reality? Not solely in a reality framed by thought? Is the other, whom he accepts and receives in this way, not solely the other framed by thought, and therefore unreal? Does the thinker of whom we are speaking hold his own with the bodily fact of otherness?

If we are serious about thinking between *I* and *Thou* then it is not enough to cast our thoughts towards the other subject of thought framed by thought. We should also, with the thinking, precisely with the thinking, live towards the other man, who is not framed by thought but bodily present before us; we should live towards his concrete life. We should live not towards another thinker of whom we wish to know nothing beyond his thinking but, even if the other is a thinker, towards his bodily life over and above his thinking —rather, towards his person, to which, to be sure, the activity of thinking also belongs.

When will the action of thinking endure, include, and refer to the presence of the living man facing us? When will the dialectic of thought become dialogic, an unsentimental, unrelaxed dialogue in the strict terms of thought with the man present at the moment?

• • •

☙§ *What Is Man?*

PROSPECT

In two significant modern attempts we have seen that an individualistic anthropology, an anthropology which is substantially concerned only with the relation of the human person to himself, with the relation within this person between the spirit and its instincts, and so on, cannot lead to a knowledge of man's being. Kant's question *What is man?* whose history and effects I have discussed in the first part of this work, can never be answered on the basis of a consideration of the human person as such, but (so far as an answer is possible at all) only on the basis of a consideration of it in the wholeness of its essential relations to what is. Only the man who realizes in his whole life with his whole being the relations possible to him helps us to know man truly. And since, as we have seen, the depths of the question about man's being are revealed only to the man who has become solitary, the way to the answer lies through the man who overcomes his solitude without forfeiting its questioning power. This means that a *new* task in life is set to human thought here, a task that is new in its context of *life*. For it means that the man who wants to grasp what he himself is, salvages the tension of solitude and its burning problematic for a life with his world, a life that is renewed in spite of all, and out of this new situation proceeds with his thinking. Of course this presupposes the beginning of a new process of overcoming the solitude—despite all the vast difficulties—by reference to which that special task of thought can be perceived and expressed. It is obvious that at the present stage reached by mankind such a process cannot be effected by the spirit alone; but to a certain extent knowledge will also be able to further it. It is incumbent on us to clarify this in outline.

Criticism of the individualistic method starts usually from the standpoint of the collectivist tendency. But if individualism understands only a part of man, collectivism understands man only as a part: neither advances to the wholeness of man, to man as a whole. Individualism sees man only in relation to himself, but collectivism does not see *man* at all, it sees only "society." With the former man's face is distorted, with the latter it is masked.

Both views of life—modern individualism and modern collectivism—however different their causes may be, are essentially the conclusion or expression of the same human condition, only at different stages. This condition is characterized by the union of cosmic and social homelessness, dread of the universe and dread of life, resulting in an existential constitution of solitude such as has probably never existed before to the same extent. The human person feels himself to be a man exposed by nature—as an unwanted child is exposed—and at the same time a person isolated in the midst of the tumultuous human world. The first reaction of the spirit to the awareness of this new and uncanny position is modern individualism, the second is modern collectivism.

In individualism the human being ventures to affirm this position, to plunge it into an affirmative reflexion, a universal *amor fati;* he wants to build the citadel of a life-system in which the idea asserts that it wills reality as it is. Just because man is exposed by nature, he is an individual in this specially radical way in which no other being in the world is an individual; and he accepts his exposure because it means that he is an individual. In the same way he accepts his isolation as a person, for only a monad which is not bound to others can know and glorify itself as an individual to the utmost. To save himself from the despair with which his solitary state threatens him, man resorts to the expedient of glorifying it. Modern individualism has essentially an imaginary basis. It founders on this character, for imagination is not capable of actually conquering the given situation.

The second reaction, collectivism, essentially follows upon the foundering of the first. Here the human being tries to escape his destiny of solitude by becoming completely embedded in one of the massive modern group formations. The more massive, unbroken and powerful in its achievements this is, the more the man is able to feel that he is saved from both forms of homelessness, the social and the cosmic. There is obviously no further reason for dread of life, since one needs only to fit oneself into the "general will" and let one's own responsibility for an existence which has become all too complicated be absorbed in collective responsibility, which proves itself able to meet all complications. Likewise, there is obviously no further reason for dread of the universe, since technicized nature—with which society as such manages well, or seems to—takes the place of the universe which has become uncanny and with which, so to speak, no further agreement can be reached. The collective pledges itself to provide total security. There is nothing imaginary here, a dense reality rules, and the "general" itself appears to have become real; but modern collectivism is essentially illusory. The person is joined to the reliably functioning "whole," which embraces the masses of men; but it is not a joining of man to man. Man in a collective is not man with man. Here the person is not freed from his isolation, by communing with living beings, which thenceforth lives with him; the "whole," with its claim on the wholeness of every man, aims logically and successfully at reducing, neutralizing, devaluating, and desecrating every bond with living beings. That tender surface of personal life which longs for contact with other life is progressively deadened or desensitized. Man's isolation is not overcome here, but overpowered and numbed. Knowledge of it is suppressed, but the actual condition of solitude has its insuperable effect in the depths, and rises secretly to a cruelty which will become manifest with the scattering of the illusion. Modern collectivism is the last barrier raised by man against a meeting with himself.

When imaginings and illusions are over, the possible and inevitable meeting of man with himself is able to take place only as the meeting of the individual with his fellow-man—and this is how it must take place. Only when the individual knows the other in all his otherness as himself, as man, and from there breaks through to the other, has he broken through his solitude in a strict and transforming meeting.

It is obvious that such an event can only take place if the person is stirred up as a person. In individualism the person, in consequence of his merely imaginary mastery of his basic situation, is attacked by the ravages of the fictitious, however much he thinks, or strives to think, that he is asserting himself as a person in being. In collectivism the person surrenders himself when he renounces the directness of personal decision and responsibility. In both cases the person is incapable of breaking through to the other: there is genuine relation only between genuine persons.

In spite of all attempts at revival the time of individualism is over. Collectivism, on the other hand, is at the height of its development, although here and there appear single signs of slackening. Here the only way that is left is the rebellion of the person for the sake of setting free the relations with others. On the horizon I see moving up, with the slowness of all events of true human history, a great dissatisfaction which is unlike all previous dissatisfactions. Men will no longer rise in rebellion—as they have done till now—merely against some dominating tendency in the name of other tendencies, but against the false realization of a great effort, the effort towards community, in the name of the genuine realization. Men will fight against the distortion for the pure form, the vision of the believing and hoping generations of mankind.

I am speaking of living actions; but it is vital knowledge alone which incites them. Its first step must be to smash the false alternative with which the thought of our epoch is shot through—that of "individualism or collectivism." Its first question must be about a genuine third alternative—by "genuine" being understood a point of view which cannot be reduced to one of the first two, and does not represent a mere compromise between them.

Life and thought are here placed in the same problematic

situation. As life erroneously supposes that it has to choose between individualism and collectivism, so thought erroneously supposes that it has to choose between an individualistic anthropology and a collectivist sociology. The genuine third alternative, when it is found, will point the way here too.

The fundamental fact of human existence is neither the individual as such nor the aggregate as such. Each, considered by itself, is a mighty abstraction. The individual is a fact of existence in so far as he steps into a living relation with other individuals. The aggregate is a fact of existence in so far as it is built up of living units of relation. The fundamental fact of human existence is man with man. What is peculiarly characteristic of the human world is above all that something takes place between one being and another the like of which can be found nowhere in nature. Language is only a sign and a means for it, all achievement of the spirit has been incited by it. Man is made man by it; but on its way it does not merely unfold, it also decays and withers away. It is rooted in one being turning to another as another, as this particular other being, in order to communicate with it in a sphere which is common to them but which reaches out beyond the special sphere of each. I call this sphere, which is established with the existence of man as man but which is conceptually still uncomprehended, the sphere of "between." Though being realized in very different degrees, it is a primal category of human reality. This is where the genuine third alternative must begin.

The view which establishes the concept of "between" is to be acquired by no longer localizing the relation between human beings, as is customary, either within individual souls or in a general world which embraces and determines them, but in actual fact *between* them.

"Between" is not an auxiliary construction, but the real place and bearer of what happens between men; it has received no specific attention because, in distinction from the individual soul and its context, it does not exhibit a smooth continuity, but is ever and again re-constituted in accordance with men's meetings with one another; hence what is experience has been annexed naturally to the continuous elements, the soul and its world.

In a real conversation (that is, not one whose individual parts have been preconcerted, but one which is completely spontaneous, in which each speaks directly to his partner and calls forth his unpredictable reply), a real lesson (that is, neither a routine repetition nor a lesson whose findings the teacher knows before he starts, but one which develops in mutual surprises), a real embrace and not one of mere habit, a real duet and not a mere game—in all these what is essential does not take place in each of the participants or in a neutral world which includes the two and all other things; but it takes place between them in the most precise sense, as it were in a dimension which is accessible only to them both. Something happens to me—that is a fact which can be exactly distributed between the world and the soul, between an "outer" event and an "inner" impression. But if I and another come up against one another, "happen" to one another (to use a forcible expression which can, however, scarcely be paraphrased), the sum does not exactly divide, there is a remainder, somewhere, where the souls end and the world has not yet begun, and this remainder is what is essential. This fact can be found even in the tiniest and most transient events which scarcely enter the consciousness. In the deadly crush of an air-raid shelter the glances of two strangers suddenly meet for a second in astonishing and unrelated mutuality; when the All Clear sounds it is forgotten; and yet it did happen, in a realm which existed only for that moment. In the darkened opera-house there can be established between two of the audience, who do not know one another, and who are listening in the same purity and with the same intensity to the music of Mozart, a relation which is scarcely perceptible, and yet is one of elemental dialogue, and which has long vanished when the lights blaze up again. In the understanding of such fleeting and yet consistent happenings one must guard against introducing motives of feeling: what happens here cannot be reached by psychological concepts, it is something ontic. From the least of events, such as these, which disappear in the moment of their appearance, to the pathos of pure indissoluble tragedy, where two men, opposed to one another in their very nature, entangled in the same living situation, reveal to one another in mute clarity an irreconcilable opposition of being, the dialogical situation can be adequately grasped only in an ontological way. But it is not to be grasped on the basis of the ontic of personal existence, or of that of two personal existences, but of that which has its being between them, and transcends both. In the most powerful moments of dialogic, where in truth "deep calls unto deep," it becomes unmistakably clear that it is not the wand of the individual or of the social, but of a third which draws the circle round the happening. On the far side of the subjective, on this side of the objective, on the narrow ridge, where *I* and *Thou* meet, there is the realm of "between."

This reality, whose disclosure has begun in our time, shows the way, leading beyond individualism and collectivism, for the life decision of future generations. Here the genuine third alternative is indicated, the knowledge of which will help to bring about the genuine person again and to establish genuine community.

This reality provides the starting-point for the philosophical science of man; and from this point an advance may be made on the one hand to a transformed understanding of the person and on the other to a transformed understanding of community. The central subject of this science is neither the individual nor the collective but man with man. That essence of man which is special to him can be directly known only in a living relation. The gorilla, too, is an individual; a termitary, too, is a collective, but *I* and *Thou* exist only in our world, because man exists, and the *I*, moreover, exists only through the relation to the *Thou*. The philosophical science of man, which includes anthropology and sociology, must take as its starting-point the consideration of this subject, "man with man." If you consider the individual by himself, then you see of man just as much as you see of the moon; only man with man provides a full image. If you consider the aggregate by itself, then you see of man just as much as we see of the Milky Way; only man with man is a completely outlined form. Consider man with man, and you see human life, dynamic, twofold, the giver and the receiver, he who does and he who endures, the attacking force and the defending force, the nature which investigates and the nature which supplies information, the request begged and granted—and always both together, completing one another in mutual contribution, together showing forth man. Now you can turn to the individual and you recognize him as man according to the possibility of relation which he shows; you can turn to the aggregate and you recognize it as man according to the fulness of relation which he shows. We may come nearer the answer to the question what man is when we come to see him as the eternal meeting of the One with the Other.

BIBLIOGRAPHY

A full bibliography is given in Maurice S. Friedman's excellent study, *Martin Buber: The Life of Dialogue* (The University of Chicago Press and Oxford University Press, 1955). The following is a selection of the major writings.

Daniel: Gespräche von der Verwirklichung (Leipzig, 1913); translated by Maurice Friedman as *Daniel: Dialogues on Realization* (New York, Holt, Rinehart & Winston, 1964)

Ich und Du (Leipzig, 1923); translated by Ronald Gregor Smith as *I and Thou* (New York, Scribner's, and Edinburgh, T. and T. Clark, 1937)

Reden über das Judentum (Frankfurt, 1923; Berlin, 1932)

Kampf um Israel: Reden und Schriften, 1921–1932 (Berlin, 1933)

Deutung des Chassidismus (Berlin, 1935); translated as *Hasidism* (New York, Philosophical Library, 1948)

Dialogisches Leben: Gesammelte philosophische und pädagogische Schriften (Zurich, 1947); translated by Ronald Gregor Smith as *Between Man and Man* (London, Fontana, 1947; New York, The Macmillan Company, 1948)

Der Weg des Menschen, nach der chassidischen Lehre (Jerusalem, 1948); translated as *The Way of Man, According to the Teachings of Hasidism* (London, Routledge and Kegan Paul, 1950)

Gog und Magog: eine Chronik (Heidelberg, 1949)

Pfade in Utopia (Heidelberg, 1950); translated by R. F. C. Hull as *Paths in Utopia* (London, Routledge and Kegan Paul, 1949; New York, The Macmillan Company, 1950)

Israel und Palestina: zur Geschichte einer Idee (Zurich, 1950); translated by Stanley Godman as *Israel and Palestine: the History of an Idea* (Oxford and New York, East and West Library, 1952)

Zwei Glaubensweisen (Zurich, 1950); translated by Norman P. Goldhawk as *Two Types of Faith* (London, Routledge and Kegan Paul, 1951; New York, The Macmillan Company, 1952)

Bilder von Gut und Böse (Köln, 1952); translated by Michael Bullock as *Good and Evil: Two Interpretations* (New York, Scribner's, 1953)

Mose (Heidelberg, 1952); published in English as *Moses* (Oxford, East and West Library, 1946)

Gottesfinsternis (Zurich, 1953); translated by Maurice S.

Friedman *et al.* as *The Eclipse of God: Studies in the Relation Between Religion and Philosophy* (New York, Harper & Row, 1952)

Hinweise: Gesammelte Schriften, 1910–1953 (Zurich, 1953); translated by Maurice S. Friedman as *Pointing the Way: Collected Essays* (New York, Harper & Row, 1956)

A representative selection of Buber's writing is given in *The Writings of Martin Buber*, selected, edited and introduced by Will Herberg (New York, Meridian Books, 1956).

MARTIN HEIDEGGER

(BORN 1889)

Sein und Zeit (1926, Eng. trans., *Being and Time*) is one of the most remarkable philosophical books of our time. It is a formidable daunting work, not least to the translator, but its detailed articulated descriptions of the basic structure of human Being in the world is a striking original achievement. Heidegger intends a new approach to ontology to take the place of traditional ontologies, which must first be destroyed because they have never properly raised the question of Being but have got stuck in categories of thought which are not ultimate. This preoccupation with the original question of philosophy which, he thinks, needs to be taken seriously again takes him back beyond classical Greek thought to the pre-Socrates, preeminently Heraclitus and Parmenides, whom he finds in agreement and not opposed. In this return, he casts back to a time when philosophy was poetry and poetry philosophy, to offset the long preoccupation with logic. At the same time his is a severely philosophical concern with ultimate structures approached by way of Husserl's phenomenology: philosophy is an inquiry into Being, ontology; and phenomenology is its method.

Those who were excited by his main work have been inclined to find the sequels thin and baffling and to feel that he has left behind and even disavowed the solid work of *Sein und Zeit* for eccentric flights into Greek philology and for habits of thought which make him as oracular and obscure as Heraclitus himself. But Heidegger never pretended in his early work to do anything else but raising the question of Being again in order to attack traditional ontology and refound it on phenomenological lines, beginning with a description of the being of man in the world as the main clue. What he is doing in later essays and their elaboration is precisely what he was proposing to do in the Introduction to *Sein und Zeit*, although the philological quirk becomes an obsession.

After acquaintance with *Being and Time*, the English reader should tackle *Introduction to Metaphysics* (1953) in the translation by Ralph Manheim (Doubleday Anchor Book, 1961), especially the fourth section, "The Limitation of Being," and most especially subsection 3, "Being and Thinking."

EXTRACTS

Because of the great difficulty of Heidegger's *Sein und Zeit* and the impossibility of representing the argument in any sample of the work, an exceptionally trustworthy account of it is reproduced, written by Dr. Werner Brock, a colleague of Heidegger at the University of Freiburg. Dr. Brock closely follows Heidegger's thought and language.

The account is taken by permission from a volume published in London by Vision Press (1949) as *Existence and Being* by Martin Heidegger, Introduction by Professor Werner Brock. The volume contains in addition to the account of *Sein und Zeit* a translation of the texts of four important and complementary essays by Heidegger, with an account of them by Werner Brock. Thus the book gives a valuable conspectus of the thought of this difficult philosopher.

An Account of *Being and Time*

1: THE THREE MAIN PROBLEMS: DASEIN, TIME AND BEING. THE PROJECT AND THE PUBLISHED VERSION

One important criterion for assessing the rank of a thinker is the relevance of the problem or problems originally envisaged by him, the intensity and consistency of thought with which he contemplates it or them and the lucidity of the exposition. Another criterion is that, under the impact of a philosophic work, the reader is induced to consider life and the world in a new way and that relevant aspects, unthought of or left in the background before, are brought into the full light of conscious reflection. A true philosopher differs from the scientist and scholar, with whom he is bound up by their common search for truth, not only through the fact that his problems are on a greater scale and more fundamental. But if his exposition is of weight, it implies a new outlook with the force of affecting, changing or stimulating that of the reader.

Judged by these criteria, M. Heidegger's *Being and Time* is a work of high rank. And it must be my first task to make its main purpose clearer.

The aim of this great work, and indeed of all of Heidegger's publications, is the re-awakening of the question: what is meant by "Being?"

This problem belongs to the tradition of European philosophy from the Greek philosophers Anaximander and Parmenides onwards; more than that, it was its central problem. In Heidegger's view, it guided the exertions of the greatest among the Pre-Socratic thinkers as well as those of Plato and of Aristotle—but after Aristotle it ceased to be the thematic problem of a genuine philosophic enquiry.

The achievement of elucidation attained until Aristotle, affected vitally the medieval discussion of the problem and the whole of the Christian theological outlook; and through many changes the tradition of the problem kept alive down to Hegel's *Logic*.

To-day, and in fact throughout the last century, the problem of "Being" has fallen into oblivion.[1]

According to Heidegger, the concept of "Being" is the most universal one, as was also realised by Aristotle, Thomas and Hegel; and its universality goes beyond that of any "genus." At the same time it is obscure and indefinable; "Being" cannot be comprehended as anything that is (Seiendes); it cannot be deduced from any higher concepts and it cannot be represented by any lower ones; "Being" is not something like a being, a stone, a plant, a table, a man. Yet "Being" seems somehow an evident concept. We make use of it in all knowledge, in all our statements, in all our behaviour towards anything that "is," in our attitude towards ourselves. We are used to living in an "understanding of Being" (Seinsverständnis), but hand in hand with it goes the incomprehensibility of what is meant by "Being."[2]

Heidegger's aim in *Being and Time* is to revive the question about the meaning of "Being," in the sense in which it was

1. Cf. *On the Essence of Truth,* Section 6 and the corresponding commentary remarks in the Introduction. [This and several following footnotes refer to other papers of Heidegger in the volume or the commentary by Dr. Brock.—Ed.]

2. The statements made in this paragraph are strictly based on *Being and Time,* pp.2/4.

the guiding problem of Greek thought until Aristotle and its express theme of enquiry. In this respect he takes the Greek thinkers as his model.

But he deviates from them fundamentally in his starting-point. They reflected upon the things encountered in the world, that could be seen and thus known. And the thing that was perceived and about which statements could be made in various relevant respects, i.e. by way of "categories," was their paradigma.

Heidegger's starting-point is not the perceptible things, but what he terms: human [illegible]," a phenomenon fundamentally, i.e. in its ontologic[illegible]ucture, not contemplated and not analysed by the Greeks or ever since in later philosophic tradition. His endeavour in this respect is to give an analysis of the "existentialia" and of the "existentialistic" structure of human Dasein in a way in which the Greek thinkers developed the "categories" of a thing that "is." But this analysis, profound and original as it is, is to him nothing but the starting-point. It is from this new angle that he intends to unfold the problem of "Being" afresh. And the final guiding aim should not be overlooked when the attention is drawn to the new starting-point. The analysis of "Dasein" is of an exclusively preparatory nature.

Heidegger realised that "Dasein"—what is usually called "human life," though both are not entirely the same—differed ontologically from all the things which are not "Dasein" in essential respects. These things, when they are there by nature, are termed "vorhanden" ("existent" in the usual sense of the word, literally: before one's hand, at hand, present); and when they are made by men, such as utensils, they are termed "zuhanden" (close at hand, in readiness, at one's disposal); but occasionally, the term "Vorhandenes" and "Vorhandenheit" applies to all that is not "Dasein."

(1) "Dasein" is always my own "Dasein." It cannot be ontologically grasped as the case or the example of a genus of beings, as can be done with things that are "vorhanden." This by itself causes considerable difficulties for the adequate ontological exposition.—Besides, the being of the kind of "Dasein" is in its Being concerned about its Being and behaves towards its Being as towards its own possibility. It chooses and decides and it may gain or may lose itself, inasfar as its Being is concerned. All this cannot be said of the things that are "vorhanden."—Two fundamental modes of Being,

authenticity and unauthenticity, are distinguished, both of them depending on the fact that "Dasein" is essentially always my own.

(2) Of all the things that are "vorhanden" it can be stated that they are of a special "genus," e.g. a house or a tree, and that they have special "qualities." In other words: their "essence" is always ascertainable. In contrast to them, the characteristics of "Dasein" are not "qualities," but possible ways of "Being." Therefore the term "Da-sein" is to express not its "essence," but its "Being"; it means "Being there." To distinguish further the kind of Being, peculiar to "Dasein," from all "Vorhandenheit," the term "Existence" is applied exclusively to it. And the fundamental characteristics of "Dasein," corresponding to the categories of "Vorhandenheit," are therefore termed "existentialia."[3]

Heidegger's own philosophic thought is grounded and deeply at home in the whole of the Occidental philosophic tradition from the earliest Greek thinkers to Kant and Hegel and beyond that to Kierkegaard, Husserl, Dilthey, Scheler and Jaspers. It would go beyond the framework of this brief introductory characterisation to consider the relatedness of *Being and Time* to any endeavour in thought of one of his great predecessors or contemporaries.[4]

But it would seem appropriate to refer in passing to its relatedness to two more recent or contemporaneous tendencies: to the Philosophy of Existence, as inaugurated by Kierkegaard and prominently represented today by Jaspers; and to the method of phenomenology, as introduced by Husserl.

Heidegger characterised his own attitude towards Kierkegaard, as follows: "In the nineteenth century S. Kierkegaard expressly seized upon and penetratingly thought out the problem of Existence as an existential one. But the existentialistic kind of problems (Problematik) is so alien to him that he is entirely under the sway of Hegel, and of the ancient philosophy seen through him, in ontological respect. Therefore more can be learnt philosophically from his 'edifying' writings than from the theoretical ones—with the exception of the treatise on the concept of dread."[5]

This distinction between "existential" (existenziell) and

3. For the last two paragraphs cf. *Being and Time*, pp.41/45.
4. For the relatedness of *Being and Time* to Kant's *Critique of Pure Reason cf.* Heidegger's own book *Kant and the Problem of Metaphysics*, especially Section 4, pp.195/236.
5. *Being and Time* (German edition), p.235.

"existentialistic" (existenzial) is a fundamental one. When Kierkegaard criticised Hegel that he had omitted the problem of the actual Existence of the individual in his apparently all-embracing speculative philosophy and when he wrote his own works of philosophical elucidation, his aim was primarily not a "theoretical" one, but he wished by his "existential" elucidations to serve and to guide other people in their conduct of life. The "elucidation of Existence" in Jaspers' philosophy [6] takes fundamentally the same line. In the meditation upon Existence the knowledge of the objects of the "world" is transcended; but such meditation aims at appealing in communication to others and to clarify, stimulate and strengthen them in their striving for Existence in their actual conduct; "Dasein," which is here taken to mean the same as life, and "Existence," which is of an absolute significance to the individual, are radically distinguished. Existential philosophy is, by its nature, inseparably related to both insight and conduct.

Heidegger's interest in "Existence" is essentially different from that of either Kierkegaard or Jaspers. He regarded it as his task to analyse "Dasein" ontologically, as had not been done by the Greeks and was never attempted afterwards. In this respect "Existence" seemed to him the fundamental characteristic of "Dasein." But one important difference between science and learning on the one hand and philosophy on the other seemed to him to consist in the fact that every kind of scientific and scholarly knowledge was concerned with a limited set of objects, of what he termed "ontic," whereas philosophy strove to envisage and analyse the far more hidden structure, and the guiding concepts, of the phenomenon basic to the "set of objects," a visualisation and an analysis which is "ontological." In this sense he states that "philosophical psychology, anthropology, ethics, 'politics,' literature, biography and history" have been the studies of some aspects of Dasein and may have been "existentially genuine" (existenziell ursprünglich). But it remained an open question whether these investigations had been carried out in an equally genuine "existentialistic" (existenzial) manner, i.e. with a philosophic insight into and grasp of the "ontological" structure of Dasein. It is therefore with the "existentialistic" structure of Dasein, with what is basic to "Existence," that Heidegger is concerned. Otherwise he could not compare the "existentialia" to

6. Cf. *Philosophy*, Volume II, 1932. The impulse to "existential" reflections and the emphasis of the import on Kierkegaard's work can be noticed in his earlier publication *Psychologie der Weltanschauungen*, 1919, to which reference is made on occasion in *Being and Time*.

the "categories," analysed by Aristotle and since, of what is "vorhanden." [7]

Similarly he adapts the method of phenomenology, as introduced by Husserl, for his own philosophic purpose. The method was applied to prevent any arbitrary and ready-made epistemological constructions and to study and describe the whole range of the phenomena given to consciousness from the standpoint of "transcendental subjectivity." In the last chapter of the "Ideas to a Pure Phenomenology and Phenomenological Philosophy" Husserl expressly discussed the problem of a formal "ontology," of the transcendental constitution of a thing and of other "regional ontologies."

Heidegger adopted this method of philosophical analysis for *Being and Time*, and he adopted the aim of a "regional ontology," namely of "human Dasein," which, however, he considered to be the fundamental one preparing for an exposition of the meaning of "Being." But his attitude is not that of a "transcendental subjectivity" and of a study of the phenomena given to consciousness in the reduced state of a "phenomenological ἐποχή." But his intention is to overcome the attitude of "subjectivity," assumed by Husserl and by most thinkers since Descartes and Kant. His aim is to analyse the structure of Dasein, as it actually is, in its relations to the things in the "world," non-human and human; and though it is a transcendental analysis and though its problem is fundamentally different from that of Greek philosophy, it may be said that it is in its spirit and standpoint much nearer to Greek thought than perhaps any other work of philosophy in our age. The terms "objective" and "realistic" in their usual sense would not seem appropriate. But Dasein is envisaged in the light of "Being" and not primarily as a theme and "transcendental object" of human consciousness and "subjectivity." The phenomenological method, as applied by Heidegger, is thus as subtle in its descriptive analyses as is that of Husserl, but the attitude in which the phenomena are studied and the final aim towards which the enquiry is directed radically differ from that of his predecessor.

If the aim of *Being and Time* is the re-awakening of the question: what is meant by Being? and if its starting-point is

7. About the concept of "ex-sistence," first introduced in the essay "On the Essence of Truth," which is likely to have played an important part in the third Section of *Being and Time*, about "Time and Being," *cf.* that essay, Section 4 and the corresponding remarks in the Introduction.

an ontological analysis of Dasein, the one main problem not yet considered is that of Time. The problem of Time is the link between the analysis of Dasein and the revival of the question of the meaning of Being. Here again Heidegger's approach seems to be in vital contrast to that of the Greeks and the ontological tradition which they initiated.

In Heidegger's view, the meaning of "Being" is intimately bound up with the phenomenon of Time and has been bound up in this way since the beginning of philosophic thought. For the Greeks the definition of the Being of the things that are was, he points out, *παρουσία* or *οὐσία*, not only in its ontological, but also in its temporal meaning. The things that are were envisaged in their Being as "present." This basis of the interpretation of the things in their Being has never been fundamentally questioned.

The temporality of Dasein, with its relations to future, past and present—to what Heidegger terms the three "ecstasies" [8] of temporality—opens up the "horizon" for the question about "Being" in an entirely new way so that this question can be re-asked only after this analysis of temporality. The relevance of Existence becomes clearer here through its prevalent relationship to the future; and it may be said that all the dominant characteristics of Dasein gain their fuller significance in the interpretation of its temporality. One trait which is discussed entirely afresh in connection with the temporality of Dasein is its "historicity" (Geschichtlichkeit); and as Heidegger's problem of "Being" as well as the whole of European civilisation are grounded in "historicity" (a phenomenon meditated upon in more recent German philosophy by Dilthey and Nietzsche), the discussion of this aspect by itself opens up a new perspective.

The aim of the exposition of the temporality of Dasein is to gain an insight into the nature of Time itself, an insight which, in Heidegger's view, has hitherto not advanced substantially beyond Aristotle's interpretation of Time in the "Physics." An analysis of Hegel's concept of Time and an expounding note on Bergson's conception of Time tend to substantiate his view. The explication of Time as the "transcendental horizon" for the problem of "Being" was to lead to the aim: the analysis of what is meant by Being.

8. About "ecstasy" in the philosophical sense *cf.* the brief remark in my Introduction to "On the Essence of Truth" in connection with the concept of "Existence" as an "ex-position."

But now it seems appropriate to state what was the original plan of the work, as set out in the beginning, and what has been published of it hitherto.

The work was to consist of two main parts. Each of them was divided into three divisions. The first part was to contain the preparatory fundamental analysis of Dasein, the analysis of the temporality of Dasein and the analysis of Time as the transcendental horizon of the problem of Being. The second part was to offer a basic outline of a phenomenological destruction of the history of ontology, guided by the problem of temporality. It was to analyse critically central doctrines of Kant, of Descartes and of Aristotle and to show where their essential limitations lay, thereby clarifying Heidegger's own exposition of Time and of Being. In this way there were to be investigated Kant's doctrine of the schematism and of Time as a preparatory stage for the analysis of the problem of temporality; the ontological basis of Descartes' "cogito sum" and his transformation of the medieval ontology into the problem of the "res cogitans"; and Aristotle's treatise on Time as the discrimen of the phenomenal basis and of the limitations of Greek ontology.

The project comprising the two parts forms a whole. Only when Aristotle's doctrine of Time was scrutinised and the limitations of Greek ontology and of their influence on the ontology of the middle ages and of later times was made plain, only when the import of the conception of subjective consciousness in Descartes' work and its bearing upon subsequent philosophy right down to Husserl was exposed and only when the analysis of the temporality of Dasein was brought into clear comparison and contrast with Kant's doctrine of Time could Heidegger's systematic enquiry stand out in full relief.

Of this project only the first two Sections, a formidable work of concentrated systematic analysis of more than 400 pages, were published. The publication breaks off at the end of the analysis of the temporality of Dasein and before the most important exposition of the work to which everything else had been preparatory: the problem of Time and Being.[9] Nor have any of the historical analyses of Kant, Descartes and Aristotle, directly concerned with the problem of *Being and Time*, been published since, though the book on *Kant and*

9. About the reason given for the fragmentary character of the work by the author himself *cf.* the end of the Introduction to "On the Essence of Truth."

the Problem of Metaphysics arose in connection with the greater work and has a close bearing on it.

This fragmentary character of the work had, inevitably, a great influence on the understanding of its readers. What was aimed at and what was guiding the whole trend of thought: the problem of Being, was mostly overlooked; and it may well be said in defence of the interested and enlightened public that at the time it could hardly be grasped in its full and absorbing significance. In contrast to this, the novel exposition of the "existentialia" of Dasein, among them an analysis of phenomena, such as dread, care, the Being-towards-one's-death, the call of conscience and resolve, held the attention of many and it was rarely realised, though plainly stated by the author, that this ontological analysis of the structure of Dasein formed nothing but the preparatory starting-point. The philosophic study of human Dasein, though here undertaken from the unusual angle of a descriptive analysis of "existentialia," seemed the more to fulfil a requirement of the age, as Nietzsche and particularly Dilthey and his school had for long demanded a "philosophy of human life," as Simmel's philosophy had tended in the same direction and as Scheler had proclaimed the task of a "Philosophical Anthropology" during the very years when *Being and Time* was prepared and published. Heidegger may well meet with a similar fate as did Hume, in that his greatest contribution to philosophic thought, held back at the time, will be recognised only very slowly and gradually, while other more congenial results of his thought found a ready acceptance and, however much distorted, helped to stimulate what is now commonly termed the movement of "Existentialism."

The fact that the actual second part of the work, the investigations of the history of European ontology, i.e. of the philosophic interpretation of Being and beings, at some of its most decisive turning-points, was not published impairs the work further. The reader is thereby deprived of an insight into the great historic tradition and perspective in which the work stands, as conceived and understood by the author himself. The "phenomenological destruction" of this history, as Heidegger points out in the Introduction to *Being and Time,* was to lay bare, under the distorting and obscuring cover of more recent problems and interpretations which stand between us and the great thinkers of the past like a barrier, the actual problems with which Kant, Descartes and Aristotle were concerned. It had thus a positive aim. But it desired at the same time to bring into the open the essential limitations implied in Kant's, Descartes' and Aristotle's approach to ontology. The historic analysis would have made the hardened and fixed tradition come to life again and would, at the same time, have enabled the philosophically-minded people of our age to realise in what essential respects the problem of "Being" and the interpretation of the things that are had not come into full grasp or had even been obscured once more in Aristotle's philosophy.

Thus *Being and Time*, in the way in which it was published in 1927, is a fragment in two important respects: it does not contain that part of the systematic enquiry to which all the preceding and preparatory analyses lead up and by which, actually, they are guided; and it does not contain the historical exposition of those great figures of the ontological tradition against the background of which the systematic work itself with its high aspirations was to be measured.

Only with this reservation, and with the repeated emphasis on the great import of the Sections that are unknown for the time being, may now a few remarks be added about the general content of the first two Sections: the ontological structure of "Dasein" and the problem of temporality. These remarks are not intended to give a proper and detailed account of the phenomena that are analysed—a task which, as has been said in the beginning, cannot be undertaken here—but only to indicate the general framework of the exposition so as to allow the reader to see in what context some phenomena, which are of import also in one or the other of the four essays, were viewed and analysed in this work.

2: SOME ASPECTS OF THE ANALYSIS OF DASEIN

Human Dasein is characterised as "Being-in-the-world." This is its fundamental constitution, its innermost essence. The characterisation is not meant in the factual, i.e., "ontic," sense. For it is not essentially necessary that a kind of being, such as human Dasein, exists factually. It may not exist. Thus taken merely ontically, the proposition would even be wrong. It is an "ontological" definition, which means that Dasein can *be* in existence, i.e. as "*Dasein*," because its essential constitution is "Being-in-the-world."

"World" is the rendering of the Greek conception of κόσμος in the sense used by Parmenides, Melissus, Heraclitus, Anaxagoras and others and indicates the "state," the "how" in which the beings are "in the whole"—a term often employed in the subsequent essays—before any special kind of beings is considered separately. "World" is that whereto Dasein "transcends" so as to be what it is.[10]

Furthermore, the term "World" designates primarily, in Heidegger's view, neither the sum total of the things of nature nor a fundamental characteristic of the community of men, a new tradition introduced by St. Paul and St. John and continued by St. Augustine and by Thomas Aquinas, and also carried on in more recent and different connotations; but it means originally the "how" in which the things are "in the whole" as implicitly related to human Dasein, though for historical reasons this relationship was not given prominence in the strictly philosophic exposition.[11]

When it is stated in the essays that man is placed amidst a multitude of other beings "in the whole" or that man "lets" the things "be" such as they are, the fundamental characterisation that human Dasein is "Being-in-the-world" is in the background; and it should be borne in mind that this proposition is essentially different from any statement that something that is "vorhanden," e.g. a tree or a star, is in the world.

"Being-in-the-world" is analysed as a unitary phenomenon. The "in" in this connection is of a nature entirely different from the "in" applied to any phenomenon that is "vorhanden." If a thing is said to be "in" something else, this relationship is "spatial." If a being of the kind of Dasein is said to be "in" something, the relationship is not meant to be primarily "spatial," but means to "dwell," to "sojourn," to "stay," in the sense of the Latin word "habitare." E.g. a match is in a box in the plain spatial sense; but if a man is in his home or in his office or in a seaside-resort, obviously this relationship is not primarily spatial.

I have expressly referred to the "in-Being" (In-Sein), as Heidegger terms this structural characteristic of human Dasein, because it plays a great part in the analysis of the first Section, with its three fundamental modes, the "*Befindlichkeit*" of Dasein and its "Gestimmtheit," the "*Verstehen*" (understanding) of Existence and of the world and "*Rede,*" i.e. speech and language; and with the "Verfallen" (the potentiality of Dasein of falling a prey to the things in the world and of becoming alienated to its own authentic possibilities, intentions and endeavours), another outstanding trait of the

10. *Cf.* "The Essence of Ground," pp.12/15.
11. "The Essence of Ground," p.25.

"in-Being" of Dasein in its everyday state. But this "in-Being" is of considerable import also for the understanding of the essays, since the "Befindlichkeit," the "Gestimmtheit" and the phenomenon of language are expressly referred to or even discussed in some detail in one or the other of them. To these traits we shall return later.

Heidegger's first concern is to analyse the "*worldliness*" of the "world" and it is noteworthy that he observes and emphasises the point that Descartes, whose conception of "res extensa" he examines critically, had omitted to analyse, the phenomenon of the "world" itself, restricting his analysis to the study of the physical and of the mental "things"; and that a similar omission belongs to the whole of European philosophic tradition as such, explicitly so in and since Parmenides.

In order to open up the philosophic study of the phenomenon of the "world" itself, his approach is a new one, different from that of the tradition, in that he analyses the constitution not of the things as given by Nature (das "Vorhandene"), but of the "utensils" ("Zeug," das "Zuhandene"), as they are encountered in daily life. This analysis offers two advantages: (1) Dasein is primarily not concerned with the things of Nature in an exclusively theoretical attitude, but in its foreground of attention and interest are the "*utensils,*" this term taken in the widest sense of a product made by man in the state of civilisation. The things of Nature were originally encountered and discovered only in connection with such practical pursuit and they commonly form its background. Thus an analysis of "utensils," as that of one kind of beings, would seem to be as good for the opening up of the problem of the phenomenon of the world as an analysis of the things of Nature and would seem more appropriate in an exposition of the constitution of human Dasein. (2) Two different kinds of beings, "Zuhandenes" and "Vorhandenes," both belonging to the phenomenon of the "world," thereby come into sight and discussion.

In the course of this enquiry, Heidegger comes to define the worldiness of the world as "the Being of the ontic condition of the possibility of the discoverability of any beings encountered in the world." [12]

On the basis of the preceding analyses of the "utensil" and

12. It is in the analysis of the actual care for a "utensil," a "Zuhandenes," that Heidegger introduces the concept "letting-be" which becomes one of the key-terms in the essay "On the Essence of Truth," *cf. Being and Time*, pp.84/85.

of "worldliness" the "spatiality" of Dasein as "Being-in-the-world" and the concept of space are discussed. It is shown that neither the space is in the subject nor the world is in space, but that space is "in" the world and a characteristic of it, inasfar as Dasein as "Being-in-the-world" is of its own spatiality and has disclosed space.

The second main concern is the question about the "*who*" of Dasein. Though this "who" was formally characterised in advance as "I," this must not be taken as an isolated "subject" or "self," independent of the "world," of what is "zuhanden" and "vorhanden," and of the other fellow-beings together with whom the "I" is there. In a similar way in which Heidegger gave an exposition of the "worldliness" of the "world" by way of an analysis of the "utensil," he starts here from the "everydayness" in which the "self" exists together with its fellow-beings and indeed in many respects not as an "Ich" (I), but as a "*Man*," i.e. as "one like many." Since it will be one of the problems of the subsequent analysis: in what way does a Dasein become "authentic"?, the averageness of the way in which the "self" is together with others in daily life, the sway which these others hold over it and the resulting levelling tendency in community life are emphasised. Primarily there is not "I" as my own "self," but the others, and "I" as one among many others, in the way of "one" (in German: "man"). I behave as "one does," I avoid doing something, because "it is not done." The "one" (or in the more common English usage of the passive tense, the "it") is the "neuter" or even the "no one," as Heidegger in his characterisation of the "man" once calls it. Yet this "one like many" is a genuine existentialistic trait of the constitution of Dasein; and the authentic self-Being (Selbstsein) is not something entirely separate from the "one like many," but is an "existential modification" of it.

"Umwelt" (the relationship to the "environment" of Dasein in its widest sense, including all that is "zuhanden" and "vorhanden") and "Mitwelt" (one's being together with a vast multitude of beings of the kind of "Dasein") as well as the rudimentary "self-being" in the form of the "one like many" are the first structural characteristics studied in this analysis of the ontological constitution of Dasein as "Being-in-the-world." They are followed up by the analyses of "in-Being," mentioned above, and of "Care" as the Being of Dasein, to which a briefer characterisation of "dread" is a preliminary.

In view of their relevance for one or the other of the essays these two structural characteristics of Dasein as "Being-in-the-world" are to be discussed in slightly greater detail.

The "in-Being" (In-Sein) of Dasein,[13] as analysed in this work, is one of the most profound and stimulating enquiries of this Section, complemented at a later stage by the equally profound investigation into the "ecstasies" of temporality in which the modes of "in-Being" are thought grounded.

The analysis of "in-Being" is to clarify what is meant by the "Da," the "There," of human Dasein, what, in Heidegger's terms, is its existentialistic constitution.

One fundamental trait of Dasein, which is expressly discussed at various points of the published work, but which is in the centre especially in the analysis of "in-Being," is its "Erschlossenheit," i.e. the "disclosed," "discovered," "unveiled" state of Dasein. Referring to the well-known metaphor of the "lumen naturale" in man, Heidegger points out that this metaphor illustrates the way in which the "Da" of Dasein actually is. Dasein is "enlightened" or "illuminated" not by another kind of being, but it itself is what sheds light. And only to an "enlightened" being (for which the shedding of light is existentialistically constitutive) is what is "vorhanden" accessible in light and concealed in darkness. It is the essential "Erschlossenheit" of Dasein, in one with that of the existence of the world, that would seem to be aimed at in the metaphor.[14]

This phenomenon of the "Erschlossenheit" of Dasein should be borne in mind, when various modes of "in-Being" are considered.

(1) The first of these "existentialia" is termed "*Befindlichkeit,*" which indicates the way in which a Dasein is "placed" in life and in the world.[15]

13. The account of the "in-Being," of "dread" and "Care" and of the whole of the structure of Temporality keeps to the text of *Being and Time* as closely as possible so that this account may assist the reader with a sufficient knowledge of German to find his way better through the text of the original and also in order to make a philosophic discussion of Heidegger's problems possible, while *Being and Time* is not available in an English translation. [Now available. See Heidegger's Works below.—Ed.]

14. This "Erschlossenheit" of Dasein is expressly in the centre of the analysis at the end of the whole of the first Section, in the discussion of the problem of truth; and it may be said to be the theme also in the essay "On the Essence of Truth."

15. *Cf.* the contrast, in Section 2 of the essay "What is Metaphysics?", between our being "placed" (Sichbefinden) amidst the multitude of things in the whole, which situation repeats itself constantly in our Dasein moment for moment, and the comprehension of the whole of the things in themselves, which is impossible for man on principle.

But this "ontological" characterisation of Dasein being "placed" in life and in the world in a specific way manifests itself in another more concrete phenomenon, or, as Heidegger would say, is the same as the well-known "ontic" phenomenon, of "Stimmung" (mood) or "*Gestimmtsein*" (being "tuned," being in a humour, spirit, mood). Thus the way in which a human being is placed in life and generally in the world would reveal itself to himself (or to others) in and through his "moods" in a very general and vague, but somehow telling manner. (The power in man of shedding a "light" on Dasein and on the beings that are met in the world will be remembered, here as in the discussion of "understanding.")

The "Befindlichkeit" and its self-revelation through "moods" is analysed in three main respects: (a) Though the "wherefrom" and the "whereto" of Dasein remain veiled, the fact "that it is," i.e. the "thrownness" (Geworfenheit) of Dasein into its "There," and that it is left to its own devices and responsibility (Ueberantwortung) is disclosed to it undisguisedly. The "mood," in its deeper meaning, brings the Dasein face to face with the "That," the fact, of the "There." (b) The "mood" has already always disclosed the "Being-in-the-world" as a whole and makes it possible that the Dasein directs itself towards, and concerns itself with, some things, persons, itself in the world. (c) The Dasein which is circumspect can be affected, impressed, and also threatened, in its "There" by the things and the persons. In the "Befindlichkeit" there is implied a disclosing persistent reference (Angewiesenheit) to the world of a somewhat compelling force; and man may encounter anything that approaches him and concerns him out of the world. He is in some way constantly exposed to the world; and this, too, is vaguely and implicitly revealed to him through his "moods."—The concepts "Befindlichkeit" and "Gestimmtheit" are explicitly referred to in some of the essays; and the problem underlying them, the "in-Being" of human Dasein in the world, is common to all of them.

In *Being and Time* itself, one special mode of "Befindlichkeit," that of fear, is analysed, to prepare for the characterisation of another mood, that of dread, which in its turn is relevant for the analysis of Care.

(2) The second of these "existentialia" of "in-Being," co-original with the first, is that of "Verstehen" (understanding). It sheds light on the "There" of Dasein in a way fundamentally different from that of the "gestimmte Befindlichkeit." Taken in its deepest and, in Heidegger's view, most original

meaning, the "understanding" discloses to the Dasein "for the sake of what" (the "Worumwillen," the τοῦ ἕνεκα) it "exists," "Existence" here understood in the strict and modern sense. Things and persons and the whole of one's "Being-in-the-world" gain their "significance" (Bedeutsamkeit) from the dominant purpose or aim, for the sake of which man understands himself to "exist."

Dasein means primarily to have the "potentiality of Being" (Seinkönnen). And "potentiality" (or "possibility") is of an essentially different meaning for Dasein and for anything that is "vorhanden." For anything that is "vorhanden" it means what is not yet real and what is never necessary. It is what is "only possible" and is ontologically less than reality and necessity. As for Dasein, on the other hand, it is the most genuine and final positive characterisation. And "understanding," as one of the "existentialia," unveils man's "potentialities" of Being to him.

Both the "Befindlichkeit" and the "Verstehen" belong together and are inseparable from one another. Dasein, as essentially "placed" in life and the world, is always face to face with some definite "potentialities," has let some of them pass and continues to do so, while it seizes upon other ones and materialises them, for good or for bad. Dasein is "thrown potentiality" through and through; and it is the potentiality of becoming free for its own and innermost potentiality of Being. Dasein as "Verstehen" always knows in some way and to some extent what is the matter with itself, i.e. with its own "potentiality of Being." But such knowledge does not arise from, and is not dependent on, introspection: it belongs to the Being of the "There," which, in one respect, essentially consists in "understanding."

However, this "understanding" of one's own potentialities does not restrict itself to the "Existence" of the individual human being. In the "light" of these potentialities what is "zuhanden" is seen and discovered in its serving function, its applicability or its harmfulness; the potentiality of the interconnectedness of all that is "zuhanden" is seen and discovered as is the "unity" of the manifold things that are "vorhanden," i.e. Nature, namely on the basis of its disclosed "potentiality."

The counter-phenomenon to the "thrownness" (Geworfenheit) of Dasein as "Befindlichkeit" is termed "project" (Entwurf). The "project" of "understanding" is always essentially concerned with "potentialities," in all possible respects. The "understanding" conceives "for the sake of what" the Being of Dasein is to be as well as the "significance" to be attached to any utensils or things or persons and to the worldliness of the world. Such "projecting" has nothing to do with a well thought-out "plan" which would only be a remote derivative of it. Dasein has always "projected" itself already and continues to "project," as long as it is. In the same way as Dasein is always essentially "thrown" into its "There," it always "projects" essentially potentialities.

The "project" concerns the full revealedness of "Being-in-the-world." But the "understanding" has two primary tendencies of dealing with this "Being-in-the-world," in accordance with the realm that is discoverable to it. It may primarily concern itself with the disclosed state of the world, i.e. Dasein can primarily understand itself from its world. Or it may primarily project itself into the "for the sake of . . ." (the "Worumwillen"), in which case the Dasein "exists" as itself. In this sense the "understanding" is either an "authentic" one, arising from one's own self as such, or an "unauthentic" one, though this does not presuppose that the self is ignored and only the world understood and though the world belongs essentially to one's self-Being.—

Starting from his exposition of "understanding" as a fundamental mode of "in-Being," Heidegger analyses in some greater detail two "derivatives" of "understanding": "interpretation" (Auslegung) as the elaboration of the understanding of something as something and of "meaning" (Sinn); and the nature of "propositions" (Aussage) as a derivative mode of interpretation.—

In contrast to the phenomena of "Befindlichkeit" and "Gestimmtheit," those of "understanding" and of "project" are not explicitly referred to in the subsequent essays. But this does not mean that they are not fundamental to the problems which are analysed there. In the concluding note to the essay "On the Essence of Truth," it is expressly emphasised that the decisive question about the "meaning," i.e. the "realm of project" (Entwurfbereich), remained intentionally undiscussed. Obviously, the aim, approach and treatment of the essay would have gained much in the way of elucidation, had this dominant and, as Heidegger calls it, "decisive" question been brought into the discussion, too; and it seems fortunate that both its relevance and its omission are clearly stated. Similarly, the conception of "project" would seem to be of great relevance for the essays on Hölderlin, especially that on the poem "Homecoming" and the outlook developed there by the poet, but also that on "Hölderlin and the Essence of Poetry," particularly in view of the great, and even extraordinary, significance which Heidegger ascribes to the work of poets for the life of the human race and its history as a whole.

(3) The third of the "existentialia" of "in-Being," co-original with "gestimmte Befindlichkeit" and "Verstehen," is "speech" (Rede). "Speaking" is the "signifying" articulation (Artikulation, Gliederung) of the "Being-in-the-world" in the way in which it is "understood." The "understanding," arising for human Dasein in the "There" in which it is "placed," expresses itself as "speech"; and the totality of the "significances" articulated by "understanding" and "interpretation" comes to "word."

"Listening" (Hören) and "silence" (Schweigen) belong as potentialities essentially together with "speech." Constitutive characteristics of "speech" are: "what is spoken of" (das Worüber der Rede, das Beredete), "what is said as such" (das Geredete als solches), "communication" (Mitteilung) and "the information given" (Bekundung). As Heidegger points out, these are not "qualities" empirically to be gathered, but existentialistic traits rooted in the constitution of Dasein, which make something such as language ontologically possible. The attempts at grasping the "essence of language" have usually taken their orientation from one or the other of these traits. The task would be to elaborate the whole of the structure of "speech" on the basis of the analytics of Dasein.

The interpretation by the Greeks of the essence of man as ζῶον λόγον ἔχον, the living being which speaks, gives point to the import of the phenomenon. For "speech," in this sense, refers not to voice and sounds, but to the way in which the world and Dasein itself are discovered.

In this connection it seems noteworthy that Heidegger points out some shortcomings of the philosophic reflections on the nature of language, which are due to the Greek tradition. The λόγος was principally grasped as "proposition" (ἀπόφανσις) and the fundamental structure of only its forms and elements was elaborated. Furthermore, the foundation of Grammar was sought in Logic and the traditional Logic, on its part, arose from the ontology of what is "vorhanden." These limitations are thought to have essentially affected the subsequent study and theory of language; in the view of the author, this kind of learning requires a genuine philosophic refoundation.—

The problem of the nature of language is discussed in the essay on "Hölderlin and the Essence of Poetry." There it may be remembered that "speech" is regarded and analysed as a fundamental mode of the "in-Being" of human Dasein, equally essential as the "Befindlichkeit" with its "moods" and the "understanding" of potentialities, of the "for the sake of what" and of "significances."—

The analysis of the three "existentialia" of "Befindlichkeit," "understanding" and "speech" forms only the first part of the characterisation of "in-Being." Its second part resumes the investigation of the "everydayness" of Dasein, i.e. the "in-Being" of the "one like many" (in German: "man"), the primary "who" of Dasein. This aspect of the analysis is of considerable import in *Being and Time,* where "authentic Existence" is to be developed from its common background of the average and levelled kind of life of the "one like many." But it has relatively little bearing on the problems of the four essays and thus it may be treated more briefly here.

Three characteristics of the "in-Being" of everyday Dasein are analysed at first: (a) "Talk" (Gerede), a modification of "speech" in which what is and what is spoken of is not so much understood, but where one listens only to what is said; it implies an indifferent and superficial, but no "genuine" understanding and moves in the wide realm of common and accepted interpretations; like the other two it is a positive and constitutive mode in which everyday Dasein understands and interprets events, things, persons, the world and Dasein itself. (b) "Curiosity" (Neugier), a modification of the "vision" (Sicht) based on the power in man of shedding forth light, a tendency of a peculiar perceptive encounter with the world, not in order to understand what is seen, but merely in order to see what things look like; the new attracts for the sake of its novelty; it is usually bound up with restlessness and distraction. (c) "Ambiguity" (Zweideutigkeit), implying the difficulty in everyday Dasein of discerning what is disclosed (erschlossen) in genuine understanding and what not; all may look as if it were genuinely understood, taken up and spoken and fundamentally this is not so, and reversely, all may look different and yet attitude and behaviour are genuine.

The fourth characteristic, the "Verfallen" of Dasein, is of a more fundamental nature and is also basic to the three forementioned ones. It means primarily that the Dasein is entirely concerned and occupied with the "world" of its care. But an undercurrent of its meaning is that the Dasein lost itself in the publicity of the "one like many" and in the "world" which belongs to its Being. Here, as everywhere, Heidegger is interested in the phenomenon not as an "ontic" peculiarity, but as an "existentialistic," i.e. "ontological," mode of "in-Being"; and he describes in a most elucidating and impressive way this mode of "unauthentic" Existence and the structure of its inner "movement."

Dasein with the publicity of the "man" in its various forms offers to itself constantly the "temptation" (Versuchung) of "Verfallen." Yet when the Dasein is actually falling a prey to the publicity of the "man," this publicity itself, and the Dasein's trust in it, exercises a profoundly appeasing influence (Beruhigung) as if everything was in the best order. But this appeasement by itself intensifies the "Verfallen," driving to a restless activity and bringing Dasein into a state of "self-estrangement" (Entfremdung) in which its own innermost "potentiality of Being" becomes concealed to it. However, this self-estrangement which denies to Dasein its authenticity and best potentialities, as it were, locking it up from what it genuinely can be, does not hand it over to something which it is not itself, but presses it into its unauthenticity, a potential mode of Being of itself; in it Dasein catches itself up and entangles itself (Sichverfangen). This way of inner movement of Dasein in its own Being is termed the "fall" (Absturz): the Dasein falls from itself to itself, namely to the groundlessness and irrelevance of unauthentic everydayness. Its kind of motion is characterised as the "whirl" (Wirbel) which swings it down into the "man." But this whirl itself reveals the "thrownness" (Geworfenheit) itself in its moving and throwing force. For thrownness is not a finished fact, but Dasein, as long as it is, remains in the state of throw and may thus be whirled into the unauthenticity of the "man."

This constitution of "Verfallen" as a mode of "in-Being" is not anything that speaks against the existentiality of Dasein, but on the contrary is a weighty proof for it. For throughout the whole of the process of "Verfallen" Dasein is concerned about nothing else than its own potentiality of "Being-in-the-world."

"Being-in-the-world" is a unitary structural whole. Up to this point the phenomenon was analysed in its various constitutive aspects: the worldliness of the world; the Being-together-with-others, the self-Being and the "one like many"; the in-Being, the "There" of Dasein. The new problem is the unity of the structural whole. The question in this "ontological" enquiry, i.e. the philosophical investigation into the Being of . . ., is: what is the Being of Dasein? It is defined as "Care"; and in preparation for its exposition the fundamental "Befindlichkeit" of dread is analysed. But the analytics of Dasein is, as we know, not the main aim, but only the starting-point. Thus we shall have to bear in mind the one guiding question: what is the meaning of Being as such? especially while the Being of one kind of beings, of Dasein, is under consideration.

The concept of "dread" (Angst), introduced into the modern philosophic discussion by Kierkegaard, prepares not only the analysis of "Care" in *Being and Time,* but forms also one important link in the sequence of arguments in the essay "What is Metaphysics?"

Both Kierkegaard and Heidegger distinguish "dread" from "fear" (Furcht). "Fear" is always the "fear of something definite."[16] "Dread" is, as Kierkegaard puts it, "the reality of freedom as a potentiality, before this potentiality has materialised"; it is "a sympathetic antipathy and an antipathetic sympathy" and its object is "the something which is nothing."[17]

Heidegger analyses fear as a special mode of the "Befindlichkeit" of "in-Being" and dread as a fundamental "Befindlichkeit" disclosing Dasein to itself in an eminent way. Both phenomena are considered neither psychologically and psychopathologically nor "existentially" with a view to their relevance for the actual life of the individual, but ontologically with regard to their bearing on Dasein as "Being-in-the-world."

Three structural aspects in the phenomenon of "fear" are especially analysed: what is feared (das Wovor der Furcht), the fearing itself (das Fürchten) and on behalf of what the fear fears (das Worum der Furcht). (a) What is feared is always something which is encountered in the world, either of the kind of the "Zuhandene" or of that of the "Vorhandene" or of that of the Dasein of others. The "What" is threatening. This implies: that it is harmful; that it concerns a definite sphere of what it can endanger; that it comes from a definite "region" which is known, but somewhat uncanny; that it approaches and is imminent; that it may hit or pass by. (b) The fearing leaves room for what is threatening in this way. It allows itself to be concerned about it. It discovers it in its

16. S. Kierkegaard, *The Concept of Dread.*

17. *Op. cit.*, p. 37. It may be of interest to some readers that Freud, in his *Introductory Lectures on Psychoanalysis,* distinguished "dread" from "fear" in a similar way: "Dread is related to the mental state as such and disregards the object, whereas fear directs its attention especially to the object"; *cf.* Chapter 25: "About Dread."

threatening nature, while and even before it approaches. The fear may then clarify the specific kind of the threat by envisaging it expressly, since the circumspection is in the "Befindlichkeit" of fear. (c) The fear fears "on behalf of" the Dasein concerned. The Dasein discloses through its fear its own endangered state and its dependence upon itself. Thus the fear always reveals the Dasein in the Being of its "There," though in different ways, e.g. concerning one's own possessions or the well-being of a friend.

The phenomenon of "dread," though somewhat akin to that of "fear," is essentially different. What is "dreaded" is something that threatens, as is what is feared. But the "something" is different. The "What" of dread is not of the kind that can be encountered in the world, "Zuhandenes," "Vorhandenes" or the Dasein of others. To clarify the nature of the "something" that is dreaded the phenomenon of "Verfallen" is found of help.

When Dasein occupies itself entirely with its world of care and gives itself up to the publicity of the "one like many," something like a flight of the Dasein from itself as from its authentic potentiality of self-Being reveals itself. What it flees in this turning away from itself is not grasped and not even attentively experienced. But the "something" from which the flight or rather the withdrawal takes place must be of a threatening nature, though it is not concrete and definite, as is any "What" of fear. The turning away from oneself and the withdrawal from one's authentic potentialities in the "Verfallen" would seem to be grounded in "dread."

What is dreaded in the state of dread is entirely indefinite. As has already been mentioned, nothing of what is "zuhanden" and "vorhanden" within the world functions as what the dread dreads. More than this: all that is discovered in either of these ways is of no interest and the world itself has assumed the character of complete irrelevance. What is dreaded is that what is threatening is nowhere. It is somehow there—and yet nowhere, very close and oppressing—and yet nowhere. What is dreaded reveals itself as "it is nothing and nowhere"; but the atmosphere of profound averseness and oppression implied in the "nothing and nowhere" indicates that what is dreaded is yet "something," namely "the world as such." What the dread dreads is the "Being-in-the-world." The dread discloses the world as world, which does not mean that the worldliness of the world is comprehended in the state of dread.

This is the first aspect of Heidegger's analysis of dread. The second one concerns the question: "for the sake of what" the Dasein is in a state of dread.

Here again it is not for the sake of one definite mode of Being and one definite potentiality of Dasein that the Dasein is in dread. It is for the sake of the "Being-in-the-world" itself or rather for the sake of its authentic potentiality of "Being-in-the-world"; for the world and the Dasein together with others as such cannot offer anything to the Dasein in dread any more. The dread isolates the Dasein for its own innermost Being-in-the-world, it opens up to Dasein Dasein as "potentiality," namely as what it can be uniquely out of itself as an isolated one in isolation. It can now project itself into potentialities by way of its understanding.

In the phenomenon of dread, therefore, both what is dreaded and for the sake of what the Dasein is in dread are substantially the same. The one is the Being-in-the-world in the state of "thrownness"; the other is the potentiality of Being-in-the-world authentically. In this way a "Befindlichkeit" of an eminent kind has become the theme of the exposition which, by its fundamental character, prepares for the subsequent exposition of the Being of Dasein.—

The problem with which the reader of the essay "What is Metaphysics?" is concerned is not the analytics of Dasein, but the problem of the nature of metaphysics. In *Being and Time* dread is analysed, as it were, as the stepping-stone to Care, representing the transition from the "nothing and nowhere" to the Being of any Dasein. Here the emphasis lies on the phenomena of dread and Care themselves. In the essay the phenomenon of "nothingness" is in the centre throughout, though it is shown to be grounded in dread. Moreover, the transposition into "nothingness" is thought to be the preliminary and indispensable state, one of "transcendence," to open up the realm of the multitude of beings in the whole and of Being itself of which nothingness is "the veil." Here again a transition, though of a very different character, from nothingness to the beings in the whole and to Being is noticeable, not wholly dissimilar to that from dread to Care. Thus the exposition in *Being and Time* and that in the essay may mutually illustrate and elucidate each other, to some extent at least. Yet the problem of the essay is infinitely vaster. Thus, while in one respect the analysis of dread, including its relation to nothingness and the "Being-in-the-world," and also that of Care would seem of especial relevance for the understanding of the essay, the whole of the analyses of the first two Sections of *Being and Time* appear to be the background for its comprehension, as is definitely so in the case of the essay "On the Essence of Truth."—

In the subsequent analyses three ontological characteristics of Dasein show themselves to be the most fundamental ones: "existentiality" with its special reference to the "potentiality of Being" (Seinkönnen), "understanding" and "project"; "Befindlichkeit" or, as it is sometimes termed with a slightly different emphasis, "Faktizität" with its special reference to the fact "*that* Dasein is," that it is "thrown" into the "There" and is in the movement of the "throw"; and the "Verfallensein," which, though it is a movement into "unauthenticity," is manifest in some respects in every Dasein. These three characteristics should not be thought three self-dependent "elements" belonging to a compound; they are in one genuine structural connection one with the others and are of one whole. But it may be well to fasten one's attention upon them when the Being of Dasein is defined as Care, this term again taken in the ontological sense. Three important aspects emerge.

(1) Dasein is a kind of being which, in its Being, is concerned about its own Being, or, as it may be phrased, is "for the sake of" its own Being. It is free for its own innermost potentiality of Being and thus for the potentialities of authenticity and unauthenticity. This relatedness to its own potentiality of Being means ontologically: Dasein is, in its Being, always already in advance of itself.

(2) But this "Being-in-advance-of-itself" is not to be taken as an isolated tendency of a "subject" without world, for it characterises one aspect of the "Being-in-the-world." It is "thrown" into a world and left there to its own devices and responsibility. It is always already in a world, being in advance of itself.

(3) However, the actual Existence of Dasein does not only consist in a "thrown" potentiality of Being-in-the-world in general and without further qualification. Dasein always engages and spends itself in the world of its care. It is actively concerned with beings that are "zuhanden," i.e. belong to the realm of civilisation, in the world. In this the "Verfallen" manifests itself. Dasein is thus, structurally: Already-Being-in-the-world, in-advance-of-itself, as the Being-concerned-with-beings-encountered-in-the-world.

This is the formula for the ontological whole of the structure of Dasein, i.e. for its Being, to which the title of care (Sorge) is given. The formula may seem formidable at first, but I hope that, once it is seen how it arises, it can relatively easily be understood in its articulated meaning.

Care, taken in this sense, may be a care of . . . if it concerns anything that is "zuhanden," or a care for . . . if it concerns the Dasein of others.

The term "Care" is not only to characterise the "existentiality" of Dasein isolated from "Faktizität" and "Verfallen," but is to comprise all of them and to indicate their unity.

In view of the import of an exposition concerning the Being of Dasein itself, two investigations of a more general significance are carried out, to make the meaning of "Care" and its philosophic relevance clearer: one into the problem of "Dasein, worldliness and reality," where the problem of the reality of the outer world, Kant's refutation of Idealism, Heidegger's attitude towards "Realism" and "Idealism" as well as to the interpretations of the nature of "reality," more recently undertaken by Dilthey and Scheler, and the problem of the relationship between "reality" and "Care" are discussed; and another one into "Dasein, its disclosed state (Erschlossenheit) and truth." An account of these two investigations cannot be attempted here; a brief reference to the second one will be made in the Introduction to the essay "On the Essence of Truth."—

It is needless to say that the concept of "Care," of which only its formal and most general characterisation could be given above, is of special import and interest whenever it occurs in one of the essays: it is used rarely and most thoughtfully.

It is referred to in the Prefatory remarks to the interpretation of Hölderlin's poem "Homecoming" as well as in the interpretation itself, briefly in the beginning and more expressly towards the end. The vocation of the poet, according to Heidegger, is "to name what is holy." His Care, therefore, is concerned with "the way in which he must tell what he contemplates he ought to communicate in his poem." The "Holy" and the "Care" in his choice of the way of its communication and wording are thus the central concern of the poet as poet.

Similarly, the thought of the thinker is considered to be "obedient to the voice of Being" and he must therefore employ all his Care for conveying it in the language which he finds to be most appropriate.

Whenever the term "Care" is used, it refers to, and may even be meant to invoke for the reader the thought of, the

Being of either the poet or the thinker or the reader himself. The brief account given above of its significance in Heidegger's main work may help to understand it more precisely in its concrete applications in the essays.

3: DASEIN AND TEMPORALITY

The first Section, the preparatory fundamental analysis of Dasein, leads up to the exposition of Care as its Being. The second Section is devoted to the problem of "Dasein and Temporality." [18]

The enquiry aims at a more fundamental (ursprünglich) ontological interpretation of Dasein than has been reached so far, in order to lay bare the "horizon" in which something such as "Being" can become understandable at all and to answer the question about the "meaning" of Being as such. In the preparatory analysis the "unauthentic" Being of Dasein, and in fact without its consideration as a "whole," was in the foreground. Two questions are therefore guiding: (a) in what way can Dasein be approached and analysed as a "whole"? and (b) in what way can it be "authentic"? Both questions are interlinked, though the one or the other of them dominates the investigation at the various stages of its progress.

The problem of "Temporality" begins to be explicitly discussed only from the middle of the third chapter onwards, i.e. in the course of the third stage of our account. But it is implicitly the one outstanding problem right from the start; and the two "guiding" questions themselves are not only related, but even subservient to it. The analysis of the phenomenon of "death" as well as of those of "conscience," "guilt" and "resolve" is carried out not so much for its own sake as rather to prepare for the exposition of "Temporality" and more especially of the "future" which, in and for Dasein,

18. Of the first Section some outstanding characteristics, such as the "worldliness" of the world with its "utensils" and the "who" of Dasein as the "one like many," were only hinted at and mainly those traits which had a more direct bearing on the problems of the essays were discussed in somewhat greater detail. Thereby the reader may have gained an inkling of the originality and intensity of the exposition, but not a clear insight into the structural complexity and unity in its variety of aspects nor into the forcefulness of the systematic procedure and into its profound consistency.

As for the second Section the subsequent representation aims at bringing this systematic procedure, and with it the treatment of the problem of "Time," before the mind of the reader. For since the exposition of the meaning of Being itself has not been published, this treatment of the problem of "Time" should at least come into clear relief, as otherwise the reader cannot gain even an "impression" of the main purpose of the work nor fully realise what the occasional reference to "Time" at some point or other in the essays signifies. At the same time, the intention of comparative brevity is maintained.

is its dominant mode. Therefore the reader may do well to bear the problem of "Temporality" in mind even during the initial stages of the enquiry, though the problem is only implicitly posed there.

(1) The first step taken to envisage, grasp and define ontologically, i.e. existentialistically, Dasein as a "whole" is the analysis not of "death" as such, but of the "Being-towards-one's-own-death" (Sein zum Tode). The meaning of the term and the reason why this is the theme of the analysis will explain itself from what follows.

"Death" is the "end" of Dasein whereby it becomes a "whole." But to arrive at this boundary of Dasein is at the same time the loss of Dasein. The transition to Dasein-no-more makes it impossible for Dasein to experience the transition and, having experienced it, to "understand" it. There is the experience of the "death" of others and this phenomenon is first characterised. But for the problem under review, i.e. death as the "end" of Dasein which always means my own Dasein, the phenomenon of the death of others is not of relevance. However much one Dasein may be able to replace another one in the activities of the community, no one can relieve another one of his own dying. Death is irreplaceable. Dasein, as long as it lasts, is always and essentially a "not yet" of what it will be; and the others who are dead are "no more" in the "There," which is an essential trait of Dasein, too, when its "end" is reached.

The first question is: in what sense must death be comprehended as the "ending" of Dasein. Such "ending" does not necessarily mean "fulfilment," but it does also not merely mean "ceasing," as of rain, or "completion," as of a work, or "vanishing." The kind of "ending" meant by death would appropriately be characterised not simply by being "*at* the end" of Dasein, as if it were the actual outer close of it, symbolised, e.g., by the cutting of the thread by one of the three Parcae, but by "Being-*towards*-the-end." For death belongs to the "Being" of Dasein; and it is a mode of its Being to which Dasein is exposed and which it must take upon itself, as soon as it is.

After this initial clarification the existentialistic analysis is distinguished from other possible interpretations of death, such as the biological one of the death of plants and animals (Verenden), the physiological and medical one of the death of Dasein (Ableben), the psychological one of the states and the ways of the experience accompanying the "Ableben," the ethnological one concerning the conceptions of death by the primitives and their attitude towards it in magic and cult, furthermore especially the "existential" attitude towards death in its great variety, the theological interpretation and the one within the larger framework of "theodicy." To all these "ontic" interpretations with the rich multitude of their material the ontological exposition is methodically prior, even though its results are of a formality peculiar to all ontological characterisations.—

The actual exposition starts by demonstrating that, and in what sense, the "Being-towards-one's-death" belongs genuinely and essentially to the "Being" of Dasein, i.e. to "Care." "Care" was analysed with regard to its three main constituent aspects: "Existentiality," "Faktizität" and "Verfallen." The "Being-towards-death" is, first of all, characterised in these three respects as well.

(Existentiality.) Death is of the character of something towards which Dasein behaves: it is an "imminence" (Bevorstand) in an eminent sense. It is a potentiality of Being which Dasein, each in its way, has to take upon itself. With death Dasein in its own and *innermost* potentiality of Being is imminent to itself. In death the "Being-in-the-world" is at stake. It is the potentiality of no more being able to be there. In this imminence Dasein is compelled to take entirely its recourse to its own potentiality of Being. For in it *all relations* to the Dasein of others are *dissolved*. This innermost potentiality, without any relationship to others or to things, is at the same time the *extreme* one. As the potentiality of Being which it is, Dasein cannot overcome the potentiality of death. For death is the potentiality of Dasein being entirely and absolutely impossible. Thus death reveals itself as the innermost (eigenst) and irrelative, i.e. absolute (unbezüglich) potentiality, not to be overcome (unüberholbar).

(Faktizität.) Dasein does not adopt this potentiality afterwards and on some occasion or other in the course of its Being nor does it arise by way of a personal attitude that is taken up by some and at some times. But whenever Dasein exists, it is also already "thrown" into this potentiality. At first and mostly, Dasein has no express, and even less a theoretical, knowledge of the fact that it is handed over to its death. The thrownness into death unveils itself more genuinely and more penetratingly in the "Befindlichkeit" of dread. The dread of death is dread of one's own innermost and irrelative potentiality of Being, not to be overcome. What is dreaded in this state of dread is the "Being-in-the-world" itself. For the sake of what Dasein is in a state of dread is the "potentiality of Being" of Dasein as such. The dread of death is no arbitrary and chance mood of the individual, but, as a fundamental Befindlichkeit of Dasein, the disclosure that Dasein exists as the thrown "Being-towards-its-end."

(Verfallen.) At first and mostly, Dasein obscures and conceals its own "Being-towards-death," fleeing from it. Dasein dies factually, as long as it exists, but at first and mostly in the mode of "Verfallen." For the actual Existence engages and spends itself always already also in the world of its care. In this state of preoccupation with what is cared for the flight from the "uncanny" announces itself, i.e. in this context, the flight from its own "Being-towards-death."—

Before Heidegger endeavours to develop the full existentialistic concept of death, he considers it first in its best known concrete mode, that of everydayness.

In the publicity of the "one like many" death is "known" as an event which constantly occurs, as something which happens "in" the world, i.e. as something which is "vorhanden," but not yet "vorhanden" for the person concerned and thus of no threatening character. "People die" (man stirbt). This "man" is "not just I"; it is "no one." The publicity of the "one like many" intensifies the "temptation" of concealing to oneself one's own "Being-towards-death" as well as the constant "appeasement" about it, even in the conventional consolation with which the "dying" is often persuaded he would escape death. The publicity of the "one like many" does not allow the courage required for the dread of death to arise. An indifferent tranquillity is expected in view of the "fact" that "one" dies. The development of such "superior" indifference "estranges" the Dasein from its innermost, irrelative potentiality of Being.

The mode of "Verfallen" is obvious in such "temptation," "appeasement" and "estrangement." The everyday Being-towards-death is a constant flight from it and has the mode of avoiding it by way of its misinterpretation, unauthentic understanding and disguise. But with all this, Dasein in its everydayness, shows itself to be essentially concerned about this innermost and irrelative potentiality of Being, if only in the mode of its care for an undisturbed indifference to the extreme potentiality of its Existence.—

In the continued examination of the Being-towards-death

in its everydayness two further essential traits emerge and are discussed: the kind of "certainty" (Gewissheit) implied in death and its "indefinable" character ("Unbestimmtheit") as to its "when."

"Certainty" is grounded in truth and one mode of certainty is conviction. But the way in which Dasein in its everydayness is mostly convinced of the "certainty" of death is that it is an "event" somehow encountered in the world. Even in serious theoretical reflection death is regarded as merely a "fact of experience" which can be observed daily and which therefore is undeniable. It is usually overlooked that Dasein, i.e. my own Dasein, must be certain of its own innermost and irrelative potentiality of Being in order to be able to be certain of death.

One way of obscuring the "certainty" of death in everyday Dasein results from its "indefinable" character as to its "when." It is interpreted and thought of as the "not yet for the time being." Dasein in its everydayness tries to cover up that death, as the "end" of one's own Dasein is imminent every moment.

Death is thus defined as the innermost and irrelative potentiality of Being, certain and indefinite as to its "when" and not to be overcome. And the problem that now arises, and for which the whole of Heidegger's preceding analysis prepares, is: in what way can Dasein "understand" its own death "authentically" and what is the "authentic" attitude and behaviour towards one's own death, i.e. the authentic "Being-towards-death"?—

The authentic "Being-towards-death" will not evade its own innermost and irrelative potentiality nor obscure or conceal it in such an escape nor misinterpret it in the way of the intelligibility of the "one like many."

It will "understand" the Being-towards-death as a Being concerned with a "potentiality" and in fact an eminent potentiality of Dasein. This potentiality, however, does not belong to the realm of what is "zuhanden" or "vorhanden," where something is to be attained or brought into control and "realised" in some way. It is a potentiality of the Being of Dasein. If it is to be "authentically understood," it must be understood, developed and endured in one's practical attitude and behaviour as a "potentiality" and no obscuring of it should be allowed.

"Expectation" is the behaviour of Dasein towards something possible in its potentiality. But this phenomenon is ambiguous in that it is mostly related to "realisation" and "reality" and to what is possible or potential there. But the attitude towards one's death is to be such that it unveils itself in and for its Being as "potentiality." Such Being towards a potentiality is termed a *"running forward in thought"* (Vorlaufen) to the potentiality. It does not aim at bringing something "real" into one's control, but approaches it in its potentiality most closely. In fact, the closest proximity of Being-towards-death is as remote from anything "real" as possible. The less this potentiality is understood in an obscured way, the more genuinely does the understanding penetrate into the potentiality as the impossibility of Existence as such. Death is the potentiality of the impossibility of every kind of behaviour towards . . . , of every mode of Existence. This "running forward in thought" to the potentiality of death makes it truly possible as such and makes the Dasein "free" for it.

Such "running forward in thought" to the potentiality of Being, as here with regard to one's death, is a very important mode of the constitution of Dasein itself, as will be seen later. As to death, Dasein discloses itself thereby in its extreme potentiality. Owing to such "running forward in thought," one's own and innermost extreme potentiality of Being can be understood, i.e. understood as the potentiality of authentic Existence.

In this perspective the five main characteristics of "Being-towards-death" are examined.

(a. Death as the innermost potentiality of Dasein.) The Being-towards-death discloses for Dasein its innermost potentiality of Being, in which the Being of Dasein is at stake. Dasein can become aware that, in this eminent potentiality of itself, it will be aloof from the "one like many" and that, in the "running forward in thought" to death, it can separate itself from this unauthentic mode, enabling itself to stand aloof.

(b. Death as the irrelative potentiality of Dasein.) Dasein can learn to understand that it has to take upon itself this potentiality of Being, involved in death, when "running forward in thought" to it. Death does not belong to Dasein in an indifferent way, but claims it in its individuality. The irrelative nature of death singles the Dasein out and refers it to itself. It makes it aware that all concern for the world of one's care and for other people fails, when one's own potentiality of Being is at stake. Dasein can be "authentic" only when it has enabled itself to be so. Dasein is "authentic" only when it is primarily concerned with its own potentiality of Being, and not with that of the "one like many," while taking care of things and of one's fellow-men.

(c. Death as the potentiality of Dasein not to be overcome.) It can learn to understand that the extreme potentiality of Existence is one of ultimate renunciation. The "running forward in thought" does not try to evade it, but makes Dasein free for it. But this liberation for one's own death frees man also from the danger of losing himself to chance possibilities and allows him to understand and choose his actual potentialities, which precede the one which cannot be overcome. Free for his own potentialities, which are determined by the "end," that is to say, are understood as "finite" ones, he will also free himself from the danger of misunderstanding the existential potentialities of others or from forcing them into the framework of his own potentialities by way of misinterpretation: for death as an irrelative potentiality singles man out and, as it were, individualises him to make him understand the potentiality of the Being of others, when he realises the inescapable nature of his own death. Because the "running forward in thought" to the potentiality that cannot be overcome implicitly discloses all the potentialities that precede it, it can envisage existentially the "whole" of Dasein, i.e. "exist" as a "whole" potentiality of Being.

(d. Death as the certain potentiality of Dasein.) The certainty of death cannot be calculated from the observation of deaths nor does it belong to the realm of the truth of what is "vorhanden": it has nothing to do with the order of degrees concerning the "evidence" of things or events that are "vorhanden." The kind of certainty, here involved, discloses itself only when the "running forward in thought" renders the potentiality of death actually potential. Then it will be found to be more "fundamental" than any kind of certainty of the things that are encountered or of formal objects. For it ascertains the Being-in-the-world itself and the innermost Being of Dasein as a "whole."

(e. Death as the potentiality of Dasein indefinite as to its when.) In realising the certainty and at the same time the "indefinite" character of death, Dasein opens up for a constant threat arising from its own "There." The mood in which it meets this threat of an absolute nature is that of dread. In it Dasein is face to face with the "nothing" of the potential impossibility of Existence and thereby discloses the extreme potentiality.

The characterisation of the "authentic Being-towards-death" is summarised as follows. "The running forward in thought reveals to Dasein that it is lost in the 'oneself' and brings it face to face with the potentiality of being itself, primarily unaided by the care of others, but itself in the passionate, actual Freedom-towards-death (Freiheit zum Tode), being certain of it and dreading it, yet being independent of the illusions of the 'one like many.'"

(2) The second step in the new enquiry is guided primarily not by the problem of Dasein as a "whole," but by that of its "authenticity." The problem is as follows. An "authentic" potentiality of the Being of Dasein, i.e. "self-Being," was presupposed in the last and most relevant formulation of the analysis of "Being-towards-death." If so, such a potentiality of "self-Being" must be "testified." With regard to this problem three phenomena are ontologically analysed: conscience, guilt and resolve.

(a. Conscience.) The essential character of conscience is found in its "call." Whereas Dasein primarily and mostly "listens" to others, gaining its restricted and unauthentic potentiality of Being and its kind of understanding in the world of its care and in the publicity of the "one like many," the "call" of conscience breaks into such "listening" of the Dasein to the anonymous "one like many" and appeals to the "self" in man to fetch it back out of this anonymity.

Heidegger considers the "call of conscience" to be a mode of "speech" in the strict sense, emphasising again that the voicing of a sound is not essential for "speech" or for a "call" like this one. "Speech" in any of its modes articulates what is "understood"; and so does, in its own way, the "call" of conscience. Heidegger refuses to accept the common interpretation which tries to trace conscience back to one of the presumed "faculties of the soul," intellect, will or feeling or to explain it as the complex product of all of them.

The "call of conscience" is characterised as a mode of speech in the following way. (a) What is spoken of is Dasein itself, not in a vague and indifferent way, but in the way in which it understands itself concretely in its everyday and average kinds of care. (b) What is appealed to is one's own "self"; not what the Dasein is reputed to be, able to do, has achieved or stood up for in the publicity of community life, which, in its "worldly" aspects, is passed by by the "call" of conscience, but the "self" which is thereby aroused, while the "one like many" collapses. This "self" is not the "object" of introspection and of self-critisism, not something which is separate from the "outer world," which likewise is passed by, but the "self" as one mode of "Being-in-the-world." (c) What is said in this "call" of conscience is in one sense nothing: it offers no information about any events nor does it open up a soliloquy or an inner negotiation. But the "call" appeals to the self's own potentiality of Being. (d) There is no sounding of a voice in this "call." Conscience speaks constantly in the mode of silence and in it alone. Yet it does not lose in audibility thereby, but, on the contrary, forces upon the Dasein which is appealed to and aroused, a silence which is to be of great relevance. (c) The "call" discloses something which is unambiguous, despite the apparent vagueness of its content, namely a sure direction of drive in which the Dasein of the "self" is to move.

The first part of the anaylsis is concerned with the nature of the "call"; the second part, with that of the "caller." According to Heidegger's interpretation, conscience is the "call" of Care. Here again only a few main points may be mentioned.

(a) Conscience calls the self of Dasein out of the state in which it is lost in the "one like many." The "self" is unambiguously and unexchangeably meant, but beyond this there remains an astonishing vagueness regarding the "What" of the call as well as its source, the "caller." The one main thing is that the call is to be "listened" to. According to Heidegger, Dasein calls in conscience for itself. (b) This call is not planned nor prepared nor voluntarily carried out by ourselves. "It" calls against one's own expectation and even one's own wishes. Yet the call comes not from any one else, but from myself and upon myself.—These characteristics of the phenomenon as such have led to two different interpretations, which go beyond the phenomenon itself: of God as the source of conscience or, as its counterpart, of explaining conscience away in a biological manner. Both of them try to interpret what is, namely the phenomenon of the call, as being "vorhanden." (c) To clarify the "it" that is calling, Heidegger refers to the "thrownness" of Dasein and to Dasein being "thrown into its Existence." The "That" is disclosed to Dasein, the "Why" is concealed. It is suggested that Dasein, being placed in the ground of its uncanniness, is the caller of the call of conscience. A number of phenomena are adduced in its favour, e.g. that the "caller" is unfamiliar to the "oneself" in its everydayness, that the call speaks in the "uncanny" mode of silence to call the self back into the silence of the "existent" potentiality of Being, that "uncanniness" is a fundamental mode of "Being-in-the-world," though concealed in everyday Dasein, and that in the call of conscience tuned by dread, which enables Dasein to "project" itself into its own potentiality of Being, the "uncanniness" follows Dasein closely and threatens its state of being lost in self-forgetfulness. (d) The final proposition is: that "conscience reveals itself as the call of Care." The caller is Dasein which dreads in its thrownness (Already-Being-in-the-world) on behalf of its potentiality of Being. What is called upon is this same Dasein appealed to in its own potentiality of Being (Being-in-advance-of-itself). And Dasein is appealed to by the call out of the "Verfallen" in the "one like many" (Already-Being-concerned-with-the-world-of-its-care).

The main aim of the enquiry at this stage is to make the phenomenon of conscience understandable as a "testimony" of Dasein's own potentiality of Being. The enquiry is continued by investigating what this call of conscience makes Dasein understand. This leads to the analysis of guilt.

(b. Guilt.) Heidegger starts from the double aspect in the "call of conscience": that it points to the Whereto and to the Wherefrom, to the potentiality of Being and to the uncanniness of "thrown" individualisation. (Whereas the "running forward in thought" to death prepares for the analysis of the future as the dominant mode of "Temporality," that of conscience, guilt and resolve prepares for that of the future, the past and the present in their unity.) As the call of conscience seems to make Dasein understand its "guilt" (Schuld, which word means also: what one owes to others, e.g. a debt) this phenomenon is first discussed in its various "ontic" meanings. Its basic ontological meaning is found to be a "deficiency," a lack of something which ought to be and can be, the ground of a "nullity" (Nichtigkeit). That Dasein is guilty (schuldig), it is pointed out, does not result from one special fault or wrong done, but, reversely, such fault is possible only on the basis of an original Being-guilty of Dasein.

It is shown in a very subtle analysis how Dasein and Care, thrownness and project, are permeated through and through by "nullity" and that "guilt" is thus grounded in the Dasein as such. In this connection Heidegger refers to the "ontological meaning of nothingness (Nichtheit)," the "ontological essence of the not as such" and the problem of the "ontological origin of nothingness" and its intrinsic conditions—a complex of problems which form the background and also the theme of "What is Metaphysics?"

To understand the call of conscience made upon the "self" (Anrufverstehen) means therefore to realise that Dasein itself, i.e. my own Dasein, is "guilty." Being guilty is a fundamental constituent of Care. Being the null ground of its null project of taking over into its own responsible Existence what it was "thrown" to be, Dasein is to be fetched back out of its lost state as a "one like many," by the call of conscience, which points forward and backward, and makes man aware that he "is guilty." Only when man projects himself also into the potentiality of being and becoming guilty (which is entirely different from making oneself actually guilty by way of a fault or a neglect), can he be open for his own potentiality of Existence and can he "choose himself" in the existential sense.

The will to have conscience is "chosen" by the self when it understands the call of conscience in the right way. Thereby it becomes free for its own "guilt" as well as for its own potentiality of Being. Understanding the call, Dasein lets its own self "act" in the way of "inner action" out of its "chosen" potentiality of Being. Only in this way can Dasein be "responsible."

(c. Resolve.) The aim of the enquiry at this second stage, the analysis of conscience, guilt and resolve, is: to characterise a "testifiable" authentic potentiality of Being, which is essentially connected with the "running forward in thought" to death so far conceived only in its ontological possibility. Such a "testimony" is found in the phenomenon of conscience and the closely allied ones of guilt and resolve. As with the phenomenon of Care before, the existentialistic structure of the authentic potentiality of Being is here in the foreground. Three main traits are emphasised.

(a) The will to have conscience is a self-understanding in one's own potentiality of Being and, in this respect, a mode of Dasein as being "disclosed" (Erschlossenheit). To understand oneself existentially means to project oneself into an actual potentiality of Being-in-the-world, which is essentially one's own. Only when one actually "exists" in the mode of such a potentiality can it be "understood."

(b) The mood that corresponds to such an "understanding" is that not of dread as such, but of a readiness for dread, in view of the uncanniness of the individualisation. In the readiness for the dread of conscience, Dasein is brought face to face with this uncanniness.

(c) The mode of speech here implied is that kind of silence in which the call of conscience brings the self to the realisation of permanent guilt and fetches it back from the talk of the intelligibility of the "one like many."

This projecting of oneself, in silence and in readiness for dread, into one's own Being-guilty—an outstanding mode of the disclosed state of Dasein, testified by conscience—is termed "resolve." The "resolve" is characterised as the "authentic self-Being," which means not a Dasein isolated from the world, but "Being-authentically-in-the-world."

The "for the sake of what" of the self-chosen potentiality of Being makes the "resolute" Dasein free for its world. The authentic fellowship of human beings depends on and arises from the authentic "self-Being" of resolve.

The "resolve" is essentially always of one actual Dasein only. The aim or the ends of the "resolve" depend on the individual Dasein and its thrown and factual potentialities. The existential resolution alone determines and defines them. But even the resolution of the individual remains related to, and in some way dependent on, the "one like many" and its world.

The "resolve" gives to Dasein a peculiar and authentic lucidity. It discovers in reality actual significant potentialities and deals with them purposefully. Two phenomena especially can be truly approached only by an individual in the attitude of "resolve": a concrete given "situation" and genuine "action."

A concrete given "situation" is the "There" disclosed in its nature by "resolve." It is essentially different from a mixture of circumstances and chance events, from general conditions and opportunities. A "situation" in the sense meant here is unknown to the "one like many." It is the call of conscience that, when arousing the self and its potentiality of Being, calls the Dasein forth into a "situation." Not an empty ideal of Existence is aimed at in the attitude of "resolve," but a situation is, and situations are, to be mastered.

In such a "situation" the Dasein of "resolve" "acts" in the genuine sense, which implies of course the potentiality of "resistance." But the term "action" is very ambiguous and may be misleading. Care, as the Being of Dasein, does not allow for a separation between a "theoretical" and a "practical" kind of behaviour. Therefore it would be a complete misunderstanding of the term "action" if resolve, situation and action were thought to be especially related to practical behaviour. Resolve, intimately related to conscience and guilt, is the "authenticity" of Care.

(3) The two preparatory stages of the investigation into the problem "Dasein and Temporality" were guided (a) by the question of Dasein as a "whole" and (b) by that of Dasein as "authentic." But the problem of Temporality as such has not been made the explicit theme. This is done, on principle at least, in this third stage of the enquiry. But at first the two most outstanding phenomena of the preceding analyses, the authentic "Being-towards-death" as the "running forward in thought" and the authentic potentiality of Being as "resolve," are interpreted in their essential interconnectedness: the "running forward in thought" is shown to be a most fundamental trait of "resolve," while death is envisaged, besides guilt, in its profound relationship to the "nullity" of Dasein. "Resolve running forward (in thought) to . . ." refers to the one phenomenon which had not yet come into full sight before: the "authentic" potentiality of Dasein as a "whole." This phenomenon had to be analysed first before the phenomenon of Temporality could be discussed.

But this unity of "authenticity" and "whole" in the phenomenon of "resolve running forward (in thought) to . . ." is not the only problem to be clarified in advance. The problem of the fundamental unity of the structure of Care, now implying the "Being-towards-the-end," conscience, guilt and resolve as well, must be elucidated, too. The traditional solution in this respect is found in the "Ego" or the "self" as the basic ground. Heidegger considers this solution to be erroneous. Only when this question of principle has been answered can the exposition of Temporality be carried out.

I am omitting here an account of the phenomenon of "resolve running forward (in thought) to . . .", to which reference will be made in connection with the exposition of "Temporality" itself, and begin my account with Heidegger's discussion of the problem: what is more fundamental, Care as the Being of Dasein or the authentic Existentiality of the self? and what is their relationship?

Heidegger tries to elucidate the problem of "selfhood" by starting from the self-interpretation of Dasein which, in its everydayness, speaks about "itself" by "saying I" (Ichsagen). This "I" is thought to be permanently the same; and as such it has been discussed by philosophers, e.g. by Kant in his doctrine of the "paralogisms." In this connection Heidegger submits Kant's teaching that the "I think" is "the form of apperception which accompanies and precedes any experience" to a critical examination. Two points are agreed to: that Kant recognises the impossibility of reducing the "I" to a substance in the "ontic" sense; and that he retains the "I" in the sense of "I think." But when Kant takes the "I" again as a "subject," Heidegger holds that he misses his point. For, in Heidegger's view, the ontological concept of the "subject" characterises not the "selfhood of the I qua self," but "the sameness and permanency of something which is always already 'vorhanden.' " Heidegger's further criticisms are: that Kant chooses the formula "I think," instead of "I think something," since the "representations" which the "I think" is said to accompany are "empirical" and not transcendental; that Kant did not characterise the nature of this "accompanying" more precisely; above all, that Kant overlooked the phenomenon of the world, though, then, he was consistent enough to keep the "representations" apart from the apriori content of the "I think," which, in its turn, leads to the result that the "I" is reduced to an isolated subject. The fundamental mistake which, according to Heidegger, Kant made was to force upon the problem of "self" the inadequate "horizon" of "categories" appropriate only for what is "vorhanden."—The fundamental criticism which Heidegger advances against the whole of the European philosophic tradition is that its "ontological" exposition was fundamentally concerned exclusively with what is "vorhanden"; and the criticism on Kant's doctrine of the "I think" is a characteristic and noteworthy instance of this fundamental and, it seems to me, most constructive criticism which pervades the whole of the work.

The criticism of Kant's theory is clarifying because the relationship between "selfhood" and "Care" must be made more lucid if the investigation is to move forward in the right direction. As Heidegger points out, the ontological constitution of the "self" cannot be traced back to either an "I-substance" or a "subject": "selfhood" can be discovered only when the "authenticity" of the Being of Dasein as "Care," especially as the "resolve that runs forward in thought to its potentialities," is analysed. But this does not mean that the "self" is the ground, or ultimate cause, of Care, thought to be permanently "vorhanden." The "self" is "permanent," because it has gained its "stand" and the firmness of its "stand," its independence, by way of its "resolve" in Care. It is the authentic counter-potentiality to the dependence of unresolved "Verfallen." Therefore, Heidegger concludes, Care does not require the foundation in a "self." "Existentiality" as one constitutive characteristic of Care implies the ontological constitution of the "self-dependence" of Dasein, to which, in accordance with the structure of Care as analysed, the actual "Verfallensein" to the dependence on others belongs as well. The enquiry, thus, moves in the direction not of "selfhood" as such, as may have been thought in view of the emphasis placed on "authenticity," but of what Heidegger terms "the ontological meaning of Care."

The phenomenon of "meaning" (Sinn) was studied by Heidegger in the context of the analyses of "understanding" and of "interpretation" when the "in-Being" was investigated. The "meaning," in the sense analysed there, is that within which the "understanding" of something is carried out and by which the "understanding" is guided, but which is not expressly and thematically envisaged as such. The "meaning" signifies the "Whereto" (Woraufhin) of the primary "project," from and by which something can be comprehended as what it is "in its inner possibility." Thus the problem of the "ontological meaning of Care" is the problem: what is the inner possibility of the articulated structural whole of Care as a whole and in its unity? The answer is: *Temporality*. And the phenomenon of "resolve running forward (in thought) to . . ." (vorlaufende Entschlossenheit) is taken as the model phenomenon of "authentic" Dasein as a "whole" to clarify in what way Temporality with its three modes enables it to be such as it is.

(a. *The future.*) "Future," in the sense meant here, does not mean a "now" which has not yet become "real" and will once "be." This is the traditional concept of the "future," based on the ontological exposition of what is "vorhanden" as carried out in Greek thought and adhered to ever since. At the last stage of this enquiry Heidegger endeavours to show how this concept of "Time" as the "sequence of nows" legitimately originates from a more genuine and fundamental kind of "Time," that of the Temporality of Dasein.

The "resolve running forward (in thought) to . . ." is the "Being towards its own eminent potentiality of Being." The reader may think of the indications given of the "Being-towards-death" or, perhaps, of the Being towards one's own profession. What makes such "resolve running forward (in thought) to . . ." possible is that "Dasein can move towards itself in its own potentiality and endures the potentiality as potentiality in this itself-moving-towards-itself." Heidegger points out that the original phenomenon of the "future" consists in this kind of "coming," namely in that Dasein comes or moves to or towards itself in its potentiality, enduring it. The "running forward (in thought)" makes Dasein authentically one with the future. But this is possible only because Dasein as such always and essentially "moves" towards itself.

(b. *The past.*) Here again the "past" does not mean the "now" which was. The "resolve running forward (in thought) to . . ." understands Dasein in its essential "Being-guilty." To take upon oneself in actual Existence such "Being-guilty," the thrown ground of nullity and thrownness as such, means to *be* authentically in such a way as Dasein always and already *was* (τὸ τί ἦν εἶναι). But the responsible acceptance of thrownness is possible only because one's future Dasein can be its own "as it already always was." Dasein can move towards itself in the mode of the "future" only by moving backwards towards its past at the same time. The fact that the call of conscience points both forward and backward, to the potentiality of Being and to the "Being-guilty" with its thrown nullity, will be borne in mind. The analysis of "historicity," too, at a later stage, will help to clarify this relationship of Dasein to both future and past.

However, for the Temporality of Dasein the future is the somehow "guiding" and dominant mode. Only when the Dasein "runs forward (in thought)" to its extreme and innermost potentiality can it, thereby, move backward in "understanding" to its own past. Inasfar as Dasein is of the future can it authentically be of the past.

(c. *The present.*) The Greek and the post-Greek ontology bases its interpretation of the nature of Time on the "present" as the "now" and on the "presence" (παρουσία, Anwesenheit) of what is "vorhanden." The "present" was conceived in that interpretation as the guiding mode. The "present" of the Temporality of Dasein must be characterised differently and, besides, it is not, as it were, its first, but its third mode.

The "resolve running forward (in thought)" discloses the concrete given "situation" in such a way that Existence "acts" with circumspection in its care of what is "zuhanden." The resolute Being-concerned-with what is "zuhanden" in such a concrete given situation is possible only when this "Zuhandene" is "rendered present" (Gegenwärtigen). Only as the "rendering present" or "presenting" can resolve be what it is, the undisguised encountering of what it actively takes upon itself.

To formulate the relationship of the three modes more precisely: Being essentially directed towards the "future" (in the sense indicated above), resolve understands from it the "past" so as to "present" the concrete situation for its circumspect action. The "past" originates from the "future" so as to engender the "present."

In the light of the nature of Temporality the three main characteristics of the structural unity of Care can be understood more appropriately.

(a) The "Being-in-advance-of-itself" of Care is grounded in the "future." The "future" enables Dasein to be concerned about its own potentiality of Being and to "project" itself into the "for the sake of itself." The primary "meaning," i.e. the inner possibility, of "Existentiality" as such is the "future."

(b) The "Already-Being-in-the-world" of Care is grounded in the "past"; and the primary "meaning" of "Faktizität" or "Befindlichkeit" with its "thrownness" is the "past" (in the fore-mentioned existentialistic sense).

(c) The "Being-concerned-with-the-world-of-one's-care" is grounded in the "present," but is of a somewhat different nature. For: the "rendering present," to which it essentially refers and in which also the "Verfallen" is primarily grounded, remains itself "embedded" in future and past. The resolute Dasein, too, which has fetched itself out of the "Verfallen" to be the more "authentically" there in a disclosed situation and to live in the fulfilled moment (Augenblick), is thus related to the future, the past and the "present" as embedded in both these modes.

Another matter of considerable import in this characterisation of Temporality on principle is the statement that Temporality is not at all anything that "is," in the sense of a "being." It "produces Time" (zeitigt sich). Moreover, the "towards itself" of the "future," the "back to" of the "past" and the "encountering of" of the "present" unveil Temporality as the "ἐκστατικόν" as such. Temporality is, as Heidegger emphasises, the original and fundamental "Outside-itself" (Ausser-sich) in and for itself. "Future," "past" and "present" are thus termed the "ecstasies" of Temporality. In the common and public "understanding" and concept of "Time," this "ecstatic" character of original Temporality is levelled.—

This first exposition of the nature of original Temporality is made more explicit in the subsequent stages of the enquiry.

Its fundamental and profoundly challenging character will, despite the brevity of the account given here, not escape the notice of the reader.

(4) The fourth stage of the enquiry is concerned with mainly two different problems. Firstly, the disclosed nature (Erschlossenheit) of the "There" of Dasein, i.e. "understanding," "Befindlichkeit," "Verfallen" and "speech," is analysed in view of its Temporality. Secondly, the Temporality of "Being-in-the-world" and the genesis of the theoretical discovery of what is "vorhanden" from circumspect care as well as the problem of the "transcendence" of the world are examined. The general tendency of the enquiry at this stage is to elucidate the problems discussed before from the basis of Temporality and to explore thereby the fundamental significance of Temporality further.

The principle of the analysis of the Temporality of "Erschlossenheit" is that Temporality "produces Time" wholly in each of its three ecstasies (future, past and present), i.e. that in the ecstasy of "future" past and present, in that of the "past" future and present, and in that of the "present" future and past, are implied. Thus it is shown that in the ecstatic unity of Temporality the structural whole of Care, i.e. Existentiality, "Faktizität" and "Verfallen," is grounded. The exposition contains a wealth of more concrete analyses.

Primarily the "understanding" is grounded in the "future." Its "authentic" mode is the "running forward (in thought) to . . .". But there is an "unauthentic" mode, too, e.g. when man becomes aware of potentialities implied in the matters of his care. This "becoming aware of" or "anticipating" (Gewärtigen) is the temporal basis of all kinds of "expectation," e.g. of one's own death in the future when it is not taken as one's own innermost and extreme potentiality.—But such "understanding," implying resolve, is also concerned with its "authentic" present, which is termed the "moment," in the fulfilled sense (Augenblick). The "unauthentic" present, where no resolve concerns itself actively with a given situation, is termed the "rendering present" (Gegenwärtigen). Whenever the understanding projects its potentiality from the matters of its care, Time is produced by rendering it present, while the "moment" arises from the authentic future.—The "authentic" past, which is taken over in resolve and understood for the sake of one's own "authentic" potentiality of Being, is termed "repetition" or "renewal" (Wiederholung).

"Wiederholung" means literally "fetching (something) back" (out of the past). Only here can Heidegger's own intention of a "repetition" or "renewal" (Wiederholung) of the question of the meaning of Being be properly "understood." The problem of Being occupied the great Greek thinkers from Thales and Anaximander to Aristotle. This problem is to be "repeated," i.e. unfolded in the spirit of the thinkers of two and a half millenniums ago by Heidegger. The "unauthentic" past is termed "oblivion" and on its ground arise one's "memories" which are "borne in mind."—The "unauthentic" way of understanding, grounded in the ecstasy of the future, is thus here analysed side by side with the "authentic" one.

The Temporality of "Befindlichkeit," grounded in the past, is analysed in a similar way. May it suffice to mention that the Temporality of the moods of fear, of dread and of hope are analysed here especially to show how the present and the future are modified, but as modified ones are implied in the ecstasy of the past.

The Temporality of "Verfallen" is the present and the phenomenon of curiosity is chosen to elucidate the "unauthentic" mode of this ecstasy.

After these analyses the problem of the Temporality of "speech" is outlined in brief. It is not primarily grounded in any one of the three ecstasies, but in language the "rendering present" is thought to have a constitutive function of preference. Special reference is made to the "tenses," and the "is" and a detailed exposition of the "origin" of "significances" is forecast as the theme of a whole chapter in the unpublished third Section.—

The second problem studied at this stage of the enquiry is that of the Temporality of the Being-in-the-world.

The investigation starts with an analysis of the Temporality of "circumspect care," where the "anticipating" (Gewärtigen), "bearing in mind" (Behalten) and the "rendering present" (Gegenwärtigen) are thought fundamental for the way in which the "Time" of the "Zuhandene" is produced, though a specific "oblivion" is essential for it, too.

To show more concretely the Temporality of the "Being-in-the-world," the genesis of the theoretical behaviour towards the "world" is traced back to the "circumspect care" of what is "zuhanden." In such a theoretical attitude, the "understanding of Being," which guides the careful handling of the "utensils," has profoundly changed. E.g. in the statement of the physicist: "the hammer is heavy," not only its character of a utensil is ignored, but also its "place" in the specific sense. Its place becomes a space-time-position, a "world-point" undistinguished from any other. What is within the environment (Umwelt) becomes "unbounded" (entschränkt) in some relevant sense. All that is "vorhanden," a phenomenon which only now fully emerges, becomes the theme.

But guided by the understanding of Being in the sense of "Vorhandenheit," what is primarily "unbounded," freed of its character as a utensil in an environment of "a-theoretical" Care, is at the same time confined once more, namely as belonging to the "region" or "realm" of what is "vorhanden." The more appropriately the Being of what is to be investigated is understood and thereby a whole kind of beings is singled out and articulated as a potential realm of matters related to one science or one branch of studies, the more precise will the perspective of methodical questions be. The classical example of such a historical development of a science is the genesis of mathematical physics, which is decisively guided by the mathematical "project" of Nature itself. Only in the light of such a "project" of Nature can "facts" be discovered and "experiments" be planned. The model character of mathematical science consists not in its specific exactness or its compulsory nature, but, more fundamentally, in its primary project of the constitution of Being with which it is concerned, in what Heidegger terms the "thematisation." The "thematisation" objectivates, i.e. frees the things in such a way that they become "objects," which can be discovered, investigated and determined.

This objectivating and scientific concern with what is "vorhanden" has the temporal character of a "rendering present" in an eminent sense. It is distinguished from the "present" of circumspection in that the discovering is "anticipating" exclusively what is "vorhanden." Existentially it is grounded in a resolve of Dasein which projects itself into the potentiality of Being in the "truth."

To make the "thematisation" of what is "vorhanden" and the scientific project of Nature possible, Dasein must "transcend" the beings that are to be thematised. "Transcendence" does not consist in the "objectivation," but the "objectivation" presupposes "transcendence." But since the thematisation of what is "vorhanden" is a modification of circumspect care, the concern with the "Zuhandene" must already be rooted in a "transcendence" of Dasein.

From this examination the analysis of the Temporality of

the "world" takes its start. The phenomenon of the world is considered to be grounded in Temporality. "The existentialistic-temporal condition of the possibility of the world is that Temporality as ecstatic unity has something such as a horizon." The "ecstasies" are not without direction. Each of them has its specific "Whereto," termed the "horizontal schema." The "ecstatic horizon" is a different one in each of them.

The schema, in which Dasein moves towards itself in the mode of the future, is the "For the sake of itself."

The schema in which Dasein is disclosed to itself as thrown into the "Befindlichkeit" is termed the "Before what" of thrownness and the "To what" to which Dasein is handed over. The horizontal structure of the past is characterised thereby.

Existing for the sake of itself and left to itself as thrown, Dasein is "rendering present" as a "Being-concerned-with . . .". The horizontal schema of the present is determined by the "In order to."

The unity of the horizontal schemata of the future, the past and the present is grounded in the ecstatic unity of Temporality. The horizon of Temporality as a whole determines in what respect the Dasein that actually exists is essentially disclosed. On the basis of the horizontal constitution of the ecstatic unity of Temporality, something such as a disclosed "world" belongs to the being which is its "There."

In the same way as the present arises out of the future and the past in the unity of Temporality, the horizon of a present arises co-original with those of the future and the past. Inasfar as Dasein produces Time (sich zeitigt), there is also a "world." Indeed, the world is neither "vorhanden" nor "zuhanden," but is there together with the "Outside-itself" of the ecstasies. If no Dasein "exists," there is also no "world" there, in the sense meant here.

Two further investigations are carried out in this connection: of the Temporality peculiar to the spatiality of Dasein, where the important point is made that only on the basis of the ecstatic-horizontal Temporality is the inroad made by Dasein into the "space" possible; and of the temporal meaning of everydayness.

(5) The next step in the enquiry is the analysis of the "historicity" of human Dasein.

So far Dasein as a "whole" has been brought into sight and

analytic grasp only with regard to its "end," its "Being-towards-death." Not only the "Being-towards-one's-beginning," i.e. birth, has been left unconsidered, but also the "extension of Dasein between birth and death." If the aim of the enquiry is to answer the question about the meaning of Being and if the meaning of Being becomes accessible in the "understanding of Being" which essentially belongs to human Dasein, the phenomenon of "historicity" is of great relevance. For not only does it essentially affect and mould the Dasein of everyone, but the "understanding of Being" is grounded in "historicity" and is handed down in human "history."

This problem of "historicity" is of especial interest to the reader of the subsequent essays, since the historic nature of human Dasein is emphasised in several places, notably in "On the Essence of Truth" and in "Hölderlin and the Essence of Poetry," and since the conception of the "historicity" of Dasein forms the background for Heidegger's communication with and his interpretations of Hölderlin's poetry. Moreover, the endeavour of the "repetition" of the question of the meaning of Being could not have been undertaken in the spirit in which it is carried out, without a profound consciousness of the "historicity" of Dasein and of philosophy.

The specific mode of motion of Dasein in its Existence is different from any kind of "motion" of something that is "vorhanden"; and this kind of "motion" in which Dasein "extends" is termed its "Geschehen," i.e. the process of happening. Its structure and its existentialistic-temporal conditions are analysed to make the nature of "historicity" understood.

The analysis starts with a distinction of four concepts of "history," all of which concern human Dasein which is "historical" in its Being: (a) history as referring to the "past" as such; (b) history as referring to the origin from the "past"; (c) history as referring to the whole of beings that change "in time" and more especially, in contrast to Nature and its kind of "changes," the whole of the changes and destinies of men, of human communities and of their civilisation and culture; and (d) history as referring to whatever is handed down by way of "tradition." After pointing out in what respects a "utensil" in the widest sense of the term or the Nature of environment as a "historical soil" are "historical," Heidegger begins to analyse "historicity" itself as an essential constitution of Dasein.

The "Geschehen" (process of happening) which defines Existence as "historical" is fundamentally implied in the phenomenon of "resolve" which projects itself, in silence and in readiness for dread, into its own Being-guilty and which is "authentic" as "running forward (in thought)" to potentialities of Being.

When Dasein, concerned about its future, moves backward in "resolve" to its "thrownness," this "resolve" discloses distinct actual potentialities of authentic Existence out of the "heritage" (Erbe) which it accepts and takes over in its state of being "thrown." Made free for death as its extreme potentiality, Dasein hands itself over to an inherited, yet freely chosen potentiality of Being, thereby entering upon the simplicity of its "fate" (Schicksal). Any choice of a potentiality of Being, made from the "heritage" and binding for the future, belongs to the "historicity" of Dasein in the genuine sense.

But since the Dasein, with its choice and fate, "exists" essentially together with others, its "Geschehen" (process of happening) takes place within the greater setting of the "Geschehen" of the community, e.g. the nation, which "Geschehen" is termed "Geschick" (destiny). The choice and the fate of the individual Dasein is guided from the start by the Dasein being together with that of others in the same world, in and with its own "generation," and by the resolve concerned with some definite and preferential potentialities.

Only when death, guilt, conscience, freedom and finiteness dwell together in the Being of a being, as they do in the Care of Dasein, can such a being "exist" in the mode of a fate, i.e. can it be "historical" in its essence. Historicity in this sense presupposes authentic Temporality. It presupposes that Dasein, in its Being, is essentially of the future so that it can "run forward (in thought)" to death as its extreme potentiality and, free for its death, is thrown back upon its actual "There." It presupposes that Dasein, being of the future, is co-original of the past so that it can hand over to itself the inherited, i.e. traditional, potentiality and can accept and take upon itself its own "thrownness." It presupposes that Dasein, being of the future and of the past, is of the present and, by adopting the inherited potentiality, lives in the moment in the fulfilled sense (Augenblick) and for its own age.

Resolve may not know expressly the origin of the potentialities into which it projects itself. But if it does know it expressly, the "repetition" of a potentiality of Existence handed down becomes the express mode of tradition, i.e. the return to potentialities which once had been. The authentic "repetition" of an existential potentiality of the past is thus grounded in the resolve which is "running forward (in thought)." Only in such a resolve does Dasein take the choice which makes it free for the faithful succession to what it considers worth repeating. Such a "repetition" is not a misguided inducement to adhere to the "past," but, on the contrary, it is the resolute and express "response" to a potentiality of past Existence, understood in its genuine originality.

Authentic historicity, thus interpreted and comprehended, has its essential weight not in the "past" nor in the "to-day" and its "connection" with the "past," but in the authentic "Geschehen" (process of happening) of Existence which originates from the "future" of Dasein, namely the "Being-towards-death" which directs Dasein back to its actual "thrownness." Both the phenomenon of the handing over of tradition to oneself and that of repetition are ultimately rooted in the future. But these very phenomena of the handing over of tradition to oneself and of repetition explain, too, why the process of happening of actual history has its weight and import in the "past," to which both the heritage of tradition and the repetition, irrespective of their deeper roots, point.—

Dasein is "Being-in-the-world" and the "historicity" of Dasein implies essentially the "historicity" of the "world" which belongs to it on the ground of the ecstatic-horizontal Temporality. Thus "utensils" and works of architecture, books and institutions have their "history" and their "fates." Nature assumes a historical significance, e.g. as the territory of settlement and exploitation, as battle-field and place of cult. This "Zuhandene" and "Vorhandene" of the "world," involved and comprised in the "historicity" of Dasein, is termed "world-historical" (Welt-Geschichtlich).

Because actual Dasein is mostly occupied with the world of its care, it understands its own history primarily in this "world-historical" sense. And as the common "understanding of Being" identifies "Being" with "Vorhandenheit" without qualification, the Being of what is "world-historical" is commonly experienced and interpreted as if it were something "Vorhandenes" that comes to pass, is happening and disappears. The kind of motion, peculiar to the process of happening in authentic historicity as well as in what is "world-historical" is usually left unconsidered.

This attitude characterises the "unauthentic" historicity of Dasein which is lost in the "one like many" and which never brought itself into the state of "resolve," in the sense described above. It lives in a mode of inner dispersal and whatever happens to it lacks inner connection. The original "extension" of the "fate" into which the individual Dasein has entered remains concealed. Without a firm stand, the "oneself" renders present the "to-day," forgetful of what had been and blind for genuine potentialities. Choice is evaded. And since nothing of what had been is being "repeated" in this "unauthentic" mode of Dasein, only the "reality" of what had been "world-historical," its remnants and the knowledge of it, are retained.

In contrast to this, the "resolve" of "authentic" Dasein brings about an "extension" of the whole Existence, a constant and permanent sameness, such that Dasein as "a fate" comprises in its Existence birth and death and their "in between." It is open for the "moment" and for the "world-historical" of its situation. In the repetition of potentialities of the past, Dasein brings itself directly back to what had been before. With the assimilation of the "heritage" even one's own birth has been encompassed in the realm of one's Existence.—"Resolve" constitutes the loyalty of Existence to one's own self. As the "resolve," ready for dread, this loyalty is at the same time potential reverence paid to the one authority which can be recognised by a free Existence: to the potentialities of Existence which are worth "repeating."—

After the characterisation of the fundamental constitution of "historicity" and of what is "world-historical," together with the attitude of unauthentic and authentic Dasein towards it, the problem of the "existentialistic" origin of history as a kind of scholarly study from the "historicity" of Dasein is outlined.

It is Heidegger's main contention that the scholarly disclosure of history is ontologically rooted in the "historicity" of Dasein and that the "idea" of history must be conceived in this light and not by way of an abstraction made from the contemporary studies of history or in an artificial adaptation to them.

History as a branch of knowledge makes it its own task expressly to disclose what is "historical." The thematisation defines its realm; the approach to it receives its methodical direction; the concepts applied in its interpretation gain their specific character. But if any historical "object" of the past is truly investigated, it must be of the constitution of a Dasein which had once been; and it presupposes the "historicity" of the Existence of the historian.

Remnants of any kind, monuments and reports are a potential "material" for such a concrete disclosure of Dasein which had once been. But their study, examination and assessment can be meaningfully carried out only on the basis of the historicity of contemporary Dasein.

In Heidegger's view, it is the "object" of history to understand the Dasein which had once been in its authentic "existential" potentiality. Such "potentiality" of the Dasein of the past is the primary and central theme of history and the "facts" which are studied are only related to it. The true historian, who treats his theme not in an "aesthetic," but in a "historical" way, can disclose the history of the past in its potentiality with such forcefulness that even its implications for the future are realised. Fundamentally, history takes its start not from "the present" nor from what is "real" only to-day, but from the future. The "selection" of what is to be an object of history is made by the actual, "existential" choice of the historicity of Dasein, i.e. of the historian, in which history arises.

Such an unveiling of the past in the "repetition" of a genuine historian must not be considered to be "subjective" in the bad sense; on the contrary, it alone guarantees the "objectivity" of history. For the "objectivity" of a science or any other branch of knowledge is thought to depend on whether the thematic object can be brought home to the "understanding" in its true Being and without disguise. With regard to a historic theme, the "historicity" of the Dasein of the historian makes such an "objectivity" possible.

The orientation by "facts" is required because the central theme of history is the potentiality of an Existence of the past and because such an Existence is always related to phenomena of the "world-historical" kind. Therefore the actual historical research concerns itself with the history of "utensils," of works, of civilisation and culture, of intellectual and spiritual life and of ideas. But the touchstone remains its proximity to its original and central theme and its treatment not in an "aesthetic," but in a genuinely "historical" manner.

An express reference is made to Nietzsche's well-known essay on "Use and Abuse of History" and to his distinction of the three kinds of history which are serving "Life": the "monumental," the "antiquarian" and the "critical" one, which Heidegger relates in a very elucidating way to the "future," the "past" and the "present" in his sense. Authentic historicity is indicated as the basis of the possible unity of these three kinds of history.—

A discussion of the investigations of W. Dilthey, Heidegger's predecessor in this field of philosophic studies, and of the ideas of Count Paul Yorck von Wartenburg, Dilthey's friend, closes this stage of the enquiry.

(6) One set of problems has been left unconsidered up to this point. Dasein counts on "Time" and is guided by "Time," even long before any scientific or scholarly research has begun. But the factor of "Time" plays also a part in the study of both history and Nature and, besides, there is the common concept of "Time" as the "sequence of nows" which deviates fundamentally from Heidegger's exposition of the nature of Temporality. If this exposition is correct, it must be shown that and how the more common concept of "Time" arises from the Temporality of Dasein itself. With this set of problems the last stage of the enquiry is concerned; and it is Heidegger's main contention that the actual Dasein counts on "Time," without understanding Temporality existentialistically, which same objection could be raised against the common concept of "Time," as developed in European philosophy. This analysis of the origin of the common concept of "Time" from Temporality is thought to be an implicit and indirect proof and justification of the interpretation given before, which characterises Temporality as the fundamental and original (ursprünglich) Time.

The investigation proceeds in three stages: (a) the way in which Dasein, grounded in Temporality, takes care of "Time" is analysed; (b) the "world-Time," concerned with what is "zuhanden" and "vorhanden" and measured by the sun and by the clock, is analysed; and (c) the common concept of Time, as first formulated by Aristotle, is analysed.

All planning, taking of precautions, preventing or calculating of Dasein in its Care says, audibly or inaudibly: "then" this is to be done; "before" that work has to be finished; "now" this has to be tried once more, after I failed in it "at that time." In the "then" the Care speaks in "anticipation," relating to the future; in the "now" in the mode of "rendering present"; in the "at that time" in the mode of "bearing in mind," relating to the past. The horizon of these three modes of everyday Care is the "later" (späterhin), the "to-day" (heute) and the "earlier" (früher). This common structure of the "now," "then" and "at that time" is termed the "datableness" (Datierbarkeit); and the problem arises how such "datableness," common as it is, is possible at all. The reason given is that the "rendering present," which is "anticipating" and "bearing in mind" at the same time, interprets itself in this way. It is this "rendering present" which interprets itself that we call "Time" and the "datableness" of the "now," "then" and "at that time" is considered to be the reflection of the ecstatic constitution of Temporality.

Another trait of this "taking care of Time" is indicated by the "until then" or "during which . . . ." Time is conceived here as a "span of time," a reflection of the "ecstatic extension of historical Temporality." In this sense an extended "span" of time is also meant by the "now," "then" and "at that time," e.g. at mealtime, in the evening, in the summer, at breakfast, during the ascent, etc.

Being occupied with the world of its care, Dasein "takes its time" over it and this is the primary and genuine mode in which "Time" is experienced, independent of and before all specific measuring of Time as the continual sequence of pure "nows." Being very busy and possibly without the attitude of genuine resolve, one "loses" one's time. Authentic Existence, on the other hand, gives to its "present" the significance of the "moment" in the fulfilled sense. Not the "rendering present" of a situation is here guiding, but the Existence is guided by its future, implying its past. The momentary Existence is embedded in a "fatefully" whole "extension," in which the self has become constant and permanent in an authentic and historical manner.

Dasein can "take" its time or "lose" its time and authentic Dasein can make use of its time in its own mode, because in the disclosed nature of the "There," grounded in the ecstatically extended Temporality, a "Time" is granted to it.—

The next problem is: what is meant by the "public Time," i.e. the "Time" of which one Dasein partakes together with that of others, and what are its characteristics?

Though time is primarily dated by way of events that occur in the environment, this takes place within the horizon of a care of time known as "chronology" in the sense of astronomy and of the calendar. This "public Time" is not the only kind of time, but that kind of time in which "Zuhandenes" and "Vorhandenes," all that is not of the kind of being such as Dasein, are encountered. This qualified definition is of the utmost import, for it points to the essential limitation involved in our common concept of Time thought to have originated from this "public Time."

The sun and its light "date" time in the first instance and the day is the first, most natural measure of Time.

The reason for this lies in the fact that the everyday circumspect "Being-in-the-world" requires the possibility of sight, i.e. light, to take care of the "Zuhandene" on the background of the "Vorhandene" and that Dasein, in its thrownness, is submitted to the change of day and night. The dawn of the day makes it possible to resume one's daily work; and similarly significant incisions of time are the sunset and the midday.

This "dating" by the sun is an indication of "Time" for "everyone." What is "dating" is at everyone's disposal and yet it is not restricted to the realm of utensils; for in it the environment of Nature and the public environment are disclosed as well. Everyone can count on this kind of "Time." But for its more precise calculation, a "measure" of it, at the disposal of the public, is required: the clock-time. It is a "Zuhandenes" which, with its regular return, has become accessible in the "rendering present" which, at the same time, is in a state of "anticipation."

Three questions arise: (a) what is implied in the "dating"; (b) what is implied in the reading of the clock; and (c) what is the nature of the "public Time."

The "dating" implies that "then" when it dawns it will be "time for" one's daily work. Time interpreted in Care is always already understood as "time for . . . ." The "now that this or that has to be done" points through the "now that" to "this" or "that" as suitable or unsuitable. In short, the "rendering present" of Care, with its "anticipation" and its "bearing in mind," understands "Time" essentially as related to some purpose or other, which itself is related to the "for the sake of what" of the potentiality of Being. In other words: the public Time unveils the "significance" of "this" or "that" by way of its purposive relations and ultimately constitutes the "worldliness" of the world. Public Time as "time for . . ." has thus essentially a character referring to the "world" and is termed "world-time." This is not to say that the "world-time" is "vorhanden," which it never can be, but to indicate that Public Time belongs to the "world" in its existentialistic-ontological sense.

In using a clock or a watch, we say expressly or inexpressively: "now" it is "time for . . ." or "now" I have still time "until. . . ." We take our time over this or that; and the reading of the clock is grounded in it and guided by it. Such an orientation in time is essentially a "saying: now" (Jetztsagen); and this "saying: now" is the articulation in speech of a "rendering present," on the basis of its unity with "anticipation" and "bearing in mind."

The dating by way of the clock-time is a "measuring" of time, which implies both an unalterable measure-rule (Massstab), with its permanent sameness for everyone, and the measured length on the dial provided with numbers, over which the hands move. This does in no way mean that the clock-time is determined by spatial lengths and the change in place of a spatial thing nor is this kind of "dating" a rendering spatial of time. It is a specific "rendering present" that makes the "measuring of time" by way of the clock possible. But with the help of the clock Time gains a publicity in a specific sense, such that it is encountered always and by everyone as "now and now and now." Thus the time made accessible through the use of clocks appears to be like a "multitude of nows," seemingly "vorhanden," though the measuring of time is never thematically concerned with Time as such.

The public time in this sense, developed by the measuring of time on the clock, is what is commonly called "the time." In Care everything is ascribed its time; and it can have its time, because anything that is is "in time." This "world-time," grounded in the ecstatic-horizontal constitution of Temporality, is of the same "transcendence" as the world itself. It is prior to any subjectivity or objectivity. "The world-time is 'more objective' than any possible object, because it is 'objectified' (objiciert) in its ecstatic-horizontal dimensions as the condition of the possibility of anything that is when the world becomes disclosed." "But the world-time is also 'more subjective' than any possible subject, because, if Care is the Being of Dasein, it contributes to making the Being of the actually existing self possible." Yet, fundamental as is this world-time which constitutes the being "in time" (Innerzeitigkeit) of what is "zuhanden" and "vorhanden," it arises from the Temporality of Dasein, as Heidegger has tried to show in this earlier part of the investigation.—

The genesis of the common concept of Time, as Heidegger points out, arises from the clock-time. Aristotle, in his "Physics," defines Time as follows. "For the time is this: what is counted in the movement in accordance with (or: in the horizon of) what is earlier and what is later." All subsequent discussion of the concept of Time is thought to keep fundamentally within the framework of the Aristotelean definition, i.e. it makes Time the theme in the way in which it shows itself in the circumspect care of what is "zuhanden" on the background of what is "vorhanden." The time is what is "counted"; and what is counted are the "nows." The common concept of Time is the "now-time," i.e. Time as the "sequence of nows."

In this interpretation of Time two fundamental characteristics are obscured: the "datableness," grounded in the ecstatic constitution of Temporality; and the "significance," opened up by the "time for . . . ." The common interpretation of "world-time" as "now-time" has not at its disposal the "horizon" to make something such as "world," "significance," "datableness" accessible. It treats the "nows," though inexpressively, as if they were "vorhanden" like things: some pass and they form the "past"; some arrive and they define the "future." Similarly the "sequence of nows" is conceived as if it were somehow "vorhanden."

Furthermore, the sequence of nows is characterised as "uninterrupted" and "without a gap," where the extended "span" of time and the "extension" of historicity are obscured; as "endless" or "infinite," where the Temporality of Dasein is ignored and the sequence of nows is treated as if it were self-dependent and absolute, obscuring especially the finite nature of Dasein and its "Being-towards-the-end"; as "passing," but not to the same extent as "arising," which, in Heidegger's view, is the faint public reflection of the Temporality of Dasein anticipating its finite future; and as an "irreversible succession," which again points to its origin from Temporality and its primary mode, that of the future.

This common characterisation of Time as an endless, passing, irreversible sequence of nows arises from the Temporality of Dasein in its mode of "Verfallen." Within its limits, it has its natural right. For it belongs to the Being of Dasein in its everydayness and to the "understanding of Being" which prevails. Thus history, too, is mostly understood in public as a process of happening "in time" in the restricted sense.

But this interpretation of Time loses its exclusive right, if it claims to indicate the "true" concept of Time and to outline the only possible horizon for the exposition of Time. It can be understood from the Temporality of Dasein and from its time-producing function why and in what way "world-time" belongs to it. But from the horizon of the common concept of Time Temporality remains inaccessible in its nature and on principle.—

A last aspect emphasised in this common experience of time

is the distinct relationship of time to the "soul" or the "spirit," as found in Aristotle, in St. Augustine, in Kant and in Hegel. This gives rise to an exposition of Hegel's conception of the relationship between Time and Spirit, which, together with a clarifying note on Bergson's conception of Time, brings the whole of the European tradition since Aristotle into perspective.—

It was the task of the enquiry in this second Section to interpret the original whole of actual Dasein, with its potentialities of authentic and unauthentic Existence, from its ground, i.e. from Temporality. The aim is the elaboration of the problem of Being as such. If the whole of the constitution of Dasein is found to be grounded in Temporality, then Temporality, as the ecstatic "Outside-itself," is most likely to render the ecstatic "project" of Being as such possible. In the very last sentence of the published fragment, Time is hinted at as the horizon of Being.

It is hoped that from the somewhat more detailed account given of the second Section the reader will gain an impression not only of the content and its originality, but also of the great power of analysis which with its sure grasp and profound consistency lays bare aspect by aspect a problem never approached before in this way.

4: SOME REFLECTIONS ON THE SIGNIFICANCE OF THE WORK

The question which would seem the most important of all, if it could be answered by any one individual at present, is: what is the actual "significance" of Heidegger's *Being and Time* as a "contribution" to European philosophy? This question can only very gradually be decided by way of the reactions of trained philosophers to the work in the future: it would become truly relevant, once a thinker of very high rank would be stimulated to the depth of his philosophic mind by the approach attempted and the problems treated in this work, so as either to develop his own problems in a kindred spirit or to criticise the work fundamentally and yet to advance his own constructive views on the basis of this criticism, as Locke may be said to have done with regard to Descartes or Kant with regard to Leibnitz and Hume. The only statement that may be ventured here is the suggestion that Heidegger's *Being and Time* is of that rank and kind that it may stimulate profoundly the thought of another original thinker in times to come.—In conclusion of the account of *Being and Time* given above, only a very few points may be made as to its possible "significance."

The work seems to have been misunderstood and misinterpreted in mainly two ways: it was taken to be either a "*Philosophical Anthropology*" or a "*Philosophy of Existence.*"

(1) A "Philosophical Anthropology" would be a philosophical analysis of what is essential to the "nature" of human life, possibly in express comparison and contrast to that of the higher animals. It would be a "regional" ontology, inasmuch as it is concerned with one kind of beings to the exclusion of other kinds.—Such a "Philosophical Anthropology" might be more especially felt to be a philosophic desideratum in an age in which the "critical" faculty of philosophy and an insight into the "limitations" of human comprehension have been highly developed, as may be said to have taken place since Locke, Hume and Kant, and in which human life is considered to be the "basis" of all kinds of thought and research concerning the great variety of things that exist or are conceived. In this sense, following Kant, the German philosopher W. Dilthey developed a Philosophy of Human Life, especially with a view to its historicity, from the basis of which all institutions and outlooks, as in religion, art and philosophy, would be more adequately understood and interpreted. Indeed, one important trend in the whole of modern thought may be said to have a direct tendency towards such a "Philosophical Anthropology"; and it is understandable that Heidegger's work, when published, was first seen in this light. For it purported to analyse human Dasein in its structural constitution.

But while Heidegger analysed relevant phenomena and traits of human Dasein, his aim was to give in no way a "regional," but a "fundamental" ontology and not to analyse "all" that is essential to the "nature" of man (if this could be analysed convincingly), but to develop the problem of the constitution of Dasein in such a way that thereby the meaning of "Being" could find its elucidation once more. The historical perspective: that what the Greek thinkers from Parmenides and Heraclitus to Plato and Aristotle had attempted, taking the things that were "vorhanden" as their starting-point and enquiring into the essence of all that is, was to be attempted once more, but this time by making human Dasein as an outstanding kind of being its starting-point and clarifying the meaning of "Being," gives an indication of Heidegger's problem and approach if the comparison is rightly understood.

Therefore not the "nature" of man as such, but Dasein as "Being-in-the-world" was analysed, this "Being-in-the-world" shown, among other points, in its relationship to the realm of "utensils" and, at a later stage, to all that is "vorhanden."—The most important turn in the enquiry, however, is taken with the analysis of "Temporality." For here, with Heidegger's analysis of "future," "past" and "present" and of their "ecstatic" unity, the inner possibility of the structural whole of Care is laid bare, so as to describe it as the "transcendental horizon" of the question about "Being"—an investigation which, by its trend of thought, transcends any study of the "nature" of man in the sense of a "Philosophical Anthropology." [19]

(2) With the publication of *Being and Time* and more especially with that of K. Jaspers' *Philosophy* (1932) a "Philosophy of Existence" had come into being—a term applied by Jaspers himself to his own way of philosophic approach and outlook—and most of what links itself up nowadays with the movement of "Existentialism" took, either directly or indirectly, its start from either of these two German thinkers, even though the original impetus and insight goes back to the Danish thinker S. Kierkegaard.[20]

In view of the import attached to "existentialia," in contrast to and as a complement of the traditional "categories," to "Existence" as the "substance" of Dasein, to the distinction between "unauthentic" and "authentic" Dasein and to phenomena, such as dread, care, death, conscience, guilt and resolve, it was almost inevitable that Heidegger was thought to be primarily concerned with the problem of "Existence" and with "Existentialism."

In this respect it should be borne in mind, first of all, that Heidegger draws a sharp distinction between "Existence," which concerns the individual human being and is something "ontic," like the physiological functions of a plant or the atomic structure of a piece of matter, and "Existentiality," which is meant to be an "ontological" characteristic of human

19. For the problem of a "Philosophical Anthropology," and its difference from a fundamental ontology, cf. Heidegger's *Kant and the Problem of Metaphysics*, pp. 193/236, where the "finiteness" in man and its relationship to the problem of the understanding of Being is placed in the centre.

20. For a general characterisation of Heidegger's and Jaspers' philosophic thought, on the background of the philosophy of Nietzsche and especially Kierkegaard as well as of Husserl, Dilthey and Max Weber and within the larger framework of a variety of other eminent figures and prominent schools in Germany cf. my own book *An Introduction to Contemporary German Philosophy*, 1935. There it was expressly emphasised that the problem of "Being" is the one main concern of Heidegger's philosophy and that the existentialistic exposition of human Dasein is only of a "preparatory" nature.

Dasein. If, e.g. the analysis of "Care" as the "Being" of Dasein is considered, the reflection is meant to dwell on the formal ontological structure in the first place and not to confuse it at once with the well-known "ontic" phenomenon.

Furthermore, if I myself were asked to explain why Heidegger places "Existentiality" so much in the foreground of his exposition of Dasein, while he purports to be primarily interested in the problem of "Being," I would give as one reason what follows.

The "Existentiality" of Dasein would seem to correspond to the "οὐσία" (substance) of what is "vorhanden," the first and most fundamental of the "categories" in Aristotle's sense; and this "οὐσία" is taken to mean the same as "παρουσία" (Anwesenheit, presence). Now, the "Existentiality" of Dasein is concerned, as we have seen, with the "potentiality of Being" (Seinkönnen), with "understanding" and with "project"; and with regard to the "Temporality" of Dasein, it is concerned with its dominant and guiding "mode," the "future." The "Faktizität" or "Befindlichkeit," with its "thrownness" into the "There" and, in regard to Temporality, with its primary relationship to the "past"; and the "Verfallen," with its concern for the world of one's care and with its primary relationship to the "present," are not independent of the "Existentiality," but closely interwoven with it. Without it, "Faktizität" and "Verfallen" could not come into sight and grasp of Dasein. "Existentiality" is the one "guiding" characteristic of Dasein, just as the "future" of Dasein is the one dominant and "guiding" mode of Temporality.

From this the statement that "Existence is the 'substance' of man" may gain some clarification. For just as "substance" in Aristotle's sense is the primary "category" of the kind of beings that are "vorhanden," "Existentiality" in Heidegger's sense is the primary characteristic of the kind of beings that are Dasein. Therefore these characteristics are termed "existentialia" and the analysis of Dasein is primarily concerned with them.

(3) Whereas I do not think that "Being and Time, Part I" should be regarded either as a "Philosophical Anthropology" or as a "Philosophy of Existence," the *analysis of the "existentialia" of Dasein,* in contrast to and as a complement of the "categories" of "Vorhandenheit," seems to me a great contribution to philosophic studies and to philosophic insight, if it is seen on the background and in the light of the Greek *ontology* from Anaximander, Parmenides and Heraclitus to Aristotle and the *transcendental* philosophy of Kant. The problem,

as posed by Heidegger, is altogether novel and the philosophically-minded reader will have to grasp the problem in its novelty first of all. The claim to the universality of the analysis, a claim implicit in any ontological analysis, will have to be scrutinised. Man is not "ontically" to be considered in his "nature," in his "social" and consequently also "historical" associations and in his "mind" and "spirit," which, at best, would lead to a "Philosophical Anthropology." But man, as Dasein, partakes of "Being" and is "Being-in-the-world." This opens up a far wider horizon. The structural constituents: (a) the realm of utensils, on the background of the things of Nature, and the worldliness of the world, (b) the self as the "one like many" with its publicity and in its primarily unauthentic Existence, (c) the in-Being with its modes of "understanding," "Befindlichkeit," "Verfallen" and "speech" and (d) the Being of Dasein, Care,—(a) characterising the "world" of the "Being-in-the-world," (b) the "who," (c) the "in" and (d) the "Being"—and the unity of the analysed structure may one day be considered fundamental in a way not altogether dissimilar to Aristotle's doctrine of "categories."

(4) Apart from the ontological analysis of the structure of Dasein and beyond it, the exposition of the "*Temporality of Dasein*" as the "inner possibility" of this ontological structure seems to me to be the most relevant "contribution" made by Heidegger in the published fragmentary portion of *Being and Time*. Kant, with his analysis of "Time" in the *Critique of Pure Reason*, undertaken from the standpoint of the "subjectivity" of man, is in this respect his immediate predecessor; and beyond it, it would seem to be the most fundamental and profound analysis of the nature of "Time" made as a "compliment" to Aristotle's analysis in his "Physics," implying a radical criticism of it. It is this exposition of the "Temporality of Dasein" that I would think is of the utmost interest to the trained philosopher, challenging all the traditional views on the problem of Time. It would have to be examined as to the correctness of insight into the "temporal" structure of future, past and present as well as to the way in which the common conception of "time," i.e. the time of what is "vorhanden" and "zuhanden," is shown to "originate" from the basic "Temporality" of Dasein. Only then would Heidegger's philosophic thought seem to be comprehended and assimilated at least in one relevant respect.

(5) The fundamental problem with which Heidegger is concerned is that of the "*meaning of Being*." For it "Tempo-

rality," in the way in which it is analysed, is said to be the "transcendental horizon." If "meaning" is to be understood here in the same sense as when Temporality is characterised as the ontological "meaning" of Care, i.e. as what makes the structural whole of "Care" in the unity of its articulated characteristics intrinsically "possible" (Ermöglichung), the exposition of "Being," with Temporality as its "transcendental horizon," would consist in analysing in what way "Being" is the "ground" and the "inner possibility" of Dasein, as well as of "Vorhandenheit," in their ontological structure. Naturally, such an analysis of the "meaning" of "Being" would have to comprise in itself a variety of detailed analyses, e.g. concerning the concept of the beings that are "in the whole" (das Seiende im Ganzen), of those of "Nature," implying on principle the constitution of those kinds of being that are not Dasein, and perhaps of "History," beyond the exposition given in the analysis of "historicity"; but especially concerning the "understanding" of "Being" itself, as it arises within the "horizon" of Temporality, as the "Outside-itself" (Ausser-sich), i.e. as "ecstatic" unity. What it meant and means that "Being" opened out in the horizon of "Time" so that all that is, with its different kinds of being, could become apparent would have to be demonstrated. The beginnings of Greek philosophy before Plato would thus be elucidated in their fundamental, and lasting, significance. Possibly the way in which the interpretation of the nature of "God" found its theoretical and theological exposition on the basis of the metaphysical tradition from Anaximander to Aristotle and Plotinus was to be clarified, on principle at least, in some context of the analysis. Man in his "Ex-sistence," which means an "ex-position" into "truth," i.e. into the discovering or unveiling of the things as they "are," belongs most definitely into the "realm of horizon" of the analysis of the "meaning" of "Being." The relatedness of "nothingness" to "Being" is likely to be another aspect of it; its import for Greek thought, e.g. for Parmenides, is apparent. It may be that the problem of "poetry" and of its relevance for the discovering and naming of the things that are was at first not included in the problem of the "meaning" of "Being"; but it may well be thought necessary to consider it in this "horizon of project," too.—The tradition of "Ontology" would receive a fundamental reorientation, in the "Metaphysica generalis," concerned with the nature of "Being," and in the "Metaphysica specialis" traditionally subdivided in a Cosmology, Rational Psychology and Natural Theology.

I myself do not know the text of the original version of the third Section of *Being and Time*. Thus it may not be thought right for me to dwell in this Introduction on the problem of the "meaning of Being." But it seems to me that something had to be said about this problem at this stage, in order not to have it deteriorate into a mere empty word as well as in view of the content of the four essays. I can only hope that the indications made are not wrong and that the problem itself can be envisaged, however faintly and inappropriately. This is of import even for the understanding of the foregoing account, since the exposition of the structure of Dasein, and that of Temporality, does not stand on its own ground, but is undertaken from the "ground" of the truth of Being.

BIBLIOGRAPHY

Die Kategorien- und Bedeutungslehre des Duns Scotus (Tübingen, 1916)

Sein und Zeit (Halle, 1927; eighth edition, Tübingen, 1957); translated by John Macquarrie and Edward Robinson as *Being and Time* (London, SCM Press, and New York, Harper & Row, 1962)

Kant und das Problem der Metaphysik (Bonn, 1929; Frankfurt, 1951)

Vom Wesen des Grundes (Halle, 1929; Frankfurt, 1949)

**Was ist Metaphysik?* (Bonn, 1929; with an afterword, Frankfurt, 1943)

Die Selbstbehauptung der deutschen Universität (Breslau, 1933)

**Hölderlin und das Wesen der Dichtung* (München, 1936)

Hölderlins Hymne: "Wie wenn am Feiertage . . ." (Halle, 1941)

Platons Lehre von der Wahrheit (Bern, 1942; second edition, with "Ein Brief über den 'Humanismus,'" 1947)

**Vom Wesen der Wahrheit* (Frankfurt, 1943; reissued 1949)

Erläuterungen zu Hölderlins Dichtung (Frankfurt, 1944; reissued 1951)

Holzwege, containing the essays "Der Ursprung des Kunstwerkes," "Die Zeit des Weltbildes," "Hegels Begriff der Erfahrung," "Nietzsches Wort 'Gott ist tot,'" "Wozu Dichter?" and "Der Spruch des Anaximander" (Frankfurt, 1950)

Der Feldweg (Frankfurt, 1950)

Einführung in die Metaphysik (Tübingen, 1954); translated by Ralph Manheim as *An Introduction to Metaphysics* (New Haven, Conn., Yale University Press, 1959; reissued by Doubleday Anchor Books, 1961)

Was heisst Denken? (Tübingen, 1954)

Vorträge und Aufsätze. Volume I: "Die Frage nach der Technik," "Wissenschaft und Besinnung," "Überwindung der Metaphysik," and "Was ist Nietzsches Zarathustra?"; Volume II: "Was heisst Denken?" "Bauen Wohnen Denken," "Das Ding," and ". . . dichterisch wohnet der Mensch"; Volume III: "Logos (Heraklit, Fr. 50)," "Moira (Parmenides, Fr. VIII, 34–41)," "Aletheia (Heraklit, Fr. 16)," and "Hinweise" (Pfullingen, 1954)

Zur Seinsfrage (Frankfurt, 1955)

Was ist das—die Philosophie? (Pfullingen, 1956); translated by W. Kluback and Jean T. Wilde with parallel German text (London, 1958)

Der Satz vom Grund (Pfullingen, 1957)

J. P. Hebel—der Hausfreund (Pfullingen, 1957)

Identität und Differenz (1957); translated as *Essays in Metaphysics* (New York, 1960)

* The starred works appear in translation in *Existence and Being* (London, 1949; Chicago, Regnery, 1949), which contains "Remembrance of the Poet," translated by Douglas Scott; "Hölderlin and the Essence of Poetry," translated by Douglas Scott; "On the Essence of Truth," translated by R. F. C. Hull and Alan Crick; and "What is Metaphysics," translated by R. F. C. Hull and Alan Crick. The translations are prefaced by a long introduction to Heidegger's work by Dr. Werner Brock.

JEAN–PAUL SARTRE

(BORN 1905)

Jean-Paul Sartre is the best-known of living existentialist philosophers because he has a public as a writer. Unlike Marcel, he has not merely written dramatic pieces to expound his philosophic thinking, he has written for the theater. And his early novel, *La Nausée* (1938) spoke to and for a generation. He is a man of impressive intellectual energy and ambitious talent, ready to challenge Kant or Freud or many contemporary American novelists, and still finding time to be almost obsessed with questions of the day. The root of his confidence and his versatility remains in his early philosophic thinking, under the influence of Husserl's phenomenology. He is the reverse of a dilettante and dabbler; as novelist, dramatist, literary critic, and publicist, he is vigorous and original because he is single-minded; he is at all times applying his fundamental insights as ontologist. This ontology is a dogmatic foundation for a humanism which has an ethic of freedom and responsibility, to replace the detached humanism of universal sympathies and disinterested interest in which, he says, three generations of Frenchmen, until World War II, had been bred.

Sartre has been called (by Iris Murdoch) a "romantic rationalist," and this is a just description. His passionate concern with politics and questions of the day creates the ethos of his philosophy, as their religious concerns do that of the "Kierkegaardian" existentialists. Philosophically, this comes out in his sustained dialogue with Marxist thinking, the main preoccupation of his later period and the theme of his last major work, *Critique de la raison dialectique* (vol. I, 1960). He accepts the practical force of Marx's historical materialism but rejects its philosophical basis. He seeks to marry phenomenology with a criticized and revised version of the dialectic; and appears as an existentialist who is a neo-Marxist.

Sartre's most interesting contribution to existentialist philosophy is as a psychologist. Psychological theories and descriptions abound in his main work, *L'être et le néant*, and two earlier psychological essays are still useful sources for his thinking: *Esquisse d'une théorie des émotions* (1939) and *L'imaginaire* (1940). This is the argument from the constitutive character of consciousness against all theories of immanence and of psychological determinism as radically mistaken. Human being, to be what it is, must transcend the world in which it exists. Its independence of and dependence on the world are equally real and certain.

EXTRACTS

A passage from "La Vie Imaginaire," the fourth part of *L'imaginaire: psychologie phénoménologique de l'imagination* (Paris, 1940). The passage is from the second section, entitled "Les Conduites en Face de l'Irréel," trans. by H. J. B.

L'être et le néant (1943) trans. by Hazel E. Barnes as *Being and Nothingness.* (New York, 1956; London, 1957.)
Part Four, "Having, Doing, and Being"
Chapter One, "Being and Doing: Freedom," III, Freedom and Responsibility.
Chapter Two, "Doing and Having," I, "Existential Psychoanalysis"; III, "Quality as a Revelation of Being."

§§ from *L'imaginaire*

BEHAVIOR IN RESPONSE TO AN UNREAL OBJECT

. . .

From all that has gone before, one can conclude that feelings in regard to a real object and feelings in regard to the image of one are different in kind. For example, love varies completely according to whether its object is present or absent.

When Annie goes away, my feelings for her change their nature. Of course I still call them love, of course I deny this change, I pretend that I love Annie as much and in the same way as when she was present. But there is no truth in it. Naturally, knowledge and general behavior remain unaffected. I know that Annie has such and such qualities, I continue to show my confidence in her, for example I write to her about everything that happens to me; if the occasion requires it, I shall defend her interests as if she were there. Moreover, the existence of genuine affective states of mind must be recognized: the sadness, melancholy, even despair into which this absence throws us. Indeed, it is not so much Annie unreal because not there as the emptiness of our life, present and real, which provokes these feelings; it is, for example, that certain movements, certain attitudes which we begin to form then collapse without a goal, leaving us with an impression of intolerable futility. But all this represents, in some way, the negative side of love. It remains that the positive element (the impulse *toward* Annie) has been profoundly modified. My love-ardor was subordinated to its object: thus I was *learning* about it all the time, it was surprising me all the time, every moment I had to remake it, readjust myself to it: it was alive with the life of Annie herself. In so far as one could believe that the image of Annie was nothing other than Annie reborn, it could seem that this Annie would provoke almost the same reactions in me as the real Annie. But we know now that Annie as an image is not to be compared with Annie given in perception. She has undergone the alteration of becoming unreal and our sentiment has undergone a corresponding modification. In the first place, it has been *fixed:* it does not "make itself" any more, it can hardly languish on in the forms which it has already taken: it has become in a sense *scholastic,* one can give it a name, classify its manifestations: they no longer overflow their definitions, they are exactly limited by the knowledge which we have of them. At the same time the sentiment has been *reduced,* for its richness, its inexhaustible depth came from the object: there was always more to love in the object than I was in fact loving, and I knew it, with the result that love as it was demonstrated in response to the real was under the unity of a directive idea in the Kantian sense: the idea that Annie as an individual reality is inexhaustible and that, correspondingly, my love for her is inexhaustible. Thus the sentiment which each moment was left behind was itself surrounded by a vast halo of possibilities. But these possibilities have disappeared just as the real object has. By an essential reversal, it is now the sentiment which produces its object, and the unreal Annie is no more than the strict correlative of my feelings for her. It follows that the sentiment *is never more than what it is.* It now has a deep poverty. In short, it has passed from the passive to the active: it plays itself, it mimics itself:

one wills it, one believes it. All the time it looks like a great effort to have Annie reborn in the flesh, because it knows well that then it would recover its own substance, it would be reincarnated. Little by little the sentiment becomes schematized and fixed in a set pattern, and correspondingly the images which we have of Annie become stale. The normal development of knowledge and of a sentiment requires that at the end of a certain time this love lose its own *nuance:* it becomes *love* in general and is in a sense rationalized: it is then that readymade sentiment which the psychologist and the novelist describe: it has gone over to the typical; it is that Annie is no longer there to give it that individuality which made it an irreducible experience. And when all the same, at that moment, I would continue to behave as if I were loving Annie, remaining faithful to her, writing to her every day, devoting all my thoughts to her, being miserable alone, something will have disappeared, my love will have undergone a radical impoverishment. Dry, scholastic, abstract, focused on an unreal object which has itself lost its individuality, it develops slowly toward absolute emptiness. It is near this point that one writes: "I no longer feel myself near you, I have lost your image, I am more separated from you than ever." That is the reason why letters are awaited with so much impatience: it is not so much for the news which they give (supposing of course that we have nothing definite to fear or hope for) as for their real and concrete nature. The notepaper, the ink marks, the scent, etc., all this takes the place of the felt object it resembles which is missing; through all this I aim at a more real Annie. We have already seen the image-making role which signs can play.

At the same time as it is impoverished and schematized, this love becomes much *easier*. With everybody whom one loves, just because of the inexhaustible richness of the actual person, there is something which is beyond our grasp, an independence, an impenetrability which exacts ever renewed attempts to get nearer. The unreal object retains none of this impenetrability: it is never more than what we know of it. At first of course we do conscientiously affirm this impenetrability, this character of the loved person as *other*. But we *feel* nothing of the kind. It is a matter of mere knowledge, which soon shrinks and remains in suspense for want of a responsive substance to which to attach itself. Thus the unreal object, in the course of being made commonplace, becomes much more conformable to our desires than the real Annie ever was. Annie's return is going to explode all this formal construction. After a period of readjustment which can be more or less long, the reduced sentiment will give way to the real sentiment. Perhaps for a moment one can regret the complaisance and the simplicity of Annie as an image. But that is only because one will have lost the memory of the impoverishment of feeling which inevitably went with it.

Thus, from the mere fact of the extraordinary difference which separates the object in imagination from reality, one can distinguish two classes of sentiment: true sentiments and *imaginary* sentiments. By this latter attribute we do not mean that they are themselves unreal, but that they never appear save in response to unreal objects and that the appearance of the real is enough to put them to flight at once, as the sun disperses the darkness. Those sentiments whose essence is to be *reduced*, poor, jerky, spasmodic, schematic need the nonexistent in order to exist. Someone in thought will set on his enemy, will make him suffer morally and physically, who will remain passive when really in his presence. What has happened? Nothing save that the enemy, present, really exists. A moment ago only the sentiment was giving meaning to the image. The unreal object was only there in order to allow the hatred to be objective. Now what is present invades the sentiment from every direction and the hatred remains in suspense, sidetracked. What was hated is not there; that hatred is not adapted to this man of flesh and blood, quite alive, fresh, unpredictable. It was hating only a phantom cut exactly to its measure and which was its own exact copy, its meaning. Proust has well shown this abyss which separates the imaginary from the real; he has made it very evident that one cannot find a way from one to the other and that the real is always accompanied by the collapse of the imaginary, even if there is not any contradiction between them, because the incompatibility comes from their nature and not from their content. It must be added that, from the very fact of the essential poverty of the images, the imaginary actions which I project have only the consequences which I want to give them. If I strike my enemy in imagination, blood will not flow or, rather, it will flow to the extent that I would like. But in front of the real enemy, in front of this real flesh, I am going to foresee that real blood will flow, and that alone will be enough to stop me. Thus there is a continual gap between the preparation for an action and the action itself.

Even if the real situation is almost what I had imagined it to be, it is still true that it is different in nature from my imaginings. I am not surprised by what happens but by the shift into a different world. At the same time the motives of the projected action disappear or change their character, for they were only imaginary. If, in spite of everything, I carry out the projected action, it usually is because I am taken unawares and have no alternative. Or yet again it is out of a sort of obstinacy which shuts its eyes and will not take account of the change which has supervened. From this comes that stiff and inflexible behavior of people who "say what they have to say" without regard to their interlocutor, in order not to quit altogether the ground of the imaginary before being engaged too deeply to be able to withdraw. Thus it is useful to distinguish in ourselves two distinct personalities: the imagining self with its inclinations and desires; and the real self. There are sadists or masochists in imagination, people who are violent in imagination. Every moment, in contact with reality, our imagining self breaks up and disappears, giving way to the real self. For the real and the imaginary, in essence, cannot co-exist. There are here two types of object, of sentiment, and of behavior incapable of being reduced.

From this we may well think that individuals should be placed in two great classes, according to whether they will prefer to lead an imaginary life or a real life. But it should be understood what preference for the imaginary means. It is not at all a preference for certain objects only. One ought not to think, for example, that the schizophrenic and, in general, pathological dreamers try to substitute for the real content of their lives an unreal content which is more attractive, more colorful, and that they seek to forget the unreal character of their images, behaving toward them as if they had to do with objects that were actually and really present. To prefer the imaginary is not only to prefer a richness, a beauty, a luxury in imagination to actual mediocrity *in spite of* their unreal character. It is also to adopt "imaginary" feelings and behavior *because of* their imaginary character. One does not only choose such and such an image, one chooses the imaginary *state of mind* with all that belongs to it; one does not escape solely from the content of the real (poverty, love deceived, frustration, etc.), one escapes from the very form of the real, its character of *being there*, the kind of response it exacts from us, the subordination of our behavior to the object, the inexhaustibility of perceptions, their independence, even the way our sentiments have of growing. This life which is artificial, frozen, arrested, scholastic, and which for most people is only accepted for want of something better, is precisely what a schizophrenic desires. The pathological dreamer who imagines himself to be a king would not adjust himself to a royal authority that was effective; not even to a tyranny in which all his desires would be complied with. Indeed, a desire is never complied with to the letter, precisely because of the abyss which separates the real from the imaginary. I may well be given the object that I desired, but it is on another level of existence to which I shall have to adapt myself. Here it is now before me: if I was not forced to act, I should hesitate a long time, surprised, not recognizing this reality packed with consequences: I should ask myself: "Is *that* really what I wanted?" The pathological dreamer, for his part, would not hesitate: *that* is not what he wanted. In the first place, the actual exacts an adjustment which he is not capable of providing; there ought even to be a kind of indeterminacy in our sentiments, a real plasticity: it is that the real is always new, always *unpredictable.*[1] I wanted Annie to come: but the Annie whom I wanted was only the correlative of my desire. Let her come and she will invade my desire on all sides, a new apprenticeship will be necessary. By contrast the feelings of the pathological dreamer are stiff and frozen; they always come in the same form and in the same manner; it has taken the patient all his time to establish them; nothing in them has been left to chance, they would not adjust themselves to the slightest variation. Correspondingly the features of the unreal objects which match them are permanently fixed. Thus the dreamer can choose from the store the sentiments which he wants to dress up and the objects which correspond to them, as the actor chooses his costumes: today it will be ambition, tomorrow amorous desire. It is the "essential poverty" alone of objects in imagination which can satisfy the feelings tamely, without ever surprising them, deceiving them, or guiding them. It is the unreal objects alone which can be extinguished when the caprice of the dreamer is over, since they merely reflect it; by themselves they have no other consequences than those one wants to draw from them. Thus one would be wrong to take the world of the schizophrenic as a torrent of

1. Not so much because, as is said, one foresees the future from the past: this argument is hardly valid except against the old conception of images. But rather because one foresees the real from the unreal, that is to say, something infinite in richness by means of outlines essentially bare.

images whose richness and splendor would compensate for the monotony of the real: it is a world that is poor and pedantic, in which the same scenes are repeated interminably, to the least detail, accompanied by the same ceremonial in which everything is regulated in advance, foreseen; in which, above all, nothing can escape, resist, nor surprise. In short, if the schizophrenic imagines so many amorous scenes, it is not merely because his real love has been deceived, but mainly because he is no longer capable of loving.

◆§ from *Being and Nothingness*

BEING AND DOING: FREEDOM

Freedom and Responsibility

Although the considerations which are about to follow are of interest primarily to the ethicist, it may nevertheless be worthwhile after these descriptions and arguments to return to the freedom of the for-itself [1] and to try to understand what the fact of this freedom represents for human destiny.

The essential consequence of our earlier remarks is that man being condemned to be free carries the weight of the whole world on his shoulders; he is responsible for the world and for himself as a way of being. We are taking the word "responsibility" in its ordinary sense as "consciousness (of) being the incontestable author of an event or of an object." In this sense the responsibility of the for-itself is overwhelming since he [2] is the one by whom it happens that *there is* a world; since he is also the one who makes himself be, then whatever may be the situation in which he finds himself, the for-itself must wholly assume this situation with its peculiar coefficient of adversity, even though it be insupportable. He must assume the situation with the proud consciousness of being the author of it, for the very worst disadvantages or the worst threats which can endanger my person have meaning only in and

1. In Sartre's terminology, being-in-the-world has two forms: being-for-itself (le *pour-soi*)—that is to say, the subjective existence of persons—and being-in-itself (l'*en-soi*)—that is to say, the objective existence of things. [Ed.]

2. I am shifting to the personal pronoun here since Sartre is describing the for-itself in concrete personal terms rather than as a metaphysical entity. Strictly speaking, of course, this is his position throughout, and the French "*il*" is indifferently "he" or "it." [Trans.]

through my project; and it is on the ground of the engagement which I am that they appear. It is therefore senseless to think of complaining since nothing foreign has decided what we feel, what we live, or what we are.

Furthermore this absolute responsibility is not resignation; it is simply the logical requirement of the consequences of our freedom. What happens to me happens through me, and I can neither affect myself with it nor revolt against it nor resign myself to it. Moreover everything which happens to me is *mine*. By this we must understand first of all that I am always equal to what happens to me *qua* man, for what happens to a man through other men and through himself can be only human. The most terrible situations of war, the worst tortures do not create a non-human state of things; there is no non-human situation. It is only through fear, flight, and recourse to magical types of conduct that I shall decide on the non-human, but this decision is human, and I shall carry the entire responsibility for it. But in addition the situation is *mine* because it is the image of my free choice of myself, and everything which it presents to me is *mine* in that this represents me and symbolizes me. Is it not I who decide the coefficient of adversity in things and even their unpredictability by deciding myself?

Thus there are no *accidents* in a life; a community event which suddenly bursts forth and involves me in it does not come from the outside. If I am mobilized in a war, this war is *my* war; it is in my image and I deserve it. I deserve it first because I could always get out of it by suicide or by desertion; these ultimate possibles are those which must always be present for us when there is a question of envisaging a situation. For lack of getting out of it, I have *chosen* it. This can be due to inertia, to cowardice in the face of public opinion, or because I prefer certain other values to the value of the refusal to join in the war (the good opinion of my relatives, the honor of my family, *etc.*). Anyway you look at it, it is a matter of choice. This choice will be repeated later on again and again without a break until the end of the war. Therefore we must agree with the statement by J. Romains, "In war there are no innocent victims." [3] If therefore I have preferred war to death or to dishonor, everything takes place as if I bore the entire responsibility for this war. Of course others have declared it, and one might be tempted perhaps to consider me as a simple accomplice. But this notion of

3. J. Romains: *Les hommes de bonne volonté;* "Prélude à Verdun."

complicity has only a juridical sense, and it does not hold here. For it depended on me that for me and by me this war should not exist, and I have decided that it does exist. There was no compulsion here, for the compulsion could have got no hold on a freedom. I did not have any excuse; for as we have said repeatedly in this book, the peculiar character of human-reality is that it is without excuse. Therefore it remains for me only to lay claim to this war.

But in addition the war is *mine* because by the sole fact that it arises in a situation which I cause to be and that I can discover it there only by engaging myself for or against it, I can no longer distinguish at present the choice which I make of myself from the choice which I make of the war. To live this war is to choose myself through it and to choose it through my choice of myself. There can be no question of considering it as "four years of vacation" or as a "reprieve," as a "recess," the essential part of my responsibilities being elsewhere in my married, family, or professional life. In this war which I have chosen I choose myself from day to day, and I make it mine by making myself. If it is going to be four empty years, then it is I who bear the responsibility for this.

Finally, as we pointed out earlier, each person is an absolute choice of self from the standpoint of a world of knowledges and of techniques which this choice both assumes and illumines; each person is an absolute upsurge at an absolute date and is perfectly unthinkable at another date. It is therefore a waste of time to ask what I should have been if this war had not broken out, for I have chosen myself as one of the possible meanings of the epoch which imperceptibly led to war. I am not distinct from this same epoch; I could not be transported to another epoch without contradiction. Thus *I am* this war which restricts and limits and makes comprehensible the period which preceded it. In this sense we may define more precisely the responsibility of the for-itself if to the earlier quoted statement, "There are no innocent victims," we add the words, "We have the war we deserve." Thus, totally free, undistinguishable from the period for which I have chosen to be the meaning, as profoundly responsible for the war as if I had myself declared it, unable to live without integrating it in *my* situation, engaging myself in it wholly and stamping it with my seal, I must be without remorse or regrets as I am without excuse; for from the instant of my upsurge into being, I carry the weight of the world by myself alone without anything or any person being able to lighten it.

Yet this responsibility is of a very particular type. Someone will say, "I did not ask to be born." This is a naive way of throwing greater emphasis on our facticity. I am responsible for everything, in fact, except for my very responsibility, for I am not the foundation of my being. Therefore everything takes place as if I were compelled to be responsible. I am *abandoned* in the world, not in the sense that I might remain abandoned and passive in a hostile universe like a board floating on the water, but rather in the sense that I find myself suddenly alone and without help, engaged in a world for which I bear the whole responsibility without being able, whatever I do, to tear myself away from this responsibility for an instant. For I am responsible for my very desire of fleeing responsibilities. To make myself passive in the world, to refuse to act upon things and upon Others is still to choose myself, and suicide is one mode among others of being-in-the-world. Yet I find an absolute responsibility for the fact that my facticity (here the fact of my birth) is directly inapprehensible and even inconceivable, for this fact of my birth never appears as a brute fact but always across a projective reconstruction of my for-itself. I am ashamed of being born or I am astonished at it or I rejoice over it, or in attempting to get rid of my life I affirm that I live and I assume this life as bad. Thus in a certain sense I *choose* being born. This choice itself is integrally affected with facticity since I am not able not to choose, but this facticity in turn will appear only in so far as I surpass it toward my ends. Thus facticity is everywhere but inapprehensible; I never encounter anything except my responsibility. That is why I can not ask, "*Why* was I born?" or curse the day of my birth or declare that I did not ask to be born, for these various attitudes toward my birth—*i.e.*, toward the *fact* that I realize a presence in the world—are absolutely nothing else but ways of assuming this birth in full responsibility and of making it *mine*. Here again I encounter only myself and my projects so that finally my abandonment—*i.e.*, my facticity—consists simply in the fact that I am condemned to be wholly responsible for myself. I am the being which *is* in such a way that in its being its being is in question. And this "is" of my being *is* as present and inapprehensible.

Under these conditions since every event in the world can be revealed to me only as an *opportunity* (an opportunity made use of, lacked, neglected, *etc.*), or better yet since everything which happens to us can be considered as a *chance* (*i.e.*, can appear to us only as a way of realizing this being which is in question in our being) and since others as transcendences-transcended are themselves only *opportunities* and *chances*, the responsibility of the for-itself extends to the entire world as a peopled-world. It is precisely thus that the for-itself apprehends itself in anguish; that is, as a being which is neither the foundation of its own being nor of the Other's being nor of the in-itselfs which form the world, but a being which is compelled to decide the meaning of being—within it and everywhere outside of it. The one who realizes in anguish his condition as *being* thrown into a responsibility which extends to his very abandonment has no longer either remorse or regret or excuse; he is no longer anything but a freedom which perfectly reveals itself and whose being resides in this very revelation. But as we pointed out at the beginning of this work, most of the time we flee anguish in bad faith.

DOING AND HAVING

Existential Psychoanalysis

If it is true that human reality—as we have attempted to establish—identifies and defines itself by the ends which it pursues, then a study and classification of these ends becomes indispensable. In the preceding chapter we have considered the For-itself only from the point of view of its free project, which is the impulse by which it thrusts itself toward its end. We should now question this end itself, for it *forms a part* of absolute subjectivity and is, in fact, its transcendent, objective limit. This is what empirical psychology has hinted at by admitting that a particular man is defined by his desires. Here, however, we must be on our guard against two errors. First, the empirical psychologist, while defining man by his desires, remains the victim of the illusion of substance. He views desire as being *in* man by virtue of being "contained" by his consciousness, and he believes that the meaning of the desire is inherent in the desire itself. Thus he avoids everything which could evoke the idea of transcendence. But if I desire a house or a glass of water or a woman's body, how could this body, this glass, this piece of property reside in my desire, and how can my desire be anything but the consciousness of these objects as desirable? Let us beware then of considering these desires as little psychic entities dwelling in consciousness; they are consciousness itself in its original projective, transcendent structure, for consciousness is on principle consciousness *of* something.

The other error, which fundamentally is closely connected with the first, consists in considering psychological research as terminated as soon as the investigator has reached the concrete ensemble of empirical desires. Thus a man would be defined by the bundle of drives or tendencies which empirical observation could establish. Naturally the psychologist will not always limit himself to making up the *sum* of these tendencies; he will want to bring to light their relationships, their agreements and harmonies; he will try to present the ensemble of desires as a synthetic organization in which each desire acts on the others and influences them. A critic, for example, wishing to explain the "psychology" of Flaubert, will write that he "appeared in his early youth to know as his normal state, a continual exaltation resulting from the two-fold feeling of his grandiose ambition and his invincible power. . . . The effervescence of his young blood was *then* turned into literary passion as happens about the eighteenth year in precocious souls who find in the energy of style or the intensities of fiction some way of escaping from the need of violent action or of intense feeling, which torments them." [4]

In this passage there is an effort to reduce the complex personality of an adolescent to a few basic desires, as the chemist reduces compound bodies to merely a combination of simple bodies. The primitive givens will be grandiose ambition, the need of violent action and of intense feeling; these elements, when they enter into combination, produce a permanent exaltation. Then—as Bourget remarks in a few words which we have not quoted—this exaltation nourished by numerous well chosen readings, is going to seek to delude itself by self-expression in fictions which will appease it symbolically and channel it. There in outline is the genesis of a literary "temperament."

Now in the first place such a psychological *analysis* proceeds from the postulate that an individual fact is produced by the intersection of abstract, universal laws. The fact to be explained—which is here the literary disposition of the young Flaubert—is resolved into a combination of *typical*, abstract desires such as we meet in "the average adolescent." What is concrete here is only their combination; in themselves they

4. Paul Bourget: *Essai de Psychologie contemporaine: G. Flaubert.*

are only possible patterns. The abstract then is by hypothesis prior to the concrete, and the concrete is only an organization of abstract qualities; the individual is only the intersection of universal schemata. But—aside from the logical absurdity of such a postulate—we see clearly in the example chosen, that it simply fails to explain what makes the individuality of the project under consideration. The fact that "the need to feel intensely," a universal pattern, is disguised and channeled into becoming the need to write—this is not the *explanation* of the "calling" of Flaubert; on the contrary, it is what must be explained. Doubtless one could invoke a thousand circumstances, known to us and unknown, which have shaped this need to feel into the need to act. But this is to give up at the start all attempt to explain and refers the question to the undiscoverable.[5] In addition this method rejects the pure individual who has been banished from the pure subjectivity of Flaubert into the external circumstances of his life. Finally, Flaubert's correspondence proves that long before the "crisis of adolescence," from his earliest childhood, he was tormented by the need to write.

At each stage in the description just quoted, we meet with an hiatus. Why did ambition and the feeling of his power produce in Flaubert *exaltation* rather than tranquil waiting or gloomy impatience? Why did this exaltation express itself specifically in the need to act violently and feel intensely? Or rather why does this need make a sudden appearance by spontaneous generation at the end of the paragraph? And why does this need instead of seeking to appease itself in acts of violence, by amorous adventures, or in debauch, choose precisely to satisfy itself symbolically? And why does Flaubert turn to writing rather than to painting or music for this symbolic satisfaction; he could just as well not resort to the artistic field at all (there is also mysticism, for example). "I could have been a great actor," wrote Flaubert somewhere. Why did he not try to be one? In a word, we have understood nothing; we have seen a succession of accidental happenings, of desire springing forth fully armed, one from the other, with no possibility for us to grasp their genesis. The *transitions*, the becomings, the transformations, have been carefully veiled from us, and we have been limited to putting order into the succession by invoking empirically established but literally

5. Since Flaubert's adolescence, so far as we can know it, offers us nothing specific in this connection, we must suppose the action of imponderable facts which on principle escape the critic.

unintelligible sequences (the need to act preceding in the adolescent the need to write).

Yet this is called psychology! Open any biography at random, and this is the kind of description which you will find more or less interspersed with accounts of external events and allusions to the great explanatory idols of our epoch—heredity, education, environment, physiological constitution. Occasionally, in the better works the connection established between antecedent and consequent or between two concomitant desires and their reciprocal action is not conceived merely as a type of regular sequence; sometimes it is "comprehensible" in the sense which Jaspers understands in his general treatise on psychopathology. But this comprehension remains a grasp of general connections. For example we will realize the link between chastity and mysticism, between fainting and hypocrisy. But we are ignorant always of the concrete relation between *this* chastity (this abstinence in relation to a particular woman, *this* struggle against a definite temptation) and the individual content of the mysticism; in the same way psychiatry is too quickly satisfied when it throws light on the general structures of delusions and does not seek to comprehend the individual, concrete content of the psychoses (why this man believes himself to be that particular historical personality rather than some other; why his compensatory delusion is satisfied with specifically these ideas of grandeur instead of others, *etc.*).

But most important of all, these "psychological" explanations refer us ultimately to inexplicable original givens. These are the simple bodies of psychology. We are told, for example, that Flaubert had a "grandiose ambition" and all of the previously quoted description depends on this original ambition. So far so good. But this ambition is an irreducible fact which by no means satisfies the mind. The irreducibility here has no justification other than refusal to push the analysis further. There where the psychologist stops, the fact confronted is given as primary. This is why we experience a troubled feeling of mingled resignation and dissatisfaction when we read these psychological treatises. "See," we say to ourselves, "Flaubert was ambitious. He was that kind of man." It would be as futile to ask why he was such as to seek to know why he was tall and blond. Of course we have to stop somewhere; it is the very contingency of all real existence. This rock is covered with moss, the rock next to it is not. Gustave Flaubert had literary ambition, and his brother Achille lacked it. That's the way it is. In the same way we want to know the properties of phosphorus, and we attempt to reduce them to the structure of the chemical molecules which compose it. But why are there molecules of this type? That's the way it is, that's all. The explanation of Flaubert's psychology will consist, if it is possible, in referring the complexity of his behavior patterns, his feelings, and his tastes back to certain *properties*, comparable to those of chemical bodies, beyond which it would be foolish to attempt to proceed. Yet we feel obscurely that Flaubert had not "received" his ambition. It is meaningful; therefore it is free. Neither heredity, nor bourgeois background nor education can account for it, still less those physiological considerations regarding the "nervous temperament," which have been the vogue for some time now. The nerve is not *meaningful;* it is a colloidal substance which can be described in itself and which does not have the quality of transcendence; that is, it does not transcend itself in order to make known to itself by means of other realities what it is. Under no circumstances could the nerve furnish the basis for meaning. In one sense Flaubert's ambition is a fact with all a fact's contingency—and it is true that it is impossible to advance beyond that fact—but in another sense *it makes itself,* and our satisfaction is a guarantee to us that we may be able to grasp beyond this ambition something more, something like a radical decision which, without ceasing to be contingent, would be the veritable psychic irreducible.

What we are demanding then—and what nobody ever attempts to give us—is a *veritable* irreducible; that is, an irreducible of which the irreducibility would be self-evident, which would not be presented as the postulate of the psychologist and the result of his refusal or his incapacity to go further, but which when established would produce in us an accompanying feeling of satisfaction. This demand on our part does not come from that ceaseless pursuit of a cause, that infinite regress which has often been described as constitutive of rational research and which consequently—far from being exclusively associated with psychological investigation—may be found in all disciplines and in all problems. This is not the childish quest of a "because," which allows no further "why?" It is on the contrary a demand based on a preontological comprehension of human reality and on the related refusal to consider man as capable of being analyzed and reduced to original givens, to determined desires (or "drives"), supported by the subject as properties by an object. Even if we were to consider him as such, it would be necessary to choose: either *Flaubert*, the man, whom we can love or detest, blame or praise, who represents for us *the Other*, who directly attacks our being by the very fact that he has existed, would be originally a substratum unqualified by these desires; that is, a sort of indeterminate clay which would have to receive them passively or he would be reduced to the simple bundle of these irreducible drives or tendencies. In either case the *man* disappears; we can no longer find "the one" to *whom* this or that experience has *happened;* either in looking for the *person*, we encounter a useless, contradictory metaphysical substance—or else the being whom we seek vanishes in a dust of phenomena bound together by external connections. But what each one of us requires in his very effort to comprehend another is that he should never have to resort to this idea of substance which is inhuman because it is well this side of the human. Finally the fact is that the being considered does not crumble into dust, and one can discover in him that unity—for which substance was only a caricature—which must be a unity of responsibility, a unity agreeable or hateful, blamable and praiseworthy, in short *personal*. This unity, which is the being of the man under consideration, is a *free unification*, and this unification can not come *after* a diversity which it unifies.

But *to be*, for Flaubert, as for every subject of "biography," means to be unified in the world. The irreducible unification which we ought to find, which is Flaubert, and which we require biographers to reveal to us—this is the unification of an *original project*, a unification which should reveal itself to us as a *non-substantial absolute*. Therefore we should forego these so-called irreducible details and, taking the very evidence of them for a criterion, not stop in our investigation before it is evident that we neither can nor ought to go any further. In particular we must avoid trying to reconstruct a person by means of his inclinations, just as Spinoza warns us not to attempt to reconstruct a substance or its attributes by the summation of its modes. Every desire if presented as an irreducible is an absurd contingency and involves in absurdity human reality taken as a whole. For example, if I declare of one of my friends that he "likes to go rowing," I deliberately intend to stop my investigation there. But on the other hand, I thus establish a contingent *fact*, which nothing can explain and which, though it has the gratuity of free decision, by no means has its autonomy. I can not in fact consider this fondness for rowing as the fundamental project of Pierre; it contains something secondary and derived. Those who portray a character in this way by successive strokes come close to holding that each of these strokes—each one of the desires confronted—is bound to the others by connections which are purely contingent and simply external. Those who, on the other hand, try to explain this liking will fall into the view of what Comte called *materialism;* that is, of explaining the higher by the lower. Someone will say, for example, that the subject considered is a sportsman who likes violent exercise and is in addition a man of the outdoors who especially likes open air sports. By more general and less differentiated tendencies he will try to explain *this* desire, which stands in exactly the same relation to them as the zoological species does to the genus. Thus the psychological explanation when it does not suddenly decide to stop, is sometimes the mere putting into relief relations of pure concomitance or of constant succession, and it is at other times a simple classification. To explain Pierre's fondness for rowing is to make it a member of the family of fondness for open air sports and to attach this family to that of fondness for sport in general. Moreover we will be able to find still more general and barren rubrics if we classify the taste for sports as one aspect of the love of chance, which will itself be given as a specific instance of the fundamental fondness for play. It is obvious that this so-called explanatory classification has no more value or interest than the classifications in ancient botany; like the latter it amounts to assuming the priority of the abstract over the concrete—as if the fondness for play existed first in general to be subsequently made specific by the action of these circumstances in the love of sport, the latter in the fondness for rowing, and finally the rowing in the desire to row on a particular stream, under certain circumstances in a particular season—and like the ancient classifications it fails to explain the concrete enrichment which at each stage is undergone by the abstract inclination considered.

Furthermore how are we to believe that a desire to row is *only* a desire to row? Can we truthfully admit that it can be reduced so simply to what it is? The most discerning ethicists have shown how a desire reaches beyond itself. Pascal believed that he could discover in hunting, for example, or tennis, or in a hundred other occupations, the need of being diverted. He revealed that in an activity which would be absurd if reduced to itself, there was a meaning which transcended it; that is, an indication which referred to the reality of man in general and to his condition. Similarly Stendhal in spite of his attachment to ideologists, and Proust in spite of his intellectualistic and analytical tendencies, have shown that love and jealousy can not be reduced to the strict desire of possessing a *particular* woman, but that these emotions aim at laying hold of the world in its entirety through the woman. This is the meaning of Stendhal's crystallization, and it is precisely for this reason that love as Stendhal describes it appears as a mode of being in the world. Love is a fundamental relation of the for-itself to the world and to itself (selfness) through a particular woman; the woman represents only a conducting body which is placed in the circuit. These analyses may be inexact or only partially true; nevertheless they make us suspect a method other than pure analytical description. In the same way Catholic novelists immediately see in carnal love its surpassing toward God—in Don Juan, "the eternally unsatisfied," in sin, "the place empty of God." There is no question here of finding again an abstract behind the concrete; the impulse toward God is no *less concrete* than the impulse toward a particular woman. On the contrary, it is a matter of rediscovering under the partial and incomplete aspects of the subject the veritable concreteness which can be only the totality of his impulse toward being, his original relation to himself, to the world, and to the Other, in the unity of internal relations and of a fundamental project. This impulse can be only purely individual and unique. Far from estranging us from the person, as Bourget's analysis, for example, does in constituting the individual by means of a summation of general maxims, this impulse will not lead us to find in the need of writing—and of writing particular books—the need of activity in general. On the contrary, rejecting equally the theory of malleable clay and that of the bundle of drives, we will discover the individual person in the initial project which constitutes him. It is for this reason that the irreducibility of the result attained will be revealed as self-evident, not because it is the poorest and the most abstract but because it is the richest. The intuition here will be accompanied by an individual fullness.

The problem poses itself in approximately these terms: If we admit that the person is a totality, we can not hope to reconstruct him by an addition or by an organization of the diverse tendencies which we have empirically discovered in him. On the contrary, in each inclination, in each tendency the person expresses himself completely, although from a different angle, a little as Spinoza's substance expresses itself completely in each of its attributes. But if this is so, we should discover in each tendency, in each attitude of the subject, a meaning which transcends it. A jealousy of a particular date in which a subject historicizes himself in relation to a certain woman, signifies for the one who knows how to interpret it, the total relation to the world by which the subject constitutes himself as a self. In other words this *empirical* attitude is by itself the expression of the "choice of an intelligible character." There is no mystery about this. We no longer have to do with an intelligible pattern which can be present in our thought only, while we apprehend and conceptualize the unique pattern of the subject's empirical existence. If the empirical attitude signifies the choice of the intelligible character, it is because it is itself this choice. Indeed the distinguishing characteristic of the intelligible choice, as we shall see later, is that it can exist only as the transcendent meaning of each concrete, empirical choice. It is by no means first effected in some unconscious or on the noumenal level to be *subsequently* expressed in a particular observable attitude; there is not even an *ontological* pre-eminence over the empirical choice, but it is on principle that which must always detach itself from the empirical choice as its *beyond* and the infinity of its transcendence. Thus if I am rowing on the river, I am nothing—either here or in any other world—save this concrete project of rowing. But this project itself inasmuch as it is the totality of my being, expresses my original choice in particular circumstances; it is nothing other than the choice of myself as a totality in these circumstances. That is why a special method must aim at detaching the fundamental meaning which the project admits and which can be only the individual secret of the subject's being-in-the-world. It is then rather by a *comparison* of the various empirical drives of a subject that we try to discover and disengage the fundamental project which is common to them all—and not by a simple summation or reconstruction of these tendencies; each drive or tendency is the entire person.

There is naturally an infinity of possible projects as there is an infinity of possible human beings. Nevertheless, if we are to recognize certain common characteristics among them and if we are going to attempt to classify them in larger categories, it is best first to undertake individual investigations in the cases which we can study more easily. In our research, we will be guided by this principle: to stop only in the presence of evident irreducibility; that is, never to believe that we have reached the initial project until the projected end appears as *the very being* of the subject under consideration. This is why we can not stop at those classifications of "authentic project" and "unauthentic project of the self" which Heidegger wishes to establish. In addition to the fact that such a classification, in spite of its author's intent, is tainted with an ethical concern shown by its very terminology, it is based on the attitude of the subject toward his own death. Now if death causes anguish, and if consequently we can either flee the anguish or throw ourselves resolutely into it, it is a truism to say that this is because we wish to hold on to life. Consequently anguish before death and resolute decision or flight into unauthenticity can not be considered as fundamental projects of our being. On the contrary, they can be understood only on the foundation of an original project of *living;* that is, on an original choice of our being. It is right then in each case to pass beyond the results of Heidegger's interpretation toward a still more fundamental project.

This fundamental project must not of course refer to any other and should be conceived by itself. It can be concerned neither with death nor life nor any particular characteristic of the human condition; the original project of a for-itself *can aim only at its being.* The project of being or desire of being or drive toward being does not originate in a physiological differentiation or in an empirical contingency; in fact it is not distinguished from the being of the for-itself. The for-itself is a being such that in its being, its being is in question in the form of a project of being. To the for-itself *being* means to make known to oneself what one is by means of a possibility appearing as a value. Possibility and value belong to the being of the for-itself. The for-itself is defined ontologically as a *lack of being,* and possibility belongs to the for-itself as that which it lacks, in the same way that value haunts the for-itself as the totality of being which is lacking. What we have expressed in Part Two in terms of lack can be just as well expressed in terms of *freedom.* The for-itself chooses because it is lack; freedom is really synonymous with lack. Freedom is the concrete mode of being of the lack of being. Ontologically then it amounts to the same thing to say that value and possibility exist as internal limits of a lack of being which can exist only as a lack of being—or that the upsurge of freedom determines its possibility and thereby circumscribes *its* value.

Thus we can advance no further but have encountered the self-evident irreducible when we have reached the *project of being;* for obviously it is impossible to advance further than *being,* and there is no difference between the project of being, possibility, value, on the one hand, and *being,* on the other. Fundamentally man is *the desire to be,* and the existence of this desire is not to be established by an empirical induction; it is the result of an *a priori* description of the being of the for-itself, since desire is a lack and since the for-itself is the being which is to itself its own lack of being. The original project which is expressed in each of our empirically observable tendencies is then the *project of being;* or, if you prefer, each empirical tendency exists with the original project of being, in a relation of expression and symbolic satisfaction just as conscious drives, with Freud, exist in relation to the complex and to the original libido. Moreover the desire to be by no means exists *first* in order to cause itself to be expressed subsequently by desires *a posteriori.* There is nothing outside of the symbolic expression which it finds in concrete desires. There is not first a single desire of being, then a thousand particular feelings, but the desire to be exists and manifests itself only in and through jealousy, greed, love of art, cowardice, courage, and a thousand contingent, empirical expressions which always cause human reality to appear to us only as *manifested* by *a particular man,* by a specific person.

As for the being which is the object of this desire, we know *a priori* what this is. The for-itself is the being which is to itself its own lack of being. The being which the for-itself lacks is the in-itself. The for-itself arises as the nihilation of the in-itself and this nihilation is defined as the project toward the in-itself. Between the nihilated in-itself and the projected in-itself the for-itself is nothingness. Thus the end and the goal of the nihilation which I am is the in-itself. Thus human reality is the desire of being-in-itself. But the in-itself which it desires can not be pure contingent, absurd in-itself, comparable at every point to that which it encounters and which it nihilates. The nihilation, as we have seen, is in fact like a revolt of the in-itself, which nihilates itself against its contingency. To say that the for-itself lives its facticity, as we have seen in the chapter concerning the body, amounts to saying that the nihilation is the vain effort of a being to found its own being and that it is the withdrawal to found being which provokes the minute displacement by which nothingness enters into being. The being which forms the object of the desire of the for-itself is then an in-itself which would be to itself its own foundation; that is, which would be to its facticity in the same relation as the for-itself is to its motivations. In addition the for-itself, being the negation of the in-itself, could not desire the pure and simple return to the in-itself. Here as with Hegel, the negation of the negation can not bring us back to our point of departure. Quite the contrary, what the for-itself demands of the in-itself is precisely the totality detotalized—"In-itself nihilated in for-itself." In other words the for-itself projects *being as for-itself*, a being which is what it is. It is as being which is what it is not, and which is not what it is, that the for-itself projects being what it is. It is as consciousness that it wishes to have the impermeability and infinite density of the in-itself. It is as the nihilation of the in-itself and a perpetual evasion of contingency and of facticity that it wishes to be its own foundation. This is why the possible is projected in general as what the for-itself lacks in order to become in-itself-for-itself. The fundamental value which presides over this project is exactly the in-itself-for-itself; that is, the ideal of a consciousness which would be the foundation of its own being-in-itself by the pure consciousness which it would have of itself. It is this ideal which can be called God. Thus the best way to conceive of the fundamental project of human reality is to say that man is the being whose project is to be God. Whatever may be the myths and rites of the religion considered, God is first "sensible to the heart" of man as the one who identifies and defines him in his ultimate and fundamental project. If man possesses a pre-ontological comprehension of the being of God, it is not the great wonders of nature nor the power of society which have conferred it upon him. God, value and supreme end of transcendence, represents the permanent limit in terms of which man makes known to himself what he is. To be man means to reach toward being God. Or if you prefer, man fundamentally is the desire to be God.

It may be asked, if man on coming into the world is borne toward God as toward his limit, if he can choose only to be God, what becomes of freedom? For freedom is nothing other than a choice which creates for itself its own possibilities, but it appears here that the initial project of being God, which "defines" man, comes close to being the same as a human "nature" or an "essence." The answer is that while the *meaning* of the desire is ultimately the project of being God, the desire is never *constituted* by this meaning; on the contrary, it always represents a particular discovery of its ends. These ends in fact are pursued in terms of a particular empirical situation, and it is this very pursuit which constitutes the surroundings *as a situation.* The desire of being is always realized as the desire of a mode of being. And this desire of a mode of being expresses itself in turn as the meaning of the myriads of concrete desires which constitute the web of our conscious life. Thus we find ourselves before very complex symbolic structures which have *at least* three stories. In empirical desire I can discern a symbolization of a fundamental concrete desire which is the person himself and which represents the mode in which he has decided that being would be in question in his being. This fundamental desire in turn expresses concretely in the world within the particular situation enveloping the individual, an abstract meaningful structure which is the desire of being in general; it must be considered as human reality in the person, and it brings about his community with others, thus making it possible to state that there is a truth concerning man and not only concerning individuals who cannot be compared. Absolute concreteness, completion, existence as a totality belong then to the free and fundamental desire which is the unique person. Empirical desire is only a symbolization of this; it refers to this and derives its meaning from it while remaining partial and reducible, for the empirical desire can not be conceived in isolation. On the other hand, the desire of being in its abstract purity is the *truth* of the concrete fundamental desire, but it does not exist by virtue of reality. Thus the fundamental project, the person, the free realization of human truth is everywhere in all desires (save for those exceptions treated in the preceding chapter, concerning, for example, "indifferents"). It is never apprehended except through desires—as we can apprehend space only through bodies which shape it for us, though space is a specific reality and not a concept. Or, if you like, it is like the *object* of Husserl, which reveals itself only by *Abschattungen,* and which nevertheless does not allow itself to be absorbed by any one *Abschattung.* We can understand after these remarks that the abstract, ontological "desire to be" is unable to represent the fundamental, *human* structure of the individual; it cannot be an obstacle to his freedom. Freedom in fact, as we have shown in the preceding chapter, is strictly identified with nihilation. The only being which can be called free is the being which nihilates its being. Moreover we know that nihilation is *lack of being* and can not be otherwise. Freedom is precisely the being which makes itself a lack of being. But since desire, as we have established, is identical with lack of being, freedom can arise only as being which makes itself a desire of being; that is, as the project-for-itself of being in-itself-for-itself. Here we have arrived at an abstract structure which can by no means be considered as the nature or essence of freedom. Freedom is existence, and in it existence precedes essence. The upsurge of freedom is immediate and concrete and is not to be distinguished from its choice; that is, from the person himself. But the structure under consideration can be called the *truth* of freedom; that is, it is the human meaning of freedom.

It should be possible to establish the human truth of the person, as we have attempted to do by an ontological phenomenology. The catalogue of empirical desires ought to be made the object of appropriate psychological investigations, observation and induction and, as needed, experience can serve to draw up this list. They will indicate to the philosopher the comprehensible relations which can unite to each other various desires and various patterns of behaviors, and will bring to light certain concrete connections between the subject of experience and "situations" experientially defined (which at bottom originate only from limitations applied in the name of positivity to the fundamental situation of the subject in the world). But in establishing and classifying fundamental desires of *individual persons* neither of these methods is appropriate. Actually there can be no question of determining *a priori* and ontologically what appears in all the unpredictability of a free act. This is why we shall limit ourselves here to indicating very summarily the possibilities of such a quest and its perspectives. The very fact that we can subject any man whatsoever to such an investigation—that is what belongs to human reality in general. Or, if you prefer, this is what can be established by an ontology. But the inquiry itself and its results are on principle wholly outside the possibilities of an ontology.

On the other hand, pure, simple empirical description can only give us catalogues and put us in the presence of pseudo-irreducibles (the desire to write, to swim, a taste for adventure, jealousy, *etc.*). It is not enough in fact to draw up a list of behavior patterns, of drives and inclinations, it is necessary also to *decipher* them; that is, it is necessary to know how to *question* them. This research can be conducted only according to the rules of a specific method. It is this method which we call existential psychoanalysis.

The *principle* of this psychoanalysis is that man is a totality and not a collection. Consequently he expresses himself as a whole in even his most insignificant and his most superficial behavior. In other words there is not a taste, a mannerism, or a human act which is not *revealing*.

The *goal* of psychoanalysis is to *decipher* the empirical behavior patterns of man; that is to bring out in the open the revelations which each one of them contains and to fix them conceptually.

Its *point of departure* is *experience;* its pillar of support is the fundamental, pre-ontological comprehension which man has of the human person. Although the majority of people can well ignore the indications contained in a gesture, a word, a sign and can look with scorn on the revelation which they carry, each human individual nevertheless possesses *a priori* the *meaning* of the revelatory value of these manifestations and is capable of deciphering them, at least if he is aided and guided by a helping hand. Here as elsewhere, truth is not encountered by chance; it does not belong to a domain where one must seek it without ever having any presentiment of its location, as one can go to look for the source of the Nile or of the Niger. It belongs *a priori* to human comprehension and the essential task is an hermeneutic; that is, a deciphering, a determination, and a conceptualization.

Its *method* is comparative. Since each example of human conduct symbolizes in its own manner the fundamental choice which must be brought to light, and since at the same time each one disguises this choice under its occasional character and its historical opportunity, only the comparison of these acts of conduct can effect the emergence of the unique revelation which they all express in a different way. The first outline of this method has been furnished for us by the psychoanalysis of Freud and his disciples. For this reason it will be profitable here to indicate more specifically the points where existential psychoanalysis will be inspired by psychoanalysis proper and those where it will radically differ from it.

Both kinds of psychoanalysis consider all objectively discernible manifestations of "psychic life" as symbols maintaining symbolic relations to the fundamental, total structures which constitute the individual person. Both consider that there are no primary givens such as hereditary dispositions, character, *etc.* Existential psychoanalysis recognizes nothing *before* the original upsurge of human freedom; empirical psychoanalysis holds that the original affectivity of the individual is virgin wax *before* its history. The libido is nothing besides its concrete fixations, save for a permanent possibility of fixing anything whatsoever upon anything whatsoever. Both consider the human being as a perpetual, searching, historization. Rather than uncovering static, constant givens they discover the meaning, orientation, and adventures of this history. Due to this fact both consider man in the world and do not imagine that one can question the being of a man without taking into account all his *situation.* Psychological investigations aim at reconstituting the life of the subject from birth to the moment of the cure; they utilize all the objective documentation which they can find: letters, witnesses, intimate diaries, "social" information of every kind. What they aim at restoring is less a pure psychic event than a twofold structure: the crucial event of infancy and the psychic crystallization around this event. Here again we have to do with a *situation.* Each "historical" fact from this point of view will be considered at once as a *factor* of the psychic evolution and as a *symbol* of that evolution. For it is nothing in itself. It operates only according to the way in which it is taken and this very manner of taking it expresses symbolically the internal disposition of the individual.

Empirical psychoanalysis and existential psychoanalysis both search within an existing situation for a fundamental attitude which can not be expressed by simple, logical definitions because it is prior to all logic, and which requires reconstruction according to the laws of specific syntheses. Empirical psychoanalysis seeks to determine the *complex,* the very name of which indicates the polyvalence of all the meanings which are referred back to it. Existential psychoanalysis seeks to determine the *original choice.* This original choice operating in the face of the world and being a choice of position in the world is total like the complex; it is prior to logic like the complex. It is this which decides the attitude of the person when confronted with logic and principles; therefore there can be no possibility of questioning it in conformance to logic. It brings together in a prelogical synthesis the totality of the existent, and as such it is the center of reference for an infinity of polyvalent meanings.

Both our psychoanalyses refuse to admit that the subject is in a privileged position to proceed in these inquiries concerning himself. They equally insist on a strictly objective method, using as documentary evidence the data of reflection as well as the testimony of others. Of course the subject *can* undertake a psychoanalytic investigation of himself. But in this case he must renounce at the outset all benefit stemming from his peculiar position and must question himself exactly as if he were someone else. Empirical psychoanalysis in fact is based on the hypothesis of the existence of an unconscious psyche, which on principle escapes the intuition of the subject. Existential psychoanalysis rejects the hypothesis of the unconscious; it makes the psychic act coextensive with consciousness. But if the fundamental project is fully experienced by the subject and hence wholly conscious, that certainly does not mean that it must by the same token be *known* by him; quite the contrary. The reader will perhaps recall the care we took in the Introduction to distinguish between consciousness and knowledge. To be sure, as we have seen earlier, reflection can be considered as a quasi-knowledge. But what it grasps at each moment is not the pure project of the for-itself as it is symbolically expressed—often in several ways at once—by the concrete behavior which it apprehends. It grasps the concrete behavior itself; that is, the specific dated desire in all its characteristic network. It grasps at once symbol and symbolization. This apprehension, to be sure, is entirely constituted by a pre-ontological comprehension of the fundamental project; better yet, in so far as reflection is almost a non-thetic consciousness of itself as reflection, it *is* this same project, as well as the non-reflective consciousness. But it does not follow that it commands the instruments and techniques necessary to isolate the choice symbolized, to fix it by concepts, and to bring it forth into the full light of day. It is penetrated by a great light without being able to express what this light is illuminating. We are not dealing with an unsolved riddle as the Freudians believe; all is there, luminous; reflection is in full possession of it, apprehends all. But this "mystery in broad daylight" is due to the fact that this possession is deprived of the means which would ordinarily permit *analysis* and *conceptualization*. It grasps everything, all at once, without shading, without relief, without connections of grandeur—not that these shades, these values, these reliefs exist somewhere and are hidden from it, but rather because they must be established by another human attitude and because they can exist only *by means of* and *for* knowledge. Reflection, unable to serve as the basis for existential psychoanalysis, will then simply furnish us with the brute materials toward which the psychoanalyst must take an objective attitude. Thus only will he be able to *know* what he *already understands.* The result is that complexes uprooted from the depths of the unconscious, like projects revealed by existential psychoanalysis, will be apprehended *from the point of view of the Other.* Consequently the *object* thus brought into the light will be articulated according to the structures of the transcended-transcendence; that is, its being will be the being-for-others even if the psychoanalyst and the subject of the psychoanalysis are actually the same person. Thus the project which is brought to light by either kind of psychoanalysis can be only the totality of the individual human being, the irreducible element of the transcendence with the structure of *being-for-others.* What always escapes these methods of investigation is the project as it is for itself, the complex in its own being. This project-for-itself can be experienced only as a living possession; there is an incompatibility between existence for-itself and objective existence. But the object of the two psychoanalyses has in it nonetheless the *reality of a being;* the subject's knowledge of it can in addition contribute to *clarify* reflection, and that reflection can then become a possession which will be a quasi-knowing.

At this point the similarity between the two kinds of psychoanalysis ceases. They differ fundamentally in that empirical psychoanalysis has decided upon its own irreducible instead of allowing this to make itself known in a self-evident intuition. The libido or the will to power in actuality constitutes a psycho-biological residue which is not clear in itself and which does not appear to us as *being beforehand* the irreducible limit of the investigation. Finally it is experience which establishes that the foundation of complexes is this libido or this will to power; and these results of empirical inquiry are perfectly contingent, they are not convincing. Nothing prevents our conceiving *a priori* of a "human reality" which would not be expressed by the will to power, for which the libido would not constitute the original, undifferentiated project.

On the other hand, the choice to which existential psychoanalysis will lead us, precisely because it is a choice, accounts for its original contingency, for the contingency of the choice is the reverse side of its freedom. Furthermore, inasmuch as it is established on the *lack of being,* conceived as a fundamental characteristic of being, it receives its legitimacy as a *choice*, and we know that we do not have to push further. Each result then will be at once fully contingent and legitimately irreducible. Moreover it will always remain *particular;* that is, we will not achieve as the ultimate goal of our investigation and the foundation of all behavior an abstract, general term, libido for example, which would be differentiated and made concrete first in complexes and then in detailed acts of conduct, due to the action of external facts and the history of the subject. On the contrary, it will be a choice which remains unique and which is from the start absolute concreteness. Details of behavior can express or *particularize* this choice, but they can not make it more concrete than is already known in a self-evident intuition. The libido or the will to power in is. That is because the choice is nothing other than the being of each human reality; this amounts to saying that a particular partial behavior *is* or expresses the original choice of this human reality since for human reality there is no difference between existing and choosing for itself. From this fact we understand that existential psychoanalysis does not have to proceed from the fundamental "complex," which is exactly the choice of being, to an abstraction like the libido which would explain it. The complex is the ultimate choice, it is the choice of being and *makes itself such.* Bringing it into the light will reveal it each time as evidently irreducible. It follows necessarily that the libido and the will to power will appear to existential psychoanalysis neither as general characteristics common to all mankind nor as irreducibles. At most it will be possible after the investigation to establish that they express by virtue of particular ensembles in certain subjects a fundamental choice which can not be reduced to either one of them. We have seen in fact that desire and sexuality in general express an original effort of the for-itself to recover its being which has become estranged through contact with the Other. The will to power also originally supposes being-for-others, the comprehension of the Other, and the choice of winning its own salvation by means of the Other. The foundation of this attitude must be an original choice which would make us understand the radical identification of being-in-itself-for-itself with being-for-others.

The fact that the ultimate term of this existential inquiry must be a *choice*, distinguishes even better the psychoanalysis for which we have outlined the method and principal features. It thereby abandons the supposition that the environment acts mechanically on the subject under consideration. The environment can act on the subject only to the exact extent that he comprehends it; that is, transforms it into a situation. Hence no objective description of this environment could be of any use to us. From the start the environment conceived as a situation refers to the for-itself which is choosing, just as the for-itself refers to the environment by the very fact that the for-itself is in the world. By renouncing all mechanical causation, we renounce at the same time all *general* interpretation of the symbolization confronted. Our goal could not be to establish empirical laws of succession, nor could we constitute a universal symbolism. Rather the psychoanalyst will have to rediscover at each step a symbol functioning in the particular case which he is considering. If each being is a totality, it is not conceivable that there can exist elementary symbolic relationships (*e.g.;* the faeces = gold, or a pincushion = the breast) which preserve a constant meaning in all cases; that is, which remain unaltered when they pass from one meaningful ensemble to another ensemble. Furthermore the psychoanalyst will never lose sight of the fact that the choice is living and consequently can be *revoked* by the subject who is being studied. We have shown in the preceding chapter the importance of the *instant*, which represents abrupt changes in orientation and the assuming of a new position in the face of an unalterable past. From this moment on, we must always be ready to consider that symbols change meaning and to abandon the symbol used hitherto. Thus existential psychoanalysis will have to be completely flexible and adapt itself to the slightest observable changes in the subject. Our concern here is to understand what is *individual* and often even instantaneous. The method which has served for one subject will not necessarily be suitable to use for another subject or for the same subject at a later period.

Precisely because the goal of the inquiry must be to discover a *choice* and not a *state*, the investigator must recall on every occasion that his object is not a datum buried in the darkness of the unconscious but a free, conscious determination—which is not even resident in consciousness, but which is one with this consciousness itself. Empirical psychoanalysis, to the extent that its method is better than its principles, is often in sight of an existential discovery, but it always stops part way. When it thus approaches the fundamental choice, the resistance of the subject collapses suddenly and he *recognizes* the image of himself which is presented to him as if he were seeing himself in a mirror. This involuntary testimony of the subject is precious for the psychoanalyst; he sees there the sign that he has reached his goal; he can pass on from the investigation proper to the cure. But nothing in his principles or in his initial postulates permits him to understand or to utilize this testimony. Where could he get any such right? If the complex is really unconscious—that is, if there is a barrier separating the sign from the thing signified—how could the subject *recognize* it? Does the unconscious complex recognize itself? But haven't we been told that it lacks *understanding?* And if of necessity we granted to it the faculty of understanding the signs, would this not be to make of it by the same token a conscious unconscious? What is understanding if not to be conscious of what is understood? Shall we say on the other hand that it is the subject as conscious who recognizes the image presented? But how could he compare it with his true state since that is out of reach and since he has never had any knowledge of it? At most he will be able to judge that the psychoanalytic explanation of his case is a *probable* hypothesis, which derives its probability from the number of behavior patterns which it explains. His relation to this interpretation is that of a third party, that of the psychoanalyst himself; he has no privileged position. And if he *believes* in the probability of the psychoanalytic hypothesis, is this simple belief, which lives in the limits of his consciousness, able to effect the breakdown of the barriers which dam up the unconscious tendencies? The psychoanalyst doubtless has some obscure picture of an abrupt coincidence of conscious and unconscious. But he has removed all methods of conceiving of this coincidence in any positive sense.

Still, the enlightenment of the subject is a fact. There is an intuition here which is accompanied by evidence. The subject guided by the psychoanalyst does more and better than to give his agreement to an hypothesis; he touches it, he sees what it is. This is truly understandable only if the subject has never ceased being conscious of his deep tendencies; better yet, only if these drives are not distinguished from his conscious self. In this case as we have seen, the traditional psychoanalytic interpretation does not cause him to attain *consciousness* of what he is; it causes him to attain *knowledge* of what he is. It is existential psychoanalysis then which claims the final intuition of the subject as decisive.

This comparison allows us to understand better what an existential psychoanalysis must be if it is entitled to exist. It is a method destined to bring to light, in a strictly objective form, the subjective choice by which each living person makes himself a person; that is, makes known to himself what he is. Since what the method seeks is a *choice of being* at the same time as a *being*, it must reduce particular behavior patterns to fundamental relations—not of sexuality or of the will to power, but *of being*—which are expressed in this behavior. It is then guided from the start toward a comprehension of being and must not assign itself any other goal than to discover being and the mode of being of the being confronting this being. It is forbidden to stop before attaining this goal. It will utilize the comprehension of being which characterizes the investigator inasmuch as he is himself a human reality; and as it seeks to detach being from its symbolic expressions, it will have to rediscover each time on the basis of a comparative study of acts and attitudes, a symbol destined to decipher them. Its criterion of success will be the number of facts which its hypothesis permits it to explain and to unify as well as the self-evident intuition of the irreducibility of the end attained. To this criterion will be added in all cases where it is possible, the decisive testimony of the subject. The results thus achieved—that is, the ultimate ends of the individual—can then become the object of a classification, and it is by the comparison of these results that we will be able to establish general considerations about human reality as an empirical choice of its own ends. The behavior studied by this psychoanalysis will include not only dreams, failures, obsessions, and neuroses, but also and especially the thoughts of waking life, successfully adjusted acts, style, *etc.* This psychoanalysis has not yet found its Freud. At most we can find the foreshadowing of it in certain particularly successful biographies. We hope to be able to attempt elsewhere two examples in relation to Flaubert and Dostoevsky. But it matters little to us whether it now exists; the important thing is that it is possible.

Quality as a Revelation of Being

. . .

What ontology can teach psychoanalysis is first of all the *true* origin of the meanings of things and their *true* relation to human reality. Ontology alone in fact can take its place on the plane of transcendence and from a single viewpoint apprehend being-in-the-world with its two terms because ontology alone has its place originally in the perspective of the *cogito*. Once again the ideas of facticity and situation will enable us to understand the existential symbolism of things. We have seen that it is in theory possible but in practice impossible to distinguish facticity from the project which constitutes it in situation. This observation can be of use to us here; we have seen that there is no necessity to hold that the "this" has any meaning whatever when considered in the indifferent exteriority of its being and independently from the upsurge of the for-itself. Actually its quality, as we have seen, is nothing other than its being. The yellow of the lemon, we said, is not a subjective mode of apprehending the lemon; it *is the lemon*. We have shown also that the whole lemon extends throughout its qualities and that each one of the qualities is spread over the others; that is what we have correctly called "this." [6] Every quality of being is all of being; it is the presence of its absolute contingency; it is its indifferent irreducibility. Yet in Part Two we insisted on the inseparability of project and facticity in the single quality. "For in order for there to be quality, there must be being for a nothingness which by nature is not being. . . . Quality is the whole of being unveiling itself within the limitations of the *there is*." Thus from the beginning we could not attribute the meaning of a quality to *being-in-itself*, since the "there is" is already necessary; that is, the nihilating meditation of the for-itself must be there in order for qualities to be there. But it is easy to understand in view of these remarks that the meaning of quality in turn indicates something as a reenforcement of "there is," since we take it as our support in order to surpass the "there is" toward being as it is absolutely and in-itself.

In each apprehension of quality, there is in this sense a metaphysical effort to escape from our condition so as to pierce through the shell of nothingness about the "there is" and to penetrate to the pure in-itself. But obviously we can apprehend quality only as a symbol of a being which totally escapes us, even though it is totally there before us; in short, we can only make revealed being function as a symbol of being-in-itself. This means that a new structure of the "there is" is constituted which is the meaningful level although this level is revealed in the absolute unity of one and the same fundamental project. This structure we shall call the metaphysical purport of all intuitive revelation of being; and this is precisely what we ought to achieve and disclose by psychoanalysis. What is the metaphysical purport of yellow, of red,

6. Part Two, ch. III, section iii.

of polished, of wrinkled? And *after* these elementary questions, what is the metaphysical coefficient of lemon, of water, of oil, *etc*? Psychoanalysis must resolve all these problems if it wants to understand someday why Pierre likes oranges and has a horror of water, why he gladly eats tomatoes and refuses to eat beans, why he vomits if he is forced to swallow oysters or raw eggs.

We have shown also, however, the error which we would make by believing that we "project" our affective dispositions *on* the thing, to illuminate it or color it. First, as was seen early in the discussion, a feeling is not an inner disposition but an objective, transcending relation which has as its object to learn what it is. But this is not all. The explanation by projection, which is found in such trite sayings as "A landscape is a spiritual state," always begs the question. Take for example that particular quality which we call "slimy." [7] Certainly for the European adult it signifies a host of *human* and *moral* characteristics which can easily be reduced to relations of being. A handshake, a smile, a thought, a feeling can be slimy. The common opinion is that first I have experienced certain behavior and certain moral attitudes which displease me and which I condemn, and that in addition I have a sensory intuition of "slimy." Afterwards, says the theory, I should establish a connection between these feelings and sliminess and the slimy would function as a symbol of a whole class of human feelings and attitudes. I would then have enriched the slimy by projecting upon it my knowledge with respect to that human category of behavior.

But how are we to accept this explanation by projection? If we suppose that we have first grasped the feelings as pure psychic qualities, how will we be able to grasp their relation to the slimy? A feeling apprehended in its qualitative purity will be able to reveal itself only as a certain purely unextended disposition, culpable because of its relation to certain values and certain consequences; in any case it will not "form an image" unless the image has been given first. On the other hand if "slimy" is not originally charged with an affective meaning, if it is given only as a certain material quality, one does not see how it could ever be chosen as a symbolic representation of certain psychic unities. In a word, if we are to establish consciously and clearly a symbolic relation be-

7. French *visqueux*. This at times comes closer to the English "sticky," but I have consistently used the word "slimy" in translating because the figurative meaning of "slimy" appears to be identical in both languages.

tween sliminess and the sticky baseness of certain individuals, we must apprehend baseness already in sliminess and sliminess in certain baseness. Consequently the explanation by projection explains nothing since it takes for granted what it ought to explain. Furthermore even if it escaped this objection on principle, it would have to face another, drawn from experience and no less serious; the explanation by projection implies actually that the projecting subject has arrived by experience and analysis at a certain knowledge of the structure and effects of the attitudes which he calls slimy. According to this concept the recourse to sliminess does not as *knowledge* enrich our experience of human baseness. At the very most it serves as a thematic unity, as a picturesque rubric for bits of knowledge already acquired. On the other hand, sliminess proper, considered in its isolated state, will appear to us harmful in practice (because slimy substances stick to the hands, and clothes, and because they stain), but sliminess then is not *repugnant.* In fact the disgust which it inspires can be explained only by the combination of this physical quality with certain moral qualities. There would have to be a kind of apprenticeship for learning the symbolic value of "slimy." But observation teaches us that even very young children show evidence of repulsion in the presence of something slimy, as if it were already combined with the psychic. We know also that from the time they know how to talk, they *understand* the value of the words "soft," "low," *etc.*, when applied to the description of feelings. All this comes to pass as if we come to life in a universe where feelings and acts are all charged with something material, have a substantial stuff, are *really* soft, dull, slimy, low, elevated, *etc.* and in which material substances have originally a psychic meaning which renders them repugnant, horrifying, alluring, *etc.* No explanation by projection or by analogy is acceptable here. To sum up, it is impossible to derive the value of the psychic symbolism of "slimy" from the brute quality of the *this* and equally impossible to project the meaning of the *this* in terms of a *knowledge* of psychic attitudes. How then are we to conceive of this immense and universal symbolism which is translated by our repulsion, our hates, our sympathies, our attractions toward objects whose materiality must on principle remain non-meaningful? To progress in this study it is necessary to abandon a certain number of postulates. In particular we must no longer postulate *a priori* that the attribution of sliminess to a particular feeling is only an image and not knowledge. We must also refuse to admit—until getting fuller information—that the psychic allows us to view the physical matter symbolically or that our experience with human baseness has any priority over the apprehension of the "slimy" as meaningful.

Let us return to the original project. It is a project of appropriation. It compels the *slimy* to reveal its being; since the upsurge of the for-itself into being is appropriative, the slimy when perceived is "a slimy to be possessed"; that is, the original bond between the slimy and myself is that I form the project of being the foundation of its being, inasmuch as it is myself ideally. From the start then it appears as a possible "myself" to be established; from the start it has a psychic quality. This definitely does not mean that I endow it with a soul in the manner of primitive animism, nor with metaphysical virtues, but simply that even its materiality is revealed to me as having a psychic meaning—this psychic meaning, furthermore, is identical with the symbolic value which the slimy has in relation to being-in-itself. This appropriative way of forcing the slimy to produce all its meanings can be considered as a formal *a priori*, although it is a free project and although it is identified with the being of the for-itself. In fact the appropriative mode does not depend originally on the mode of being of the slimy but only on its brute being there, on its pure encountered existence; it is like any other encounter since it is a simple project of appropriation, since it is not distinguished in any way from the pure "there is" and since it is, according to whether we consider it from one point of view or the other, either pure freedom or pure nothingness. But it is precisely within the limits of this appropriative project that the slimy reveals itself and develops its sliminess. From the first appearance of the slimy, this sliminess is already a response to a demand, already a *bestowal of self;* the slimy appears as already the outline of a fusion of the world with myself. What it teaches me about the world, that it is like a *leech sucking me,* is already a reply to a concrete question; it responds with its very being, with its mode of being, with all its matter. The response which it gives is at the same time fully appropriate to the question and yet opaque and indecipherable, for it is rich with all its inexpressible materiality. It is clear inasmuch as the reply is exactly appropriate; the slimy lets itself be apprehended as that which I lack; it lets itself be examined by an appropriative inquiry; it allows its sliminess to be revealed to this outline of appropriation. Yet it is opaque because if the meaningful form is evoked in the slimy by the for-itself, all its sliminess comes to succour and replenish it. We are referred then to a meaning which is full and dense, and this meaning releases for us first being-in-itself in so far as the slimy is at the moment that which is manifesting the world, and second an *outline of ourselves,* in so far as the appropriation outlines something like a founding act on the part of the slimy.

What comes back to us then as an objective quality is a new *nature* which is neither material (and physical) nor psychic, but which transcends the opposition of the psychic and the physical, by revealing itself to us as the ontological expression of the entire world; that is, which offers itself as a rubric for classifying all the "thises" in the world, so that we have to deal with material organizations or transcended transcendences. This means that the apprehension of the slimy as such has, by the same stroke, created for the in-itself of the world a particular mode of giving itself. In its own way it symbolizes being; that is, so long as the contact with the slimy endures, everything takes place for us as if sliminess were the meaning of the entire world or the unique mode of being of being-in-itself—in the same way as for the primitive clan of lizards all objects *are* lizards.

What mode of being is symbolized by the slimy? I see first that it is the homogeneity and the imitation of liquidity. A slimy substance like pitch is an aberrant fluid. At first, with the appearance of a fluid it manifests to us a being which is everywhere fleeing and yet everywhere similar to itself, which on all sides escapes yet on which one can float, a being without danger and without memory, which eternally is changed into itself, on which one leaves no mark and which could not leave a mark on us, a being which slides and on which one can slide, which can be possessed by something sliding (by a rowboat, a motor boat, or water ski), and which never possesses because it rolls over us, a being which is eternity and infinite temporality because it is a perpetual change without anything which changes, a being which best symbolizes in this synthesis of eternity and temporality, a possible fusion of the for-itself as pure temporality and the in-itself as pure eternity. But immediately the slimy reveals itself as essentially ambiguous because its fluidity exists in slow motion; there is a sticky thickness in its liquidity; it represents in itself a dawning triumph of the solid over the liquid—that is, a tendency of the indifferent in-itself, which is represented by the pure solid, to fix the liquidity, to absorb the for-itself which ought to dissolve it.

Slime is the agony of water. It presents itself as a phenomenon in process of becoming; it does not have the permanence within change that water has but on the contrary represents an accomplished break in a change of state. This fixed instability in the slimy discourages possession. Water is more fleeting, but it can be possessed in its very flight as something fleeing. The slimy flees with a heavy flight which has the same relation to water as the unwieldy earthbound flight of the chicken has to that of the hawk. Even this flight can not be possessed because it denies itself as flight. It is already almost a solid permanence. Nothing testifies more clearly to its ambiguous character as a "substance in between two states" than the slowness with which the slimy melts into itself. A drop of water touching the surface of a large body of water is instantly transformed into the body of water; we do not see the operation as buccal absorption, so to speak, of the drop of water by the body of water but rather as a spiritualizing and breaking down of the individuality of a single being which is dissolved in the great All from which it had issued. The symbol of the body of water seems to play a very important role in the construction of pantheistic systems; it reveals a particular type of relation of being to being. But if we consider the slimy,[8] we note that it presents a constant hysteresis in the phenomenon of being transmuted into itself. The honey which slides off my spoon on to the honey contained in the jar first sculptures the surface by fastening itself on it in relief, and its fusion with the whole is presented as a gradual sinking, a collapse which appears at once as a *deflation* (think for example of children's pleasure in playing with a toy which whistles when inflated and groans mournfully when deflating[9]) and as *display*—like the flattening out of the full breasts of a woman who is lying on her back.

In the slimy substance which dissolves into itself there is a visible resistance, like the refusal of an individual who does not want to be annihilated in the whole of being, and at the same time a softness pushed to its ultimate limit. For the *soft* is only an annihilation which is stopped half way; the

8. Although slime has mysteriously preserved *all* fluidity in slow motion, it must not be confused with purées where fluidity, roughly outlined, undergoes abrupt breaks and blocks and where the substance, after a preliminary plan of pouring, rolls abruptly head over heels.

9. In the original the reference is to gold-beater's skin, a thin membrane used in making gold leaf. Tr.

soft is what furnishes us with the best image of our own destructive power and its limitations. The slowness of the disappearance of the slimy drop in the bosom of the whole is grasped first in *softness,* which is like a retarded annihilation and seems to be playing for time, but this softness lasts up to the end; the drop is sucked into the body of the slimy substance. This phenomenon gives rise to several characteristics of the slimy. First it is *soft* to touch. Throw water on the ground; it *runs.* Throw a slimy substance; it draws itself out, it displays itself, it flattens itself out, it is *soft;* touch the slimy; it does not flee, it yields. There is in the very fact that we cannot grasp water a pitiless hardness which gives to it a secret sense of being *metal;* finally it is incompressible like steel. The slimy is compressible. It gives us at first the impression that it is a being which can be *possessed.* Doubly so: its sliminess, its adherence to itself prevents it from escaping; I can take it in my hands, separate a certain quantity of honey or of pitch from the rest in the jar, and thereby *create* an individual object by a continuous creation; but at the same time the softness of this substance which is squashed in my hands gives me the impression that I am perpetually *destroying* it.

Actually we have here the image of destruction-creation. The slimy is *docile.* Only at the very moment when I believe that I possess it, behold by a curious reversal, *it* possesses me. Here appears its essential character: its softness is leech-like. If an object which I hold in my hands is solid, I can let go when I please; its inertia symbolizes for me my total power; I give it its foundation, but it does not furnish any foundation for me; the For-itself collects the In-itself in the object and raises the object to the dignity of the In-itself without compromising itself (*i.e.,* the self of the For-itself) but always remaining an assimilating and creative power. It is the For-itself which absorbs the In-itself. In other words, possession asserts the primacy of the For-itself in the synthetic being "In-itself-For-itself." Yet here is the slimy reversing the terms; the For-itself is suddenly *compromised.* I open my hands, I want to let go of the slimy and it sticks to me, it draws me, it sucks at me. Its mode of being is neither the reassuring inertia of the solid nor a dynamism like that in water which is exhausted in fleeing from me. It is a soft, yielding action, a moist and feminine sucking, it lives obscurely under my fingers, and I sense it like a dizziness; it draws me to it as the bottom of a precipice might draw me. There is something like a tactile fascination in the slimy. I am no longer the master in *arresting* the process of appropriation. It continues. In one sense it is like the supreme docility of the possessed, the fidelity of a dog who *gives himself* even when one does not want him any longer, and in another sense there is underneath this docility a surreptitious appropriation of the possessor by the possessed.

Here we can see the symbol which abruptly discloses itself: there exists a poisonous possession; there is a possibility that the In-itself might absorb the For-itself; that is, that a being might be constituted in a manner just the reverse of the "In-itself-For-itself," and that in this new being the In-itself would draw the For-itself into its contingency, into its indifferent exteriority, into its foundationless existence. At this instant I suddenly understand the snare of the slimy: it is a fluidity which holds me and which compromises me; I can not *slide* on this slime, all its suction cups hold me back; it can not slide over me, it clings to me like a leech. The sliding however is not simply denied as in the case of the solid; it is *degraded*. The slimy seems to lend itself to me, it invites me; for a body of slime at rest is not noticeably distinct from a body of very dense liquid. But it is a trap. The sliding is *sucked* in by the sliding substance, and it leaves its traces upon me. The slime is like a liquid seen in a nightmare, where all its properties are animated by a sort of life and turn back against me. Slime is the revenge of the In-itself. A sickly-sweet, feminine revenge which will be symbolized on another level by the quality "sugary." This is why the sugar-like sweetness to the taste—an indelible sweetness, which remains indefinitely in the mouth even after swallowing—perfectly completes the essence of the slimy. A sugary sliminess is the ideal of the slimy; it symbolizes the sugary death of the For-itself (like that of the wasp which sinks into the jam and drowns in it).

But at the same time the slimy is *myself*, by the very fact that I outline an appropriation of the slimy substance. That sucking of the slimy which I feel on my hands outlines a kind of continuity of the slimy substance in myself. These long, soft strings of substance which fall from me to the slimy body (when, for example, I plunge my hand into it and then pull it out again) symbolize a rolling off of myself in the slime. And the hysteresis which I establish in the fusion of the ends of these strings with the larger body, symbolizes the resistance of my being to absorption into the In-itself. If

I dive into the water, if I plunge into it, if I let myself sink in it, I experience no discomfort, for I do not have any fear whatsoever that I may dissolve in it; I remain a solid in its liquidity. If I sink in the slimy, I feel that I am going to be lost in it; that is, that I may dissolve in the slime precisely because the slimy is in process of solidification. The *sticky* would present the same aspect as the slimy from this point of view, but it does not have the same fascination, it does not compromise because it is inert. In the very apprehension of the slimy there is a gluey substance, compromising and without equilibrium, like the haunting memory of a *metamorphosis*.

To touch the slimy is to risk being dissolved in sliminess. Now this dissolution by itself is frightening enough, because it is the absorption of the For-itself by the In-itself as ink is absorbed by a blotter. But it is still more frightening in that the metamorphosis is not just into a thing (bad as that would be) but into slime. Even if I could conceive of a liquefaction of myself (that is, a transformation of my being into water) I would not be inordinately affected because water is the symbol of consciousness—its movement, its fluidity, its deceptive appearance of being solid, its perpetual flight—everything in it recalls the For-itself; to such a degree that psychologists who first noted the characteristics of *duration* of consciousness (James, Bergson) have very often compared it to a river. A river best evokes the image of the constant interpenetration of the parts by a whole and their perpetual dissociation and free movement.

But the slimy offers a horrible image; it is horrible in itself for a consciousness to *become slimy*. This is because the being of the slimy is a soft clinging, there is a sly solidarity and complicity of all its leech-like parts, a vague, soft effort made by each to individualize itself, followed by a falling back and flattening out that is emptied of the individual, sucked in on all sides by the substance. A consciousness which became slimy would be transformed by the thick stickiness of its ideas. From the time of our upsurge into the world, we are haunted by the image of a consciousness which would like to launch forth into the future, toward a projection of self, and which at the very moment when it was conscious of arriving there would be slyly held back by the invisible suction of the past and which would have to assist in its own slow dissolution in this past which it was fleeing, would have to aid in the invasion of its project by a thousand parasites until finally it completely lost itself. The "flight of ideas" found in the psychosis of influence gives us the best image of this horrible condition. But what is it then which is expressed by this fear on the ontological level if not exactly the flight of the For-itself before the In-itself of facticity; that is, exactly temporalization. The horror of the slimy is the horrible fear that time might become slimy, that facticity might progress continually and insensibly and absorb the For-itself which *exists it*. It is the fear not of death, not of the pure In-itself, not of nothingness, but of a particular type of being, which does not actually exist any more than the In-itself-For-itself and which is only *represented* by the slimy. It is an ideal being which I reject with all my strength and which haunts me as *value* haunts my being, an ideal being in which the foundationless In-itself has priority over the For-itself. We shall call it an *Antivalue*.

Thus in the project of appropriating the slimy, the sliminess is revealed suddenly as a symbol of an antivalue: it is a type of being not realized but threatening which will perpetually haunt consciousness as the constant danger which it is fleeing, and hence will suddenly transform the project of appropriation into a project of flight. Something has appeared which is not the result of any prior experience but only of the pre-ontological comprehension of the In-itself and the For-itself, and this is the peculiar meaning of the slimy. In one sense it is an experience since sliminess is an intuitive discovery; in another sense it is like the discovery of an adventure of being. Henceforth for the For-itself there appears a new danger, a threatening mode of being which must be avoided, a concrete category which it will discover everywhere. The slimy does not symbolize any psychic attitude *a priori;* it manifests a certain relation of being with itself and this relation has originally a psychic quality because I have discovered it in a plan of appropriation and because the sliminess has returned my image to me. Thus I am enriched from my first contact with the slimy, by a valid ontological pattern beyond the distinction between psychic and non-psychic, which will interpret the meaning of being and of all the existents of a certain category, this category arising, moreover, like an empty skeletal framework *before* the experience with different kinds of sliminess. I have projected it into the world by my original project when faced with the slimy; it is an objective structure of the world and at the same time an antivalue; that is, it determines an area where slimy objects will arrange themselves. Henceforth each time that an object will manifest to me this relation of being, whether it is a matter of a handshake, of a smile, or of a thought, it will be apprehended by definition as slimy; that is, beyond its phenomenal context, it will appear to me as constituting along with pitch, glue, honey, *etc.* the great ontological region of sliminess.

Conversely, to the extent that the *this* which I wish to appropriate, represents the entire world, the slimy, from my first intuitive contact, appears to me rich with a host of obscure meanings and references which surpass it. The slimy is revealed in itself as "much more than the slimy." From the moment of its appearance it transcends all distinctions between psychic and physical, between the brute existent and the meanings of the world; it is a possible meaning of being. The first experience which the infant can have with the slimy enriches him psychologically and morally; he will not need to reach adulthood to discover the kind of sticky baseness which we figuratively name "slimy"; it is there near him in the very sliminess of honey or of glue. What we say concerning the slimy is valid for all the objects which surround the child. The simple revelation of their matter extends his horizon to the extreme limits of being and bestows upon him at the same stroke a collection of clues for deciphering the being of all human facts. This certainly does not mean that he *knows* from the start the "ugliness," the "characteristics," or the "beauties" of existence. He is merely in possession of all the *meanings of being* of which ugliness and beauty, attitudes, psychic traits, sexual relations, *etc.* will never be more than particular exemplifications. The gluey, the sticky, the hazy, *etc.*, holes in the sand and in the earth, caves, the light, the night, *etc.*—all reveal to him modes of pre-psychic and presexual being which he will spend the rest of his life explaining. There is no such thing as an "innocent" child. We will gladly recognize along with the Freudians the innumerable relations existing between sexuality and certain matter and forms in the child's environment. But we do not understand by this that a sexual instinct already constituted has charged them with a sexual significance. On the contrary it seems to us that this matter and these forms are apprehended in themselves, and they reveal to the child the For-itself's modes of being and relations to being which will illuminate and shape his sexuality.

To cite only one example—many psychoanalysts have been struck by the attraction which all kinds of holes exert on the child (whether holes in the sand or in the ground, crypts, caves, hollows, or whatever), and they have explained this attraction either by the anal character of infant sexuality, or by prenatal shock, or by a presentiment of the adult sexual act. But we can not accept any of these explanations. The idea of "birth trauma" is highly fantastic. The comparison of the hole to the feminine sexual organ supposes in the child an experience which he can not possibly have had or a presentiment which we can not justify. As for the child's anal sexuality, we would not think of denying it; but if it is going to illuminate the holes which he encounters in the perceptual field and charge them with symbolism, then it is necessary that the child apprehend his anus as a hole. To put it more clearly, the child would have to apprehend the essence of the hole, of the orifice, as corresponding to the sensation which he receives from his anus. But we have demonstrated sufficiently the subjective character of "my relation with my body" so that we can understand the impossibility of saying that the child apprehends a particular part of his body as an objective structure of the universe. It is only to another person that the anus appears as an orifice. The child himself can never have experienced it as such; even the intimate care which the mother gives the child could not reveal the anus in this aspect, since the anus as an erogenous zone, or a zone of pain is not provided with tactile nerve endings. On the contrary it is only through another—through the words which the mother uses to designate the child's body—that he learns that his anus is a *hole*. It is therefore the objective nature of the hole perceived in the world which is going to illuminate for him the objective structure and the meaning of the anal zone and which will give a transcendent meaning to the erogenous sensations which hitherto he was limited to merely "existing." In itself then the *hole* is the symbol of a mode of being which existential psychoanalysis must elucidate.

We can not make such a detailed study here. One can see at once, however, that the hole is originally presented as a nothingness "to be filled" with my own flesh; the child can not restrain himself from putting his finger or his whole arm into the hole. It presents itself to me as the empty image of myself. I have only to crawl into it in order to make myself exist in the world which awaits me. The ideal of the hole is then an excavation which can be carefully moulded about my flesh in such a manner that by squeezing myself into it and fitting myself tightly inside it, I shall contribute to making a fullness of being exist in the world. Thus to plug up a hole means originally to make a sacrifice of my body in order that the plenitude of being may exist; that is, to subject the passion of the For-itself so as to shape, to perfect, and to preserve the totality of the In-itself.[10]

BIBLIOGRAPHY

Philosophy:

L'Imagination (1936); translated by Forrest Williams as *Imagination: A Psychological Critique* (Ann Arbor, Mich., 1962)

Esquisse d'une théorie des émotions (1939); translated by Philip Mairet as *Sketch for a Theory of the Emotions* (London, 1962) and by Bernard Frechtman as *The Emotions: Outline of a Theory* (New York, 1948)

L'Imaginaire, psychologie phénoménologique de l'imagination (1940); translated as *The Psychology of Imagination* (New York, 1948; London, 1950)

L'Être et le néant: essai d'ontologie phénoménologique (1943); translated by Hazel E. Barnes as *Being and Nothingness* (New York and London, 1957)

L'Existentialisme est un humanisme (1945); translated by Philip Mairet as *Existentialism and Humanism* (London, 1948)

Critique de la raison dialectique (volume 1, 1960)

Criticism:

Beaudelaire (1947); translated by Martin Turnell (London, 1949; New York, 1950)

Réflexions sur la question juive (1947); translated by Erik De Mauny as *Portrait of the Anti-Semite* (London, 1948) and by George J. Becker as *Anti-Semite and Jew* (New York, 1948)

Situations (volumes I, II, and III). Literary and political essays, mostly reprinted from *Les Temps Modernes*. The first volume includes studies of Faulkner, Nizan, Denis de Rougement, Camus, Bataille, Parain, Giraudoux, Blanchot, Ponge, Jules Renard. Volume II contains for the most part political articles, while Volume III includes the essay "Qu'est-ce que c'est la littérature?" Translated selections from these volumes include: *What Is Literature*, translated by Bernard

10. We should note as well the importance of the opposite tendency, to poke through holes, which in itself demands an existential analysis.

Frechtman (New York, 1949; London, 1950); *Literary and Philosophical Essays,* translated by Annette Nicholson (New York and London, 1955); and *Essays in Aesthetics,* translated by Wade Baskin (New York, 1963)

Saint Genêt, comédien et martyr (1952); translated by Bernard Frechtman (New York, 1963)

Prose Fiction:

La Nausée (1938); translated by Lloyd Alexander as *Nausea* (New York, 1949) and *The Diary of Antoine Roquentin* (London, 1949)

Le Mur (1939); translated by Lloyd Alexander as *Intimacy* (London, 1949; New York, 1952)

L'Âge de raison (1945); translated by Eric Sutton as *The Age of Reason* (New York and London, 1947)

Le Sursis (1945); translated by Eric Sutton as *Reprieve* (New York and London, 1947)

La Mort dans l'âme (1949); translated by Gerard Hopkins as *Iron in the Soul* (London, 1950) and *Troubled Sleep* (New York, 1951)

Plays:

Les Mouches (1943); translated by Stuart Gilbert as *The Flies*

Huis-clos (1944); translated by Stuart Gilbert as *No Exit*

Morts sans sépultures (1946); translated by Lionel Abel as *The Victors* and by Stuart Gilbert as *Men Without Shadows*

La Putain respectueuse (1946); translated by Lionel Abel as *The Respectful Prostitute* and by Kitty Black as *The Respectable Prostitute*

Les Mains sales (1948); translated by Lionel Abel as *Dirty Hands* and by Kitty Black as *Crime Passionel*

Le Diable et le bon Dieu (1951); translated by Kitty Black as *The Devil and the Good Lord*

Kean, ou Désordre et génie (1954); translated by Kitty Black as *Kean, or Disorder and Genius*

Nekrassov (1953); translated by Sylvia and George Leeson

Les Séquestrés d'Altona (1959); translated by Sylvia and George Leeson as *Loser Wins* (London, 1960) and *The Condemned of Altona* (New York, 1961)

Autobiography:

Les Mots (1963); translated by Tony White as *Words* (London, 1964) and by Bernard Frechtman as *The Words* (New York, 1964)

Critical and biographical material:

Sartre: Romantic Rationalist by Iris Murdoch (Cambridge, Bowes and Bowes, and New Haven, Yale University Press, 1953)

The Tragic Finale: An Essay on the Philosophy of Jean-Paul Sartre by Wilfrid Desan (Harvard University Press, 1954)

Jean-Paul Sartre: The Existentialist Ethic by Norman N. Greene (University of Michigan Press, 1960)

Jean-Paul Sartre: A Literary and Political Study by Philip Thody (London, Hamish Hamilton, 1960; New York, The Macmillan Company, 1961)

Sartre: A Collection of Critical Essays, edited by Edith Kern (Englewood Cliffs, New Jersey, Prentice-Hall Spectrum Books, 1962)

Biographical material also appears in the three volumes of Simone de Beauvoir's autobiography.

MAURICE MERLEAU-PONTY

(1907–1961)

Maurice Merleau-Ponty is bracketed with Sartre and Simone de Beauvoir as cofounder of *Les Temps Modernes* in 1945. In this monthly review these writers addressed their young contemporaries emerging from the war and made their world and the circumstances of their lives intelligible to them. The recognition of Merleau-Ponty as a philosopher of the highest academic rank after the publication of his *Phénoménologie de la Perception* was sealed in 1952 by his election to the chair of philosophy at the Collège de France, after he had been professor of philosophy for three years at the Sorbonne.

A philosopher of the highest academic rank, but not an academic philosopher, he exhibits splendidly what is meant by existentialist "engagement," at the intellectual level. He tries patiently and honestly to come to practical terms with Marxist Communism in *Humanisme et Terreur* (1947), an exploration of the complexities and contradictions of the situation in which one has to act without self-deception, striving to understand and to meet the others and to work out the problems with them and reach agreement and union in a world in which hope is possible because it is a world that remains open and waits on human action, although not a world whose problems can be resolved by reason in terms of the "given." With Sartre, he is occupied with Marxism and "the communist problem," as the others are occupied with faith and the religious implications of the problem of Being.

Merleau-Ponty is the least famous of these eight existentialists, but certainly not the least attractive, and perhaps the closest and clearest thinker. His full contribution to thought was prevented by premature death.

EXTRACTS

Phénoménologie de la Perception, trans. by Colin Smith as *Phenomenology of Perception* (London, 1962) Preface.

Passage from the inaugural lecture at the Collège de

France, 1953, *Éloge de la Philosophie,* trans. by John Wild and James M. Edie.

☙ from *Phenomenology of Perception*

PREFACE

What is phenomenology? It may seem strange that this question has still to be asked half a century after the first works of Husserl. The fact remains that it has by no means been answered. Phenomenology is the study of essences; and according to it, all problems amount to finding definitions of essences: the essence of perception, or the essence of consciousness, for example. But phenomenology is also a philosophy which puts essences back into existence, and does not expect to arrive at an understanding of man and the world from any starting point other than that of their "facticity." It is a transcendental philosophy which places in abeyance the assertions arising out of the natural attitude, the better to understand them; but it is also a philosophy for which the world is always "already there" before reflection begins—as an inalienable presence; and all its efforts are concentrated upon re-achieving a direct and primitive contact with the world, and endowing that contact with a philosophical status. It is the search for a philosophy which shall be a "rigorous science," but it also offers an account of space, time and the world as we "live" them. It tries to give a direct description of our experience as it is, without taking account of its psychological origin and the causal explanations which the scientist, the historian or the sociologist may be able to provide. Yet Husserl in his last works mentions a "genetic phenomenology,"[1] and even a "constructive phenomenology."[2] One may try to do away with these contradictions by making a distinction between Husserl's and Heidegger's phenomenologies; yet the whole of *Sein und Zeit* springs from an indication given by Husserl and amounts to no more than an explicit account of the "natürlicher Weltbegriff" or the "Lebenswelt" which Husserl, towards the end of his life, identified as the central theme of phenomenology, with the

1. *Méditations cartésiennes,* pp. 120 ff.
2. See the unpublished *6th Méditation cartésienne,* edited by Eugen Fink, to which G. Berger has kindly referred us.

result that the contradiction reappears in Husserl's own philosophy. The reader pressed for time will be inclined to give up the idea of covering a doctrine which says everything, and will wonder whether a philosophy which cannot define its scope deserves all the discussion which has gone on around it, and whether he is not faced rather by a myth or a fashion.

Even if this were the case, there would still be a need to understand the prestige of the myth and the origin of the fashion, and the opinion of the responsible philosopher must be that *phenomenology can be practised and identified as a manner or style of thinking, that it existed as a movement before arriving at complete awareness of itself as a philosophy.* It has been long on the way, and its adherents have discovered it in every quarter, certainly in Hegel and Kierkegaard, but equally in Marx, Nietzsche and Freud. A purely linguistic examination of the texts in question would yield no proof; we find in texts only what we put into them, and if ever any kind of history has suggested the interpretations which should be put on it, it is the history of philosophy. We shall find in ourselves, and nowhere else, the unity and true meaning of phenomenology. It is less a question of counting up quotations than of determining and expressing in concrete form this *phenomenology for ourselves* which has given a number of present-day readers the impression, on reading Husserl or Heidegger, not so much of encountering a new philosophy as of recognizing what they had been waiting for. Phenomenology is accessible only through a phenomenological method. Let us, therefore, try systematically to bring together the celebrated phenomenological themes as they have grown spontaneously together in life. Perhaps we shall then understand why phenomenology has for so long remained at an initial stage, as a problem to be solved and a hope to be realized.

It is a matter of describing, not of explaining or analysing. Husserl's first directive to phenomenology, in its early stages, to be a "descriptive psychology," or to return to the "things themselves," is from the start a rejection of science. I am not the outcome or the meeting-point of numerous causal agencies which determine my bodily or psychological make-up. I cannot conceive myself as nothing but a bit of the world, a mere object of biological, psychological or sociological investigation. I cannot shut myself up within the realm of science. All my knowledge of the world, even my scientific knowledge, is gained from my own particular point of view, or from some experience of the world without which the symbols of science would be meaningless. The whole universe of science is built upon the world as directly experienced, and if we want to subject science itself to rigorous scrutiny and arrive at a precise assessment of its meaning and scope, we must begin by reawakening the basic experience of the world of which science is the second-order expression. Science has not and never will have, by its nature, the same significance *qua* form of being as the world which we perceive, for the simple reason that it is a rationale or explanation of that world. I am, not a "living creature" nor even a "man," nor again even "a consciousness" endowed with all the characteristics which zoology, social anatomy or inductive psychology recognize in these various products of the natural or historical process—I am the absolute source, my existence does not stem from my antecedents, from my physical and social environment; instead it moves out towards them and sustains them, for I alone bring into being for myself (and therefore into being in the only sense that the word can have for me) the tradition which I elect to carry on, or the horizon whose distance from me would be abolished—since that distance is not one of its properties—if I were not there to scan it with my gaze. Scientific points of view, according to which my existence is a moment of the world's, are always both naïve and at the same time dishonest, because they take for granted, without explicitly mentioning it, the other point of view, namely that of consciousness, through which from the outset a world forms itself round me and begins to exist for me. To return to things themselves is to return to that world which precedes knowledge, of which knowledge always *speaks*, and in relation to which every scientific schematization is an abstract and derivative sign-language, as is geography in relation to the countryside in which we have learnt beforehand what a forest, a prairie or a river is.

This move is absolutely distinct from the idealist return to consciousness, and the demand for a pure description excludes equally the procedure of analytical reflection on the one hand, and that of scientific explanation on the other. Descartes and particularly Kant *detached* the subject, or consciousness, by showing that I could not possibly apprehend anything as existing unless I first of all experienced myself as existing in the act of apprehending it. They presented consciousness, the absolute certainty of my existence for myself, as the condition of there being anything at all; and the act of relating as the basis of relatedness. It is true that the act of relating is nothing if divorced from the spectacle of the world in which relations are found; the unity of consciousness in Kant is achieved simultaneously with that of the world. And in Descartes methodical doubt does not deprive us of anything, since the whole world, at least in so far as we experience it, is reinstated in the *Cogito*, enjoying equal certainty, and simply labelled "thought about. . . ." But the relations between subject and world are not strictly bilateral: if they were, the certainty of the world would, in Descartes, be immediately given with that of the *Cogito*, and Kant would not have talked about his "Copernican revolution." Analytical reflection starts from our experience of the world and goes back to the subject as to a condition of possibility distinct from that experience, revealing the all-embracing synthesis as that without which there would be no world. To this extent it ceases to remain part of our experience and offers, in place of an account, a reconstruction. It is understandable, in view of this, that Husserl, having accused Kant of adopting a "faculty psychologism," [3] should have urged, in place of a noetic analysis which bases the world on the synthesizing activity of the subject, his own "*noematic reflection*" which remains within the object and, instead of begetting it, brings to light its fundamental unity.

The world is there before any possible analysis of mine, and it would be artificial to make it the outcome of a series of syntheses which link, in the first place sensations, then aspects of the object corresponding to different perspectives, when both are nothing but products of analysis, with no sort of prior reality. Analytical reflection believes that it can trace back the course followed by a prior constituting act and arrive, in the "inner man"—to use Saint Augustine's expression—at a constituting power which has always been identical with that inner self. Thus reflection itself is carried away and transplanted in an impregnable subjectivity, as yet untouched by being and time. But this is very ingenuous, or at least it is an incomplete form of reflection which loses sight of its own beginning. When I begin to reflect my reflection bears upon an unreflective experience; moreover my reflection cannot be unaware of itself as an event, and so it appears to itself in the light of a truly creative act, of a changed structure of consciousness, and yet it has to recognize, as having priority over its own operations, the world which is given to the

3. *Logische Untersuchungen, Prolegomena zur reinen Logik*, p. 93.

subject, because the subject is given to himself. The real has to be described, not constructed or formed. Which means that I cannot put perception into the same category as the syntheses represented by judgements, acts or predications. My field of perception is constantly filled with a play of colours, noises and fleeting tactile sensations which I cannot relate precisely to the context of my clearly perceived world, yet which I nevertheless immediately "place" in the world, without ever confusing them with my daydreams. Equally constantly I weave dreams round things. I imagine people and things whose presence is not incompatible with the context, yet who are not in fact involved in it: they are ahead of reality, in the realm of the imaginary. If the reality of my perception were based solely on the intrinsic coherence of "representations," it ought to be for ever hesitant and, being wrapped up in my conjectures on probabilities, I ought to be ceaselessly taking apart misleading syntheses, and reinstating in reality stray phenomena which I had excluded in the first place. But this does not happen. The real is a closely woven fabric. It does not await our judgement before incorporating the most surprising phenomena, or before rejecting the most plausible figments of our imagination. Perception is not a science of the world, it is not even an act, a deliberate taking up of a position; it is the background from which all acts stand out, and is presupposed by them. The world is not an object such that I have in my possession the law of its making; it is the natural setting of, and field for, all my thoughts and all my explicit perceptions. Truth does not "inhabit" only "the inner man," [4] or more accurately, there is no inner man, man is in the world, and only in the world does he know himself. When I return to myself from an excursion into the realm of dogmatic common sense or of science, I find, not a source of intrinsic truth, but a subject destined to be in the world.

All of which reveals the true meaning of the famous phenomenological reduction. There is probably no question over which Husserl has spent more time—or to which he has more often returned, since the "problematic of reduction" occupies an important place in his unpublished work. For a long time, and even in recent texts, the reduction is presented as the return to a transcendental consciousness before which the world is spread out and completely transparent, quickened

4. In te redi; in interiore homine habitat veritas (Saint Augustine).

through and through by a series of apperceptions which it is the philosopher's task to reconstitute on the basis of their outcome. Thus my sensation of redness is *perceived as* the manifestation of a certain redness experienced, this in turn as the manifestation of a red surface, which is the manifestation of a piece of red cardboard, and this finally is the manifestation or outline of a red thing, namely this book. We are to understand, then, that it is the apprehension of a certain *hylè,* as indicating a phenomenon of a higher degree, the *Sinngebung,* or active meaning-giving operation which may be said to define consciousness, so that the world is nothing but "world-as-meaning," and the phenomenological reduction is idealistic, in the sense that there is here a transcendental idealism which treats the world as an indivisible unity of value shared by Peter and Paul, in which their perspectives blend. "Peter's consciousness" and "Paul's consciousness" are in communication, the perception of the world "by Peter" is not Peter's doing any more than its perception "by Paul" is Paul's doing; in each case it is the doing of pre-personal forms of consciousness, whose communication raises no problem, since it is demanded by the very definition of consciousness, meaning or truth. In so far as I am a consciousness, that is, in so far as something has meaning for me, I am neither here nor there, neither Peter nor Paul; I am in no way distinguishable from an "other" consciousness, since we are immediately in touch with the world and since the world is, by definition, unique, being the system in which all truths cohere. A logically consistent transcendental idealism rids the world of its opacity and its transcendence. The world is precisely that thing of which we form a representation, not as men or as empirical subjects, but in so far as we are all one light and participate in the One without destroying its unity. Analytical reflection knows nothing of the problem of other minds, or of that of the world, because it insists that with the first glimmer of consciousness there appears in me theoretically the power of reaching some universal truth, and that the other person, being equally without thisness, location or body, the Alter and the Ego are one and the same in the true world which is the unifier of minds. There is no difficulty in understanding how *I* can conceive the Other, because the I and consequently the Other are not conceived as part of the woven stuff of phenomena; they have validity rather than existence. There is nothing hidden behind these faces and gestures, no domain to which I have no access, merely a little shadow which owes its very existence to the light. For Husserl, on the contrary, it is well known that there is a problem of other people, and the *alter ego* is a paradox. If the other is truly for himself alone, beyond his being for me, and if we are for each other and not both for God, we must necessarily have some appearance for each other. He must and I must have an outer appearance, and there must be, besides the perspective of the For Oneself—my view of myself and the other's of himself—a perspective of For Others—my view of others and theirs of me. Of course, these two perspectives, in each one of us, cannot be simply juxtaposed, *for in that case it is not I that the other would see, nor he that I should see.* I must be the exterior that I present to others, and the body of the other must be the other himself. This paradox and the dialectic of the Ego and the Alter are possible only provided that the Ego and the Alter Ego are defined by their situation and are not freed from all inherence; that is, provided that philosophy does not culminate in a return to the self, and that I discover by reflection not only my presence to myself, but also the possibility of an "outside spectator"; that is, again, provided that at the very moment when I experience my existence—at the ultimate extremity of reflection—I fall short of the ultimate density which would place me outside time, and that I discover within myself a kind of internal weakness standing in the way of my being totally individualized: a weakness which exposes me to the gaze of others as a man among men or at least as a consciousness among consciousnesses. Hitherto the *Cogito* depreciated the perception of others, teaching me as it did that the I is accessible only to itself, since it defined *me* as the thought which I have of myself, and which clearly I am alone in having, at least in this ultimate sense. For the "other" to be more than an empty word, it is necessary that my existence should never be reduced to my bare awareness of existing, but that it should take in also the awareness that *one* may have of it, and thus include my incarnation in some nature and the possibility, at least, of a historical situation. The *Cogito* must reveal me in a situation, and it is on this condition alone that transcendental subjectivity can, as Husserl puts it,[5] *be* an intersubjectivity. As a meditating Ego, I can clearly distinguish from myself the world and things, since I certainly do not exist in the way in which things exist. I must even set aside from myself my body understood as a

5. *Die Krisis der europäischen Wissenschaften und die transzendentale Phänomenologie,* III (unpublished).

thing among things, as a collection of physico-chemical processes. But even if the *cogitatio*, which I thus discover, is without location in objective time and space, it is not without place in the phenomenological world. The world, which I distinguished from myself as the totality of things or of processes linked by causal relationships, I rediscover "in me" as the permanent horizon of all my *cogitationes* and as a dimension in relation to which I am constantly situating myself. The true *Cogito* does not define the subject's existence in terms of the thought he has of existing, and furthermore does not convert the indubitability of the world into the indubitability of thought about the world, nor finally does it replace the world itself by the world as meaning. On the contrary it recognizes my thought itself as an inalienable fact, and does away with any kind of idealism in revealing me as "being-in-the-world."

It is because we are through and through compounded of relationships with the world that for us the only way to become aware of the fact is to suspend the resultant activity, to refuse it our complicity (to look at it *ohne mitzumachen*, as Husserl often says), or yet again, to put it "out of play." Not because we reject the certainties of common sense and a natural attitude to things—they are, on the contrary, the constant theme of philosophy—but because, being the presupposed basis of any thought, they are taken for granted, and go unnoticed, and because in order to arouse them and bring them to view, we have to suspend for a moment our recognition of them. The best formulation of the reduction is probably that given by Eugen Fink, Husserl's assistant, when he spoke of "wonder" in the face of the world.[6] Reflection does not withdraw from the world towards the unity of consciousness as the world's basis; it steps back to watch the forms of transcendence fly up like sparks from a fire; it slackens the intentional threads which attach us to the world and thus brings them to our notice; it alone is consciousness of the world because it reveals that world as strange and paradoxical. Husserl's transcendental is not Kant's and Husserl accuses Kant's philosophy of being "worldly," because it *makes use* of our relation to the world, which is the motive force of the transcendental deduction, and makes the world immanent in the subject, instead of *being filled with wonder* at it and conceiving the subject as a process of transcendence towards the

6. *Die phänomenologische Philosophie Edmund Husserls in der gegenwärtigen Kritik,* pp. 331 and ff.

world. All the misunderstandings with his interpreters, with the existentialist "dissidents" and finally with himself, have arisen from the fact that in order to see the world and grasp it as paradoxical, we must break with our familiar acceptance of it and, also, from the fact that from this break we can learn nothing but the unmotivated upsurge of the world. The most important lesson which the reduction teaches us is the impossibility of a complete reduction. This is why Husserl is constantly re-examining the possibility of the reduction. If we were absolute mind, the reduction would present no problem. But since, on the contrary, we are in the world, since indeed our reflections are carried out in the temporal flux on to which we are trying to seize (since they are *sich einströmen*, as Husserl says), there is no thought which embraces all our thought. The philosopher, as the unpublished works declare, is a perpetual beginner, which means that he takes for granted nothing that men, learned or otherwise, believe they know. It means also that philosophy itself must not take itself for granted, in so far as it may have managed to say something true; that it is an ever-renewed experiment in making its own beginning; that it consists wholly in the description of this beginning, and finally, that radical reflection amounts to a consciousness of its own dependence on an unreflective life which is its initial situation, unchanging, given once and for all. Far from being, as has been thought, a procedure of idealistic philosophy, phenomenological reduction belongs to existential philosophy: Heidegger's "being-in-the-world" appears only against the background of the phenomenological reduction.

A misunderstanding of a similar kind confuses the notion of the "essences" in Husserl. Every reduction, says Husserl, as well as being transcendental is necessarily eidetic. That means that we cannot subject our perception of the world to philosophical scrutiny without ceasing to be identified with that act of positing the world, with that interest in it which delimits us, without drawing back from our commitment which is itself thus made to appear as a spectacle, without passing from the *fact* of our existence to its *nature,* from the Dasein to the Wesen. But it is clear that the essence is here not the end, but a means, that our effective involvement in the world is precisely what has to be understood and made amenable to conceptualization, for it is what polarizes all our conceptual particularizations. The need to proceed by way of essences does not mean that philosophy takes them as its object, but, on the contrary, that our existence is too tightly held in the world to be able to know itself as such at the moment of its involvement, and that it requires the field of ideality in order to become acquainted with and to prevail over its facticity. The Vienna Circle, as is well known, lays it down categorically that we can enter into relations only with meanings. For example, "consciousness" is not for the Vienna Circle identifiable with what we are. It is a complex meaning which has developed late in time, which should be handled with care, and only after the many meanings which have contributed, throughout the word's semantic development, to the formation of its present one have been made explicit. Logical positivism of this kind is the antithesis of Husserl's thought. Whatever the subtle changes of meaning which have ultimately brought us, as a linguistic acquisition, the word and concept of consciousness, we enjoy direct access to what it designates. For we have the experience of ourselves, of that consciousness which we are, and it is on the basis of this experience that all linguistic connotations are assessed, and precisely through it that language comes to have any meaning at all for us. "It is that as yet dumb experience . . . which we are concerned to lead to the pure expression of its own meaning." [7] Husserl's essences are destined to bring back all the living relationships of experience, as the fisherman's net draws up from the depths of the ocean quivering fish and seaweed. Jean Wahl is therefore wrong in saying that "Husserl separates essences from existence." [8] The separated essences are those of language. It is the office of language to cause essences to exist in a state of separation which is in fact merely apparent, since through language they still rest upon the ante-predicative life of consciousness. In the silence of primary consciousness can be seen appearing not only what words mean, but also what things mean: the core of primary meaning round which the acts of naming and expression take shape.

Seeking the essence of consciousness will therefore not consist in developing the *Wortbedeutung* of consciousness and escaping from existence into the universe of things said; it will consist in rediscovering my actual presence to myself, the fact of my consciousness which is in the last resort what the word and the concept of consciousness mean. Looking for the

7. *Méditations cartésiennes,* p. 33.
8. *Réalisme, dialectique et mystère,* l'Arbalète, Autumn, 1942, unpaginated.

world's essence is not looking for what it is as an idea once it has been reduced to a theme of discourse; it is looking for what it is as a fact for us, before any thematization. Sensationalism "reduces" the world by noticing that after all we never experience anything but states of ourselves. Transcendental idealism too "reduces" the world since, in so far as it guarantees the world, it does so by regarding it as thought or consciousness of the world, and as the mere correlative of our knowledge, with the result that it becomes immanent in consciousness and the aseity of things is thereby done away with. The eidetic reduction is, on the other hand, the determination to bring the world to light as it is before any falling back on ourselves has occurred, it is the ambition to make reflection emulate the unreflective life of consciousness. I aim at and perceive a world. If I said, as do the sensationalists, that we have here only "states of consciousness," and if I tried to distinguish my perceptions from my dreams with the aid of "criteria," I should overlook the phenomenon of the world. For if I am able to talk about "dreams" and "reality," to bother my head about the distinction between imaginary and real, and cast doubt upon the "real," it is because this distinction is already made by me before any analysis; it is because I have an experience of the real as of the imaginary, and the problem then becomes one not of asking how critical thought can provide for itself secondary equivalents of this distinction, but of making explicit our primordial knowledge of the "real," of describing our perception of the world as that upon which our idea of truth is for ever based. We must not, therefore, wonder whether we really perceive a world, we must instead say: the world is what we perceive. In more general terms we must not wonder whether our self-evident truths are real truths, or whether, through some perversity inherent in our minds, that which is self-evident for us might not be illusory in relation to some truth in itself. For in so far as we talk about illusion, it is because we have identified illusions, and done so solely in the light of some perception which at the same time gave assurance of its own truth. It follows that doubt, or the fear of being mistaken, testifies as soon as it arises to our power of unmasking error, and that it could never finally tear us away from truth. We are in the realm of truth and it is "the experience of truth" which is self-evident.[9] To seek the essence of perception is to declare that

9. *Das Erlebnis der Wahrheit (Logische Untersuchungen, Prolegomena zur reinen Logik)* p. 190.

perception is, not presumed true, but defined as access to truth. So, if I now wanted, according to idealistic principles, to base this *de facto* self-evident truth, this irresistible belief, on some absolute self-evident truth, that is, on the absolute clarity which my thoughts have for me; if I tried to find in myself a creative thought which bodied forth the framework of the world or illumined it through and through, I should once more prove unfaithful to my experience of the world, and should be looking for what makes that experience possible instead of looking for what it is. The self-evidence of perception is not adequate thought or apodeictic self-evidence.[10] The world is not what I think, but what I live through. I am open to the world, I have no doubt that I am in communication with it, but I do not possess it; it is inexhaustible. "There is a world," or rather: "There is the world"; I can never completely account for this ever-reiterated assertion in my life. This facticity of the world is what constitutes the *Weltlichkeit der Welt*, what causes the world to be the world; just as the facticity of the *cogito* is not an imperfection in itself, but rather what assures me of my existence. The eidetic method is the method of a phenomenological positivism which bases the possible on the real.

We can now consider the notion of intentionality, too often cited as the main discovery of phenomenology, whereas it is understandable only through the reduction. "All consciousness is consciousness of something"; there is nothing new in that. Kant showed, in the *Refutation of Idealism*, that inner perception is impossible without outer perception, that the world, as a collection of connected phenomena, is anticipated in the consciousness of my unity, and is the means whereby I come into being as a consciousness. What distinguishes intentionality from the Kantian relation to a possible object is that the unity of the world, before being posited by knowledge in a specific act of identification, is "lived" as ready-made or already there. Kant himself shows in the *Critique of Judgement* that there exists a unity of the imagination and the understanding and a unity of subjects *before the object*, and that, in experiencing the beautiful, for example, I am aware of a harmony between sensation and concept, between myself and others, which is itself without any concept. Here the subject is no longer the universal thinker of a system of ob-

10. There is no apodeictic self-evidence, the *Formale und transzendentale Logik* (p. 142) says in effect.

jects rigorously interrelated, the positing power who subjects the manifold to the law of the understanding, in so far as he is to be able to put together a world—he discovers and enjoys his own nature as spontaneously in harmony with the law of the understanding. But if the subject has a nature, then the hidden art of the imagination must condition the categorical activity. It is no longer merely the aesthetic judgement, but knowledge too which rests upon this art, an art which forms the basis of the unity of consciousness and of consciousnesses.

Husserl takes up again the *Critique of Judgement* when he talks about a teleology of consciousness. It is not a matter of duplicating human consciousness with some absolute thought which, from outside, is imagined as assigning to it its aims. It is a question of recognizing consciousness itself as a project of the world, meant for a world which it neither embraces nor possesses, but towards which it is perpetually directed—and the world as this pre-objective individual whose imperious unity decrees what knowledge shall take as its goal. This is why Husserl distinguishes between intentionality of act, which is that of our judgements and of those occasions when we voluntarily take up a position—the only intentionality discussed in the *Critique of Pure Reason*—and operative intentionality (*fungierende Intentionalität*), or that which produces the natural and antepredicative unity of the world and of our life, being apparent in our desires, our evaluations and in the landscape we see, more clearly than in objective knowledge, and furnishing the text which our knowledge tries to translate into precise language. Our relationship to the world, as it is untiringly enunciated within us, is not a thing which can be any further clarified by analysis; philosophy can only place it once more before our eyes and present it for our ratification.

Through this broadened notion of intentionality, phenomenological "comprehension" is distinguished from traditional "intellection," which is confined to "true and immutable natures," and so phenomenology can become a phenomenology of origins. Whether we are concerned with a thing perceived, a historical event or a doctrine, to "understand" is to take in the total intention—not only what these things are for representation (the "properties" of the thing perceived, the mass of "historical facts," the "ideas" introduced by the doctrine)—but the unique mode of existing expressed in the properties of the pebble, the glass or the piece of wax, in all the events of a revolution, in all the thoughts of a philosopher. It is a matter, in the case of each civilization, of finding the Idea in the Hegelian sense, that is, not a law of the physico-mathematical type, discoverable by objective thought, but that formula which sums up some unique manner of behaviour towards others, towards Nature, time and death: a certain way of patterning the world which the historian should be capable of seizing upon and making his own. These are the *dimensions* of history. In this context there is not a human word, not a gesture, even one which is the outcome of habit or absent-mindedness, which has not some meaning. For example, I may have been under the impression that I lapsed into silence through weariness, or some minister may have thought he had uttered merely an appropriate platitude, yet my silence or his words immediately take on a significance, because my fatigue or his falling back upon a ready-made formula are not accidental, for they express a certain lack of interest, and hence some degree of adoption of a definite position in relation to the situation.

When an event is considered at close quarters, at the moment when it is lived through, everything seems subject to chance: one man's ambition, some lucky encounter, some local circumstance or other appears to have been decisive. But chance happenings offset each other, and facts in their multiplicity coalesce and show up a certain way of taking a stand in relation to the human situation, reveal in fact an *event* which has its definite outline and about which we can talk. Should the starting-point for the understanding of history be ideology, or politics, or religion, or economics? Should we try to understand a doctrine from its overt content, or from the psychological make-up and the biography of its author? We must seek an understanding from all these angles simultaneously, everything has meaning, and we shall find this same structure of being underlying all relationships. All these views are true provided that they are not isolated, that we delve deeply into history and reach the unique core of existential meaning which emerges in each perspective. It is true, as Marx says, that history does not walk on its head, but it is also true that it does not think with its feet. Or one should say rather that it is neither its "head" nor its "feet" that we have to worry about, but its body. All economic and psychological explanations of a doctrine are true, since the thinker never thinks from any starting-point but the one constituted by what he is. Reflection even on a doctrine will be complete only if it succeeds in linking up with the doctrine's history and the extraneous explanations of it, and in putting back the causes and meaning of the doctrine in an existential structure. There is, as Husserl says, a "genesis of meaning" (*Sinngenesis*),[11] which alone, in the last resort, teaches us what the doctrine "means." Like understanding, criticism must be pursued at all levels, and naturally, it will be insufficient, for the refutation of a doctrine, to relate it to some accidental event in the author's life: its significance goes beyond, and there is no pure accident in existence or in co-existence, since both absorb random events and transmute them into the rational.

Finally, as it is indivisible in the present, history is equally so in its sequences. Considered in the light of its fundamental dimensions, all periods of history appear as manifestations of a single existence, or as episodes in a single drama—without our knowing whether it has an ending. Because we are in the world, we are *condemned to meaning*, and we cannot do or say anything without its acquiring a name in history.

Probably the chief gain from phenomenology is to have united extreme subjectivism and extreme objectivism in its notion of the world or of rationality. Rationality is precisely measured by the experiences in which it is disclosed. To say that there exists rationality is to say that perspectives blend, perceptions confirm each other, a meaning emerges. But it should not be set in a realm apart, transposed into absolute Spirit, or into a world in the realist sense. The phenomenological world is not pure being, but the sense which is revealed where the paths of my various experiences intersect, and also where my own and other people's intersect and engage each other like gears. It is thus inseparable from subjectivity and intersubjectivity, which find their unity when I either take up my past experiences in those of the present, or other people's in my own. For the first time the philosopher's thinking is sufficiently conscious not to anticipate itself and endow its own results with reified form in the world. The philosopher tries to conceive the world, others and himself and their interrelations. But the meditating Ego, the "impartial spectator" (*uninteressierter Zuschauer*)[12] do not rediscover an already given rationality, they "establish themselves,"[13] and establish

11. The usual term in the unpublished writings. The idea is already to be found in the *Formale und transzendentale Logik*, pp. 184 and ff.
12. *6th Méditation cartésienne* (unpublished).
13. Ibid.

it, by an act of initiative which has no guarantee in being, its justification resting entirely on the effective power which it confers on us of taking our own history upon ourselves.

The phenomenological world is not the bringing to explicit expression of a pre-existing being, but the laying down of being. Philosophy is not the reflection of a pre-existing truth, but, like art, the act of bringing truth into being. One may well ask how this creation is *possible*, and if it does not recapture in things a pre-existing Reason. The answer is that the only pre-existent Logos is the world itself, and that the philosophy which brings it into visible existence does not begin by being *possible;* it is actual or real like the world of which it is a part, and no explanatory hypothesis is clearer than the act whereby we take up this unfinished world in an effort to complete and conceive it. Rationality is not a *problem*. There is behind it no unknown quantity which has to be determined by deduction, or, beginning with it, demonstrated inductively. We witness every minute the miracle of related experiences, and yet nobody knows better than we do how this miracle is worked, for we are ourselves this network of relationships. The world and reason are not problematical. We may say, if we wish, that they are mysterious, but their mystery defines them: there can be no question of dispelling it by some "solution," it is on the hither side of all solutions. True philosophy consists in relearning to look at the world, and in this sense a historical account can give meaning to the world quite as "deeply" as a philosophical treatise. We take our fate in our hands, we become responsible for our history through reflection, but equally by a decision on which we stake our life, and in both cases what is involved is a violent act which is validated by being performed.

Phenomenology, as a disclosure of the world, rests on itself, or rather provides its own foundation.[14] All knowledge is sustained by a "ground" of postulates and finally by our communication with the world as primary embodiment of rationality. Philosophy, as radical reflection, dispenses in principle with this resource. As, however, it too is in history, it too exploits the world and constituted reason. It must therefore put to itself the question which it puts to all branches of knowledge, and so duplicate itself infinitely, being, as Husserl says, a dialogue or infinite meditation, and, in so far as it remains faithful to its intention, never knowing where it is

14. "Rückbeziehung der Phänomenologie auf sich selbst," say the unpublished writings.

going. The unfinished nature of phenomenology and the inchoative atmosphere which has surrounded it are not to be taken as a sign of failure, they were inevitable because phenomenology's task was to reveal the mystery of the world and of reason.[15] If phenomenology was a movement before becoming a doctrine or a philosophical system, this was attributable neither to accident, nor to fraudulent intent. It is as painstaking as the works of Balzac, Proust, Valéry or Cézanne —by reason of the same kind of attentiveness and wonder, the same demand for awareness, the same will to seize the meaning of the world or of history as that meaning comes into being. In this way it merges into the general effort of modern thought.

☙ from *In Praise of Philosophy*

The life and the death of Socrates record the difficult relations which the philosopher maintains—when he is not protected by the immunity of books—with the gods of the City; that is to say, with other men and with the rigid absolute which they represent for him. If the philosopher were a rebel, he would offend less. For, after all, everybody knows in his heart that the world is unacceptable as it is; one likes to see that registered, for the honor of humanity, and be free to forget it when one returns to practical affairs. Therefore revolt does not displease. With Socrates, it was another matter. He taught that religion is true, and he was seen to offer sacrifices to the gods. He taught that one should obey the City and was the first to obey it to the end. What he was reproached with was not so much what he did as his manner, his motive. There is in the *Apology* a saying which explains everything, when Socrates says to his judges: "Athenians, I believe as none of those who accuse me." An oracular utterance: he believed *more* than they, but also he believed *otherwise* than they and in a different sense. The religion which he called true is one in which the gods are not in the battle, in which the omens remain ambiguous—since, after all, as the Socrates of Xenophon says, it is the gods, not the birds, who foresee the future—in which the divine is revealed, like the daemon of Socrates, only by a

15. We are indebted for this last expression to G. Gusdorf, who may well have used it in another sense.

warning silence recalling to man his ignorance. Religion is true, then, but with a truth of which it is unaware, true as Socrates thought it and not as it is thought to be true. And the same when he justified the City: it was for reasons of his own and not by the reasons of State. He did not run away, he appeared before the tribunal. But there is scant respect in the reasons he gave for it. First, he said, at my age the passion to live is not at stake; moreover, I should not be better provided for elsewhere; anyhow, I have always lived here. There was of course the famous argument about the authority of the laws. But that should have close inspection. Xenophon makes Socrates say: one can obey the laws while wishing them changed, as one serves in war while wishing for peace. It is not that the laws are good, then, but that they constitute order, and one has need of order to change the order. When Socrates refused to flee, it was not that he acknowledged the tribunal, it was the better to refuse to recognize its competence. In fleeing, he would become an enemy of Athens, he would make the sentence true. In remaining, he secured, acquitted or condemned, that he would prove his philosophy in making it accepted by the judges, or prove it anyhow in accepting the sentence. Aristotle, seventy-six years later, said on going into exile that there was no sense in allowing the Athenians to commit another affront to the dignity of philosophy. Socrates formed a different idea of philosophy: it was not like an idol whose keeper he would be and which he would put in a safe place; it existed in his living relationship with Athens, in his absence in being present, in his disrespectful obedience. Socrates had a way of obeying which was a way of resisting, as Aristotle disobeyed with decorum and dignity. Everything Socrates did was based on this secret principle which irritated because it baffled. Always offending by his excess or by his deficiency, always more simple and less arbitrary than others, more submissive and less accommodating, he put them in a state of uneasiness, he inflicted on them that unpardonable injury of making them doubt themselves. In everyday life, in the Assembly of the people, as in front of the tribunal, he was there, but in such a way that one could make nothing of him. No eloquent speeches, not even a prepared defense, for that would be to give ground to the accusation by taking part in the game. But no defiance either, for that would be to forget that in a sense the others could hardly judge him otherwise than as they did. The same philosophy obliged him to appear before the judges and made him different from them, the same freedom which bound him to them cut him off from their prejudices. The same principle made him universal and unique. There was a part of him by which he was kin to them all; it was called reason, and it was invisible to them, it was for them, as Aristophanes said, vapor, vacuity, chatter. The commentators sometimes say: it was a misunderstanding. Socrates believed in religion and in the City in spirit and in truth—the others believed in them to the letter. He and his judges were not *on the same plane.* To explain all, one has only to see that he was not seeking new gods and that he was not neglecting those of Athens: he was only giving them a meaning, he was interpreting them. The trouble is that this operation is not so innocent. It is in the universe of the philosopher that one saves the gods and the laws by understanding them, and, to maintain on earth the *plane* of philosophy really requires philosophers like Socrates. Religion interpreted was, for the others, religion abolished, and the accusation of impiety was the view of him from the standpoint of the others. He gave reasons for obeying the laws, but to have reasons for obeying is already too much: reasons raise other reasons in opposition, and respect disappears. What was expected of him was exactly what he could not give: willing assent to the thing itself, and without justifications. He, on the contrary, appeared before the judges, but only in order to explain to them what the City is. As if they did not know it, as if they *were* not the City. He did not plead for himself, he pleaded the cause of a city which would receive philosophy. He transposed the roles and said to them: it is not myself that I am defending, it is you. In the final analysis, the City was in him, and they were the enemies of the laws; it was they who were judged, and he who judged. This reversal was inevitable with the philosopher, since he justifies the external by the values which come from within.

What can be done if one can neither plead nor defy? Speak in a way that makes freedom appear through the marks of respect, dissolve hatred with a smile—a lesson for our philosophy, which has lost its smile with its tragic actuality. It is what is called irony. The irony of Socrates is a relationship with the other which is distant but true; it expresses the fundamental truth that each one is himself alone, inescapably, and nevertheless recognizes himself in the other; it tries to release the one and the other for freedom. As in tragedy, both adversaries are justified and true irony makes use of a double meaning which is rooted in the state of affairs. Thus there is no presumption, the irony hits oneself no less than the others. Hegel well says that it is *naive*. The irony of Socrates does not consist in understatement in order to have more effect by showing strength of mind or by hinting at some esoteric knowledge. "Every time I convince somebody of ignorance," the *Apology* says sadly, "those present think that I know what he does not know." He does not know *more* than they, he only knows that there is no absolute knowledge and that it is through this gap that we are open to the truth. Hegel opposes to this fine irony a romantic irony which is ambiguity, deceit, insolence. It draws on the ability we do indeed have, if we like, to give no matter what meaning to whatever it may be: it makes things meaningless, it plays with them, it permits everything. The irony of Socrates is not this delirium. Or at any rate, if there is with him any trace of noxious irony, it is Socrates himself who teaches us to correct Socrates. When he says: "I make myself hated, it is proof that I speak the truth," he is wrong according to his own principles: all good reasoning gives offense, but everything that gives offense is not true. Again, when he says to his judges: "I shall not cease to philosophize, *when I ought to die several times*," he is taunting them, he is tempting their inhumanity. Thus he does sometimes give way to the caprice of insolence and of mischief, to personal loftiness and the aristocratic spirit. It is true that no other resources than himself were left to him. Again as Hegel said, he appeared "at the epoch of the decadence of Athenian democracy; he escaped from actual existence and took refuge in himself to seek there the just and the good." But, indeed, that was just what he was forbidden to do, since he thought that one cannot be just by oneself, that in being so by oneself one ceases to be so. If it was truly the City which he defended, he could not be concerned only about a City within himself, he was concerned about that actual City in the midst of which he was. The five hundred men who were assembled to judge him were not all stuffed shirts or fools: two hundred and twenty-one of them voted for his acquittal, and thirty brought over would have saved Athens from dishonor. Also, there were all those to be thought of, after Socrates, who would run the same danger as he. He might perhaps be free to bring on his own head the anger of fools, to forgive them with contempt and to transcend his life; he was not free to absolve in advance the evil which would be done to others and to transcend *their* life. It was necessary therefore to give the tribunal its chance to understand. While we live with others, no judgment of ours on them is possible which exempts us and separates us from them. To say *all is vain,* or *all is evil,* as moreover to say *all is good,* which is hardly to be distinguished from it, does not belong to philosophy.

BIBLIOGRAPHY

La Structure du Comportement (Paris, Presses Universitaires de France)

Sens et Non-sens (Paris, Nagel)

Phénoménologie de la Perception. Gallimard; translated by Colin Smith as *Phenomenology of Perception* (London, 1962)

Humanisme et Terreur: essai sur le problème communiste (Paris, Gallimard, 1947)

Éloge de la Philosophie: Leçon inaugurale faite au Collège de France, 15 janvier 1953 (Paris, Gallimard, 1953)

See also Colin Smith, "The Notion of Object in the Phenomenology of Merleau-Ponty," *Philosophy* (vol. xxxix, no. 148, April, 1964); and Colin Smith, *Contemporary French Philosophy* (London, 1964).